Devastation and Renewal

HISTORY OF THE URBAN ENVIRONMENT

Martin V. Melosi and Joel A. Tarr, Editors

Devastation *and* Renewal

AN ENVIRONMENTAL HISTORY OF PITTSBURGH AND ITS REGION

EDITED BY
Joel A. Tarr

University of Pittsburgh Press

Published by the University of Pittsburgh Press, Pittsburgh, Pa., 15260

Copyright © 2003, University of Pittsburgh Press

Manufactured in the United States of America

Printed on acid-free paper

First paperback edition, 2005

10 9 8 7 6 5 4 3 2 1

ISBN 0-8229-5892-9

An earlier version of Lynne Page Snyder, "The Death-Dealing Smog over Donora, Pennsylvania: Industrial Air Pollution, Public Health Policy, and the Politics of Expertise, 1948–1949," was published by *Environmental History* and is reprinted here with permission.

CONTENTS

PREFACE

The idea for this book originated with the publication of Andrew Hurley's pioneering edited work on St. Louis environmental history, *Common Fields: An Environmental History of St. Louis* (St. Louis: Missouri Historical Society, 1997). I realized at that time that an edited work would be the best way to present material about Pittsburgh environmental history in as expeditious a manner as possible. I therefore approached the H. J. Heinz Family Foundation about the possibility of funding a conference and a book on the subject. Andrew McElwaine, then director of Environmental Programs for the Heinz Endowments, now director of the Pennsylvania Environmental Council and the author of the essay dealing with Nine Mile Run in this volume, generously agreed to sponsor such a project. I am grateful to him and to the Heinz Endowments for their support.

On September 16–17, 2000, a conference entitled "Pittsburgh's Environment: A Historical Perspective," was held at the Senator John Heinz Pittsburgh Regional History Center. All but one of the papers delivered at that conference are represented in this volume. In addition, a panel composed of Andrew Hurley from the University of Missouri at St. Louis, Anthony Penna from Northeastern University, Adam Rome from The Pennsylvania State University, and Christine Rosen from the University of California at Berkeley, discussed Pittsburgh's environmental history in comparative perspective. Unfortunately, time for the panel was very limited, but among the valuable observations made were comparisons between St. Louis and Pittsburgh's similar political economies but differing industry mix and geological site structures, contrasts with Boston's strikingly different environmental history, and the manner in which Pittsburgh's culture imposed a pattern of "path dependency" on environmental decision making as compared to other locales.

In the preparation of illustrative material for the conference and for the book, Tim Collins and Reiko Goto of the Studio for Creative Inquiry, Carnegie Mellon University, were extremely helpful and generous of their time. Priya Lakshmi, also of the studio, did an excellent job of creating maps for the book. Environmental historians Martin Melosi and Char Miller both made insightful suggestions in regard to the final editing. Over the years I have received inspiration from my colleagues in urban environmental studies and from my graduate students in urban and environmental history, several of whom are represented in this volume. My largest professional debt is to Edward "Ted" Muller of the Department of History, University of Pittsburgh. Not only did Ted prepare an essay for this book on Pittsburgh's rivers and co-author one with me on the Pittsburgh landscape, but in spite of his busy schedule he was always available to provide advice and wisdom. I am greatly in his debt.

Finally, this book is dedicated to my wife, Tova Brafman Tarr, who created the idea for an event called "Mandala: Healing the Environment," held in November 2002 at the Pittsburgh Center for the Arts. This event, featuring the building of a sand mandala by Tibetan monks and an environmental art exhibit organized by artist Reiko Goto, was dedicated toward the healing of past environmental wounds and the renewing of the balance of nature in Pittsburgh and the world.

Tibetan monks offer blessed mandala sand at the confluence point of the three rivers, summer, 2003.
Photo by Joel A. Tarr

Devastation and Renewal

Introduction

Some Thoughts about the Pittsburgh Environment

JOEL A. TARR

A Walk around a Pittsburgh Park

ONE EARLY JUNE morning in 2002, while preparing the introduction for this book, I took a stroll in Schenley Park, which adjoins my university office. It was a beautiful morning, with the sun glistening through the leaves of trees that still held rain droplets from the previous day's evening shower. The park itself is a marvel, 454 acres and based on land donated to the city in 1889 by Mary Schenley, an heir to a Pittsburgh landed fortune, at a time when Pittsburgh had no parks. On a high pedestal at the entrance to the park stands the statue of the man who had persuaded her to donate the land, Edward Bigelow, director of the Department of Public Works. Bigelow was an admirer of Central Park and modeled Schenley after Frederick Law Olmsted's and Calvert Vaux's masterpiece. He is revered as the father of Pittsburgh's parks.[1]

As I walked through the park I visited the outdoor gardens of the Phipps Conservatory and Botanical Gardens, a massive greenhouse with silvered domes and glass vaults donated to the city by Henry Phipps, a partner of Andrew Carnegie, and opened in 1893. Beautifully arranged and landscaped on several levels, the gardens display varieties of flowering plants, spices, and shrubs. Outside the garden I was saddened to see the stump of a large elm tree that a fierce storm (an act of nature) had toppled just two weeks before. A sign placed next to the stump by the Conservatory noted in gratitude that the tree had provided shade to park visitors for over a hundred years—it would be sorely missed. Here we had an example of how nature had given to Pittsburghers (although perhaps the tree had been planted by the park's landscapers) and then taken away.

My path then wound around two rectangular landscaped ponds planted with water lilies (one graced with a statue of Neptune spewing out water), and took me across a road busy with morning traffic and then to an overlook from which I could view the deep valley and thick woods (but secondary growth) of Panther Hollow. All panthers, except for the four sculpted by Giuseppe Moretti that guard the entrances to a nearby bridge, have long since vanished. In idle moments, I speculate about the possibility of returning panthers to the Hollow just as wolves and buffalo have been brought back to Yellowstone, only to realize the implausibility of such a return of first nature to the city.

Wending my way up the road, I came upon the Westinghouse Memorial Fountain, dedicated on October 6, 1930, by sixty thousand Westinghouse employees to show their "esteem, affection and loyalty" to the great inventor and entrepreneur. At the head of the pond surrounding the fountain is a statue of a young George Westinghouse, looking intently at a triptych of brass panels, each bearing etched images of his most famous inventions and projects: the air brake, alternating current, the electric locomotive, and the Niagara Falls power house. Surrounding the pond is a spectacle of nature—weeping willows, bushes, and grass—sculpted and landscaped and complementing the hymn to industry inscribed by the monument.

My walk in the park on that June morning reminded me of the many contradictions presented in Pittsburgh's environmental history. Schenley Park is beautiful, but the initial landscaping had eliminated many of the site's rugged features in order to present a more pastoral setting and not jar elite and middle-class sensibilities as well as to have a civilizing influence on visiting Pittsburgh immigrant workers. During the park's initial years, however, it was difficult to access, and not easily available to workers who frequently lived in crowded and dilapidated housing near the mills, suffering from poor air and water. Edward Bigelow may have been the father of Pittsburgh's parks, but for many years he was closely associated with the notoriously corrupt political machine of William Flinn and Christopher Magee.[2] The name of Flinn's construction company adorns many pieces of park infrastructure. Phipps Conservatory lightens the spirit with the beauty of nature, especially in the dark winters, but the smoke produced by Carnegie Steel, from whence the money for the Conservatory came, and by other coal burners, had harsh effects on the city's atmosphere and defoliated many wooded hills. In the park itself smoke necessitated the use of pollution-resistant trees—hence the rows of ginkgo trees that line the park road overlooked by Bigelow's statue.

The ginkgo trees, however, have outlived all but one of Carnegie's steel mills, and the other mills have succumbed to human demolition. Now they are either awaiting renewal or have spouted new elements of the built environment. The electrical and transportation-related industries spawned by George Westinghouse helped transform our cities with light and transportation, giving jobs to generations of workers, but the great Westinghouse industrial empire is all but gone. The streams and land of Pittsburgh's "electric valley" have yet to recover from the damage inflicted upon them by industrial wastes, and many of the old Westinghouse works are empty and deteriorating. Eventually they, too, will be demolished or refurbished and the land put to other uses. Then, very possibly, more nature will return to the site and coexist in a symbiotic relationship with the forces of urbanization and industrialization.[3]

The City and the Natural Environment in Historical Perspective

All cities possess environmental stories, but there is no city that surpasses Pittsburgh in terms of the scope of its air, land, and water pollution history and the extent to which its landscape has been altered and shaped. Over the past two centuries, commentators who have encountered the city have noted its particular ambience. Consider, for instance, the following quotations:

James Parton, 1866: Pittsburgh is "Hell with the lid taken off."

Willard Glazier, 1883: "In truth, Pittsburg [sic] is a smoky, dismal city, at her best. At her worst, nothing darker, dingier or more dispiriting can be imagined."

Herbert Spencer, 1882: "6 months residence here [Pittsburgh] would justify suicide."

R. L. Duffus, Atlantic Monthly, 1930: "From whatever direction one approaches the once lovely conjunction of the Allegheny and the Monongahela the devastation of progress is apparent. Quiet valleys have been inundated with slag, defaced with refuse, marred by hideous buildings. Streams have been polluted with sewage and the waste from the mills. Life for the majority of the population has been rendered unspeakably pinched and dingy. . . . This is what might be called the technological blight of heavy industry."[4]

Today Pittsburgh has managed to overcome many aspects of this history although the tasks ahead remain considerable.

Human-produced environmental blight has marred not only this city but also other urban and metropolitan landscapes. Some are recovering but others make slow if any progress. During the past decade or so, the attention of environmental and urban historians, as well as researchers from other disciplines, has begun to focus on the subject of the city and its relationship to the natural environment. The roots of this concern actually go back to the 1960s but the volume of literature published has accelerated in recent years as new research agendas are developed.[5]

Urban history and environmental history are both relatively new subfields of American history, with urban history emerging as a sustained focus of study in the 1960s and 1970s and environmental history originating in the 1970s and 1980s. Both fields were largely outgrowths of the events and turmoil of their own times rather than evolving from the independent study of the past. Urban history, in this respect, reflected concern over the growth, decay, and future of cities in an age of urban disruption and decline, while environmental history emerged during an era of heightened concern over the quality of the environment and threats to nature and human health. Initially the two fields appeared to be largely concerned with separate spheres. After all, urban history was about cities and built environments, while environmental historians largely studied natural environments and different manifestations of wilderness. As the distinguished environmental historian Donald Worster comments, environmental history was about "the role and place of nature in human life."[6] And, for most environmental historians in the first decade of the field's development, "nature" was something that was found in the American West or rural areas rather than the heavily urbanized parts of the nation.

Reflection tells us, however, that it would be difficult to write urban history without touching on environmental elements. Americans founded their cities in locations where nature offered various attractions—on coastlines where the land's contours created harbors, on rivers and lakes that served for transportation, water supplies, and waste disposal, and in fertile river valleys with plentiful food and animal resources. Cities have always placed demands on their sites and their hinterlands and, as the chapters in this book illustrate, Pittsburgh's demands were large.[7]

All cities, including Pittsburgh, were interested in extending their usable territory. Municipal governments, urban developers, industries, and railroads often reshaped natural landscapes, leveling hills, filling valleys and wetlands, and creating large areas of reclaimed land along the edges of rivers, lakes, and bays. On this new land they constructed a built environment of paved streets, squares, parks, parking lots, railroad tracks, and viaducts, as well as erecting structures such as houses, warehouses, factories, office buildings, and churches. In the process they altered urban ecosystems for their own purposes, killing off animal populations, eliminating native species of flora and fauna, and introducing new and foreign species. They also disrupted local hydrological patterns, damming rivers, dredging their bottoms, and culverting streams. Thus urbanites constructed a built environment that both replaced the natural environment and created a local microclimate, with different temperature gradients and rainfall and wind patterns than those of the surrounding countryside.

As the field of urban-environmental history emerged during the last decade, six primary themes emerged: the study of the construction of the built environment and of urban infrastructure and their effect on the natural environment; the study of societal responses to these impacts and efforts to alleviate environmental problems; analysis of land use patterns, including the reshaping of the landscape; exploration of the attempts to bring elements of the natural environment to the city; analysis of the relationship between cities and their hinterlands; and the investigation of the interplay of the factors of gender, class, and race with environmental issues. Also explored were topics such as the political economy of cities and provision of environmental services, the effect of political and economic power on environmental decision making and considerations of environmental justice. All of these themes are involved in the environmental history of Pittsburgh and are implicit if not explicit in the chapters included here.

Of special note are three immediate predecessors to this volume—that is, three books whose authors initiated the compilation of articles and essays dealing with the environmental history of a specific city: *Common Fields: An Environmental History of St. Louis* (1997), a pioneering volume edited by Andrew Hurley; *Transforming New Orleans and Its Environs: Centuries of Change* (2000), edited by geographer Craig E. Colten; and *On the Border: An Environmental History of San Antonio* (2001), edited by Char Miller.[8] At this point other volumes on cities such as Boston, Houston, and Los Angeles are under preparation.

This book focuses on the environmental history of the city of Pittsburgh and its hinterland. Readers will find that Pittsburgh and its region share some features with the cities mentioned above—St. Louis, New Orleans, and San Antonio—but there are also a number of differences stemming from factors such as geographical location, climate, and resource endowment. Pittsburgh, as might be expected, is more similar to industrial cities located primarily in the eastern and midwestern parts of the nation. But every city, while sharing common elements with other cities, has its own unique environmental history. Pittsburgh stands out for its site characteristics, rivers, and resource endowment, especially coal; extensive industrialization and massive iron and steel complexes; distinctive history of pollution; attempts at creating a "Renaissance" for the industrial city; and, most recently, sweeping deindustrialization and attempts at redevelopment, which have powerful implications and promise for renewing aspects of the natural environment. Elements of these issues will be dealt with in the chapters in this book. First, however, I wish to present some basic geographical and demographic facts.

Pittsburgh sits astride the Monongahela and Allegheny rivers at the mouth of the Ohio River, just west of the ridges of the Allegheny Mountains—one of the world's great city locations. George Washington visited the future site of Pittsburgh in November 1753 and commented in his journal that, "I spent some time in viewing the rivers, and the land in the fork; which I think extremely well situated for a fort, as it has absolute command of both rivers." He might also have noted that it was an ideal location for a city. Both the French and the British built forts on the peninsula between the rivers—Fort Duquesne and Fort Pitt being the most substantial—and they played a critical role in the French and Indian War of the 1760s.[9] Fort Pitt proved the most durable, and eventually the settlement around it grew into a city. Pittsburgh was incorporated as a borough in 1794 and applied for and received its city charter from the Commonwealth of Pennsylvania in 1816.

Over approximately two centuries the city has grown into the center of a major six-county metropolitan area that extends 40 to 50 miles from a highly concentrated downtown. The city occupies an area of 56 square miles (144 sq. km.) while the metropolitan area—which for our purposes is equivalent to the Pittsburgh region—is 3,650 square miles (11,976 sq. km.). The population of Pittsburgh in 2000 was 334,563 persons, down from a high of 676,806 in 1950, while the metropolitan population was 2,358,695 in 2000, slightly up from 2,213,236 in 1950. Thus the city, after growing for much of its history, has lost half its population in the last half-century, while the region's population, after peaking in 1970, has been stable. Urban uses of the land expanded as population grew, but even when population growth halted, suburbanization continued to consume greenfields at the periphery of the metropolitan area, putting pressure on rural areas and on the natural environment.[10]

From an ecological perspective, many other aspects of the history of the region are critical. Its particular geological history and topography are essential background factors in its environmental history, and these are touched upon in several chapters. The region's natural history, its biological and botanic features, are also vital, but unfortunately no comprehensive study of the natural history has been compiled.

The Pittsburgh region has a temperate climate, and while winters can be severe and snowfall heavy, this is the exception. An absence of extremes is also characteristic of rainfall patterns and summer temperatures. The land occupied today by the metropolitan area was originally heavily forested, largely with the so-called mixed oak forest, including various oaks, American chestnut, flowering dogwood, as well as mountain laurel. The area was timbered over several times, but, aside from the built-up areas, is again heavily forested.[11] A limited number of wetlands existed in the region before dense settlement, but most of these, especially near rivers and streams, have disappeared. Many varieties of fish species swam in the Pittsburgh rivers before the twentieth century, but by the 1920s sewage, mine acid, and industrial pollution had created long stretches of river dead zones. Today, however, the rivers are again abundant with species of fish, some reintroduced or newly introduced.[12] Prior to European colonization, sixty-nine species of mammals existed in what is today the state of Pennsylvania, and one can assume that most of these species were present in the Pittsburgh region. Some, such as the beaver, were exterminated but have been reintroduced. Today there are sixty-five species of land mammals in Pennsylvania.[13]

From an environmental perspective, we are concerned with the manner in which the physical and economic growth of this city has shaped its location, penetrated its regional hinterland, and impacted the natural environment. Like most American cities, the site of Pittsburgh was originally used and occupied at different times by various tribes of Amerindians, including the Delaware, the Shawnee, and various tribes from the Iroquois nation.[14] By the early nineteenth century, settlers, most of whom were English and Scotch-Irish, with the assistance of the U.S. Army, had largely pushed the various tribes out of the region's heart and taken over the land. The city and its site went through various stages of development after its colonial and military beginning, providing a major commercial and transshipment center for travelers moving west into the Ohio Valley; furnishing important natural resources, especially relating to energy, to cities and industries; becoming one of the nation's premier industrial centers; and experiencing rapid deindustrialization in recent decades.[15]

Each of these stages affected the environment, as commercial and industrial development and the construction of the built environment impacted and shaped the natural environment in the mediums of water, air, and land. These issues are dealt with in various chapters throughout this volume. The first chapter, "The Interaction of Natural and Built Environments in the Pittsburgh Landscape," by Edward K. Muller and myself, provides an overview of the city's history over two centuries. This chapter is followed by three chapters that deal explicitly with issues relating to water: Muller's chapter on the history of the region's major rivers; my chapter with Terry Yosie exploring the critical decisions relating to water supply and wastewater disposal; and Nicholas Casner's chapter examining attempts to deal with one of the region's worst water pollutants—mine acid.

The second section of the book deals with air quality. Pittsburgh is famous as the "smoky city," and the three chapters presented here examine several aspects of this issue. Angela Gugliotta's penetrating chapter shows how smoke, over time, was regarded as having both costs and benefits. Subjecting attitudes toward coal smoke to social and cultural analysis, she challenges the reader to comprehend the complexity of the environmental issue and not to view it only from a perspective of problem creation and solution. Lynn Snyder's chapter on Donora, originally published in 1994 in the *Environmental History Review* but presented here with a new introduction, discusses the manner in which the Donora smog episode produced a set of contradictory results—a focus on exploration of the health effects of industrial pollution rather than a call for federal leadership in pollution regulation and prevention. In the final chapter in this section, Sherie Mershon and I explore the variety of forces, including a strong smoke control ordinance and market-driven fuel change, behind Pittsburgh's elimination of heavy smoke in the 1940s, and contrast this with the limited approach to controlling air pollution from industrial sources in Allegheny County after 1949.

Pollution of the land has also been a major factor in the Pittsburgh area, resulting in the cutting up and reshaping of the landscape. Elements of this are dealt with in Muller's and my landscape chapter, especially how the creation of a built environment of roads, streets, and tunnels altered the physical landscape. Industry has an equally important role in reshaping the landscape in order to meet both its transportation and production needs and to dispose of its wastes. In his chapter, "Slag in the Park," Andrew McElwaine deals with the latter issue comprehensively in his study of the fate of the beautiful Nine Mile Run valley, converted to a dump for slag produced by the steel industry.

A constant theme in most of the chapters is the use of power to cause or avoid change; that is, who benefited from actions that produced environmental degradation and pollution and who bore the health and nuisance costs? In some cases the answer is obvious—industry altered and scarred the environment, and the poor and the immigrant and African American working class suffered the most. But in other cases cultural and political forces as well as economics came into play, and responsibility for harm was not always clear. Cultural attitudes helped shape the industrial workforce's position on smoke and water purity. Industry's position was also not always uniform: some were heedless in their willingness to use air, water, and land as sinks for their wastes, while others found that degraded air and water quality raised their costs and damaged their products.[16]

A consideration of the exercise of power also involves the exploration of who sought positive change and why they did so. These chapters examine positive improvements in many aspects of environmental quality as well as its degradation, and the authors explore and explain the success and failure of these reform attempts. Much of the movement toward environmental improvement over time was led by elites, professionals such as engineers and physicians, and women's groups who became involved in campaigns to control air, water, and land pollution. The motivations of these groups are not always obvious and they cannot easily be assumed to have always been self-interested. More recently, representatives of industrial unions and minorities concerned with environmental justice issues have played a role in seeking to control pollution.[17]

The stories presented here tell of many positive environmental outcomes, even though change frequently required decades to come to fruition. The air and water are far cleaner today than in a century and many species of fish fill the rivers. The hills that were barren for years have become richly revegetated, endowing the city with a green ambience. The rivers themselves are being opened to recreational use, and old industrial sites along their shores have been redeveloped. Even the slag-filled Nine Mile Run valley is now being redeemed with the construction of housing and building of a green corridor to the river. And there is even movement toward "daylighting" long buried urban streams. In balance, the trend has been positive even though significant air, water, and land environmental problems remain, as do others that relate to environmental equity issues. Pittsburgh boosters like to trumpet the city's environmental accomplishments, but least they become too self-congratulatory about their achievements, eminent environmental historian Samuel P. Hays, a former long-term resident of the city and an environmental activist for forty years, scolds them in this volume's final chapter. Hays argues that not only have the city's politicians and elites exaggerated their environmental accomplishments but they have also been in an "environmental lethargy" for the past thirty years. Legislative actions on the state and local level have been limited, and the region's environmental organizations, he charges, have been overly cautious, with no strong leadership emerging to set environmental goals and to invigorate the region's environmental culture.

While some who identify themselves as proponents of environmental quality will dispute Hays's criticisms, his words are worthy of serious consideration. Strong leadership and consistent movement toward higher goals of environmental quality need constant reaffirmation. However, it must also be recognized that, in its own way over time, through the actions of concerned citizens and groups, Pittsburgh has managed to remediate many of the damages that its built environment and industry inflicted upon its natural environment. How far such healing will go, however, is unclear. Cities are human artifacts, subject to the various pulls of economic, political, and cultural forces, and these often result in compromises that produce less than ideal results.

The Interaction of Natural and Built Environments in the Pittsburgh Landscape

EDWARD K. MULLER

and JOEL A. TARR

The capacity for being seen with the eye in the large ... is the birthright of Pittsburgh. Where from so many different points one sees the involved panorama of the rivers, the various long ascents and steep bluffs, the visible signs everywhere of movement, of immense forces at work, —the pillars of smoke by day, and at night the pillars of fire against the background of hillsides strewn with jets of light, —one comes to have the convincing sense of a city which in its ensemble is quite as real a thing as are the separate forces which go to make it up.

—Robert A. Woods, 1909, from The Pittsburgh Survey

THERE IS PROBABLY no city in the nation that can match the dramatic landscape changes that have marked the city of Pittsburgh during the last two centuries. The natural environment itself provided a striking panorama of flowing rivers and streams, steep bluffs, and deep valleys that would shape the configuration of the built environment. With nineteenth- and twentieth-century technology and the characteristic American disregard for the natural environment, however, Pittsburghers engineered and abused the landscape to accommodate the imperatives of industrial production, efficient transportation, communication, and city building such that it often became difficult to discern the land's original configuration. Early in the twentieth century, Pittsburgh elites, concerned with the perceived relationship between environmental degradation and a deteriorating civic culture, set in motion a countertrend toward consciously planning urban growth and controlling damages to the natural environment. In the decades after the Second World War, a public-private coalition made further attempts at restoration, driven in this case by fears of economic decline. Most recently, the collapse of the steel industry has again suggested possibilities for renewal, although the scope and quality of these endeavors are still open questions.

Many Americans have difficulty conceiving of an urban-industrial landscape because "landscape" conjures up images of natural scenery. For the geographer, however, "landscape" becomes the central organizing concept in contemplating both natural and built environments. It includes the physical properties of the land, flora and fauna, and climate, as well as human-built features. The construction of an industrial city on a complex natural site produced a landscape that encapsulated inherent conflicts and tensions over issues of environmental quality and ecological protection.

We will explore some of these conflicts and tensions by examining Pittsburgh history over time, illuminating the city's impacts upon its physical landscape. Many of these changes were deliberate, resulting from the construction of a built environment designed to either control or re-form the natural environment of rivers, steams, and landforms. At times the forces of city building and industry were able to shape the rivers and landforms of the region to meet their needs, but at other times nature's forces surged out of control, wreaking havoc on the landscape.

Encountering the Western Pennsylvania Region

In the eighteenth and early nineteenth centuries, westward-bound Euro-American settlers in Pennsylvania found themselves challenged by a massive mountain barrier—what the Native American populations called the "endless mountains"—the ridges and valleys of the Appalachian Mountains. After climbing the abrupt 1,500-foot-high Allegheny front that separated the mountain chain from the broad Appalachian Plateau stretching far to the west, they confronted two more ridges and a sea of hilltops as far as they could see. Descending down into that "sea," these pioneers encountered mature forests draped over a complex network of knobby hills and steep valleys. Small creeks, larger streams, and rivers further impeded their progress except where long floodplains offered some respite from the hills. The many small creeks flowing down steep grades to the larger rivers and streams cut a complicated pattern of sharply sloped, narrow ravines. They were, in fact, traversing the eastern province of the great Appalachian Plateau.[1]

As the pioneers looked westward from atop the most western ridge, they might have noticed that most hilltops unfolding before them were nearly the same height. This uniformity, roughly 1,200 to 1,300 feet above sea level, is the plateau; the complexity of hills and valleys derives from the protracted erosion of this upland surface by the many streams and rivers. In short, the hill and valley character of southwestern Pennsylvania is really a dissected upland. Over millions of years fluctuating inland seas laid down layer upon layer of sedimentary rocks. When the seas periodically retreated, dense vegetation, peat swamps, and marshes emerged and flourished, only to be submerged again when the seas rose once more. The seas deposited strata of sand, mud, shells, and pebbles, which turned into layers of sandstone, shale, slate, limestone, and conglomerates. Under the increasing weight of this layering, the decomposed vegetation and peat became coal, petroleum, and gas intermingled with the layers of sedimentary rock. Strata of clay, some soft, sticky, and unstable like the red-bed clays, complete the profile. Compared to regions of the Appalachian Plateau to the west, the soils of this region are thin, sandy, rocky, and relatively acidic.[2]

Two more geological events shaped southwestern Pennsylvania's natural landscape. Buckling of the earth's crust thrust upward the two long parallel ridges—Chestnut and Laurel ridges—running northeast to southwest across the region's eastern edge. Later, across the northern portion of the region, north of a line from Beaver to Warren, glaciers covered the land and disrupted the original northward flow of the major rivers. They created the now familiar and distinctive three rivers geographical framework for the settlement and development of the region—the Allegheny River flowing southward to meet the northward flowing Monongahela River to form the Ohio River, which courses generally westward to the Mississippi Valley. The glaciers also widened and deepened the Allegheny River valley, filling it with the sand and gravel detritus of glacial scouring action. After the glaciers retreated, the river cut into this sediment, leaving relatively broad, fertile terraces and deep gravel deposits below the riverbed. All three rivers flow in broad, sweeping meanders that create alternating, arch-shaped floodplains on the inside of the curves and steep bluffs on the outsides.[3]

Given this geological history, southwestern Pennsylvania's potential for commercial agriculture paled in comparison to that of regions to the west or to the east in southeastern Pennsylvania, which possessed richer soils and flatter lands. However, the regional landscape still contained abundant resources to attract pioneer settlement. While eighteenth-century Euro-American explorers, traders, and trappers depended on the region's natural resources, they caused relatively minor and spatially concentrated impacts on the landscape, much like the Native Americans they encountered.

At the time of Euro-American contact, Native Americans only sparsely settled the region and the area was a crossroads for hunting and trading. This settlement pattern resulted from conflict between the powerful Iroquois, who claimed the land, and eastern tribes such as the Delaware and Shawnees, whom whites forced to migrate westward.[4] Village sites, small crop plots, and overland trails were probably the most recognizable human imprints, though Native Americans sometimes burned forest undergrowth for hunting and agricultural purposes. Traders and trappers, trading for beaver and other animal hides, attached themselves to this pattern. In the 1760s, Generals Braddock and Forbes's armies constructed roads through the wilderness, probably having more of an impact on the environment than any Native American activity. Both of these roads became major overland routes in subsequent years.[5]

In the second half of the eighteenth century, major clashes for regional control occurred among Native Americans, French and British traders and troops, and American colonists. By the end of the century permanent Euro-American occupancy was assured and regional development accelerated, thus beginning a dramatic transformation of the landscape.[6] Southwestern Pennsylvania settlers exploited the waters, forests, and wildlife of the region, while the primary rivers provided serviceable transportation routes during large portions of each year for migrants as well as access to slowly emerging markets.

Between the 1780s and 1830s, settlers carved farms out of the hills and valleys of southwestern Pennsylvania, wherever reasonably level or moderately sloped land permitted. Slowly they cleared the trees from arable land. Self-sufficient at first, the spreading market economy allowed farmers to add some cash crops, especially wheat and rye, and make whiskey from grain for an especially marketable product. Compared to highly productive agricultural regions, however, southwestern Pennsylvania was not especially fertile or densely settled, and travelers frequently commented on the "rough and uncultivated" character of the land.[7]

Some observers, often from the more fortunate social classes, described the landscape in the picturesque terms fashionable after the first third of the century. A few eyewitnesses painted romantic views of the region's streams and countryside, while local painters of the Scalp Level School, such as George Hetzel, painted sublime landscapes of the western

Pennsylvania wilderness in a manner derivative of the Hudson River School.[8] As Rina C. Younger notes in her study of art and industry in Pittsburgh, local artists turned to nature at a time "when the city stood as an antithesis to pastoral values in its steady encroachment of the landscape along the three rivers."[9]

The growing commercial city of Pittsburgh presented a striking contrast with these wilderness and pastoral landscapes. Commercial activity focused on the busy Monongahela wharf, a mudflat stretching down to the river while urban development spread across the point of land formed by the convergence of the Allegheny and Monongahela Rivers. Organized by a gridiron street plan and the centering of trade around the wharf, the city featured artisan shops, inns and taverns, small offices, and residences, which were crammed densely into the confined space. Only church spires and steamboat stacks broke the uniformly low skyline of two- and three-story brick and frame buildings. Small industries occupied the riverfronts around the edges of this settlement core. More rapid economic and population growth after 1830, especially with the opening of the terminal basins of the Pennsylvania Main Line Canal, pushed new manufacturing firms up both the Allegheny and Monongahela floodplains and across these rivers. Many settled in communities that Pittsburgh later annexed, such as Allegheny City on the north bank of the Allegheny River (annexed 1907) and several smaller towns (annexed in 1872 and called Pittsburgh's South Side) on the south bank of the Monongahela River.[10]

Even in the initial decades of the nineteenth century, visitors remarked on the pall of smoke lingering over the basin formed by the hills surrounding the city. As one visitor to the city noted in 1829, "After traveling for two weeks through white, clean, cheerful-looking villages and towns, to come all at once upon dirty streets and dark, filthy looking houses stretching away in rows continuously ahead and enveloped in an atmosphere of smoke and soot which blackened everything in sight, was not a pleasant transition."[11] Although only covering a land area of less than two miles in radius from the Monongahela wharf, this collection of several contiguous communities housed nearly eighty thousand residents at midcentury.

Emergence of the Industrial Landscape

Although Pittsburgh's massive industrialization occurred primarily in the second half of the nineteenth century, its identification with industry and industrial landscapes actually emerged at a relatively early time in its history. The rich diversity of minerals embedded in the sedimentary rock layers of the Appalachian Plateau supported the city's growth. Local manufacturers fashioned the region's clay into pottery wares and bricks. Others used local sand for making glass products, and Pittsburgh for a time was the nation's leading manufacturer of glass. Iron masters refined the iron ore of Chestnut and Laurel ridges in nearby blast furnaces fueled with charcoal made from hardwood trees. The pig iron product of these country blast furnaces was usually sent to Pittsburgh foundries and rolling mills. Most important of all, however, was cheap energy, as outcroppings of coal or easily worked shallow drift mines provided fuel for local industries and residences.[12]

The focus on iron manufacture was so prominent that as early as 1821 British visitor George W. Ogden observed that the city could be called the "Birmingham of America." Views of Pittsburgh painted by various artists before the Civil War also began to feature industrial scenes, as they felt less compelled to emphasize picturesque subjects. Especially striking, for instance, is Sherman Day's "Pittsburgh from the Northwest, 1843," which highlights the smoke and industrial buildings that dominated the city when viewed from Mount Washington. William Schuchman's view of "Pittsburgh, Pa., 1859," also profiles industries such as iron works, foundries, and cotton mills as well as riverfront activity.[13]

Much of Pittsburgh's industry up to the 1870s was concentrated within the city or close to it in the neighboring city of Allegheny and in the South Side communities of Birmingham, East Birmingham, and South Pittsburgh. Otto Krebs's 1870s paintings, for instance, reflect the density of industry in these towns. In the late nineteenth century, as railroads increasingly penetrated the region and the rivers were made navigable through the construction of locks and dams (slack watered), large firms spread up and down the rivers, locating particularly in the river meanders. It is in this context that Pittsburgh's "meta-landscape" emerged, as is fully illustrated in representations of the industrial city in the major journals of the late nineteenth century.[14]

In his enlightening study, *Metropolitan Corridor: Railroads and the American Scene,* historian John R. Stilgoe discusses the growth of what he calls the "industrial aesthetic" that emerged in the industrial zone outside cities east of the Rocky Mountains after 1880 or so.[15] One of the major features of these zones was the shift in the scale of enterprises. Even though Pittsburgh had had major industrial complexes before the late nineteenth century, they paled in comparison to those that emerged after this date, and the Pittsburgh region became renowned for presenting an unmatched urban-industrial landscape to those that encountered it.

The most striking examples of the industrial aesthetic in the Pittsburgh region were its integrated steel mills.[16] These enormous complexes, each covering several hundred acres and sometimes both sides of the river, presented a chaotic assemblage of huge brick and metal sheds, towering blast furnaces, hot ovens, Bessemer converters, open hearth furnaces, rolling mills, giant ore loaders, and ore yards, all framed by river and rail. Most observers commented on fiery, dramatic displays of the converters and furnaces: "Particularly remarkable is the weird spectacle presented at night, with the furnaces fiercely gleaming, the fresh ingots smoking hot, the Bessemer converter 'blowing off,' the great cranes moving about like things of life, bearing giant kettles of molten steel." In a recent description, writer Laurie Graham captures the bewildering mass and complexity of a steel mill:

The view on approaching the mill was of another world—the looming plant sheds, the convoluted tubing of blast furnaces, the trusswork of ore bridges over mounds of reddish ore, the winding roads through hundreds of acres of buildings large and small, metal platforms and stairs, ductwork and railroad tracks, trucks and locomotives, torpedo and thimble and other types of railroad cars. . . . Plumes of water vapor rose from rooftops as steam issued into the cold winter air.[17]

Many other industries, including glass and refractory makers, locomotive and railroad equipment manufacturers, carriage builders, metals fabricators, and electrical equipment firms, operated out of large, brick, multistoried structures that covered a full block or more, providing a solidity to the urban landscape.[18]

Stilgoe notes that travelers passing through the industrial zones found them "extraordinary, intriguing, beautiful places. Refineries, steel mills, locomotive plants, coal breakers, and mysterious factories combined . . . to make an awesome landscape of built forms." For many, the zone "hummed with enterprise," and these landscapes drew an appreciative response in trade journals, engineering magazines, and even more general circulation periodicals. Booster publications and materials prepared for Pittsburgh's many conference visitors proudly illustrated the industrial strengths of the city through facts and figures and multiple drawings and photographs.[19]

Whether it was greeted with praise or blame, however, depended upon the perspective of the viewer. For Paul U. Kellogg, director of the Pittsburgh Survey, a "matrix" of pipelines, electric, telegraph, and telephone wires, mile-long river barge tows, and extensive railroad tracks had almost completely obliterated the natural features of Pittsburgh's rivers, hills, and valleys—in short, the industrial environment had replaced the natural environment.[20] Others, however, found it a fascinating landscape, reflecting the power and authority of dedicated human forces.

Critical to this industrial complex, of course, were the railroads, which came to form a ubiquitous part of the Pittsburgh landscape.[21] The first railroad to enter Pittsburgh was the Pennsylvania and Ohio, which linked the city with Philadelphia in the east in 1852. It was soon followed by other major trunk line railroads including the Baltimore & Ohio from the south, the Allegheny Valley from the north, and the Pittsburgh & Lake Erie. By World War I, the city was served by six major trunk lines and sixteen industrial and switching-railroads.[22] In addition to the trunk line railroads, many short lines and feeder lines also honeycombed throughout the Pittsburgh region.

The railroads blanketed the city, tunneling through the hills, bridging the rivers and ravines, and usurping the riverbanks. Seeking flat land in order to run their tracks, they occupied both sides of the river valleys and the bottoms of ravines. In some places two lines shared the same narrow shelf along the river. The Pennsylvania Railroad, which carried more passengers and freight than any other Pittsburgh line, was four-tracked throughout the city and much of the region. Up until the first decades of the twentieth century, the railroads disrupted city traffic flows with numerous grade crossings; trains actually ran down Liberty Avenue through the middle of downtown to terminals at the Point until 1905.[23]

The railroads built massive freight and marshalling yards, roundhouses, and shops at convenient locations. The largest marshalling yard in the region until 1952 when the Pennsylvania Railroad established the Conway Yard, was the Pennsy's Pitcairn Yard, built in 1892 on a 250-acre site east of the city. On this site four major tracks fanned into thirty-six tracks to make possible the assembly of freight trains up to fifty cars long.[24] Other marshalling yards were scattered at points throughout the region, including sites close to the downtown.

The railroads established their presence downtown by locating their stations at important throats and disgorging thousands of commuting passengers into city streets every weekday morning. These architecturally prestigious stations furnished major landmarks in the city's downtown, surrounded by cabs, omnibuses, private vehicles, and horse-drawn drays, all competing for space. Railroad smoke formed a large fraction of the city's air pollution burden, creating especially bad conditions at locations such as marshalling yards, roundhouses, and terminals. Not until after World War II did diesel-electric engines replace the smoke-belching steam locomotives.[25] The shriek of the steam locomotive whistles pierced the

Pittsburgh atmosphere day and night as they wended their way through the torturous Pittsburgh topography hauling long trains of cars filled with coal, coke, and other goods.

Fueling the Industrial Landscape: Coal and Coke

Without coal, Pittsburgh would have remained a relatively small commercial city for, as Willard Glazier wrote in 1883, all of Pittsburgh's industry was "rendered possible by the coal which abounds in measureless quantities in the immediate neighborhood of the city."[26] The rapid growth of steam railroads, steam-powered manufacturing plants, and the iron and steel industry, especially after midcentury, led to a burgeoning demand for coal and the development of the bituminous coal and coke industry across the region. Pittsburgh possessed magnificent coal resources, especially the Pittsburgh seam, which extended throughout southwestern Pennsylvania. Coal outcroppings and seams close to the surface in the city itself and in its outskirts were mined first, but as demand increased mining spread rapidly. Coal production in the four southwestern Pennsylvania counties of Allegheny, Westmoreland, Fayette, and Washington mushroomed from less than half a million tons in 1850 to 5.5 million tons in 1870, 11.6 million in 1881, and 66.5 million in 1911.[27] By the early 1900s, coal mines and coke plants pockmarked the region's hills and valleys, existing uneasily with the earlier agricultural landscape in some areas and supplanting it in others.

The coal industry had major impacts on the landscapes of both the natural and built environments. Coal mining scarred the natural environment wherever it took place, as men and technology ripped the coal out of the hills. As mining proceeded, huge heaps of mining wastes or slate dumps (also called gob piles) accumulated near the mines and loomed over the patch towns. Debris from mining filled the streams and disrupted water supplies. Acid drainage from the mines turned the water in nearby streams rust colored and coated the hillsides with rivulets of orange and rust colored drainage, and land often subsided in areas where deep mines had been dug.[28]

Structures relating to mining were scattered over the landscape. The most recognizable structural feature of the mining complex was the coal tipple standing high above the landscape near the mine entrance or protruding from a riverbank. Depending on the age and size of the mine, other structures also stood nearby, including a head frame, hoist house, boiler house or powerhouse, fan house, repair shop, lamp house, and mine office.[29]

Near the mine complex, most coal firms built small company towns called "patches" or "patch towns." The companies owned and operated these patches in order to attract workers to inaccessible mine sites, have a stable labor supply, increase control over the workers, and turn a profit. Usually companies erected rows of cheaply built, identical wooden houses for workers and their families in a linear pattern along a road leading to the mine or on a grid plan rising up a hillside. The houses were generally two-story, semidetached structures on large lots equipped with double out-houses and coal bins in the backyards. Mine managers occupied more elaborate houses in a separate row. The largest building, mostly brick, was the company store. Streets and walkways were unpaved, except for rust colored waste ("red dog") from the "gob" pile or coke ash that was spread on the surface to keep down dust.[30]

The towns presented a drab, monotonous, and temporary scene, for the companies believed the town would lose its utility when the coal was exhausted and the mine closed. Ironically, in the years after World War II when many mines were shut down, tenants often bought their homes, which they usually had upgraded with running water, indoor plumbing, and electricity. Those patches enveloped by urban development remained low-income housing and frequently deteriorated. In the rural areas, they evolved into residential pockets amid the countryside.[31] Many of the other physical remains of the coal industry, however, such as the large gob piles that had loomed over the towns and streams tainted with mine acid, often remained as disfigurements on the landscape.

While much coal was shipped directly to markets, coal used for the coking process presented a different picture. Carbon was a basic require-ment of iron making, and for approximately the first half of the century iron manufacture took place primarily on charcoal iron plantations that drew on surrounding forest resources. After the 1850s, however, coke made from bituminous coal increasingly substituted for charcoal as a source of carbon, making it possible to locate iron blast furnaces in the city. The best coking coal in the world—the so-called Connellsville Coke—was discov-ered in southwestern Pennsylvania in a narrow seam that ran approxi-mately forty miles from northeast to southwest.[32]

From about 1850 to 1920, most coke was made by distilling bituminous coal in beehive coke ovens at high temperatures to drive out the volatiles (oils, gases, and tars) through holes at the top, leaving a high carbon resi-due that could be used in iron making. Therefore, it made economic sense to process it near the mines and ship it to the city by river and rail.[33] Opera-tors built rows of beehive ovens into hillsides called "bank" ovens or in free-standing rows or blocks of fifty ovens, with some installations holding as many as three hundred ovens. The dome-shaped ovens had a base diameter of approximately twelve feet and rose to about seven feet in height. The coal cooked for forty-eight to seventy-two hours, and was then removed from the oven by laborers or, after 1900 or so, by mechanical unloaders.[34]

When the demand warranted, the ovens operated around the clock. The coke plants themselves were dirty, noxious operations of several hundred ovens, busy railroad yards, and a proximate mine complex and gob pile, with cinders and ash everywhere. With thousands of ovens of several operators working in a relatively small area, the smoke, fumes, and ash cast a pall over the valleys. Muriel Sheppard captured the scene well:

It depends on the wind and weather, the season, the time of day, and the coke market how much there is to see from the Chestnut Ridge lookout. Early on an autumn morning with a damp wind blowing up plumes of smoke raveling sideways, a violet curtain full of moving particles of soot blots out the valley. The spring smoke is apt to be whitish-blue, that of winter brown or gray, and any time of year it ranges from pinkish-lavender to gun-metal tinged with purple at evening. . . . It is a country of extremes, ugly by day with banks of coke ovens, tipples, sidings, and fields gnawed to the rock with strip-coal operations: luridly beautiful by night when the glare of the ovens paints the sky and works magic with head frames and sooty buildings.[35]

A regional urban network of towns arose to service the coal and coke industry, including administrative offices, repair facilities, and stores of machinery and parts. Estimates for 1910 suggest a population of more than 100,000 in the two major coke areas, including the urban centers. The railroads and, after 1900, interurban cars provided some connections within the region. And the rivers, railroads, and capital tied the whole area to Pittsburgh, which in ownership of the number of coal mines, coke plants, and coke ovens dominated the industry. In this manner Pittsburgh capitalists controlled the coke region, although considerable local fortunes were also made.[36]

In the years after 1910, the making of coke in by-product ovens began to emerge as an important alternative to beehive ovens. The by-product oven was a narrow slot oven constructed in batteries in which coking chambers alternated with heating chambers. Coal was charged through openings in the top of the oven and the coke pushed out by a power-driven ram at the end of the combustion process, to be quenched outside the oven. The gas evolving from the coal supplied the heat required for distillation and was also used for other purposes throughout the mill. The by-product oven had the advantage of capturing the volatile elements such as coke oven gas, tar, and ammonia freed by the coking process, as well as producing a higher coke yield per ton of coal than the beehive.[37]

While beehive coke ovens were customarily located close to the mines, by-product coke oven works were sited closer to the mills in or near urban areas. The various by-products could thus be utilized not only in the integrated steel mills but could also be sold to various users such as municipalities. U.S. Steel opened the first full by-product coking plant in the region in 1916 at Clairton, twenty miles south of Pittsburgh on the Monongahela River. The plant occupied a riverfront site 5,200 feet long and 1,800 feet in width, the largest plant in the world at the time of its construction. The Clairton Works had 1,500 by-product ovens that consumed enormous amounts of coal, largely moved to the plant by river barge. Jones & Laughlin Steel (J & L) constructed a by-product coke oven between 1918 and 1920 at its Hazelwood complex. While not as extensive as the Clairton Works, the location of the J & L plant within the city made it both highly visible and a producer of extensive air pollution and odor that plagued the nearby community. On a windy day, the odor of sulphur would carry far beyond the mill communities into middle-class neighborhoods.[38]

The by-product coke works, then, along with the iron and steel mills, consumed huge amounts of land along the rivers, using the latter for purposes of cheap transportation and wastewater disposal as well as sources of process water. Their presence was indicated not only by the flaring of waste gases and columns of black smoke, but also by plumes of white steam that rose as the red-hot coke was cooled with process and river water. Since the plants worked twenty-four hours a day, these plumes constantly appeared in the visible landscape. In addition, the companies constructed major networks of pipes to ship the coke oven gas to the linked steel mills and to other users, often running these pipes along the sides of hills of the river valleys. The plumes of steam and the pipelines provided additional visible evidence of the impact of industrialism on the landscape.[39]

The Rivers

The three rivers, especially the point of land they form which signifies the beginning of the Ohio River, have always been a defining feature of the Pittsburgh landscape. Although the rivers' relentless current makes them seem like the one constant amid the ever-changing, man-made industrial landscape, the river landscape itself, in fact, also underwent significant changes. In the city's initial fifty years or so when its economy depended on being the "gateway to the West," river commerce dominated the urban scene. The city's street plan, merchant houses, and goods handling together focused on the busy Monongahela mudflat, that is, the city's wharf.

All kinds of craft, but mostly steamboats as the years went on, tied up at the wharf, which was a beehive of activity. The solid row of brick two- and three-story merchant buildings along Water Street at the top of the wharf was the city's face to the river and the world. Boatyards and manufactories claimed the riverfronts away from the wharf, and the riverbanks reverted to their natural state at the urban periphery, where the recreational activities of fishing, hunting, rowing, and picnicking took place.[40]

Industrialization changed the river landscape as profoundly as it did the rest of the urban area. Shippers, mine owners, and industrialists demanded greater control over the rivers' flow in order to enhance the shipping of resources, especially coal, essential to the region's burgeoning industries. Beginning with the Monongahela River in the 1840s, private and public construction of locks and dams successfully created slack water pools between the dams on all three rivers. Slack watering the river through the construction of dams and locks raised average water levels, narrowed their fluctuations, and thereby extended the navigation season. By the late nineteenth century huge rows of many barges lashed together (a "tow"), characteristically piled high with coal and pushed by powerful steamboats, plied the region's waters. Loaded barges were moored to enormous round piers or mooring cells, queued up for unloading or waiting for river conditions to be favorable for navigation.[41]

As railroads, mills, and factories spread for miles on every available floodplain, vegetation largely disappeared from the riverbanks, and the river edges became hardened with man-made structures. Industries built wood, brick, and concrete bulkheads; cranes towered over the river shorelines; industrial waste, sewage, and storm water outflow pipes stuck through the banks; and mooring cells rose above the river surface near the shores. Some industries dumped fill beyond the river edges to extend the floodplain and then built bulkheads against erosion around the new land. The Pittsburgh municipal government raised the levels of many streets near the rivers with fill in order to diminish flood damage. Industrial and urban growth increased the release of toxic chemicals, effluent, and storm water into the rivers, and the water often took on a muddy brown color. Discarded rubbish and garbage littered the riverbanks along with abandoned barges and other debris stranded during high water episodes. At the same time, urban industrial development required the erection of numerous railroad and highway bridges over the rivers with their massive stone piers thrust into the channels. By the early twentieth century and for decades thereafter, the rivers became increasingly inaccessible to residents, unsightly and unnatural in appearance and fact.[42]

Creating a Technical Network Above and Below Ground:
Streets, Streetcars, and Sewers

Much of the city building process took place above the surface of the ground with the construction of various networks—streets, transportation lines, and electrical, telegraph and telephone wires, as well as buildings. By the late nineteenth century, canopies of wires shrouded downtown streets while steel tracks ran along the surface. At the same time, other construction activities took place below ground with the placement of water and sewer pipe networks as well as tunnels of various sorts. All of these features of the built environment had to cope with the constraints imposed by the natural environment.[43]

Pittsburgh's topography prevented a typical gridiron street pattern. Even without this constraint, however, streets were badly designed and configured. Correspondent Ernie Pyle wrote that, "Pittsburgh is undoubtedly the cockeyedest city in the United States. Physically, it is absolutely irrational. It must have been laid out by a mountain goat."[44] Nineteenth-century streets, aside from major corridors, were often narrow and poorly integrated with the street grid, frequently having very steep grades. The municipality made major efforts in the first quarter of the twentieth century to widen streets, align them, reduce steep grades, and pave them. Beginning in 1899, it constructed several boulevards, reflecting an attempt to improve communication between districts. In addition, because of the threat of flooding, the city raised a number of streets along the floodplain between eight and ten feet.

In the years after 1859, streetcar systems increasingly traversed the city streets, becoming a major element in the Pittsburgh landscape. Horse-drawn streetcars first appeared in that year, and by 1888 entrepreneurs had built fifty-six miles of track in Pittsburgh and surrounding towns, with their cars carrying twenty-three million passengers for the year. In the 1890s, traction companies replaced the horsecars with electric streetcars and cable cars and extended their lines throughout the region. The replacement of the horsecar by the electric trolley was a great environmental improvement. It helped eliminate the manure, urine, and carcasses that dirtied the streets because of the previous dependence on the horse.[45] By 1902, 469.5 miles of track linked city neighborhoods and regional towns, carrying 168,632,339 passengers for the year. Thus, the trolley became a constant feature of the urban landscape, occupying major streets, forming a large part of downtown street congestion, and running precariously on trestles along the slopes of steep hills.[46]

Other aspects of the landscape and its alteration were related to the reshaping of the city's hydrological patterns. This change involved the physical transition from a hilly landscape cut by many streams to one in which most streams were placed in culverts, becoming part of the sewerage system.[47] Initially the streams themselves were used to dispose of domestic wastes and storm waters, but in the late nineteenth century the city began to develop an extensive combined sewer system. This system was based upon the natural drainage basins of the region and required the Pittsburgh Department of Public Works to culvert most of the city's streams. By 1910, the sewers drained over seven thousand acres of the city, discharging into the neighboring rivers. The outlets ranged in size from fifteen-inch terra cotta pipes to twelve-foot brick sewers. Forty-seven public sewer outlets flowed into the Monongahela River, with another ninety-eight flowing into the Ohio and Allegheny Rivers. As of 1910 the four major streams that were still unculverted or only partially culverted, Nine Mile Run, Street's Run, Becks Run, and Saw Mill Run became open sewers, serving as the receptacles for sewage from both private and public sewers.[48]

Urban development, therefore, created a need to dispose of both storm water and domestic wastes. This need transformed the hydrological landscape of the city from one marked by flowing streams and a healthy stream ecology into a site almost completely devoid of waterways except for the large rivers that transected it. The floodplains, valleys, and ravines where the runs had flowed were transformed into corridors for infrastructure including sewer systems, railroads lines, and highways, as well as for industry. Increasingly, the untreated sewage and industrial wastes flowing into the rivers consumed their oxygen, destroyed fish and plant life, and transformed them into open sewers rather than environmentally healthy natural water bodies (see Tarr and Yosie, this volume).

Hillsides and Valleys

Dense development in the city was initially confined to the level lands of the river floodplains where the construction of infrastructure to provide for transportation and communication was not problematic. Expansion of settlement and infrastructure beyond the Point and low-lying areas of the sibling communities across the rivers often confronted the region's pervasive hills and valleys. Some adventuresome Pittsburghers attempted early on to move out of the flats. In 1843, for instance, traveler Mary Ann Corwin wrote in her diary that "the town with the surrounding hills and subberbs [sic], the roads winding up the hills, and houses up the sides of the hills, and on the top of some of them," was "the grandest sight we have had."[49] As population grew, however, dealing with what the Department of Public

Works called the city's "broken" topography was not easy. In his 1910 plan for Pittsburgh, Frederick Law Olmsted Jr. succinctly stated the problem: "No city of equal size in America or perhaps the world, is compelled to adapt its growth to such difficult complications of high ridges, deep valleys and precipitous slopes as Pittsburgh." Tributary stream valleys offered routes to many of the areas beyond the Point, but eventually the hills had to be climbed or breached, and ravines bridged.[50]

The steep slopes of many hillsides not only presented a barrier to transportation, but also meant that they were not usable for either commercial or residential purposes. Olmsted reported that "excessively steep hillsides" comprised "as much as 30 to 35 percent" of the Pittsburgh district outside of downtown and East Liberty. During the course of the nineteenth century, hillside forests were largely cut down for fuel and building materials. Acrid industrial and railroad smoke further harmed vegetation. The deforested hillsides eroded, gullies formed, earth slumped, and small landslides plunged to the valley floors. Billboards sprouted up on some as if a new species was taking its place with the scrubby vegetation of secondary growth. People illegally and surreptitiously dumped trash and garbage on many hillsides. Olmsted observed, "In far too many cases they [hillsides] are apt to be wholly uncared for and to become shabby, dirty, and altogether unsightly, depreciating adjacent property and contributing largely to the slatternly conditions in the midst of which so many of Pittsburgh's working people . . . are compelled to live."[51]

Building a road up a hill was either impossible or created a grade so steep as to be impractical. Nonetheless, a few incredibly steep roads such as Rialto Street to Troy Hill and Negley Avenue in the East End still exist today to intimidate the unwary driver. Local governments and private transportation companies turned to more elaborate engineering solutions to get around the hills. Although expensive, tunnels provided the most direct route. In 1831 an 810-foot-long tunnel was dug to connect the Pennsylvania Main Line Canal from its tidal basin near the Allegheny River across the east end of downtown through Grant's Hill (later referred to as the Hump) to the Monongahela Wharf.[52] In the second half of the nineteenth century, railroad companies built many tunnels around the region. In 1899, a major tunnel penetrated Mount Washington (Coal Hill) for streetcar use, opening up areas beyond the bluff for settlement.

In the early twentieth century, public officials realized that an automobile tunnel through the escarpment of Mount Washington would, like the 1899 street railway tunnel, accelerate suburbanization of the South Hills. While consensus existed on the need for the tunnel, debate raged for years over its trajectory. Proponents for a lower-level tunnel into downtown won the political battle, and the 5,889-foot-long Liberty Tunnel (also known as the Liberty Tubes), the longest vehicular tunnel of its day, opened in 1925 at the cost of nearly six million dollars. The Liberty Bridge connecting the tunnels to downtown was completed three years later.[53] Two more tunnels for automobiles (the Squirrel Hill Tunnel and the Fort Pitt Tunnel) opened after World War II; together the three tunnels defined the commute to downtown. Despite the successful penetration of the hills, the tunnels functioned as bottlenecks in the flow of traffic during rush hours, with cars queued up in long lines behind the entrances. In contrast, the exits from both the Fort Pitt and Liberty Tunnels facing the Pittsburgh Point treated the motorist to dramatic views of the downtown landscape.[54]

Cuts across the sides of hills became the commonest means of getting around the hilly barriers. While the earliest roadways wended along valley floors, subsequent development and congestion in the valleys led to the placement of higher speed highways such as Bigelow Boulevard (1916) and the Boulevard of the Allies (1922) along the hillsides. These cuts destabilized the slopes, especially when the red-bed clay strata were exposed. Because these strata are not porous, soils above them move along the slippery red clay and plunge downward at the cut. Although the secondary growth of vegetation on the hillsides enhanced stability, enormous retaining walls of wood, stone, or reinforced concrete provided the best deterrent of falling debris and landslides. In 1876, the city enacted an ordinance permitting the city's Bureau of Engineering to build on private property when grading streets. Many embankments extended for more than a mile. Along West Carson Street, for instance, on the city's South Side, the Bureau of Engineering constructed over 6,600 feet of reinforced concrete retaining walls from 13 to 17.5 feet high to buttress the hillside. Other parts of the city similarly required extensive construction of retaining walls, some of which were in need of constant reinforcement. Large sandstone blocks, which absorbed soot from smoke and turned black, were used for many and became an especially striking feature of the urban landscape.[55]

Smaller hills that obstructed traffic flows were sometimes simply lowered or removed. The most famous instance involved Grant's Hill, known as "the Hump," on the east end of downtown. Grant's Hill had been partially reduced in the first half of the nineteenth century, the dirt removed being used to fill in ponds in the downtown area, but it still posed difficulties since it had a steep enough grade to impede the smooth flow of traffic and discourage higher value retail and office development. Nonetheless, street, sewer, gas, water, and street railway infrastructure, as well as buildings, were already in place on the Hump. On the downtown edge of the Hump stood architect Henry Hobson Richardson's 1888 Allegheny

County Courthouse, which some consider among his finest buildings. Across the street stood industrialist Henry Clay Frick's 1902 skyscraper, designed by D. H. Burnham. Lowering the streets of this area would incur not only the considerable disruption and typical costs of excavation and street reconstruction, but also the extraordinary expense of replacing infrastructure and the reimbursement for damages to the buildings. As a result, the Hump project remained the subject of debate for several years. Proponents, including Olmsted, argued for cutting the Hump and simultaneously widening the major streets in order to provide major routes to the city's rapidly developing East End neighborhoods. The director of the Department of Public Works in his 1912 annual report observed that the Hump cut was a "proposition of such magnitude and everlasting benefit . . . that the public will only realize its vast importance after . . . [its completion when] the city will be so greatly improved in appearance, convenience, and increased property valuation."[56]

Begun in 1912 with the funding of a council bond issue, the project involved an area of twenty acres, parts of eight streets, cuts as much as sixteen feet deep, and the demolition of many buildings. The entrances of extant buildings such as the courthouse and Frick Building had to be reconfigured to accommodate the new street levels. The total cost of the project to the city exceeded three million dollars at its completion in 1913. Today the rise eastward along the streets is very gradual; few people suspect that the Hump had existed.[57]

Although Olmsted aptly recognized that the steepness of many hillsides prevented residential development, numbers of Pittsburghers did build houses precariously sited on precipitous slopes. As development consumed the floodplains, people often turned to the hills for housing sites that were still within walking distance to factories and mills but also above the densest smoke. Many of these homes were owner built rather than constructed by professional builders.[58] Two and two-and-a-half story rowhouses, built in party wall clusters or freestanding, climbed some hillsides along streets crossing the slopes at sharp angles or rose nearly straight up the slope along a stairway street. In some instances, houses sat isolated on hillsides. Others seemed to cling perilously to hilltop edges. Houses with two stories fronting on a street sometimes had a few more stories and/or outdoor terraces on the back side running down the hill. The slopes and instability of the hillsides forced these homeowners to build retaining walls made from a variety of materials to secure small yards, gardens, stairs, and driveways.

While over the years some of these hillside communities became affectionately embraced as emblematic of Pittsburgh's landscape, heavy smoke pollution, scarred hillsides, and inadequate incomes during the industrial era rendered a less favorable residential landscape. In 1927, H. L. Mencken, Baltimore's renowned journalist, commented on this hillside residential landscape in his signature overheated style: "By the hundreds and thousands these abominable houses cover the bare hillsides, like gravestones in some gigantic and decaying cemetery. . . . On their deep sides they bury themselves swinishly in the mud. Not a fifth of them are perpendicular. They lean this way and that, hanging on to their bases precariously."[59]

Some residents of the hills could reach their homes and jobs by another man-made feature of the Pittsburgh landscape, the incline. The inclines were steep rail viaducts constructed along the hillsides to transport coal, freight, and passengers, and to open up hilly areas to settlement. Steam engines powered drums that operated endless cables pulling the cars. The Monongahela Incline, the first intended for passengers alone, was opened in 1870. Eventually, fifteen inclines operated in the city, hauling passengers and freight to and from hilly areas. The largest number of inclines was on the city's South Side where the steep bluff of Mount Washington raised a formidable four-hundred-foot wall several hundred yards from the river shore, but they could be found in other parts of the city.[60]

Other steep slope residents had to reach their homes by traversing precipitous wooden and concrete stairways. Stairways began appearing in the nineteenth century but the first year for which we have a measure of their length is 1937, when thirteen miles of stairways were recorded. By 1952 the total had reached twenty-nine miles, of now mostly concrete steps. In hundreds of cases, sets of these steps were legal streets, complete with street names, and they provided the only access to steep slope homes. During the nineteenth and the early twentieth centuries stairways were sometimes the only way that working-class families could access water supplies and privy vaults. The steps were the responsibility of the municipal Bureau of Steps and Boardwalks, part of the Public Works Department. In the year 1999, sixty-six of Pittsburgh's identified ninety neighborhoods possessed steps.[61]

The valleys of tributary streams (usually named creeks or runs) to the region's primary rivers presented a different set of problems than did the hillsides. Early settlers established roads in these valleys or hollows, as they are often called. After the mid-nineteenth century, railroads appropriated space in the valley floors as well. Mines, factories, homes, and commercial enterprises soon followed. In the broader valley floodplains close to the mouths of the tributary streams, small neighborhoods or suburban, often industrial, towns occupied the level land. But the valleys narrowed and rose quickly toward the stream sources, forcing development into linear patterns with buildings aligned along road, rail, and stream. In search of space, some working families built homes on the lower portion of the adjacent hillsides, terracing upwards for yard and garden space. The irregular placement of these houses contrasted with the linearity along the valley floor. Inadequate sanitary and storm sewers, if any at all, periodic flooding, bald hillsides, and the proximity of industry led to deteriorating and at times squalid environments. Municipalities placed many streams in culverts to contain the flow, and numerous small bridges crisscrossed them for access to homes and industry. Long high-level bridges passed overhead to connect developments on the adjacent hilltops with each other, bypassing the congested valleys below.

These linear valley or hollow settlements became isolated communities unto themselves. In 1909 the Pittsburgh Survey highlighted the dilapidated houses of Skunk Hollow, tucked out of the way below the Bloomfield neighborhood, as one illustration of the city's atrocious housing conditions for low-income families. In 1926 residents of a small Italian community, sometimes called Basso La Vallone, or down in the hollow, inhabited a collection of wooden houses along a dirt road, Chianti Way, in a valley well below the large Italian Larimer neighborhood. The Meadow Street bridge passed high overhead. Besides the dirt road, steps rose upward to connect the hollow residents with the Larimer community.[62]

Although picturesque in natural or park settings, countless small ravines were perceived as land that inhibited travel and defied development. The "useless ravines," as one engineer termed them in 1909, attracted illegal dumping such as industrial waste and sewage and were candidates for filling with earth removed by excavations, rubble from construction and demolition, street sweepings, and a myriad of other sources.[63] Filled ravines created level, usable land. The filling of St. Pierre's Ravine in the years before World War I illustrates the propensity to not just alter but obliterate this characteristic topographical feature of the region, even at substantial cost. It also reflects the elite's desire to manipulate the landscape for social and aesthetic goals, as well as economic ones.

St. Pierre's Ravine in the city's Oakland area was a small offshoot of two larger valleys that formed the western edge of the new major city park, Schenley Park. With the establishment of the park and Andrew Carnegie's library, Museum of Natural History, and concert hall in the 1890s, a developer, a public official, and an architect self-consciously set out to develop Oakland as a civic center in the current fashionable style of the City Beautiful movement. In addition to being a good investment opportunity, Oakland was to be a counterpoint to the haphazard and deleterious landscape of the industrial city. St. Pierre's Ravine commanded the key site at the entrance to Schenley Park and front of the Carnegie Library. In recognition of this location, the city in 1898 erected at considerable expense a long stone arch bridge with balconies on each side for enjoying the view of the ravine.[64] But the increasing civic pride in the emerging civic center and blossoming park during the subsequent ten years sparked interest in a more formal design than the picturesque bridge and ravine presented. Partially at the request of Mayor William Magee, who apparently already had a plan before him on his desk, Olmsted advanced two proposals for the ravine; one that he favored involved filling the ravine and making it a grand plaza. Although some filling may have already occurred, the Department of Public Works directed thousands of loads of fill to the ravine in 1913 and 1914 (some of which reputedly came from the Hump cut project). Meanwhile, the city's Art Commission sponsored a competition for a plan of the filled site. With the bridge buried and ravine filled, a plaza and grander park entrance was ultimately completed in 1923.[65]

Few people today could imagine the site's original topography. The tension between development and conservation of the region's hilly topography continues today in the constant drive to flatten and extensively grade hills, as well as fill ravines and wetlands, for new building sites. One critic of the plan to fill St. Pierre's Ravine captured this dilemma when he wrote in 1910:

Here in the foot hills of the mountains we possess a feature of natural beauty which we should appreciate and treasure—the ravine. Throughout this city the practical problems of transportation have demanded the filling up of ravines. . . . But here [St. Pierre's Ravine], in our little oasis, . . . why should the hand of man try to improve that refreshing slope, so restful to the eye of the jaded victim of the transportation system. . . . Shall we have beds of red geraniums and coleus in geometrical rows to mark the grave of our ravine?[66]

Akin to the filling of ravines was the wanton depositing on the land of wastes of various sorts, including steel mill slag, coal mine debris, ashes, and garbage. These wastes have historically marked and shaped the landscape of the Pittsburgh region in the form of huge slag mountains or gob piles of coal wastes, filled in wetlands, altered riverbanks, and open garbage dumps. These practices are well illustrated in another chapter in this volume by Andrew McElwaine that explores the destruction of the beautiful valley of Nine Mile Run, which Frederick Law Olmsted Jr. identified as a perfect opportunity for a park but instead was used by the steel industry as a dump for the waste product of slag from iron and steel manufacturing.

Bridges

The numerous rivers and streams in the region, along with the sharp valleys and ravines, created a particular need for bridges in the Pittsburgh region. As Allen T. Burns wrote in the Pittsburgh Survey in 1911, "No city in America, if in the world, has had such physical obstacles to overcome in securing free communication and access between its different parts. Not only the rivers, but also hills, gorges, cliffs, and precipices cut the land into separate districts."[67] Pittsburgh became known as "The City of Bridges," or a "bridge museum," spanned by many bridges of different styles.[68] Thus bridges, many of "great architectural and engineering skill and beauty," became a distinctive feature of the Pittsburgh landscape.

The first bridge built in Pittsburgh was the Monongahela Bridge, completed in 1818, followed by the Allegheny Bridge in 1819. Both were covered wooden toll bridges. Other bridges were constructed in subsequent years, three by the famous engineer John Roebling. By the 1850s, five bridges crossed the Allegheny and two the Monongahela River. Perhaps the most striking was Roebling's Sixth Street Bridge (1859), which previewed his Brooklyn Bridge in its suspension cables and tall towers. All were private bridges aside from the suspension aqueduct Roebling constructed in 1844 for the Pennsylvania Main Line Canal, the first bridge he ever built.

Entrepreneurs continued to build toll bridges of various styles over the rivers in the coming decades, but in the twentieth century Pittsburgh bridges became public, free of tolls. Many reflected unusual styles, such as Gustav Lindenthal's Smithfield Street Bridge (1883), which featured a lenticular truss, the Point Bridge (1876) of Edward Hemberley, a suspension bridge that utilized pairs of Howe trusses as stiffening features, and George Richardson's George Westinghouse Memorial Bridge (1932), with the longest span in a reinforced concrete arch in the United States. By 1916 the city owned ninety bridges and was continuing to build new ones and replace deteriorating structures with more elaborate bridges.[69]

Railroad bridges are another type of structure that marks the Pittsburgh landscape. Within a few years of the railroad's initial entry into Pittsburgh in 1852, a dozen railroad bridges crossed the district's main rivers. These bridges were largely deck and through-truss bridges. An especially unique type of Pittsburgh bridge was the hot metal span, constructed to transport molten iron from blast furnaces on one side of the Monongahela River to Bessemer and open hearth furnaces on the other. All rail bridges were designed to carry heavy loads, but the hot metal bridges had especially heavy construction. In addition to spans over water, the serrated Pittsburgh landscape required land bridges to connect sections of the city that were otherwise divided. They crossed railroads, streets, ravines, and streams, and were constructed and maintained by the city. In 1930, the city owned and maintained 149 land bridges, of which 33 were for pedestrian travel and 119 for vehicles. They ranged in size from spans of fifteen feet to a half a mile in length.[70]

Allegheny County as well as the city of Pittsburgh constructed many bridges in the twentieth century. In the eight-year period between 1924 and 1932, the county built ninety-nine bridges.[71] Today the county claims to possess over two thousand bridges of more than eight feet in length, of which more than half are small single-span metal and masonry structures. These bridges reflected many types of design, including covered wooden, arch, cantilevered, suspension, and truss, with many design variations within these categories. Bridges, therefore, form a seemingly ubiquitous aspect of the region's landscape, taken for granted by residents but noticed by visitors.

Reshaping the Landscape in the Twentieth and Twenty-first Centuries

By the early twentieth century, many of Pittsburgh's elites were becoming concerned about the shabby appearance of their industrial city. In concert with the Progressive spirit of the times, they believed that a good natural and social environment not only boosted their city's economy, but also uplifted the physical and moral health of the citizenry.[72] The Chamber of Commerce, the Civic Club of Allegheny County, the local chapter of the American Institute of Architects, and other voluntary groups entered into a public conversation about civic improvement, which by 1900 included, among many other issues, the beautification and civic design goals of the then fashionable City Beautiful movement. Although the city government had been developing a grand park system in the 1890s roughly following the principles of Frederick Law Olmsted Sr., it had not yet addressed the many design concerns of these advocacy groups. However, before the end of the decade the city adopted planning and beautification as part of its formal responsibility. This emerging partnership between private groups and government, though fluctuating in character over the century, has had a significant impact on the region's landscape.[73]

In 1904, for example, the Civic Club established a Forestry Committee that encouraged the municipality to protect and maintain the city's trees and undertook a program to educate the public about the benefits of tree planting along the streets. In 1909, the city established a Shade Tree Commission within the Department of Public Works. The commission built a tree nursery, which by the end of 1914 had 5,400 trees growing in it. In the first four years of operation, it planted over 7,000 trees along city streets, which had to be regularly pruned, sprayed, watered, and replaced when vandalism, disease, and other factors such as pollution killed them. The commission optimistically viewed its ability to transform the landscape when it reported, "The coming generation will behold the wonderful transformation of the desiccated scarred hills of Allegheny County reverting to their former glory of forested crowns of green, and traversed not by wagon roads of former days but by miles of boulevards and broad avenues lined with symmetrical rows of fruit and shade trees."[74] The Shade Tree Commission assiduously continued to pursue its mission through years of fluctuating budgets. With improving air pollution conditions and the determined tree planting program, the city's streetscape inevitably became greener in the later decades of the twentieth century. Pittsburgh is a reforested city.

If the urging of voluntary organizations succeeded in getting the city to undertake the greening of its streetscapes, their advocacy for the beautification of the shabby hillsides had much less success. Both the Chamber of Commerce and Civic Club formed committees to study the proliferation of billboards at key intersections and on deforested hillsides. They tried to educate the public about the nuisance and to prod, without success, the city government to regulate the industry.[75] In 1910, Olmsted argued in his city plan that "the City ought to pursue a definitely active policy" in the case of shabby hillsides. It should "insist upon the maintenance of such vacant lands in a clean and orderly condition," and acquire some hillsides for return to "natural vegetation" and for views, terracing, walkways, and places to sit. Moreover, he recommended a number of designs based on European precedents for roads and even houses on those slopes not too steep for at least some development. Despite the new City Planning Commission's advocacy of "the beautification of the bluffs and hillsides," few of Olmsted's hillside recommendations were implemented in the following decades.[76] Three decades after Olmsted's recommendations, for example, a new nonprofit organization, the Greater Pittsburgh Parks Association, finally tackled the landscaping of the bald and unstable hillsides along one of the city's main boulevards. Bigelow Boulevard was opened in 1916 not only as a main artery to the East End, but was also intended as a parkway to Schenley Park in the manner of the famous designs of Frederick Law Olmsted Sr.[77]

Other design issues advocated by the private groups involved the refurbishment of downtown waterfronts, creation of a civic center, and rejuvenation of the Point, which had deteriorated into a rundown area of railroad yards, traffic congestion, warehouses, and other unsightly structures. Discussion of these concerns led to the mayor's appointment of the Pittsburgh Civic Commission, another voluntary elite organization, which engaged Frederick Law Olmsted Jr. in 1910 to prepare a city plan. The decade-long conversation over environmental, social, and design issues along with the completion of the Olmsted plan resulted in the creation of the Pittsburgh City Planning Commission and an Art Commission in 1911 to plan for the long-range physical development of the city. During the next three decades, the city and Allegheny County tackled an ambitious highway and bridge program. But, as with Olmsted's hillside recommendations, design plans for public spaces such as the Point infrequently left the drafting table, and few serious reforms of environmental problems materialized.[78]

Since World War II, however, two developments have markedly reshaped Pittsburgh's landscape. The first involved a reformulated public and private partnership that undertook a series of developments known as the Pittsburgh Renaissance. This partnership between an elite but corporate-dominated nonprofit organization and the city government attempted to reshape the city landscape in a number of ways both physically and environmentally. The most striking of these changes, which was essential for improving Pittsburgh in other ways, addressed the city's greatest environmental need, the elimination of the heavy smoke (which is dealt with in a chapter by Mershon and Tarr in this volume). Other major projects involving the environment included the erection of eight flood control dams (the first in 1941, the next seven after the war) by the U.S. Army Corps of Engineers and the formation of the Allegheny County Sanitary Authority (1946) with the mission to construct a regional sewage collection and treatment system.

Alterations of the built landscape under Renaissance programs involved the construction of new skyscrapers, downtown parks, automobile "parkways" along the rivers, and in the late 1940s and 1950s the clearing of the structures and railroad tracks that desecrated Pittsburgh's historic Point. The latter action made possible the creation of Point State Park and the adjacent Gateway Center high-rise office complex. In the 1960s and 1970s, two new bridges, a new stadium (Three Rivers Stadium), and a dramatic fountain at the Point joined the earlier redevelopment. Travelers entering the city from the west through the Fort Pitt tunnel and bridge were presented with a striking view of the confluence of the rivers and downtown.[79]

Other significant landscape changes, often with less positive overtones, resulted from large-scale urban renewal projects. The most infamous one, the Lower Hill renewal, occurred in the 1950s. This project took place in what was one of the most densely inhabited areas of the city adjacent to downtown. Residences and businesses involving over five thousand persons (80 percent African American) were demolished and replaced with the Civic Arena, a major sports arena surrounded by surface parking lots. A crosstown boulevard separated the renewal area from downtown. Two other massive demolition and renewal projects destroyed and reconfigured major neighborhood business districts of the city.[80] Thus, while the city's air and water quality were markedly improved and its infrastructure greatly upgraded, changes to the built landscape largely replaced densely congested nineteenth-century areas with mid-twentieth-century modernistic open and geometrically designed spaces.

Renaissance II, which lasted from approximately 1978 to 1988, produced further landscape changes in the downtown. Most striking here were major skyscraper additions to the city skyline, further enhancing Pittsburgh's dramatic city entrance. In addition, the movement to preserve rather than demolish historic structures (which had begun in 1971 with the symphony's movement to Heinz Hall, a converted downtown movie palace) gained momentum, while the growing recognition of the aesthetic quality and advantage of river locations resulted in the municipal construction of the Allegheny Landing and Sculpture Garden in 1984.[81]

Even as the municipality and its private partners labored to reshape the city, devastating changes to the region's economy dramatically affected the industrial landscape. Structural change in the national economy, notably deindustrialization, destroyed much of the region's manufacturing base, especially the major steel firms and allied manufacturing businesses in areas such as the by-product coking industry, machinery production, and railroad and electrical equipment. From approximately the mid-1970s through the late 1980s, mills and industries lining the riverbanks closed down, eliminating many thousands of jobs; some closings continued into the 1990s. Thousands of acres of shuttered factories, rusting steel mills, abandoned rail yards, and vacant land contrasted starkly with the vibrant scene of decades earlier, which John Stilgoe had described. Adjacent to the mills, city working-class neighborhoods and suburban towns sputtered, and their business districts began to deteriorate. The human cost was incalculable.[82] As the flow of investment capital shifted, the emerging brownfields of inactive industrial sites along the rivers contrasted markedly with the sprawling office parks, retail shopping centers, and residential developments sprouting up on suburban greenfields near the interstate highways on the urban periphery.

Clearing of the brownfield sites began slowly during the latter part of the 1980s and into the 1990s. The Urban Redevelopment Authority, which had coordinated much of the renewal of the Pittsburgh Renaissance, cleared sites in the city. Private salvaging firms and a regional nonprofit organization called the Regional Industrial Development Corporation (RIDC), working under the direction of county government, undertook redevelopment of brownfields around the county. The primary goals were to attract new tenants and provide for new taxes and jobs. This single-minded focus resulted in the sweeping destruction of the old industrial landscape and, except for a few isolated structures, almost a complete disregard for the history of the region.[83]

A new landscape began to emerge on these sites along the rivers, although only some of them took advantage of their river location. The Research and Development Park, a high-tech office project developed through the cooperation of the Urban Redevelopment Authority, Carnegie Mellon University, and the University of Pittsburgh on the former site of the LTV (formerly Jones & Laughlin Steel) integrated steel mill on the north bank of the Monongahela River near downtown, is designed as a suburban office park and makes only a limited attempt to take advantage of its river location. Although paying more attention to the river, the private Waterfront development on the mammoth site of the famous Homestead Steel Works on the Monongahela River southeast of Pittsburgh is a retail, entertainment, office, and light industrial complex seemingly designed to be more at home in a landlocked suburb than a river-based former mill town.[84]

In contrast to these brownfield redevelopments are several projects in the city and a few former industrial towns that do recognize the opportunities of river locations.[85] The redevelopment of a former slaughterhouse and industrial site on Herr's Island, renamed Washington's Landing to distance it from its industrial past and tie it to the region's more distant history, uses proximity to downtown and great river views for housing, light industrial and commercial facilities, a marina and rowing club, along with space devoted to the public for biking, walking, and other recreational possibilities. The success of this project has helped to make city riverside real estate very attractive. The city reoriented its vastly expanded convention center in downtown to the Allegheny River and placed its two new sports stadiums on the opposite shore. The nonprofit Cultural Trust, enjoying the city's full cooperation, has expanded its orchestration of a downtown cultural district to include a linear park on the south shore of the Allegheny River. As a result of this focus on the Allegheny River, private firms are busily planning or erecting new projects in the river corridor. And another elite sponsored nonprofit organization, the Riverlife Task Force, has proposed a river park for the segments of the three rivers surrounding downtown with the imaginative concept of the rivers as the park's core.

In addition to these major redevelopment projects, the river landscape is changing in many smaller, but no less profound ways. Despite the deteriorated conditions of Pittsburgh's industrial rivers prior to the mid-twentieth century, they remained a landscape of recreational interest and romance to some boaters. Recreational boating grew in the years after World War II. A few marinas hugged riverbanks protected from powerful currents by proximate islands or sought the calmer waters of tributary streams where they widened near their confluence with the main rivers. In recent decades, the improving environmental quality of both water and air along with the collapse of "smokestack" industries has encouraged the proliferation of pleasure boating, boat tours, and cruises. Increasingly, they have replaced the diminishing number of commercial tows on the rivers. Marinas with lattices of docks occasionally dot the river shores; boat storage yards and launch facilities sit on the banks above the docks, although public access to the rivers is limited to only a few sites. Crews row past the new river-oriented stadiums, convention center, and restaurants of the city's core. Beyond this central area, riverbanks and edges are softening again with rapid revegetation, biking trails on former railroad track beds, and new community riverfront parks. Residences, office buildings, and even a shopping center are replacing the industrial character of riverfront land uses. Fishermen and picnickers again share the river shorelines with the blossoming flora and reviving fauna. Indeed, the river water more often is blue these days than the muddy brown characteristic of the industrial era.[86]

The former industrial riverfronts are not the only sites of renewal. Most dramatic, perhaps, are the developments of a regional shopping mall and an upscale housing complex on massive slag dumps. But, for every brownfield that has sprung back to life with new activity, many more await redevelopment. Suburban office and industrial parks still prove to be more attractive to businesses than settings in older industrial parts of the region. While industrial sources of air and water pollution have been largely eliminated, toxic residues remain in riverbeds and former industrial sites. Moreover, despite improving river conditions, the region still has nearly half of its days during the recreational season when sewage plunges water quality below acceptable levels.[87] And, like other American cities dependent on fossil fuels for power and mobility, Pittsburgh constantly struggles to meet clean air standards, particularly during the hot and humid summer season.

Even though the distinctive industrial structures of the region's coal and steel days have largely disappeared from the built landscape, some river infrastructure and commercial, residential, and public buildings remain along with the engineered river and land contours. Developers who propose new concepts for older areas frequently encounter a battle between those wanting to preserve the built landscape and those wishing to present a modern appearance free of the smoky past. This struggle over the city's image once again pits powerful public and private interests, informed by experts on both sides, against each other for control over shaping the landscape.

In the past, as today, average working-class Pittsburghers had little to say about the shape of the environment in which they lived. Low incomes, inadequate housing, and pedestrian mobility constrained workers in industrial Pittsburgh to live in noisy, congested, and smoky neighborhoods, while middle-class families rode streetcars to leafy, less crowded communities that were still vulnerable on certain days to industrial soot and odors. While the upper class hired landscape architects to fashion plush gardens and grounds from the region's complex topography, working families had to make do with the industrialists' perceptions of a productive economic and social landscape in an individualistic, private society. But that does not mean that workers did not exercise agency in their landscape. Small vegetable and flower gardens, some with religious icons, represented only a small portion of the fashioning of ethnic and racial landscapes. Churches, fraternal societies, and small shops marked the neighborhoods more explicitly. Some workers trespassed onto industrial sites to fish and swim in the rivers; others by the 1930s became passionate hunters in the Pennsylvania mountains and golfers on local public courses. There is another landscape to be discovered and described, which existed outside that of the industrialists' world.

We have written in this chapter about the transformation of the Pittsburgh region's natural landscape by the creation of a built environment and the forces of industrial capitalism. Many of these changes were made to ensure and regulate the workings of the city—to guarantee that traffic would flow, that water would be available where needed, that wastes would be removed, and that streets would not flood. Urban civic leaders and experts such as engineers and planners competed with political interests (often unsuccessfully) to attempt to shape the ideal of a more orderly and efficient urban system. The powerful currents of industrial capitalism also reshaped the landscape, but driven more by the imperative of productivity rather than urban efficiency concerns. The two forces of the city-planned and efficient and the city-productive often clashed, even though there was considerable overlap in their aims. Over time, the pendulum, driven both by conscious planning and economic decline, has gradually swung toward coexistence with and regeneration of the natural environment rather than its mastery. How far these changes will be reflected in the landscape of the future has yet to be seen.

·

River City

EDWARD K. MULLER

WATER COVERS LESS than 2 percent of the area of the Pittsburgh metropolitan region, and yet one always seems to encounter water when traveling about the region. The existence of the three major rivers, three sizable secondary rivers, and a host of small tributary streams explain this paradox.[1] Because major highways, for example, wend their way through the river and stream valleys, motorists are frequently reminded of the rivers' presence, especially when traffic converges, and often slows, to cross bridges. These rivers have been crucial throughout history in the development of the metropolitan region. They have not only sculpted Pittsburgh's physiography, but have also shaped, or at least influenced, daily lives, patterns of settlement, the built landscape, and the regional economy. In turn, Pittsburghers have shaped the rivers, altering flow characteristics, water composition, and river edges. In our efforts to bend the rivers to our will, we have changed the riverine ecology. Thus, the rivers and man are intimately intertwined, no less today than in the past.

In the initial century of the city's development, Pittsburghers recognized their dependence on the rivers for their livelihood. As the premier transportation route to the frontier West, the rivers, especially the Ohio River, provided the basis for the city's burgeoning interregional trade. They also

The Allegheny

The Ohio

★ Pittsburgh

The Monongahela

FIG. I. The rivers and streams of Allegheny County, Pennsylvania

provided essential resources for everyday life. With the shift to an industrial economy after the mid-nineteenth century, the role of the rivers changed and in the minds of many Pittsburghers diminished to a subordinate one in the city's economic world. Through technological means, the rivers were engineered and controlled, reduced in function to serve industry, and made less accessible, both physically and psychologically, to city residents. In the second half of the twentieth century, the rivers staged a modest resurgence in local consciousness for both their symbolic importance and recreational potential, and by the beginning of the twenty-first century they have become once again increasingly recognized as central to the region's economic future and postindustrial life.

Rivers of Empire

Visitors to Pittsburgh often remark on the region's rugged terrain, sometimes even describing it as mountainous. This nomenclature is inaccurate. Pittsburghers do not use the term "mountain" in everyday talk, except for the designation of Mount Washington, the hilltop overlook across from downtown Pittsburgh from which tourists view the city. In fact, the metropolitan region (southwestern Pennsylvania) is an ancient plateau dissected by rivers and streams into a complex mosaic of steep hills, narrow valleys, and modest floodplains. Geologist Henry Leighton captured this succinctly seventy-five years ago:

Standing upon any of the higher hills in Pittsburgh . . . and looking out at the hilltops in all directions, one cannot fail to be impressed with the uniform skyline or equal elevation of the high hilltops. It is evident that the whole region represents an ancient plateau, through which the large rivers and even their smaller tributaries have cut deep gashes. The hills are flat-topped and the stream-valleys are steep-sided. Such a region is called a dissected plateau, representing an elevated plain, over which streams have passed and through the long centuries have carved out their channels and formed tributaries in every direction, until now large or small streams penetrate almost the whole of the area.[2]

The region's most striking physical feature is the convergence of the Allegheny and Monongahela Rivers to form both a small peninsula of land between them known as the Point and the larger Ohio River that flows westward for 981 miles to the Mississippi River.[3] The Allegheny springs to life in the north-central Pennsylvania mountains, flows briefly north and westward into New York state and then courses swiftly 325 miles southwestward through western Pennsylvania to its junction with the Monongahela. Far to the south in the West Virginia mountains, the Tygart and West Fork Rivers join together at Fairmont to form the Monongahela. The Monongahela, locally called the Mon, then flows lazily in sweeping curves for 128 miles northward to its mouth, where, marked often by a muddy brown color, it slowly merges with the bluer waters of the Allegheny. The Point and these three rivers—the Allegheny, Monongahela, and the Ohio—have been the physical framework around which settlement of the Pittsburgh region has unfolded. The three secondary rivers—the Beaver, Kiskiminetas, and Youghiogheny—as well as dozens of tributary streams, creeks, or runs augment this riverine structure.

By the middle of the eighteenth century, both Europeans and American colonists recognized the strategic importance of the Ohio River and the Point for controlling access to the continent's interior. When Euro-Americans crossed the Allegheny Mountains to explore the continent, map out feasible routeways, and harvest valuable animal pelts, they encountered Native Americans who had traversed, hunted, and lived in the region for centuries. The three rivers long served Native Americans as corridors for movement. The junctions of overland trails from the east with the rivers leading to the west made the region an important crossroads in the Native American transportation network, just as it would also be during later Euro-American settlement. By the early eighteenth century, a variety of Native American tribes from the north and east—Seneca, Delaware, Shawnee, and Mingo—hunted in southwestern Pennsylvania, occupied temporary camps, and established approximately a dozen permanent villages, especially at junctions of the river network. Some of these villages became points where Euro-American traders and fur trappers conducted business with them.[4]

French and English leaders, concerned with their aspirations of empire, also understood the strategic significance of the three primary rivers of southwestern Pennsylvania. Their attempts to control the Point, and therefore access to the western interior via the Ohio River, sparked a final struggle (the War for Empire) in the 1750s between the two longtime rivals over their conflicting continental ambitions. Adjacent to their respective forts at the Point, the French and English encouraged crude settlements, which proved to be the embryo of the city of Pittsburgh.[5] After England's victory in the struggle for empire, Virginians initially pressed the settlement of southwestern Pennsylvania and crossed the mountains from the southeast, reaching the navigable, at least by raft and canoe, Monongahela River. Arable land accessible to the mid–Monongahela Valley in counties now south of the city attracted the Virginian settlers, and small urban centers on the Monongahela became points for conducting trade. At the same time, Pennsylvanians trekked over the mountains from the east in smaller numbers until disagreements and even conflict with the Virginians over the definition of provincial boundaries was resolved in 1780 and the jurisdiction of local authorities was thereby firmly established. Pennsylvanians then migrated to the region in increasing numbers. Although Native American raids and skirmishes persisted for several years after 1780, frontier settlement grew rapidly, requiring a variety of urban services.[6]

Laid out and named Pittsburgh in the closing years of the War for Empire, the town outside Fort Pitt on the shores of the Monongahela remained not much more than a frontier outpost, a collection of crude cabins, until the conclusion of the American Revolution. However, Pittsburgh's future looked bright, for the town at the Point commanded the logical point of transfer between the overland eastern roads and the river highway to the western interior of the new nation, where settlers were discovering tremendous opportunities. The first two city plans for Pittsburgh recorded the centrality of the rivers for this urban speculation. In 1764, Colonel John Campbell marked out a small gridiron plan of four blocks oriented to the Monongahela River, where it was easiest to land boats. Twenty years later at the direction of the Penn family, George

Woods and his assistant Thomas Vikeroy surveyed a plan for the entire Point. In keeping with Philadelphia's plan, the nation's largest city and primary model for urban planning at the time, the two surveyors used the gridiron street plan and oriented it to the prospective city's main function of river commerce.[7] Retaining Campbell's original layout, they expanded the grid back from a base of Water Street, which ran parallel to the Monongahela River. The mudflat rising gradually from the river's edge to Water Street formed the wharf. However, Woods and Vikeroy encountered a problem for their scheme at its northern edge because the Allegheny River cut across the peninsula area at an angle as viewed from Water Street. Recognizing the importance of waterfronts for early American urban settlement, they marked out a second gridiron oriented to the Allegheny River, creating an awkward convergence of the two street layouts at Liberty Avenue.[8] The resulting angular intersections have vexed traffic engineers concerned with the smooth flow of vehicles through the confined space of downtown. In contrast to the engineers, architects and pedestrians have enjoyed the landscape aesthetics arising from the disruption of canyonesque streetscapes normally formed when gridirons seem to trail off endlessly into space.

The Commercial City

During the first half of the nineteenth century, civic leaders tried to carry out the vision of Pittsburgh as the commercial emporium for the western frontier by taking advantage of the city's strategic river location. Migrants journeying westward found the small city at the Point a welcome respite from the arduous crossing of the "endless" Allegheny Mountains. Here, they could regain their strength, engage water transportation for the next phase of their journey, replenish provisions, purchase necessary tools and goods (often replacing those jettisoned in the mountains), and gather information about potential destinations. In the early years, the federal government also bought goods locally to supply its western army troops that skirmished for several years with Native Americans in the Ohio Valley. Thus, Pittsburgh provided a market for the surplus of regional farmers, the products of wood, leather, and metal-working artisans, and the services of river men, innkeepers, and hostelries.[9]

As settlement took hold on the western frontier with the new states of Kentucky, Ohio, Indiana, and Illinois being formed between 1792 and 1818, the frontier market assumed a greater importance for Pittsburgh than its simply supplying the military and western migrants. Trade at Pittsburgh reveals the city's pivotal role in both a regional network and the interregional flow of goods between the east and west. People and goods collected at the Monongahela wharf for the river journey to the continental interior, so that Pittsburgh became known as the gateway to the West. Early river commerce floated mostly downriver on rafts and flatboats, while much smaller amounts moved slowly upstream on keelboats. The breakthrough for commercial growth came with the proliferation of steamboats on western waters after 1820. Historian Catherine Reiser reports that the more than 22,000 tons of goods moving to and from Pittsburgh in 1825 grew fifteen times to 380,000 tons in 1848. More than 1,600 boats, both flatboats and steamboats, arrived in 1837 at the Monongahela wharf from the Ohio Valley, and another 190 boats came down to Pittsburgh on the Monongahela and Allegheny Rivers. From the west came furs, cotton, wool, tobacco, sugar, molasses, hemp, and the processed farm products of barreled flour, lard, pork, cheese, and butter. From the east destined for the frontier were dry goods, coffee, spices, hardware, textiles, and a variety of other merchandise.[10]

In the midst of this burgeoning interregional traffic, in which the city's merchants acted as brokers and commission agents, a sizable regional trade developed and added to business down the Ohio. The two regional rivers brought agricultural goods and raw materials to city merchants, artisans, and manufacturers. Whiskey, coal, lumber, salt, farm produce, and pig iron came down the Allegheny and Monongahela Rivers and overland by wagon.[11] Artisans turned out a great variety of goods, while larger manufacturers produced textiles, glasswares, and iron products for frontier markets down the Ohio. Regional boat builders supplied vessels of all kinds. Boatyards at Pittsburgh and nearly a dozen other towns along the Monongahela built rafts, keelboats, barges, and steamboats. In the twenty-five years between 1811 and 1836, historian John Kudlik reports that 252 steamboats were launched at Pittsburgh yards. Boatbuilders at McKeesport, Brownsville, and other points completed several hundred more.[12] By 1850 manufacturing for the frontier, especially by ironworks, garnered a reputation for the city rivaling its gateway distinction.

Despite the relative efficacy of the three rivers for transportation, Pittsburgh merchants and shippers sought both to overcome obstacles to navigation that hindered trade and to improve connections to the east. Normal fluctuations in river flow limited navigation on the rivers for several months each year. Droughts perilously extended low water seasons for shippers and merchants, while rapidly rising waters and floods also interrupted navigation. Ice, shoals and boulders, snags, sandbars, rapids (ripples), and constantly shifting channels at all times of the year routinely made navigation dangerous. Interest in improving navigation began in the late eighteenth century. Pennsylvania declared the three rivers and the secondary rivers as public highways, and thereby to be free of privately erected obstructions and to be improved for navigation. After 1790, Pennsylvania initiated a program to clear obstructions on the Monongahela, Youghiogheny, and Allegheny Rivers, but lasting improvement did not result from these early efforts.[13] The construction of the National Road to Wheeling, West Virginia, which threatened Pittsburgh's gateway position, focused attention on the Ohio River. Poor navigability of the Ohio below Pittsburgh could have made Wheeling a preferable transfer point between the new interregional road and the western rivers. Between 1817 and the 1850s, both the Pennsylvania and the federal government attempted to clear and deepen the Ohio's channel. In 1824 Congress gave responsibility for improving navigation on interstate inland rivers to the Army Corps of Engineers. Snags were pulled, boulders and ripples blasted, bars dredged, and wing dams erected to divert more water over the channels. None provided permanent improvement; floods, ice, and even normal current continually created new hazards. Banks routinely caved in, new snags and bars formed, and channels shifted. In the face of opposition from lumber rafters and high projected expenses, nothing besides surveying was done on the Allegheny. On the Youghiogheny River, locks and dams built in 1850 to provide pools of slackwater behind the dams succumbed to high maintenance costs. However, the Monongahela Navigation Company's slackwater project begun in 1838, consisting of six locks and dams between Brownsville and Pittsburgh, did generate profits for investors and extended the navigation season, especially for coal haulers. Although the overall success of improved navigation was spotty at best, the considerable political pressure, several surveys, and prodigious improvement efforts demonstrated the rivers' paramount role in the minds of southwestern Pennsylvanians.[14]

Pittsburgh's civic leadership expended political capital supporting state legislative efforts to build canals to improve upon the limitations of river navigation and overland travel within the state. Although a financial disaster for the state, the Pennsylvania Main Line Canal, connecting Philadelphia and Pittsburgh, was a boon to trade after its completion in 1834. It traversed the Pittsburgh region via its own man-made channel in the Allegheny and Kiskiminetas river valleys. By increasing enormously the volume of goods moving over the mountains, the canal enhanced Pittsburgh's strategic position in the interregional commercial network. The opening in the 1840s of a canal through the Beaver River valley between the town of Beaver on the Ohio River and Warren, Ohio, further expanded market horizons for Pittsburgh manufacturers and merchants.[15]

The river trade had direct effects on Pittsburgh's spatial development. Since the gateway to the West was the basis of the city's economy, the Monongahela wharf was the focal point for daily life. With the steady growth in trade, the wharf became more and more congested. In 1825 the city passed an ordinance creating a wharf master charged with directing river traffic, collecting a tonnage tax, and maintaining the wharf. The wharf presented a cacophony of sights, sounds, and smells. The newspaper, the *Advocate*, described the scene in May 1838:

one of the most animated scenes we have witnessed in a long time. . . . The whole of our broad levee . . . is closely dotted with drays and wagons, hurrying to the margin of the river from every point of access, burdened with the valuable products of our factories or with Eastern goods. Some half a dozen of the steamers are puffing away ready to start. The margin of the wharf is absolutely covered to the height of a man with freight in all its varieties, while higher up on the footwalks and streets the fronts of the great forwarding houses are blocked by piles of boxes, bales and barrels in beautiful disorder. Shippers, porters, draymen and steamboat clerks blend their hurried voices at once—one is actually deafened with their cheerful din and rush of business.[16]

Businesses gravitated to the streets near the wharf and the markets along Market Street. While artisans, combining their shop and residence in one building, were scattered widely about the town, larger manufactories occupied flat lands along the rivers in both directions away from the wharf. As room ran out along the north shore of the Monongahela, glassmakers and iron masters crossed to the floodplain of the southern shore and occupied the riverbanks of both shores of the Allegheny. A devastating fire that burned nearly a third of the Point area hastened this movement of industry across the rivers. By the early 1850s, the growth of iron and glass factories on the southern shore of the Monongahela led to the formation of five municipalities, collectively called the South Side after annexation to Pittsburgh in the early 1870s. Directly across the Allegheny River from Pittsburgh, the broad floodplain of the sibling community of Allegheny City also attracted many manufacturers. The Pennsylvania Main Line Canal, which ran parallel to the Allegheny River's north shore, enhanced the locational attraction of this rival city, and the small industrial communities of Millvale, Etna, and Sharpsburg developed a few miles further up the river and canal. In Allegheny City, the canal split with one branch ending in a basin in Allegheny City and the other crossing over the river by aqueduct to a basin in the northeast corner of Pittsburgh. This latter basin attracted warehouses and artisans. Over the ensuing years some manufacturers moved from the basin area eastward up the broad floodplain of the Allegheny's south shore, a district known successively as Bayardstown, Northern Liberties, and today the Strip District. The main overland road to eastern Pennsylvania passed through this floodplain as well. Thus, by midcentury the river corridors contained both overland transportation routes and new urban development.[17]

If the rivers provided the foundation for urban growth and its spatial expression, they also influenced life in the city in other important ways. The growing city soon outstripped the ability of private wells and water haulers to supply water. Businesses, craftsmen, and homeowners needed water for work, fire protection, and household use. In the 1820s, the city turned to the Allegheny River for water to pump into a hilltop gravitational reservoir for distribution in the city. The city expanded the water system twice more in the 1840s. Even as the city increasingly drew water out of the Allegheny, primitive waste disposal methods and storm water runoff fouled the rivers. Most wastewater went into privy vaults and cesspools, but private contractors removing solid waste sometimes dumped their loads into the rivers. In 1844, the city assigned a barge tied up at the Allegheny River as its solid waste dump. Of course, the barge's loads were emptied further downstream. Without sewers, storm water frequently drained into the rivers. The first underground sewers were constructed in the late 1840s, but they, too, had outlets in the rivers. In short, the volume of waste and wastewater grew with the city's rapid development and increasingly fouled the rivers (see Tarr and Yosie, this volume).[18]

The rapid growth of new communities across the rivers from Pittsburgh raised demands for more serviceable means of communication than ferryboats. The first bridges went up over the Monongahela and Allegheny Rivers in 1818 and 1819, respectively. They were wooden toll bridges built by private companies with state aid. From these modest beginnings, bridging became an important part of the landscape and economy. Seven bridges spanned the Monongahela and Allegheny Rivers by the end of the 1850s, three of which the innovator of cable wire and famous bridge engineer, John Roebling, built.[19] As industry, railroads, and population spread over the metropolitan region, more and more bridges were erected over the primary rivers, smaller tributaries, and even the many ravines of tiny creeks. In 1928, forty-five bridges spanned the primary rivers of Allegheny County, and this one county alone has today approximately nine hundred bridges, some of which cross railroads and highways rather than water.[20] In the early twentieth century federal, state, and local governments became responsible for building and maintaining most bridges. Further, they replaced bridges in response to demand for increased capacity or the requirement of the Army Corps of Engineers and the War Department for higher bridge clearance over the rivers to facilitate commercial navigation. In the mid-1920s, Allegheny County initiated a major highway and bridge building program that resulted in the construction of nearly one hundred bridges, including a dozen of considerable architectural merit.[21]

The most infamous bridge replacement project to accommodate bigger towboats involved the long debate and final erection of the "Three Sisters" bridges between downtown and the North Side over the Allegheny River between 1926 and 1928. Older low bridges forced towboats to lower their stacks in order to pass beneath them; in high water periods the vessels simply could not pass underneath. As Frederick Law Olmsted Jr. pointed out in his 1910 study of the issue, the Army Corps of Engineers' request to raise the height of the bridges created problems related to the traffic crossing the bridges. Greater elevations caused steeper grades, slowing traffic, and resulted in longer approaches to the bridges, which altered streetscapes and effected land uses on both sides of the river. Since by Olmsted's estimate thirty times more tonnage crossed the bridges than went under them, these concerns were critical for the merchants, haulers, and citizens that would be affected. Other questions raised by replacement bridges involved relationships to proposed flood control measures, the placing of new piers in the navigation channels, and expense. Moreover, the Pittsburgh Arts Commission had approval power over the appearance of the bridges. In 1918, the War Department ordered the erection of new, higher bridges over the Allegheny River. After three decades of debate, the solution finally came with the county's building in the mid-1920s of the prize-winning Three Sisters—self-anchored suspension cable bridges.[22]

Although before the mid-nineteenth century the rivers hindered close interaction among the emerging towns, even with the initial bridges, individuals enjoyed accessibility to them and the many pleasures that water afforded. Pittsburghers boated, fished, hunted, and swam in the rivers. The earliest scientific observations of riverine fauna recorded diverse and abundant fishes and mussels in the region's waters. Local markets commonly sold fish to their customers.[23] Young Henry Oliver, eventually to become one of Pittsburgh's steel titans, fondly remembered swimming in the Allegheny River in the protected waters between a sandbar and the riverbank in Allegheny City.[24] Walking and picnicking along the riverbanks outside of the urban area were also frequent pastimes. More organized recreational activities emerged as the city grew larger. Rowing, first boats and then sport sculling, became popular by midcentury and evolved into rowing clubs and competitions that drew throngs of spectators.[25] Recreational "gardens" at riverside locations a mile or so up the Monongahela River provided venues, albeit with an admission price, for outdoor sports and leisure activities for working-class families. Entrepreneurs promoted cruises on the rivers, while folks who could bear the expense took steamboats on day trips up the Allegheny River. A few upper-class families built summer homes along the rivers.[26] The rivers were fundamental to the city's way of life, and the rhythm of the seasons, manifested through the rivers' different moods, affected people's economic, recreational, and daily lives. If ever the label "river city" applied to Pittsburgh, this was the era.

The Industrial Era

On December 10, 1852, Pittsburghers congregated in the Strip District on the floodplain of the Allegheny River to celebrate the opening of the Pennsylvania Railroad's service to Philadelphia. Within a few years, trains left for the City of Brotherly Love three times a day and covered the distance in an average of fifteen hours. The Pennsylvania Railroad also made connections with the Fort Wayne Railroad to Cleveland and Chicago. This new technology soon negated Pittsburgh's strategic role as the transfer point at the head of the Ohio River, puncturing its inflated commercial aspiration as the great trans-Appalachian emporium. As the city's commercial role declined and heavy industry, especially iron and steel, became its main business, the rivers' role and people's perceptions of them changed. The rivers became more industrial, more utilitarian, more engineered, and less accessible to residents. Their physical characteristics changed to reflect their new roles. Yet, they still had important impacts on people's lives and on the metropolitan region.

The railroads carried merchandise, agricultural products, and people destined either to the west or east through Pittsburgh without the need for stopping. As the railroad network expanded, the city's middleman and break-in-bulk functions withered away. Former commission merchants and canal boat merchants changed their businesses, often moving, as Benjamin F. Jones did, initially into the iron trades and subsequently into iron manufacturing, where Pittsburgh's future lay.[27] While Jones built the large and successful Jones & Laughlin Steel Corporation, business at the Monongahela wharf progressively declined during the second half of the nineteenth century, and smaller packet lines working a limited, regional river trade in what was known as the headwaters or Pittsburgh district remained the wharf's habitués. By the 1920s portions of the wharf had become a parking lot for automobiles. The wharf and the surrounding blocks of warehouses, once the focus of the city's business, deteriorated into a backwater of downtown. Capital moved to the interior blocks of the Golden Triangle along Fourth Avenue, the city's new financial district, and around Grant Street in tall, corporate headquarters office buildings.[28]

The demise of Pittsburgh's gateway function did not diminish the total tonnage carried on the rivers. Tonnage increased enormously for the rest of the century as coal, oil, sand, gravel, other raw materials, and industrial products moved in tows of heavy barges lashed together and pushed by steam-propelled boats. Prior to the 1850s merchants had transported the finished products of iron and glass manufacturers down the Ohio River to frontier markets. In the late 1850s, however, the city's iron manufacturers, who had primarily operated forges, foundries, and rolling mills until that point, expanded into the new railroad rail markets, supplied iron products and armaments for the Civil War, built enormous blast furnaces to produce their own pig iron for the first time, erected much larger puddling and rolling mills, and after 1875 entered the mass production steel industry. The astounding success of these initiatives, along with the growth of the glass, railroad equipment, oil refining, and electrical equipment industries, transformed Pittsburgh from a commercial city to an industrial metropolis.[29] Even though the railroads were essential to the industrialization of the region, transportation along the rivers remained critical to many industries as well. In the 1860s and 1870s small oil refineries relied on crude oil floated down the Allegheny River from the northwestern Pennsylvania oil fields. The immense iron and steel industry of the Pittsburgh region consumed enormous quantities of coal and coke brought down the rivers, particularly the Monongahela River, to the mills and power plants. By the 1920s more than twenty million tons of goods moved along the Monongahela, approximately 80 percent of which was coal. Several million more tons moved along the Ohio and Allegheny Rivers. The Army Corps of Engineers estimated that Pittsburgh industries had by 1928 invested approximately forty million dollars in river terminals and craft. The three rivers' shipbuilding industry with origins in the early years of frontier development evolved along with river shipping. After building ironclad craft in the Civil War, local shipbuilders turned to barges, towboats, and workboats. By one account, five shipyards launched nearly four hundred hulls in 1928 alone, including crane and dredging boats, sand diggers, dump scows, towboats, and a few hundred steel barges.[30] Moreover, many industries depended on the rivers for water supply and waste disposal. By one estimate, it took seventy tons of water to make one ton of steel, eighteen barrels of water to refine one barrel of oil, and seven barrels of water to brew one barrel of beer.[31]

As a result of the growing dependence of shippers and industries on the three rivers, efforts to improve navigation and the reliability of water supply revived after the Civil War. Pressure on Congress produced more legislation and some financial support for new surveys, removal of snags, dredging, and more diversion dams. As earlier, however, these measures failed to provide adequate improvements for the rapidly increasing volume of traffic, and it became increasingly clear that only a more sophisticatedly engineered system of locks and dams that kept a slackwater depth of six, and later nine feet, offered a permanent solution. Congress authorized the construction of locks and dams for the Ohio River in 1875. Ten years later the Army Corps of Engineers completed the Davis Island Lock and Dam five miles below Pittsburgh. With a 1,223-foot wicket dam across the river, this dam created a six-foot pool for the Pittsburgh harbor. Its success encouraged the lobbying for canalization of the Ohio. By 1899, Congress authorized erecting Locks 2 through 18 to Marietta, Ohio. At the same time, locks and dams extended navigation on the Monongahela and Allegheny Rivers. Congress authorized locks and dams on the entire Ohio River in 1910, but the expense, perception of them as pork-barrel projects, and some stakeholder opposition prevented completion until the 1920s. Under tremendous pressure from steel corporations that wanted to take greater advantage of the river to market their products, Congress finally funded the completion of the fifty-three locks and dams along the Ohio, which Pittsburgh celebrated with great fanfare in October 1929.[32] Ironically, Pittsburgh's great era of industrial growth had already ended.

The rivers not only supported the industrialization of Pittsburgh's economy, they also shaped the spatial structure of the emerging industrial metropolis. Due to the explosive industrialization that began in the 1850s, the population of the urban area grew from approximately eighty thousand in 1850 to more than one million in 1920. Manufacturers, shipbuilders, and shippers initially expanded along the river edges in the city of Pittsburgh, but soon faced limited opportunities for adequate sites on floodplains that narrowed toward the city boundaries. Beginning with Andrew Carnegie's construction of his highly successful, trendsetting Edgar Thomson steel mill at Braddock Fields nine miles up the Monongehela River, industrialists wishing to build large, modern, mass production plants, such as integrated iron and steel works, looked well beyond the city for floodplain locations. Railroads snaking down valleys of tributary streams such as Turtle Creek also attracted manufacturers such as George Westinghouse to their smaller, narrow floodplains. By World War I industrial towns stretched twenty to thirty miles from downtown Pittsburgh along each of the three rivers, alternating from one riverbank to the other with each sweeping river bend.[33] While residential suburbs spread onto and over the hills away from the rivers and smaller industries lined the narrow tributary creek valleys, the characteristic Pittsburgh industrial landscape was a broad, rounded floodplain on the inside of a river curve hemmed in by flanking hillsides. Across the river facing the mill town site, a steep, often wooded, hillside arose from the river's edge, leaving only room for a railroad track. The alternating geography of these mill towns from one side of the river to the other has been likened to "beads on a string" and, when viewed on a map of urban development, gave the Pittsburgh region a starfish spatial pattern.

Age-old fluvial processes of erosion and deposition from the rivers cutting down through the Allegheny Plateau account for the distinctive settlement pattern of the metropolitan region. As the region's rivers reached lower elevations with gentler gradients, they tended to diminish their rate of downward cutting or erosion and increase their widening action or horizontal spread. The rivers began to meander in broader curves, taking a more serpentine course. The faster flow of water occurring on the outside of curves cut into the riverbank, while the resulting load of silt, sand, and gravel deposited by the slower waters on the inside of curves further downstream created floodplains. Thus, steep hills formed on the outside of river curves where erosion was taking place, and floodplains were built up on the inside of the curves where deposition occurred.[34] Industries and railroads acquired the riverfront sites in the floodplains; towns developed adjacent to the industries and expanded up the flanking hillsides. The opposing steep hillsides across the river usually remained undeveloped. In some instances, the trees on these hills had been harvested for fuel and building materials or damaged by air pollution from the mills, leaving scarred and eroded landscapes that have only recently been reforested.

The expansion of industry along the river floodplains and industry's dependence on the rivers for transportation, water supply, and often waste disposal had significant impacts on the rivers and the residents' ability to use them. In general, industrialization increased the engineering of the rivers. The canalization of the rivers with the construction of locks and dams, along with the erection of cement and wooden bulkheads for river terminals and flood control walls, altered river levels and flow. Locks and dams slowed river flow rates, raised water levels, and in effect created a series of controlled pools. In this manner seasonal low water extremes were diminished and deeper channels maintained, but riverbanks were altered and normal fluvial processes disrupted such that new areas of erosion and deposition were created. At the same time, businesses and communities used "fill" from excavations, trash disposal, and land grading to extend land into the rivers and even to close back channels to nearby islands. Both the Carnegie and Jones & Laughlin steel corporations, for example, expanded mills on Monongahela River sites, such that the sloping riverbanks were extended beyond the original water line, raised as much as twenty feet, and thereby turned into flat land.[35]

This engineering of the rivers, riverbanks, and floodplains greatly altered the lowland riverine environment, disrupting natural systems. Higher water levels submerged mudflats, beaches, and wetlands, while dredging for navigation and draining and filling for development not only destroyed wetland sedges, rushes, and other plants, but also the vegetation complex of sycamore, silver maple, slippery elm, and black willow trees that traditionally occupied the slightly higher and drier alluvial floodplains. Placing smaller streams in culverts had a similar impact on their ecology. The destruction of wetlands diminished the natural processes of cleaning, retaining, and slowly releasing water. Dredging, filling, and pollution disrupted the river bottom environment for many species of mussels, fish, and other aquatic life. For example, the commercial opportunities for sand and gravel have sustained the dredging of the Allegheny River's glaciated materials down to today.[36] Large fish kills and the dismally small number of fish species left in the rivers in the 1950s indicated the severely degraded quality of water.

Rapid urbanization and industrial growth also led to the degradation of water quality. Pittsburgh and the surrounding industrial and residential communities relied on water carrying waste to the rivers for disposal. Beginning in the mid-nineteenth century, the city of Pittsburgh built underground sewers that emptied into the rivers. In the later 1880s, the city began constructing combined sanitary and storm water sewers, completing more than four hundred miles in little more than twenty years (see Tarr and Yosie, this volume). By the 1920s, more than a hundred communities upriver from Pittsburgh also disgorged their sewage into the rivers, and many manufacturers dumped their wastewater as well. Adding to this deteriorating situation, hundreds of thousands of tons of sulfuric acid drained from mines into the watershed, destroying aqua life and fauna, damaging waterworks, bridges, industrial machinery, and pipes, and tainting drinking water (see Casner, this volume). As a result, Pittsburgh's rivers and tributary streams became severely polluted; at the turn of the century the city had the nation's worst death rate from typhoid fever. Since the city and many suburban communities pumped their water supply from the rivers, they had to consider expensive water treatment facilities. Pittsburgh, for example, began operating a state-of-the-art slow sand filtration plant in 1908, after which the typhoid death rate significantly declined. However, treating water encouraged engineers and politicians to avoid treating sewage. The city only stopped dumping and began treating sewage in 1959 (see Tarr and Yosie, this volume).

Locks and dams diminished, but did not end flooding. Seasonal floods remained a recurrent nuisance and expense for most of the industrial era, while disastrous floods periodically wreaked havoc with river communities and industries. Those living close to the river, such as the young Henry Oliver and his family who lived on the "First Bank" above the Allegheny River in Allegheny City, experienced annual flooding and established routines for evacuation, protection of household belongings, and cleaning up. Henry's father and older brother remained in their home's second floor to guard their property, while Henry, the younger children, and his mother moved to higher ground away from the river. When the waters receded, mud had to be shoveled out of the house.[37] Between 1832 and 1907, eleven major floods destroyed property and caused deaths. The devastating flood of March 1, 1907, covered an estimated 53 percent of downtown and idled more than 100,000 workers for a week. The event precipitated the Pittsburgh Chamber of Commerce to appoint a Flood Commission. The commission observed that flood frequency and severity had intensified in recent years, and with increasing urbanization the value of losses was skyrocketing. It predicted that a forty-foot flood was probable at some date in the future. In its 1912 final report the commission laid out a flood control plan involving the creation of at least seventeen impoundment reservoirs, construction of a strategically placed flood wall in downtown Pittsburgh, the filling in of three back channels of islands close to the Point, and the establishment of forest preserves in the headwater areas of the Monongahela and Allegheny Rivers. Once again dependence on federal action led to little accomplishment.[38] As predicted, the forty-foot flood level was, indeed, surpassed in the Saint Patrick's Day flood of 1936. This disastrous flood killed forty-seven people, injured an estimated 2,800, left tens of thousands homeless, and caused approximately fifty million dollars in property loss across the region. It finally galvanized political leaders in Pittsburgh and Washington to build the recommended impoundment reservoir system to protect lives and property.[39] Although floods still occur, the frequency and severity have significantly declined along with their impact on people's lives and property in the region.

The development of industry and railroads along miles of riverfront eventually blocked easy access to the rivers for most residents. Pittsburgh vacated streets that once ended at the river edges in order to provide industries with land for expansion and the erection of railroad ramps, sidings, and switching tracks.[40] In order to get to the rivers, people had to cross dangerously busy railroad tracks and trespass on industrial property, some of which was cordoned off from the public for security reasons. Heavy river traffic, polluted waters, high bulkheads, and banks littered with debris and abandoned barges made the rivers themselves less and less appealing. Recreational activities such as swimming, fishing, rowing, and pleasure boating declined and what did persist moved to settings beyond the urban area. Even in the early 1920s, the city of Pittsburgh maintained some riverfront beaches despite warnings about the unhealthy water quality. These were soon closed.[41] A few individuals still swam, fished, or boated at considerable risk or in the case of teenagers with much relish at defying authorities or parental instructions. Drownings happened every year. As a result of the overall deterioration of the river environment, people increasingly viewed the rivers as industrial rivers—economically important, unnaturally engineered, picturesque perhaps, but not scenic, and no longer accessible. This perception hardened over the years. Those who had the time and income sought the pleasures of water recreation at Atlantic Ocean beaches, the Lake Erie shore, the lake regions of Ontario, or the streams and rivers of the Allegheny Mountains.[42]

The Rivers in the Postindustrial Economy

Despite evidence of weakness in Pittsburgh's industrial activity by the 1930s and the prediction in 1963 of absolute decline, manufacturing, especially of primary metals, continued to dominate the region's economy and river landscapes until the early 1980s. In the city's post–World War II redevelopment, small changes in the region's orientation to the rivers did occur. Fundamental change only began to surface in the 1980s when deindustrialization devastated the region's heavy industries; but it has taken more than a decade to reverse negative perceptions of the rivers, comprehend their importance to the city's future, and prepare a strategy for taking advantage of this resource.

In the early 1940s, as civic leaders assessed the gloomy prospects of their city after the war, they concluded that Pittsburgh's environmental, infrastructural, and economic problems would have to be addressed effectively. Five decades of reform agitation, civic organizing, and municipal planning had not resulted in a great deal of change. The city was still smoky, dirty, congested, unsightly, unhealthy, and overspecialized in primary metal industries. In order to retain and attract new major corporations and talented personnel, civic leaders organized to rid the skies of smoke, improve sanitation, build new highways, revitalize downtown, and attract new kinds of businesses. With the tacit partnership of the city's two most powerful political and corporate leaders and the creation of a new civic organization comprised of corporate presidents, the city embarked on a twenty-year redevelopment program in 1946 known as the Pittsburgh Renaissance, which addressed many of these problems with varying success. Smoke control legislation and the emerging economic advantages of natural gas over bituminous coal brightened the skies. As new buildings, parks, and highways began to appear by the mid-1950s, a renewed spirit swept through many, though not all, segments of the population. Pittsburgh was enjoying a renaissance in image, infrastructure, and some parts of the built environment.[43]

The civic leadership did not intend to transform Pittsburgh's basic economy; after all, they primarily led the established industries. Rather, their strategy was to strengthen and diversify the regional economy. Accordingly, the rivers remained an important industrial transporter, and factories and mills continued to line the riverbanks. The completion of the flood control system and a sewage collection and treatment plant for Allegheny County improved both conditions on river floodplains for businesses and residents and water quality, even though many mills and communities continued to dump waste in the rivers. Along with generally rising incomes and increased leisure time resulting from the success of unionization and postwar prosperity, the clearly improving environmental conditions encouraged more pleasure boating on the rivers. By the mid-1970s, there were fifty-one wharves, marinas, and boat launching ramps in Allegheny County, most privately operated, to accommodate fifteen thousand licensed pleasure boats.[44] Moreover, urban redevelopment at the Point replaced the warehouses, abandoned and run-down buildings, and railroad facilities with a state park that symbolized the geographical and historical significance of the confluence of the rivers: the beginning of the Ohio and the birth of the city. The park's designers wished to encourage active participation in the park, as well as to provide vistas of the rivers and a place to moor pleasure craft. The symbolic and participatory orientation to the rivers dramatically reversed the utilitarian approach of the previous seventy-five years.

Despite the celebration of the rivers at Point State Park, basic attitudes about, and perceptions of, the rivers did not significantly change. When new expressways and parking lots were built after World War II, they were often placed on the riverfronts, where they further inhibited access to the rivers for recreation. In 1910, Frederick Law Olmsted Jr. had proposed combining European style promenades and scenic linear parks along downtown's riverfronts with necessary traffic arteries.[45] However, as plans were formulated in the 1920s and 1930s, traffic priorities prevailed. Implementation of these plans before and after World War II turned the Monongahela wharf into a parking lot, flood wall, and expressway. In the 1950s, a major river study noted the terrible conditions of the riverbanks used as dumps, marred by abandoned river terminal facilities and barges, and appropriated by ragtag shantyboats, scrap yards, and small boat repair operations. The study recommended minor changes based on the assumption, undoubtedly widely held, that since floodplains must be the home of industry, additional river recreational opportunities must be found in a manner that does not "detract from industry."[46]

In the 1970s, two major public developments were built on riverfront land along the Allegheny River in the heart of the city, where blight was taking hold. Tellingly, neither project took advantage of the river. Despite its name, Three Rivers Stadium, completed in 1970, failed to open to the rivers and the city's signature vista of the fountain in Point State Park framed by downtown's redeveloped skyline. Only adjacent Roberto Clemente Park, a small, hard-edged concrete linear river park with little real connection to the stadium, acknowledged the river's existence.[47] A few years later in 1977 the new convention center was finished with its back—its loading docks and windowless walls—to the river. The postwar renaissance improved the city's environment, some active groups in the city adopted the new environmental values sweeping across the nation, and a few citizens enjoyed the small riverfront parks of a handful of suburban towns and the recreational use of a couple of islands. Nonetheless, civic leaders and most Pittsburghers still could not conceive of the region's rivers beyond their industrial function of the past hundred years.[48]

Despite earlier warnings and even evidence of industrial decline, the dramatic and rather sudden collapse of Pittsburgh's steel industry and several other traditional manufacturing plants in the late 1970s and 1980s changed the economic role and ecological conditions of the rivers in the region. Shipments of mostly coal and some of the same bulk products like sand and gravel, primary metals, and petrochemicals through the port of Pittsburgh have remained strong at fifty-three million tons in 1998.[49] Nonetheless, a declining proportion of the region's economy is dependent on the rivers.

Water quality has markedly improved with the diminution of industrial waste in the river and the greater enforcement of clean water regulations. The restoration of local fisheries since the 1970s, including prized game fish such as sauger, smallmouth black bass, and walleye pike, has generated optimism for the rejuvenation of the rivers.[50] A recent study of water quality in the main Pittsburgh pool of the rivers indicates that they meet reasonable standards during dry weather conditions, but not during wet weather conditions. The tributary streams do not meet the standards in either weather situation. Traces of toxic chemicals in fish, the occasional fish kill, and frequent summer advisories to avoid contact with the water, especially after rainstorms, remind the optimists that additional remedial efforts and continued regulatory vigilance are warranted.[51] Despite the need for continued improvement of water quality, trees and plants have flourished along the riverbanks in recent years though invasive species such as Japanese knotweed have displaced many native ones. Further, the increasing abundance and diversity of mammals, reptiles, amphibians, birds, and waterfowl signify a more healthy riverine ecology.

Just as importantly, the shuttering of factories, warehouses, and mills along miles and miles of riverbanks raised the potential for both reuse of the valuable floodplain sites and revived access to the rivers. While a few river enthusiasts advocated imaginative reuse of the region's riverfronts in the 1980s, civic leaders thought mostly along traditional lines of creating as soon as possible new jobs, manufacturing or otherwise, for the abandoned industrial sites. Under enormous political pressure from economically depressed neighborhoods and towns, politicians did not have the luxury of considering environmental, recreational, historic preservation, and design issues and solutions, which seemed peripheral to the explicit demand for new jobs. Moreover, the abandoned industrial buildings and lands, known as brownfields, frequently had serious toxic waste problems that raised public health, costly remediation, and liability issues, and suffered from inadequate highway access by modern standards. The financially distressed and socially disorganized adjacent mill towns, many of which had begun to decline several years before the plant closures, further detracted from the brownfield sites' development potential.[52]

The region's inability to attract much development capital, as well as the palpable sense of economic decline and population loss, allowed the former industrial sites to lie inactive or undergo demolition. This delay in redevelopment and the growing recognition that manufacturing would never return to most of these lands provided the opportunity for those advocating the reconceptualization of the rivers and riverfronts to organize, make their case, and develop plans for alternative uses. At the same time, some civic leaders began to see the success of waterfront redevelopment in other American cities, reassess the environmental advantages of the region's water resources, and understand, however slowly and inconsistently, that the heralded new economy at the end of the twentieth century depended in part on environmental and outdoor recreational quality of life issues. In the late 1980s and early 1990s, public and nonprofit-sponsored studies, one after another, promoted accessibility to the rivers and river edges as one way to make Pittsburgh a more attractive place to live and work. Although clearing skies, improving water quality, and increased river access came at cost to Pittsburgh's industrial economy, severely distressing the workforce and badly impacting working families, the changes also pointed to one way to build a new future.[53]

Several successful river projects appearing between the mid-1980s and the mid-1990s contributed to the changing attitudes about the rivers. Joseph Bendel, former city planner and longtime mayor of the small industrial city of McKeesport, located twelve miles upriver from Pittsburgh at the junction of the Monongahela and Youghiogheny Rivers, saw the advantage of redeveloping the riverfront long before other local politicians envisioned a greener future for their waterfronts. Mayor Bendel patiently worked the labyrinth of governmental grants to develop a riverside park, marina, and hiking and biking trail that filled in a leg of the Pittsburgh-to-Washington, D.C. trail slowly emerging across southwestern Pennsylvania. Down the river a few miles from McKeesport, a water slide park arose on the brownfield site of the former Mesta Machine Corporation works in the unlikely setting of the tired industrial town of West Homestead. The instant success of the city of Pittsburgh's modest boat launch and linear park on the South Side's riverfront in 1983 revealed pent-up popular demand for river access and reflected the development of sport fishing and pleasure boating around the region. At the same time, the huge crowds generated by the annual river regatta each summer and the profitability of the Gateway Clipper cruise boats demonstrated the tourist potential of the rivers. And, across from downtown, the Urban Redevelopment Authority of Pittsburgh constructed Allegheny Landing in 1984 as a small riverfront park and sculpture garden adjacent to a new privately developed complex of office buildings. This project showed the possibilities of riverfront sites for extending downtown development across the rivers that had once been only utilitarian boundaries to the Golden Triangle.

The popularity of the initial rails-to-trails projects supported the Friends of the Riverfront effort to place a twelve-mile riverfront trail from the city's northeastern boundary on the Allegheny River, westward around the Point, and eastward again up the Monongahela River to the city's southeastern boundary.[54] With the inauguration of Mayor Tom Murphy in 1993, this trail, the Three Rivers Heritage Trail, officially became a city project. Finally, the successful redevelopment of Herr's Island, the site of a former cattle yard and slaughterhouse, into Washington's Landing, an office and residential complex based on its proximity to downtown, striking views of the river, and access to riverfront trails, a marina, and a popular rowing club, probably did more than anything else to accelerate the rethinking of the rivers' role in the region. Here was the successful demonstration of the viability of building housing on a brownfield site along the rivers. Like the popularity of artificially created lakes around the country, these engineered rivers are increasingly perceived by the public as a valuable "natural" resource.

By the mid-1990s, civic leaders had begun to incorporate the rivers explicitly into the city's redevelopment strategy. Public investments in new baseball and football stadiums and an enlarged and reoriented convention center emphasized a river corridor of entertainment activity along the Allegheny. The stadiums and convention center now open to the rivers. The bridge from downtown over the Allegheny River to the stadiums is closed to vehicles on game days and used for street vending and programming. These new projects complement the Pittsburgh Cultural Trust's fifteen-year-long development of a performing arts district in a fourteen-square-block area of downtown paralleling the Allegheny River. At the same time, the city is actively encouraging private projects on the river shores, including apartments, office buildings, and restaurants. Foremost in the advancement of these efforts is the recent completion of the Alcoa Corporation's new headquarters building across from downtown on the Allegheny riverfront. Along with the Cultural Trust's riverfront park development on the southern shore of the Allegheny, the Riverlife Task Force, a new nonprofit organization with governmental participation and private funding, is exploring innovative park designs to tie the various activities of the river corridor together.[55] The North Shore Corridor, as the city is calling the area, is envisioned as the signature complex of the new, river-based Pittsburgh.

Other towns in the region are also turning to the rivers for new development. From Kittanning at the metropolitan region's northeastern edge on the Allegheny River to Brownsville at the southern edge on the Monongahela, riverside parks, trails, marinas, public river landings, water taxis, and guided tours are in operation, under construction, in planning, or being discussed. While light industrial and office parks are emerging on some brownfield sites adjacent to the rivers, others are (where location within the metropolitan region is advantageous) becoming shopping centers, residential neighborhoods, and recreational complexes. Not all developers and public officials are taking advantage, or full advantage, of riverine resources.[56] Older land use and design values linger on, so that the finite opportunities along the river are fragile. Besides the prospect of the city of Pittsburgh's North Shore planning currently underway, no grand design guides or even influences these developments. Instead, a broad consensus is slowly evolving which recognizes that a healthy and diverse physical environment of flora and fauna, outdoor recreational opportunities and amenities, and the aesthetics of water resources are essential in the region's strategy to compete with other metropolitan regions for businesses and people.

Whereas the rivers were once instrumental in the city's economic success as the gateway to the West and then as an industrial powerhouse, they are gaining importance again for Pittsburgh's future in the postindustrial economy. Additionally, location with respect to the rivers, which exercised a powerful influence on the region's spatial structure through the commercial and industrial eras, is again becoming a force. Once the outlines of the industrial metropolis had been established by World War I and many riverfront sites built up, new residential, commercial, and industrial developments from the 1920s to the 1970s most often sought available sites served by railroad, and increasingly motor vehicles, which were not oriented toward the rivers. The new importance of the rivers in the current era strengthens development of river floodplains, and local officials hope this emphasis on the rivers will enhance the adjacent former mill towns, which have been declining since the 1950s because of suburbanization. Moreover, more and more Pittsburgh residents are reclaiming accessibility to the rivers, making them important to their everyday lives. During the region's industrial heyday, the rivers were critical to economic success, but through the intensive industrial development of the riverfronts and waterways and through their engineering, the rivers became remote from many people's sense of place, of what was important to them, just as people across industrial American felt removed from their environments. With the collapse of the industrial economy, the rivers and the people are being reunited. It has, perhaps, been more difficult to awaken people's sensitivity to the value of their environment and its potential for their future in the once heavily industrialized and economically weakened Pittsburgh region than it has been in many other American cities. But, with the growing realization of the importance of the rivers and the riverine environment for its future, Pittsburgh may be in its residents' minds a river city once again.

Critical Decisions in Pittsburgh
Water and Wastewater Treatment

JOEL A. TARR

and TERRY F. YOSIE

ONE OF THE MOST serious environmental problems facing
Pittsburgh throughout its history has been pollution of its
neighboring rivers. This pollution, from both domestic and
industrial sources, has severely impacted the quality of the
water drawn from the rivers for drinking water and for industrial purposes as well as sharply curtailing the availability of the rivers for recreational uses. All cities have to deal
with the problem of their metabolism—providing a supply
of fresh water for domestic and commercial and industrial
purposes, for street cleaning, and for fire-fighting—and then
disposing of this water in a manner that will not endanger
the health of their citizens or the surrounding ecosystem.
Because of its position as a riverine city, Pittsburgh has been
blessed by abundant supplies but also cursed by the extensive pollution of these supplies resulting from their use as
sinks for waste disposal. This chapter will review the history
of water supply and wastewater disposal and treatment in
Pittsburgh, paying particular attention to critical turning
points, public health issues, and organizational and political
questions.[1]

Water Supply

Like other urbanites at the beginning of the nineteenth century, Pitts-burghers drew their water from local sources such as springs, ponds, and the rivers, as well as from rainwater gathered in cisterns. From almost the beginning of the municipality, there were major issues as to whether water would be furnished by public or private providers. In 1802, for instance, the Pittsburgh Select and Common Councils passed an ordinance allowing the borough to construct four public wells and to purchase private wells "in useful and necessary parts of the Borough." At the same time, private water suppliers operated, and in 1815 the city directory listed five water carters who provided water to those able to afford the service. As the city grew in population, its needs increased rapidly, making it clear that more ample sources would have to be found. The major issue continued to be, as it was in other cities, whether water would be furnished by public or private providers.[2]

In 1818 the councils refused to approve an attempt by private interests to obtain a municipal water franchise, expressing a preference for public supply. In 1821, reflecting this sentiment, sixty-one prominent citizens suc-cessfully petitioned the councils to provide new wells and to make all ex-isting pumps public, while in the following year citizens petitioned the councils requesting that the municipality build a waterworks to supply Allegheny River water to the city. The petitions maintained that municipal ownership was required to guarantee improved fire protection and to se-cure lower fire insurance rates, to service domestic and manufacturing needs, and to meet public health requirements.[3]

After extensive debate, in 1826 the Pittsburgh Select and Common Councils approved the construction of a waterworks that would provide protection against fire and "beneficial effects to every manufactory and . . . family in the city." The city completed the waterworks in 1828. It utilized a steam pump to draw water from the Allegheny River and to raise it to a million-gallon reservoir located on Grant Hill for gravity distribution throughout the city. The councils appointed a joint standing committee to supervise the system, as well as three water commissioners and a superin-tendent.[4]

The councils expanded the system in 1844 and again in 1848 in response to the inadequacies revealed by the Great Fire of 1845 and the needs of the territories annexed in 1845 and 1846. By the end of 1850 the city had laid twenty-one miles of water pipe serving 6,630 dwellings, stores, and shops. The pipe network continued to expand, especially after the large annexations of territory in 1867 and 1872. In 1879 the city opened a new water-works that pumped water from the Allegheny River and stored it in two reservoirs, one on Highland Avenue and the other on Herron Hill, for gravity distribution throughout the city. From 1889 to 1900, it built a yearly average of 15.4 miles of pipe; by 1895 the system was 268 miles in length and by 1915, 743 miles. Extensive waste and leaky pipes, however, plagued the system, resulting in frequent water shortages. In the 1890s, the Department of Public Works began installing water meters in order to reduce waste, but the city continued to have one of the highest rates of per capita water consumption of any city in the nation.[5]

Waterworks funding was the single largest expenditure made by the city during its first fifty years, with the initial cost of construction constituting 40 percent of all municipal spending from 1827 to 1833. In 1854, the council's Water Committee estimated the total cost of the system as $677,709, with $243,240 paid out of annual appropriations and $377,069 borrowed at 6 percent interest. Pittsburgh was not unusual in the extent to which waterworks costs constituted a substantial part of the total municipal budget. The building of New York's Croton Aqueduct in 1842, for instance, increased the city's debt from $500,000 to over $9 million and caused many citizens to predict financial disaster.[6] Waterworks were usually the most expensive capital project undertaken by nineteenth-century American cities. Pittsburgh's willingness to make such a large expenditure for a public good can be explained by the combination of a variety of interest groups—merchants and industrialists, homeowners, fire insurance companies, and those concerned with the public health—to demand an adequate supply of water.

Access to water services, however, was unevenly distributed throughout the city. Working-class districts generally had poorer water supplies than did affluent neighborhoods, often relying on local springs or wells. Many neighborhoods in the heavily industrial South Side, for instance, utilized springs for water that were located close to privy vaults. The South Side was also served by the privately owned Monongahela Water Company, which drew its supplies from the Monongahela River. The company's intake pipe was located below Beck's Run, a tributary to the Monongahela that was badly polluted with night soil from overflowing privy vaults. In addition, extension of the shoreline along the river meant that the intake pipe could "hardly reach the current." Tenement house residents often had to access their water supplies from backyard spigots located near privy vaults rather than through indoor plumbing. The infamous Painter's Row, tenements owned by U.S. Steel on the South Side, had one spigot in a yard serving ninety-one families.[7]

An 1872 administrative ruling exacerbated the situation in regard to disparities in water access. In that year the newly created City Water Commission ruled that the size of the pipe laid on a particular street would be determined by the amount of potential revenue. This ruling resulted in either insufficient supply or no supply to poor neighborhoods. Such a policy was common for nineteenth-century American cities. Historian Robin L. Einhorn calls it the "segmented system"—one that provided benefits to those who paid for them but which also "made the American urban landscape a physical expression of political inequality."[8]

Constructing a Sewerage System

A supply of potable water was only one part of the city's metabolic system—wastewaters from households and industries as well as storm water had to be disposed of. Pittsburghers normally placed household wastes and wastewater in cesspools and privy vaults, not in the sewers. The 1804 borough charter gave the municipality the right to regulate these receptacles, and in 1816 citizens' complaints about overflowing filth and smells from privy vaults caused the councils to approve fines in the case of nuisances. Private scavengers under city contract were responsible for cleaning privy vaults and removing garbage, but they continually fouled the streets and polluted the rivers with the wastes. In 1875 the Pittsburgh Board of Health observed that the major health issue facing the city were privy vault nuisances, and in 1880 it reported almost 1,300 full "privy-wells," of which 176 were leaking and another 154 "foul." The county engineer noted in the same year that the South Side was "full of cess-pools [sic], and the soil is so saturated with the filth that you can smell it."[9]

The provision of running water to households and their adoption of water-using appliances such as sinks, showers, and water closets exacerbated the problem of overflowing cesspools and privy vaults. Improving the availability and volume of water supply was a benefit, but it also had a devastating effect on the public health.[10] In many cases, in order to dispose of the wastewater householders connected these appliances to the existing wastewater disposal sinks—cesspools and privy vaults. In 1881, for instance, about 4,000 of the 6,500 water closets were connected to privy vaults and cesspools and only about 1,500 to street sewers.[11]

Such conditions raised the possibility of epidemic disease and highlighted the need for improved sanitation and construction of a sewerage system. Concern over cholera, for instance, had led the councils in June 1832 to establish a Sanitary Board to "direct all such measures as they think necessary for averting the introduction of the frightful epidemics." The board had the power to "cause the streets, lanes, alleys, buildings, lots and shores of the rivers to be explored, cleansed and purified in an efficient manner." It organized the city into sanitary districts, attempted to clean the streets, and sought to control unsanitary privy vaults and cellars. The councils also enacted ordinances to improve waste collection and to extend the water system.[12] The city's response to the public health threat, however, remained limited, and conditions soon reverted to their normal unsanitary state. Thus, fear of epidemic disease alone could not persuade the councils to make the large expenditures necessary to build a sewerage system. In addition to costs, confusion over disease etiology as well as uncertainty about the technical and design requirements for an efficient system had a discouraging effect.

By the 1840s, demands for improved services, particularly from the city's commercial interests, had accelerated. In 1848 and 1849 the municipality constructed underground sewers in the commercial district and by 1866 it had a "fairly adequate" system of main sewers. Other areas of the city tended to be provided with services in a much more uneven and haphazard fashion. By 1875 the city had constructed about twenty-five miles of sewers (thirteen miles of brick sewers and eleven miles of pipe sewers), mostly for storm water drainage. These sewers suffered from design faults and were often either undersized or oversized and subject to constant clogging. Sewers did not conform to topography nor follow an overall engineering plan. The municipality commonly built sewers as a result of council members' attempts to meet constituent demands. Householders often constructed their own sewers, many of which were unrecorded, and the city lacked topographical maps until the 1870s. "You have no sewers; you don't know where they are going, or where they are to be found," commented noted New York civil engineer J. J. R. Croes to an 1881 meeting of the Engineers' Society of Western Pennsylvania.[13]

Until the 1890s, sewers were almost completely lacking in the newly annexed areas of the East End and the South Side. An 1887 East End citizens' committee complained that "in warm weather many parts of the East End are absolutely unfit for habitation owing to the polluted atmosphere arising from open runs of filth of every description." Conditions in the South Side, where population density and industrial development were greater, were even more unsanitary, with the district suffering from epidemics of diphtheria and typhoid. In 1890 the chief clerk of the Bureau of Health appealed to the councils to install sewers in the South Side and thereby "number the lives which could be saved to the community, saying nothing else of the value of the thousands of days lost by the attendant sickness."[14]

Even with agreement about the desirability of a sewerage system, debate raged about its design. Should it be a separate, small pipe system that carried only domestic and industrial wastes, the technology advocated by the famous sanitarian Colonel George E. Waring Jr.? Or, should it be a larger, combined system that could accommodate both wastewater and storm water in one pipe, a design favored by many noted sanitary engineers? The city's public health and engineering professionals divided over the question. Physicians argued that the separate system was preferable because it would protect health by removing wastes from households before they had begun to generate disease-causing sewer gas. They considered storm water a secondary matter, best handled by surface conduits. Engineers took a different position and maintained that sanitary wastes and storm water were equally important; therefore, a large pipe system that would accommodate both was more economical. After years of debate, the superior storm water removal virtues of the combined system convinced city officials, and by the late 1880s Pittsburgh had begun to build a system of large combined sewers.[15]

Between 1889 and 1912, civil engineers from the Bureau of Engineering of the Public Works Department constructed over 412 miles of sewers, almost all of the combined type. The construction of the planned centralized sewerage system signified a movement away from the "piecemeal, decentralized approach to city-building characteristic of the 19th century."[16] In constructing a large, centralized, combined sewer network Pittsburgh was following the lead of other big American cities such as Boston, Chicago, and New York.

Not all citizens were willing to abandon their old disposal technologies. Some attempted to keep their privy vaults and cesspools and resisted connections to the new sewer lines because of assessment costs. The Board of Health was compelled to use the sanitary code to compel connection. In 1888 the councils barred the construction of cesspools where sewer service was available and in 1901 they outlawed water closets from draining into privy vaults and prohibited the connection of privy wells to a public sewer. The bureau ordered the cleaning or removal of thousands of privies, but a small staff of inspectors and collusion between inspectors and scavenger firms limited the effectiveness of the order. Private sewers persisted in use, especially on the South Side, illustrating the difficulties of creating a uniform system of sanitary infrastructure throughout the city.[17]

Part of the problem was the several different ways the city financed sewer construction. Up to the middle of the 1890s, the city assessed the cost of main sewers to whole neighborhoods while charging the cost of lateral sewers to abutting property owners. In 1895, however, the Supreme Court declared the city's assessment practices in regard to main sewers unconstitutional and forced the municipality to assume the whole burden. To fund their liabilities and to provide for future needs, the city resorted to bonds, some of which required the voters' approval (People's Bond Issues) and some of which were voted by the councils (Councilman's Bond Issues). Lateral sewers were still financed by assessing abutting property holders, who complained incessantly about inequities.[18]

Typhoid Fever and Water Filtration

Pittsburgh drew its water supply from the Allegheny and Monongahela Rivers and discharged its untreated sewage into these same rivers as well as into the Ohio. Communities upstream of Pittsburgh were also building sewers and discharging their wastes into the Allegheny and Monongahela. By 1900, for instance, more than 350,000 inhabitants in seventy-five upriver municipalities discharged their untreated sewage into the Allegheny River, the river that provided drinking water for most of Pittsburgh's population. Some of Pittsburgh's own sewers discharged into the river at locations above its water supply pumping stations. The resulting pollution gave Pittsburgh the highest death rate from typhoid fever of the nation's large cities—well over 100 deaths per 100,000 people from 1873 to 1907. In contrast, in 1905, the average for northern cities was 35 per 100,000 persons.[19]

Typhoid fever death rates were highest in working-class immigrant and African American living areas. Of the nine wards with the highest typhoid death rates in the 1890s, seven were working class. In the years after 1900, the so-called "Strip" and "the Hill" neighborhoods attracted large numbers of new immigrants and African Americans. Typhoid rates soared in these wards. In 1907 the Pittsburgh Health Department noted that the death rate for the foreign-born and their children was nearly twice that of native-born whites.[20] The Health Department advised that drinking water be boiled but new immigrants often ignored such advice since they viewed the water as uncontaminated. "You cannot make the foreigner believe that Pittsburgh water is unwholesome," observed one physician, noting that roughly half of all foreign-born men became sickened with typhoid within two years of arriving in the city.[21] Pittsburgh had one of the highest rates of bottled water consumption in the nation but these supplies were out of reach for most working-class people. Thus, as a 1909 Pittsburgh Survey article observed, "those who could not afford to buy bottled water continued to drink filth." According to the municipal Health Department, Pittsburgh appeared "as two cities, one old and congested with a high mortality, and the other new and spacious with a very low death rate."[22]

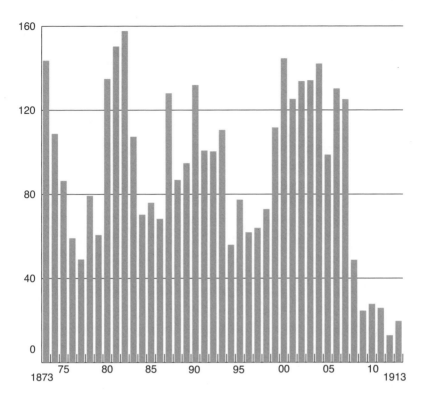

FIG. 2. Typhoid deaths per 100,000 of the population

The Board of Health became concerned with the growing typhoid death rates in the late 1880s, and by the early 1890s several professional, business, and women's groups were agitating about the need to protect the water supply from infectious disease. A variety of motives drove them, including evidence derived from the use of the new science of bacterial water analysis concerning the sewage pollution of the Allegheny River, related health concerns, and a desire to protect the city's reputation. In early 1893, the Engineers' Society of Western Pennsylvania, the Allegheny County Medical Society, the Chamber of Commerce Committee on Water Supply, and the Iron City Microscopical Society joined to form a joint commission to study the question of water pollution and water quality. The commission's report, issued early in 1894 and based on chemical, bacteriological, and statistical methods, found Pittsburgh and Allegheny City water supply "not only not up to a proper standard of potable water but . . . actually pernicious." After considering various options such as an upcountry water supply, the commission recommended that the water of both Pittsburgh and of Allegheny be treated using a slow sand filtration system. Their recommendation was based on the success in reducing infectious waterborne disease of a slow sand filtration plant installed in 1893 at Lawrence, Massachusetts.[23] Engineer James Otis Handy, who had been secretary of the joint commission, suggested building a demonstration filter using Allegheny River sand and gravel to illustrate the filtering process. After seeking the advice of Allen Hazen, the nation's leading water filtration expert, the filter was constructed on the lot of the Unitarian Church on Craig Street near Fifth Avenue. The experimental tank clearly demonstrated "that Allegheny River water could be purified satisfactorily by means of a filter containing Allegheny River sand," and aroused public interest in the process.[24]

In 1896, the councils approved an ordinance authorizing the mayor to create a Pittsburgh Filtration Commission to further study the matter and make public policy recommendations. The commission members were prominent Pittsburghers, and they hired as their consultants several of the nation's leading sanitary engineers and public health specialists, including Allen Hazen, William T. Sedgwick of the Massachusetts Institute of Technology, and sanitary engineer Morris Knowles, also an MIT graduate. Hazen and Knowles had worked on the slow sand filter constructed at Lawrence. The commission performed bacterial analyses of local rivers, tested slow sand and mechanical filtration technologies, and explored the feasibility of obtaining water from deep wells or piping it from Indian Creek in the mountains, about sixty miles southeast of the city. These investigations reconfirmed the link between water and disease, and the commission's 1899 report recommended construction of a slow sand filtration plant as the most economical means of dealing with the public health problem.[25]

Voters approved a bond issue for plant construction in 1899, but several factors blocked action. One involved individuals who refused to accept the validity of the scientific analysis concerning the relationship between typhoid and the city's water supply. Edward Bigelow, director of the Public Works Department argued that the city's water did not cause typhoid and warned that impugning its quality would discourage investment in the city.[26] In addition, disputes among political factions within the Republican Party over control of the construction contracts brought further delay and political battles. Bigelow also played a key role here, insisting that the filtration contracts, rather than being awarded to the construction firm of political boss William Flynn, be granted in open bidding. And a third factor involved disputes over source and technology choices, with some advocating bringing water to the city by aqueduct from Indian Creek, while others argued for a mechanical rather than slow sand filtration system. The

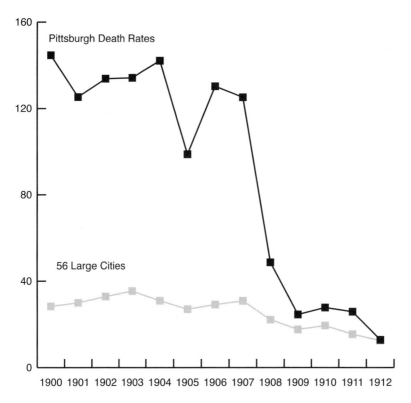

160

Pittsburgh Death Rates

120

80

56 Large Cities

40

0

1900 1901 1902 1903 1904 1905 1906 1907 1908 1909 1910 1911 1912

FIG. 3. Comparison of typhoid deaths per 100,000 of the population

disputes necessitated a vote on a second bond issue, approved by voters in 1904, with the beginning of construction in 1905. In December 1907, the water department delivered the first filtered water and the city's typhoid rates began to drop. In 1912, the city began chlorinating its water supply and Pittsburgh's death rate from typhoid fever soon dropped to the level of the national average for large cities.[27]

In 1909, Frank E. Wing, associate director of the Pittsburgh Survey, published an article on "Thirty-Five Years of Typhoid" in *The Survey Magazine*. Wing charged that 1,538 lives had been unnecessarily lost to typhoid fever due to political infighting between Republican Party factions that had delayed construction of the filtration plant after voters had approved the funds.[28] While there is no doubt that political conflict was an important factor in the delay, the full explanation is more complicated. Such disputes over construction of expensive filtration facilities were not unique to Pittsburgh, and cities such as Cincinnati, Philadelphia, and St. Louis experienced similar disputes and consequent delays. In Cincinnati, for instance, reformers opposed the construction of a new waterworks because they feared possible political corruption more than they did polluted drinking water and successfully marshaled city voters to defeat the bond issue.[29] Almost a decade was to pass before the Queen City finally constructed a new waterworks and filtered its water. In Philadelphia city councilmen skeptical of the validity of the germ theory feared that criticism of the city's water supply was hurting the city's image. Other councilmen raised questions about the cost of filters while some argued for having a private firm supply pure water from an upcountry source via an aqueduct. Again, decades of delay in the provision of clean water resulted.[30]

These delays in implementing filtration technology that would have produced a more healthful water supply need to be understood in the context of a modernizing society struggling with new ideas concerning the role of government and of scientific expertise. Bacterial analysis in regard to water supply was a new science, still disputed by those who clung to the validity of chemical tests of water quality and to anticontagionist theories of disease propagation. Some believed that only a protected upstream source could bring pure water to the city or were convinced that mechanical filtration was superior to slow sand filters. Contests between different groups of politicians and reformers who were seeking to rationalize and systematize municipal government complicated issues of technological choice. Achieving political power and structural change rather than constructing improved water systems were the primary goals of these contending groups. The confluence of these issues not only in Pittsburgh but also in other major cities helps explain the delays in the protection of water supplies that ultimately cost many hundreds of lives.[31]

Retaining the Rivers as Sewers

Water filtration provided one safety net in regard to polluted water but many sanitarians and public health physicians believed it also necessary to treat the city's sewage for maximum protection. Professional, business, and medical groups protested against sewage disposal by dilution in streams. They demanded that municipalities treat their sewage and agitated for state laws against stream pollution. In the years after the turn of the century, states such as Connecticut, Massachusetts, Minnesota, New Hampshire, New Jersey, New York, Ohio, Pennsylvania, and Vermont, responding to a series of unusually severe typhoid epidemics, gave state boards of health increased power to control sewage disposal in streams.[32]

The Pennsylvania act "to preserve the purity of the waters of the State for the protection of the public health" (the Pure Waters Act), passed by the state legislature in 1905 in response to the severe 1903 Butler typhoid epidemic, typified these laws. It forbade the discharge of any untreated sewage into state waterways by new municipal systems. While it permitted cities already discharging to continue the practice, it required them to secure a permit from the State Department if they wished to extend their systems.[33] Engineering opinion largely disagreed with these prohibitions. As the *Engineering Record* noted in 1909, "it is often more equitable to all concerned for an upper riparian city to discharge its sewage into a stream and a lower riparian city to filter the water of the same stream for a domestic supply, than for the former city to be forced to put in sewage treatment works."[34]

Although Pittsburgh was filtering its own water after 1907, the city continued to dump its untreated sewage into its neighboring rivers, endangering the water supply of downstream communities. In the beginning of 1910, the city requested the State Department of Health to grant it a permit allowing it to extend its sewerage system. The department, headed by Dr. Samuel G. Dixon, responded by requesting a "comprehensive sewerage plan for the collection and disposal of all of the sewage of the municipality" before it would grant the permit. In addition, the department argued that in order to attain efficient treatment, the city should consider changing from a combined to the separate system. F. Herbert Snow, the department's chief engineer, maintained that the plan was needed to protect the public health of communities that drew water supplies from rivers downstream from Pittsburgh. "The baneful effect of Pittsburgh's sewage on the health of the brightest citizens at her door," wrote Snow, "admonishes city and state authorities alike of the futility of defying nature's sanitary laws."[35]

The city of Pittsburgh responded to Dixon's order by hiring the engineering firm of Allen Hazen and George C. Whipple to act as consultants for the required study. Hazen had been the chief consultant to the city's Filtration Commission while Whipple was one of the nation's most distinguished sanitary engineers. The engineers focused their study upon an evaluation of the costs of building a treatment system and of converting Pittsburgh sewers to the separate system. In their report, issued on January 30, 1912, they argued that a Pittsburgh sewage treatment plant would not free the downstream towns from threats to their water supplies nor from the need to filter them, since other communities would continue to discharge raw sewage into the rivers. The method of disposal by dilution in the rivers, they maintained, sufficed to prevent nuisances, particularly if storage reservoirs were constructed upstream from Pittsburgh to augment flow during periods of low stream volume. Hazen and Whipple argued that there was no case "where a great city has purified its sewage to protect public water supplies from the stream below."[36] "Rivers are the natural and logical drains and are formed for the purpose of carrying the wastes to the sea," argued N. S. Sprague, superintendent of the Pittsburgh Bureau of Construction in forwarding the Hazen-Whipple report to the director of Public Works. "When the amount of such wastes discharged into the rivers produces a nuisance it is then time to adopt remedial measures . . . this time has not arrived."[37]

Hazen and Whipple's most powerful argument concerned the lack of economic feasibility for converting Pittsburgh's sewerage system to separate sewers and building a sewage treatment plant. There was no precedent, they claimed, for a city replacing the combined system by the separate system "for the purpose of protecting water supplies of other cities taken from the water course below." They calculated that financing such a project would cause the city to exceed its municipal indebtedness level and thus violate state law. Moreover, because the sewage treatment plant was intended for the protection of the downstream communities, it would not give Pittsburgh any direct benefits while downstream cities would still have to filter their water to protect against waterborne pathogens. Hence, they concluded, "no radical change in the method of sewerage or of sewage disposal as now practiced by the city of Pittsburgh is necessary or desirable."[38]

While the engineering press received the Hazen and Whipple report with enthusiasm, Pennsylvania Health Commissioner Dixon found it an insufficient response to his original request for a long-range plan for a comprehensive regional sewerage system. He argued that water pollution had to be viewed from a health rather than a nuisance perspective, and that the immediate costs of sewage treatment would be outweighed by the long-range health benefits. The time had come, Dixon stated, "to start a campaign in order that the streams shall not become stinking sewers and culture beds for pathogenic organisms."[39] Given the political context, however, and the financial limitations upon the city, Dixon had no realistic means by which to enforce his order. In 1913 he capitulated and issued Pittsburgh a temporary discharge permit.

This particular case had implications beyond Pittsburgh. The dispute pitted public health physicians against sanitary engineers and illustrated their different conceptions of the choices dictated by the urban environment. Sanitary engineers believed that they had a superior conception of the "relative needs and values" of cities in regard to public health because of their understanding of municipal financial limitations—thus sewage treatment was a luxury, less critical than other urban public health needs. It should be delayed until nuisance conditions became unacceptable.[40]

Many public health officials believed, however, that sewage disposal was not a proper use of streams, especially if drinking water quality was involved. The so-called New Public Health rested on confidence in laboratory-derived methods of bacterial analysis that helped identify the dangers of sewage pollution. Possible health effects, rather than nuisance alone, were the major considerations.[41] From the longer perspective of urban metabolism and urban sustainability, the position of the engineers appears shortsighted, however driven by fiscal necessities, while that of the State Department of Health seems prescient. The power of those possessing strong environmental values, however, was not yet great enough to force what now retrospectively appears to have been an environmentally desirable if costly policy.[42]

Pittsburgh Treats Its Sewage

For Pittsburgh to be compelled to treat its sewage would require major policy and value changes on the part of both government officials and the public. In 1923 state policy in regard to river pollution took what most sanitary engineers considered to be a forward step but which, from the perspective of Pittsburgh river quality, was a move in the opposite direction. In that year the Pennsylvania General Assembly enacted legislation proposed by Governor Gifford Pinchot that created, within the Department of Health, a Sanitary Water Board whose function was to balance economic growth and improved water quality. The board created a stream classification system that designated streams into three categories for municipal and industrial users. These classifications included streams that were relatively clean and pure, streams in which pollution existed but could be controlled, and streams that were so polluted that they could not be used as public water supplies without treatment or for fishing and recreational purposes and therefore could continue to be used for the discharge of untreated wastes. Decisions were to be made on a case-by-case basis. Pittsburgh rivers fell under the third category—that is, they were to continue to be used as open sewers.[43]

While some improvements were made in Pennsylvania water quality during the 1920s, Pittsburgh conditions remained static. The Depression retarded the possibility of any substantive advances, although the federal government, operating through the Civil Works Administration and the Works Progress Administration, funded a Metropolitan Drainage Survey and supplied funds for improving water and sewage collection systems. Hard-pressed municipalities and the state, however, could do little on their own, and the rivers became increasingly polluted with both municipal sewage and industrial wastes. By 1934, 85 percent of Pennsylvania waterways suffered from various degrees of degradation, although the drinking water supplies of 80 percent of the state's population were treated.[44]

By the end of the decade, however, advocates of clean streams had increased in number and strength. The deterioration of stream quality offended many interests, but especially sportsmen's groups and conservation advocates who were especially strong in the state. Kenneth A. Reid, national director of the conservationist Izaak Walton League, editor of *Outdoor America,* and a member of the Pennsylvania Board of Fish Commissioners, wrote, for instance, that "Vilely polluted streams throughout the . . . nation furnish mute but convincing testimony . . . that existing methods of control by state and local agencies have proved utterly inadequate."[45] Industries that required clean water in their manufacturing processes as well as railroads also demanded stricter pollution control. In response to pressure from these groups, in 1937 the Pennsylvania General Assembly passed the Clean Streams Act. This act gave power to the Sanitary Water Board to issue and enforce waste treatment orders to all municipalities and most industries but exempted acid drainage from coal mines.[46]

As early as 1930, the Sanitary Water Board had sought to compel Pittsburgh to submit a comprehensive plan for the collection, treatment, and disposal of the city's sewage, but without success. Now, faced by a state law that provided the board with enforcement power, the city had to act. The previous argument that state spending limits prevented spending for sewage treatment plants could no longer be used, since new legislation and court decisions in 1934 and 1935 permitted local governments to create authorities and to utilize user charge financing to provide public services such as sewer treatment.[47]

In December 1937, Mayor Cornelius Scully called a meeting of Allegheny County municipalities to discuss possible collective action. Scully appointed a General Committee on Sewage of the Municipalities of Allegheny County, which met on July 28, 1939. The committee approved several resolutions including a recommendation for joint participation by municipalities and industries in the construction and operation of intercepting sewers and treatment works, formation of a municipal authority to undertake and finance waste treatment, and investigation of possible state and federal funding for metropolitan waste disposal. The committee also submitted the so-called Koruzo report—prepared by John Koruzo, director of the Pittsburgh Public Works Department—to the municipalities. The report analyzed pertinent wastewater and population data and recommended the construction of nineteen individual sewage disposal works with intercepting sewers in the three major county watersheds. The Sanitary Water Board was unenthusiastic about the Koruzo recommendation for decentralized treatment centers, and the onset of World War II delayed any action on sewage treatment.[48]

In 1944, with the war ending, the Sanitary Water Board announced comprehensive plans to reduce pollution of Pennsylvania streams. In a major step, it required that all municipalities treat their sewage "to a primary degree," thus abandoning its former classification scheme.[49] In preparation for the announcement of waste treatment orders in the postwar period, the Sanitary Water Board held pollution abatement hearings in Pittsburgh in June 1944. These hearings revealed sharply divergent views among municipal officials concerning how to proceed with pollution abatement at the local level. Most towns preferred that some other municipality than themselves take the lead in initiating sewage treatment. The Sanitary Water Board argued, however, that since Pittsburgh was the largest population entity and pollution source within Allegheny County, it bore a tacit obligation to initiate a pollution control program and to coordinate its proposals with those of surrounding communities.[50]

While the general public had been apathetic about pollution issues during the Depression, by the late 1930s the return of prosperity had generated more concern about water quality from both an aesthetic and a health perspective.[51] Offensive sights and smells from the rivers had increased, as sewage from the city as well as from upstream communities overwhelmed the oxidation capacity of the streams. In addition, gross pollution levels in streams impacted health. While filtration and chlorination had sharply reduced typhoid death rates, diarrhea and enteritis death rates remained elevated. In the period 1933–1937, the mean rate of mortality from typhoid was .74 per 100,000 of the population; diarrhea and enteritis, however, claimed 8.3 victims per 100,000 inhabitants. In addition, mine acid drainage increased the costs of water filtration for the residents of Pittsburgh. And complaints from downstream populations concerning Pittsburgh waste disposal practices also had an effect. These factors increased citizen awareness that water pollution produced adverse economic consequences as well as reductions in environmental quality and damages to public health, but the persistence of weak environmental values impeded action to solve the problem.[52]

By 1945, however, sewage pollution was only one of the several serious issues facing Pittsburgh. Its population was stagnating, its industries were exhausted by the war effort and badly in need of renewal, its physical plant was deteriorating, and its air and land, as well as its water, were badly polluted. Both corporate and municipal officials recognized that only a large-scale renewal could avert a massive exodus of population and industry from the city. Reacting to this sense of crisis, various civic groups formulated plans and sponsored programs for redevelopment. The most important of these organizations, the Allegheny Conference on Community Development (ACCD), campaigned for smoke abatement, flood control, clean streams, cultural improvement, and the renewal of downtown Pittsburgh. The Pittsburgh Regional Planning Association, which often functioned as the technical arm of the ACCD, issued land-use, parking, and transit studies and developed a number of master plans for municipalities surrounding Pittsburgh. In addition, the Pennsylvania Economy League analyzed financial issues and reported upon the revenue base of the city in relation to its expenditure patterns.[53]

These local urban and environmental improvement efforts coincided with actions taken by state officials in connection with their postwar planning programs. The Sanitary Water Board, for instance, acting under the authority granted it under the provisions of the Clean Streams Act of 1937, initiated a Clean Streams Program to improve levels of water quality throughout Pennsylvania. In June 1945, it issued the long-awaited orders to the city of Pittsburgh and to 101 other municipalities, as well as to more than ninety Allegheny County industries, to cease the discharge of untreated wastes into the state waterways. State officials decreed that these communities submit their final plans for a waste disposal program by July 1, 1946, and fully comply with the treatment orders by May 16, 1947.[54]

Municipal and county officials reacted with consternation to the state waste treatment orders, as they confronted a number of administrative and technological issues. Among the most vital were questions as to whether sanitary policy should be determined by each municipality or by a regional agency, how sewage treatment should be financed, whether a central treatment facility or multiple disposal plants would be most efficient, and what form of treatment technology made the most sense given the existing system of sewage collection and drainage and local conditions of population density and topography.[55]

The county commissioners proceeded to survey affected Allegheny County municipalities to determine if they would support the incorporation of a special district governmental authority to plan and implement a waste disposal program. Commissioner John J. Kane argued that a county-wide waste treatment agency financed by revenue bonds could service participating localities without increasing their level of bonded indebtedness. User charges collected from households and industries connected to the treatment system could provide a self-financing mechanism for efficient and professional waste disposal service. Finally, these officials pointed out that the construction of an authority-managed treatment system would benefit the Pittsburgh metropolitan economy because of the demands it would create for building materials, labor, and technicians.[56]

As a result of a set of meetings sponsored by the County Board of Commissioners with Allegheny County municipalities, a pro-authority consensus developed. Seventy-four communities in receipt of state treatment orders resolved that their individual waste disposal problems could be best solved "on a county-wide basis." This provided the support that the county commissioners needed, and on December 19, 1945, acting under the recently passed Pennsylvania Municipal Authorities Act, the commissioners adopted a resolution to create a sanitary authority. Three months later, in March 1946, the secretary of the commonwealth officially approved the formation of the Allegheny County Sanitary Authority (ALCOSAN).[57] The county commissioners proceeded to choose a board of directors to manage the new authority, balancing off individuals with prior managerial and engineering experience with those having city or county political backgrounds. They appointed John P. Laboon, who had previously served as Allegheny County public works director, as chief engineer; at the Authority's first board meeting on March 15, 1946, the board members elected Laboon as chairman.[58]

The ALCOSAN research staff conducted a number of studies and made recommendations in 1945–1946 that looked toward the creation of an integrated sewage treatment system that utilized activated sludge technology. An investigation by the Sanitary Authority showed that county municipalities and industries with a population of 678,000 discharged an estimated wastewater flow of 65 million gallons per day. The Authority decided to remove 50 percent of the biochemical oxygen demand generated by wastes entering its proposed activated sludge treatment plant, thereby complying with or exceeding the discharge standards promulgated by the Sanitary Water Board. The research staff recommended that the plant itself be located on a site situated on the north bank of the Ohio River beneath the McKees Rocks Bridge. Sanitary officials believed that a single plant would be more cost-effective than multiple plants and lead to fewer siting and odor objections from local populations. A centralized unit would also operate more efficiently and assimilate greater quantities of industrial residuals.[59]

The authority staff was also responsible for construction of an extensive intercepting sewer system, a series of conduits that would connect various outfalls throughout the service district and transport wastes to the treatment works. This would be a difficult task, since the region's rough topography complicated the excavation for sewer lines, while its densely populated and intensively developed landscape offered few open areas to construct a new system of conduits. Because the building of the interceptors promised extensive disruptions of transportation and industrial activity, ALCOSAN officials recommended subaqueous sewer construction.[60]

To finance the cost of its proposed treatment project, estimated at $82 million (1948 dollars), the Authority recommended the utilization of a pay-as-you-go system which it calculated would save approximately $17 million in capital costs over alternative methods of finance. Specifically, ALCOSAN officials requested that member communities authorize them to levy partial, pre-service sewerage charges on municipal sewers to pay for pre-service operating costs. They also sought to assume billing and collection responsibilities from local water companies as a means of generating operating capital. To amortize the long-term construction and other costs of the waste treatment system, ALCOSAN proposed to issue nondebt revenue bonds serviced by the imposition of sewage treatment charges upon individual households and industrial plants. Such charges, also known as sewer rentals, enabled municipal authorities, under the provisions of the 1935 Sewer Rentals Act, "to charge and collect annual rentals" and to retire operating and depreciation expenses of sewer facilities as well as other forms of indebtedness.[61]

While the financial and construction details of ALCOSAN were essential, the Authority would only become feasible through delicate political negotiations with the city of Pittsburgh and with county municipalities jealous of their independence. Here two individuals were key: Pittsburgh Mayor David L. Lawrence and ALCOSAN Board Chairman John P. Laboon.[62] Lawrence, who assumed the office of mayor in January 1946, was also the powerful leader of the Democratic organization. A master politician, Lawrence believed in the importance of regionwide pollution abatement but also wanted to maximize the city's political influence by gaining control of the Sanitary Authority. Laboon occupied a less influential institutional base than the mayor. He possessed, however, strong personal qualities and was a talented engineer and a skilled conflict mediator. He was strongly committed to creating a countywide sewage disposal system.

Policy differences surfaced between the two men because they represented differing constituencies and because they frequently disagreed over the methods to achieve countywide sewage treatment. Pittsburgh officials, for example, worried that city taxpayers would bear a disproportionate share of the financial burden while Laboon and ALCOSAN officials sought to protect the other county municipalities from excessive Pittsburgh influence. Heated battles between the city and ALCOSAN occurred in 1947–1949 in regard to financing powers and treatment plans, and the city consequently refused to sign a binding commitment to the Authority. The city's action delayed movement toward the acceptance of the Authority's program by neighboring communities. Those critical of the Lawrence administration charged that the city's failure to sign revealed its preoccupation with electoral politics and a desire to secure patronage appointments at the expense of an effective waste treatment policy.[63]

In June 1949, ALCOSAN experienced its most serious crisis. Not only had the agency failed to execute service agreements with Pittsburgh and neighboring municipalities, but its operating funds, derived from loans from the city, were almost exhausted. As a result, ALCOSAN and its waste treatment program faced an imminent collapse. Intensive negotiations, however, brought about agreements between the city and ALCOSAN ("Project Z"), the essence of which was to enlarge the number of communities permitted into the service district and to increase city control over the board. City officials agreed to loan the Sanitary Authority an additional $2 million to continue its survey work and operations while ALCOSAN agreed that the city would select the agency that would ultimately build and maintain the treatment system. The culmination of these developments revealed the political skill of David Lawrence, for he had masterminded a major political coup against the Sanitary Authority. By providing the Authority with its sole source of income through loans, the mayor and the City Council rendered it dependent upon the city for its very existence. Pittsburgh officials had demonstrated their commitment to a sewage treatment program but they had also increased their political control over ALCOSAN and reduced the financial burden of waste treatment upon city residents.[64]

Other changes in the construction plans for the proposed system also occurred at this time. These included a reduction in the number of miles of interceptor sewers and the abandonment of plans for subaqueous interceptors. The latter change was a result of U.S. Army Corps of Engineers' concerns over interference with navigation. The Sanitary Authority substituted a method of sewer installation utilizing special floating equipment and divers to connect preassembled sewer pipe through trenches and tunnels excavated along instead of within the riverbanks. Finally, ALCOSAN adopted a new system for the disposal of sewage sludge—the so-called Laboon Process—through preheating.[65]

But while some financial and technical issues were resolved, other problems resulted relating to ratification of the plan by several Allegheny County communities and even members already in ALCOSAN. Outlying areas, for instance, such as Verona, Blawnox, O'Hara Township, and Penn Township, objected to paying higher service charges than city residents due to higher unit costs of construction and treatment. These uncertainties regarding the number of participating communities and industries impeded the preparation of construction plans, while delays in building added to overall costs.[66]

Officials at ALCOSAN used a carrot-and-stick approach to persuade municipal officials to negotiate service contracts. On the one hand, they generated media and public interest support for sewage treatment and emphasized the financial and service economies, as well as the aesthetic improvements, local governments would realize from participation in the pollution control program. "It is to the singular advantage of your municipality," wrote the Authority to officials from the Borough of McKees Rocks, "to enter into a long-term contract with the Sanitary Authority to do the job on a cooperation basis covering the whole county. . . .The combined effort of all the municipalities will produce the cheapest and best solution."[67] On the other hand, the board petitioned state officials to pressure municipalities to achieve their compliance deadlines for waste treatment. While the state refused to require that communities in receipt of treatment orders join ALCOSAN, it indirectly supported such action by notifying local governments that "signing an agreement with the Authority is considered compliance with the State order." Faced with such waste disposal decrees as well as the cheaper long-term waste treatment service provided by the Authority, a majority of the affected municipalities decided to join. By February 1956, a total of sixty-eight communities and industries comprising about 80 percent of the county population had negotiated service contracts.[68]

Pittsburgh delayed its formal entry into ALCOSAN until it had clearly demonstrated its dominance over the board and designated the agency that would build and maintain the waste treatment system.[69] As Laboon and the ALCOSAN board had agreed earlier, Mayor Lawrence's Study Commission on Water Supply and Sewage Disposal would have the final word about who would build and operate the system. ALCOSAN officials initiated an elaborate campaign for the selection of their agency. Writing to Mayor Lawrence and to members of City Council, the Authority argued that its staff was "especially qualified by education, experience, and training to design, construct and operate not only sewage works but also water supply systems." More significantly, John Laboon offered to give the city direct control of the Sanitary Authority by the reorganization of its five-person governing board.[70]

Having achieved his objective to control ALCOSAN, Mayor Lawrence approved the Authority's plan for the reorganization of its board of directors, authorized the appointment to the board of three Pittsburgh representatives, and committed the city to officially join the Authority's service district. The rapid-fire series of events that transpired from the fall of 1954 to early spring of 1955 constituted the final resolution of issues enabling the city of Pittsburgh to exercise de jure as well as de facto control of the Sanitary Authority.[71]

The final act in the drama was financing the project, not an easy task given the fact that ALCOSAN was the largest sewage treatment project ever proposed. In order to secure financing, the city and ALCOSAN decided to utilize nondebt revenue bonds financed by the imposition of waste treatment charges upon those households and industrial plants located within the service district. To determine service charges, sanitary officials metered water consumption levels at the household tap or plant site. State legislation required water utilities to furnish water meter readings to ALCOSAN and empowered the agency to terminate water service to individual customers delinquent in their payment of sewage treatment bills.[72] Poor bond market conditions and investor concerns about the use of revenue bonds for sewage treatment not supported by authority power to tax, however, caused problems. ALCOSAN represented, not only the biggest metropolitan waste disposal unit ever established but also the largest one to finance its revenue bonds solely through sewer rentals. These factors, along with the huge sums of money involved (by August 1953, estimates of the final costs of the project had risen to $88 million), caused interest rates for ALCOSAN's bonds to increase by an additional 3 to 4 percent above the average, a not inconsiderable financial burden for local residents.[73]

Officials from both the city of Pittsburgh and the Sanitary Authority balked at the prospect of marketing revenue bonds under these unfavorable financial conditions. Mayor Lawrence advised sanitary officials to delay its construction timetable until interest rates subsided and John Laboon concurred in this position. Mayors of cities downstream of Pittsburgh in the Ohio River Valley, however, as well as Edward Cleary, the director of the Ohio River Valley Water Sanitation Commission (ORSANCO), complained about the delay. The Authority and representatives of Mellon Bank and Trust Company resolved the stalemate when Mellon offered a loan with below market interest rates and ALCOSAN agreed to accept it. In October 1955, the Sanitary Authority and Mellon Bank and Trust Company announced a four-year loan that totaled $100 million. Altogether, this agreement involved twenty-three banking concerns in Pittsburgh, New York, Cleveland, and Philadelphia and represented the largest loan for a sewage treatment system in American history. Contemporary banking commentators viewed this loan as the most "unique method in the history of authority finance."[74]

By the latter part of 1955, ALCOSAN had hurdled the majority of the financial and political obstacles impeding completion of its waste treatment system. In February 1956, the Sanitary Authority awarded construction contracts totaling $82,082,000, and on March 1 of the year, workers began to build the treatment system. In the spring of 1959, ALCOSAN processed sewage charges on 250,000 accounts within the service district. The "shakedown period" during which engineers tested the disposal facility for efficiency and reliability commenced on April 30; on October 1, the official dedication of the plant occurred. Waste treatment in the Pittsburgh region had become a long-awaited reality.[75]

⤳

This chapter has traced the history of the interaction of water supply and wastewater disposal and treatment in Pittsburgh from approximately 1800 through 1958. As Edward K. Muller has illustrated in his chapter on Pittsburgh area rivers, the rivers have shaped Pittsburgh's destiny in many different ways. Among these, none has been more important than the fact that the rivers have provided both a source of water and a sink where the city disposed of its wastes. Four major issues are consistent across this history of water supply and wastewater disposal decisions: technology choice, public health, costs, and the political and institutional context.

The city's decision to obtain its water supply from its neighboring rivers rather than from a protected upcountry source cost it dearly in terms of lives once these rivers became wastewater disposal sinks. The technological decision—to build combined rather than separate sewers—had short- and medium-term benefits but long-term environmental and health costs. While other river cities made similar choices, the character of Pittsburgh rivers made them particularly dangerous in terms of bacterial contamination. The slow sand filtration system that began operating in 1907 served the city well for a long period of time, providing high-quality drinking water. However, its very success in dealing with typhoid fever meant the city delayed in treating its sewage and also its industrial wastes. Pittsburgh's refusal to treat its own wastes offered no encouragement to other cities in its watershed to treat theirs.

The negative consequences of technological decisions for public health and the environment, as well as a willingness to ignore the destructive effects of industrial pollution, were exacerbated by institutional and political structures in the city and the county. A major factor in the decision-making space, political factionalism, helped delay the city's movement toward filtering and improving its drinking water quality. Cooperation in meeting environmental goals was impeded by political competition between city and county as well as rivalry and provincialism on the part of the county's many municipalities. The damaging effects of this political fragmentation were demonstrated throughout the twentieth century in regard to environmental issues and impeded the formation of new institutions such as ALCOSAN created to deal with pollution issues.

From a policy perspective, Pittsburgh's environmental history bears heavily on the present in regard to water quality. Here the concept of path dependency is useful because it illuminates the burdens that the present bears from the continued use of imbedded water and sewer technologies.[76] The city's water distribution and combined sewer systems are both old, and suffering from various problems, although over the past decade more attention has been paid to the former rather than the latter. The city has been free of waterborne disease for some decades, and has been fortunate enough to escape episodes of exposure to *Giardia* or *Cryptosporidium* from which other cities such as Milwaukee have suffered. The earlier history of exposure to waterborne disease may make the Pittsburgh Water and Sewer Authority especially proactive in consistently upgrading its treatment systems.

The situation in regard to the legacy of the city's combined sewer system is less positive. Pittsburgh today has more combined sewer overflow outlets than any other city in the nation, leading to rising fecal coliform rates in the rivers at times of wet weather. The fecal pathogen contamination is a threat to recreational users of the region's waterways, and from 1994 to 2001, the Allegheny County Health Department issued warnings on 37 percent of days during the recreational boating season. However, this is not only a Pittsburgh problem, and the city, county, and region, under prodding from the Environmental Protection Agency, have moved to study and seek alternative options to deal with it.[77] In order to remedy this situation, the city and other municipalities in the region may have to absorb the costs of one of several options, including enlarging treatment capacity, constructing holding tanks, or even building a parallel system of sanitary sewers.

Finally, the history of Pittsburgh water supply and wastewater disposal reveals the constant importance of political and institutional factors within the city and the county. The city has experienced political factionalism and competition between departments with different goals over the years. Within Allegheny County there has been competition between city and county, between city and suburb, and among different municipalities. Within the region, there has been competition between different counties.

These situations have shaped the character and timing of the water and wastewater decisions that have been made. The creation of ALCOSAN in the 1950s suggests that it is only through regional cooperation that we will be able to realize the full potential that our rivers and their waters provide to the region.

Acid Mine Drainage and
Pittsburgh's Water Quality

NICHOLAS CASNER

IN 1803, T. M. HARRIS, traveling through Pittsburgh, noted the poor quality of the city's water: "But the spring water, issuing through fissures in the hills, which are only masses of coal, is so impregnated with bituminous and sulphurous particles as to be frequently nauseous to the taste and preju-dicial to the health."[1] From the earliest days of Pennsylvania history, sulfur-laden water confirmed the presence of coal as an abundant natural resource. The taste and smell of water flowing through or over exposed coal beds signaled a poten-tial for enormous wealth unrealized for centuries after its first recognition. With the exploitation of that wealth in the industrial age, sulfur or acidic water flowing from mines produced a pollution problem of colossal magnitude and complexity. By the 1920s, when an estimated 2.5 million tons of sulfuric acid annually flowed into the Ohio River at Pitts-burgh, the problem threatened the natural environment of the region as well as the industrial economy coal created.[2]

This chapter focuses on the environmental problems associated with acid mine drainage.[3] Particular attention will be paid to the pollutant's destructive power and efforts to stem damages in the natural and human environments. Aside from its destructive nature, acid drainage advanced a wider purpose in that it required government, industry, and impacted citizens to confront a costly and threatening environmental issue. These attempts to deal with the problem of acid drainage played a significant role in the development of state and national pollution policies during the 1920s and 1930s. These decades represent an important juncture for the creation of pollution policy and environmental awareness in the first half of the twentieth century.

The sulfuric discharge from coal mines has been the most pervasive and widespread water pollution problem in Pittsburgh's industrial history. It destroyed or altered the flora and fauna along small streams and in major rivers, extracted millions of dollars in damages from domestic and industrial water users, and represented a key issue in the evolution of state and federal pollution policy. The volume of waste and associated problems caused by acid mine drainage parallel the nineteenth-century expansion of the coal-driven industrial economy. By the early twentieth century the costs of the pollutant, considered by many as an unfortunate but necessary trade-off for economic prosperity, demanded concerted actions by lawmakers as well as industrialists to protect the region's water resources. As prominent Johnstown mining engineer Andrew Crichton argued, "no more important question" existed for coal producers "than the prevention of stream pollution by mine drainage."[4] One could easily go further and argue that "no more important question" existed for the environmental health of the region.

Acid Mine Drainage

The formation of acidic water from coal is not dependent on mining; it is a natural process resulting from oxidation of iron pyrite or marcasite found in coal. Acid water is created in any exposed outcropping of coal, but becomes particularly problematic with the exposing of a large amount of acid-forming substances. Pyrite is found in especially great quantities in the overburden of coal beds and in the coal itself. When exposed to air, these mineral sulfides are transformed into soluble sulfates that create sulfuric acid when combined with water. Discharges, such as groundwater pumped from mines or small streams or rain making contact with coal debris, introduced acids in watersheds. In water, further oxidation may take place and produce iron hydroxide deposits commonly referred to as "sulfur mud" or "yellow boy." The yellow mud has been, until recent years, a very common site along the state's waterways.[5]

Pennsylvania's bituminous coal has a high sulfur content and therefore produces enormous acid loads. Drainage from thousands of exposed outcroppings, thousands of small "country bank" mines—used for local domestic purposes—thousands of commercial mining operations, and an unknown number of abandoned mines contributed to stream degradation. Acid production does not depend on fresh exposures; played-out mines and tailings piles produce the substance for decades.

There are a number of methods used to prevent damage from acid mine drainage, though studies from the turn of the century to the present indicate that there is no one ideal prevention method. Alkaline materials, usually crushed limestone, lime marl, or soda ash, neutralized the discharges. Municipal and industrial water suppliers used such methods to neutralize their supplies in the first decades of the twentieth century. Other methods to neutralize acids have included using chemical inhibitors, dilution, flooding of abandoned workings, the introduction of sulfur-consuming bacteria, and the construction of wetlands to filter water near mine discharge points. In the 1930s, the Federal Mine Sealing Program (to be discussed later in more detail) targeted abandoned mines in the Appalachian coal region. The program, a New Deal public works project, represented the first attempt by the U.S. government to physically stop an industrial pollutant at its source. The program sealed abandoned mines in an effort to prevent oxidation and discharges but proved of little benefit. In 1965, Pennsylvania, after decades of debate, enacted stream legislation requiring working coal mines to treat effluents with neutralizing processes.[7]

Mining and Acid Production

Early mining generally developed when wood supplies for iron making dwindled, especially if favorable transportation for coal to markets existed. The first mines typically began where outcroppings had appeared in hillsides, especially if located near a river. Pennsylvania's first coal workings appeared upon the banks of the Susquehanna and Monongahela Rivers in locations close to cities. Howard Eavenson, in *The First Century and a Quarter of the American Coal Industry,* quotes an eighteenth-century Pittsburgh visitor: "The banks of the Monongahela on the west, or opposite side of Pittsburgh, are steep, close to the water and about two hundred yards high. About a third of the way from the top is a vein of coal . . . burnt in the town and considered very good."[8]

In the nineteenth century, as coal replaced wood as a prime source of energy and coke replaced charcoal in steelmaking, mining production soared and streams degraded. Acid loads corresponded with the volume of coal mined. Expansion of the coal industry also took place as a result of improved transportation methods achieved through road construction and railroad expansion; improvements to navigable waterways also opened up new areas for extraction. Mines were often concentrated within a specific locale, producing higher and more concentrated acid quantities that overwhelmed the dilution capacity of local streams. Local mining communities and neighboring cities received the brunt of the water problems associated with coal production. As an industrial center located at the convergence of three rivers that extended through mining country, Pittsburgh endured a major burden from the pollutant.

Following the Civil War, the American coal industry began a spectacular period of growth. Bituminous coal production soared, reaching a peak in 1918. From that point onward, the industry began to grope with a number of complex and threatening issues. Competition from oil and gas, greater efficiencies in coal burned, and overproduction from hundreds of large and small competitive producers imperiled an industry vulnerable to cyclical slumps in the national economy. Challenged on these fronts, the industry paid scant attention to water pollution issues. It rather depended on the common law and the absence of legislative antipollution statutes to protect it from having to take remedial actions. In the years from the end of the Civil War to the 1920s, massive environmental degradation resulted. To a society bent on economic growth, energy demands took precedence over aesthetics and, at times, public health and property rights. Pollution symbolized prosperity. Business and government considered negative environmental impacts an unfortunate by-product, but considered it to be the price of affluence.

Impacts in the Natural and Urban/Industrial Environment

Water pumped from mines naturally followed the path of least resistance into nearby streams. Acidic discharges from those mines had an immediate impact. Flora and fauna of coal region streams quickly died off; the discharges eliminated practically all aquatic life from microorganisms to fish and killed vegetation on stream banks. Therefore, on small streams, it produced a double impact by reducing life in the stream and also altering stream dynamics. Wildlife tended to avoid the water. In highly impacted regions, bird populations dropped dramatically. Livestock also refused the water, forcing farmers to find alternative sources.[9]

As the volume of acidic water increased, the destruction moved farther from the mines and through tributaries into major rivers. Massive fish kills often first heralded the arrival of acid waste to previously untainted areas, an increasingly common phenomenon in the late nineteenth century. These kills were attributed to "acid slugs," which formed when a mine began pumping a large volume of highly acidic water into streams. This occurred especially when mines were closed for a period and then reopened. The idle workings accumulated a large body of water that was pumped from mines to allow access. Large acid loads diminished a stream's natural dilution capacity and therefore the discharges often remained at high concentrations for great distances.

The loss of game fish such as trout produced a growing concern early in the twentieth century. In his 1910 survey of the impact of acid water on the Monongahela River, Colonel Thomas P. Roberts, U.S. Army Corps of Engineers, stated that since "the advent of acid in the Monongahela River the salmon [sic] and bass, which formerly abounded in its waters and in those of its large tributaries, have become practically extinct."[10] The growth of outdoor recreation and sportsmen's desires for abundant fish and wildlife populations drove many into organized conservation groups that patronized stream protection programs. These groups, discussed later, were instrumental in the promotion of government water policy throughout the twentieth century.

In Pittsburgh, problems associated with acid had a long history. In his Army Corps of Engineers report, Colonel Roberts observed acid clarification as early as 1882 at the mouth of the Youghiogheny River at McKeesport, Pennsylvania.[11] In 1899, sanitary engineer Allen Hazen, in his report for the Pittsburgh Filtration Commission, noted that acid conditions existed intermittently in the city's rivers, and especially in the Monongahela River.[12] Roberts claimed that by 1910 acid conditions on the Monongahela River drainage existed 130 miles upstream from Pittsburgh. Four years later, the U.S. Public Health Service found occasional acid conditions for extending 170 miles down the Ohio River to Marietta, Ohio.[13]

"The Most Heavily Treated Water Supply in the World"

While environmental degradation caused some early concern, the real threat converged on human populations. Industrial wastes hindered the development of potable water supplies in an era that grasped the relationship between contamination and poor health. The Pittsburgh region followed a typical pattern in the creation of a water supply and waste removal system. Mortality rates from waterborne diseases in the region were among the highest in the nation from approximately 1880 to 1907 (see Tarr and Yosie, this volume).[14] A United States Geological Survey characterized the region as a "a hotbed for water-borne disease," with death rates consistently over 100 per 100,000 per year at the turn of the century.[15] To combat the health menace, municipal governments constructed facilities that filtered and chemically treated water and occasionally built sewerage systems for the removal of domestic wastes.

The city began filtering its water in 1907–1908 and commenced chlorinating it in 1912. These treatments caused a dramatic reduction of the death rates from infectious disease: the city's typhoid mortality rate fell from 120 per 100,000 in 1900 to 21.7 in 1910 and 2.7 in 1920.[16] Such success confirmed Progressive era arguments that applied science could improve the human condition while preserving economic prosperity. However, problems created by industrial waste presented a complex situation for public water officials since these pollutants required different treatment processes from those of domestic sewerage. Industrial wastes often nullified the benefits of municipal water treatment by imparting tastes to water, damaging equipment, and, if acidic, disrupting biological processes of water filtration and sewer treatment.

Industrial pollution presented a danger to health, but in the early twentieth century public health officers and sanitary engineers believed that waterborne infectious disease constituted a more direct threat. Water contaminated with industrial wastes often became unpalatable, and water supplies that contained twelve grains of sulfuric acid per gallon became undrinkable. At lower levels, municipal waters treated with chlorine reacted with acidic compounds and phenolic wastes, imparting "obnoxious tastes and odors," which frequently forced consumers to alternative sources such as wells or bottled water.[17] In more than one instance, the well water used as an alternative source proved to be a fatal carrier of contagious disease. Water users on the Monongahela River near Pittsburgh experienced this taste and odor problem relatively frequently. On the South Side of Pittsburgh and in communities upstream, local and federal health officials attributed high typhoid morality rates to the use of alternative shallow wells and other contaminated water supplies.[18]

In addition to diminished drinking quality, acid also retarded water delivery; as its corrosive action destroyed pipes and pumps. The cost of such damage was a key factor in the erection of neutralizing plants as a component of overall water treatment. The savings provided by neutralization offered a considerable return on the investment, not only at treatment plants, but also in the communities using the water, since the acidic water also destroyed domestic plumbing.

The impact on municipal water supplies is aptly illustrated by the experience of McKeesport, Pennsylvania. The city located thirteen miles upstream from Pittsburgh at the junction of the Monongahela and Youghiogheny Rivers was one of the region's most important steel production centers. McKeesport supplied its municipal water needs from wells and from the Youghiogheny. That river's drainage contained one of the most active coal mining districts in the nation. The combination of large volumes of manufacturing wastes and domestic sewage mixed into high concentrations of acid drainage produced, according to the United States Geological Survey, "the worst water in the United States."[19] In a 1906 *Water-Supply and Irrigation Paper,* the survey characterized McKeesport's water as "dangerous and in no sense potable or fit for consumption by human beings." Alternatives to municipal supplies included bottled and frequently contaminated well water. In 1903 McKeesport's typhoid-attributed mortality of 112 per 100,000 confirmed USGS condemnation.[20]

In 1908, McKeesport put into operation one of the first municipal water treatment plants designed to filter particulates, kill bacteria through chlorination, neutralize acid, and soften water. The plant treated ten million gallons daily. The financial return on the city plant's investment clearly depicted the extent of acid water damage. Prior to its use, the McKeesport distribution system—including households—lost nearly half of its water supply to corrosive leaks, with high plumbing expenses for domestic and industrial users. The new system reportedly saved the community an estimated $250,000, and improvements reduced the number of plumbers from 156 to 46 a year later.[21] According to the water department's chief chemist, Edward Trax, McKeesport achieved these benefits by becoming the "most heavily treated domestic water supply in the world."[22]

Total costs of pollution are difficult to estimate because damage is often subtle and not directly connected to the effluents. A 1910 pollution survey conducted by the Army Corps of Engineers estimated that acid drainage cost the Pittsburgh district $3 million a year. The corps itself experienced $50,000 a year in damages to its river structures, primarily steel bridge supports. In a study conducted between 1914 and 1917, the United States Public Health Service suggested the total cost of damages from acid drainage may have been as high as $10 million a year.[23]

Acid water not only destroyed domestic plumbing but also caused other damages to households. Consider clothing, for example. Acidic wash water disintegrated fabric. Even neutralized water remained "hard" and corrosive. In addition, hard water required more soap to produce the desired cleansing action. Therefore, the pollutant increased the costs of clothing and cleaning for working-class as well as white-collar families. The high sulfur content of the region's atmosphere likewise damaged clothing and necessitated more frequent cleaning. Beyond these costs, acidic water required women to devote more attention to washing and clothing maintenance than was necessary under normal conditions. Some investigations cited incalculable costs such as damage to domestic appliances and a "de-cidedly acid taste" which destroyed the flavor of food.[24]

Industry and Acid Mine Drainage

Industry paid a considerable price for the pollutant. The most immediate impact of acid water took place at the mines themselves. The corrosive action of the acid destroyed the pipes and pumps installed to remove wa-ter. Damaged machinery raised expenses and hindered coal extraction on a timely basis. Even without acid problems, the mines incurred consider-able expense pumping water. According to various industry surveys, the volume of water removed from mines in the bituminous region ranged on average from a few hundred to several thousand gallons per acre daily. The removal of water required the use of steam-driven pumps that used on average approximately 10 percent of the coal mined: some mines used up to 40 percent of their coal for pumping energy.[25] Leaks caused by corrosion increased the cost of energy production and also damaged equipment. By the late nineteenth century mining engineers were advising the industry to use wooden pipe linings. In highly acid workings, expensive bronze and lead linings and covers protected equipment.[26]

Pipes and pumps could be shielded to a degree but not boilers. Since the highest concentration of acid appeared in mine effluents, the greatest potential for damage occurred near the collieries. In a study of 208 Pitts-burgh coal seam mines, for instance, the pH level in two-thirds of the mines ranged from 2.9 to 3.0. Sulfuric acid and the related sulfates caused pitting in iron, and high temperatures and pressure exacerbated this action. Under some circumstances a boiler could be eaten through in as little as three weeks.[27]

Damages from acid forced operators to develop water neutralization methods for boiler feed. Adding lime lessened the corrosive effect of the acid, but increased the hardness of the water and formed scale in boilers. To combat this effect, soda ash, which precipitated the hardness, was in-troduced, but in large quantities it produced foaming that also reduced pressure. Unfortunately, the process yielded another troublesome waste product: acidic sludge—a "slimy mud, too thick to pump and too thin to shovel." Coal operators disposed of the sludge by dumping it in sumps or nearby streams, thus adding to the streams' pollution burden. Treatment costs were high, a special burden for small companies. The construction of treatment facilities ran about a hundred dollars for each one thousand gal-lons of capacity, and chemical costs of fifty to ninety cents per ton of wa-ter further boosted expenses.[28]

Trouble at the mines was merely the first of the acidic water problems industry faced. As the discharges moved downstream other industries encountered degraded water. Manufacturing required large quantities of reasonably pure water and when acid pollution became more acute, treatment became a necessity. While most, if not all, industries in the areas were impacted, the effect on steel and on the railroads was most severe.

The steel industry began treating acidic water supplies in the first years of the twentieth century. The National Tube Company built a treatment plant at the same time as the city of McKeesport. The damage at the mills included the destruction of pipes and pumps, but acid water also complicated cooling processes and the quenching of coke at the region's by-product coke ovens. By the end of the decade, all of the mills had constructed treatment plants. One of the largest steel mills located on the Monongahela River, for instance, consumed up to 60 million gallons a day. Usually only water for boilers received treatment, but during high acid conditions the entire volume required neutralization, especially to prevent pitting during steel cooling. The investment reduced costs and company engineers calculated that treatment made it possible to "produce steam for $7 per horse power per annum cheaper than was possible before."[29]

Steel mills and other manufacturing establishments requiring treated water could build large, stationary facilities to provide supplies on site. Railroads, however, were at a relative disadvantage since their equipment did not remain stationary. The rolling stock of early twentieth-century railroads depended on steam energy, which required frequent water stops. As the production of coal expanded in the area, acceptable boiler feed became harder to find. In the 1870s the American Railway Master Mechanics Association studied the expense brought on by unsuitable water supplies. The study found that the region's hard water cost $750 annually per locomotive. These expenses included larger coal bills, boiler repairs, and cleaning. By 1914, industry surveys fixed the annual expense of acid water at $1,618 per locomotive. For two large Pittsburgh area railroads, the total cost amounted to nearly $800,000 per year, not including that resulting from delays caused by acid damaged equipment.[30]

American railroads built treatment plants in an effort to stem these costs. In 1904 rail lines maintained 257 water treatment plants. Thirty years later, the number of plants had grown to 1,200, treating 90 billion gallons a year. Many of these plants were treating acid water in the Appalachian coal regions. The Baltimore & Ohio Railroad, for example, operated 113 plants on its lines, and reported savings in equipment of over $1 million annually. Other railroads developed water supply systems by building reservoirs above mining districts and running pipelines along rail networks. Several lines resorted to purchasing treated water. For a number of railroads and for steamboats plying the Monongahela River, an expensive alternative was to haul extra water.[31]

Water dependent industries did not passively accept the negative impacts of mine acid on their businesses. Many corporate leaders complained—at times bitterly—over the growing nuisance and expense precipitated by acid waste. These complaints took place regardless of the fact that both the steel industry and the railroads maintained extensive coal holdings and mining operations as well as being significant polluters in other ways. The steel industry, for example, castigated coal operators for acidic discharges that raised treatment cost, but defended its "right" to dump "pickling" waste into the same rivers on which it built water treatment facilities.[32] By the 1920s, these industries as well as municipalities and recreational users began pushing the government for solutions to counter the growing burden of acid mine drainage.

For government policy makers, acidic water offered an engineering and policy dilemma. The pollutant hindered effective water treatment and presented an indirect health threat. However, the economic importance of coal inhibited coercive action. The coal industry argued emphatically that no "suitable" method existed for the treatment of mine water. And, even if authorities contemplated action, the industry had achieved a legal protection.

Mining's great environmental and political influence became evident when the 1905 Pennsylvania legislature passed "An Act to Preserve the Purity of the Waters of the State for the Protection of the Public Health." This law applied primarily to the dumping of domestic wastes from new sewage systems and excluded existing systems. The Purity of Waters Act pertained to individuals, municipalities, and corporations. The legislature specifically exempted "waters pumped or flowing from coal mines."[33] The act shielded the industry from regulations and likewise complicated the dilemma for health officials, domestic water users, and even coal dependent industries. This legislation was built around the recognized multifaceted value of coal and supported by an infamous nineteenth-century legal precedent.

Pollution and Common Law: *Sanderson v Pennsylvania Coal Co.*

In 1886, the Pennsylvania Supreme Court ruled in favor of the coal industry in a case involving acid mine drainage. This case, *Pennsylvania Coal Company v Sanderson and Wife,* concerned mine acid damages to a family farm near Scranton, Pennsylvania. The Sanderson farm was situated downstream from the company's Gypsy Grove mine, which corrupted the farm's water supply, killing crops and wrecking the domestic water system.

The Sandersons sued for injunctive relief and damages. In February 1878, the Luzerne County Court found in favor of the mine, stating that "the exigencies of the great industrial interest must be kept standing in view . . . and for slight inconvenience or occasional annoyances, they ought not be held responsible." The Sandersons appealed the decision and secured a reversal. However, Pennsylvania Coal sought an appeal of that decision and the Pennsylvania Supreme Court finally settled the issue, in the process creating a powerful precedent. The court maintained that "the right to mine coal is not a nuisance in itself," and that the acidic substances entered the stream via natural forces beyond the company's control. Justices also considered the importance of the coal industry, which included labor. It followed then that "the trifling inconvenience to particular persons must sometimes give way to the necessities of a great community."[34]

The *Sanderson* decision is one of the most cited water pollution cases in American law. Since the decision offered a positive affirmation of industrial actions, the precedent emerged in a legion of pollution suits. The doctrine, considered extreme by many courts, found strict support in only a few cases outside Pennsylvania.[35] However, in Pennsylvania the case carried a dramatic effect, since it protected industrial polluters—coal in particular—from potential environmental liability. Thus, in 1905, when the Pennsylvania legislature passed the Purity of Waters Act it acknowledged a protected zone for coal and the natural forces involved. Unrestricted pollution supposedly encouraged the economy, but with the result noted by another jurist twenty-five years later that acid drainage corrupted "nearly every stream in the western end of the state, and it has become a serious problem how to obtain pure water sufficient to supply the inhabitants."[36]

The Sanitary Water Board

By 1920, water pollution, and acid mine drainage in particular, created enough concern throughout the state to receive serious political recognition. In 1923 the newly elected governor, Gifford Pinchot, proposed an administrative code that would, among other things, establish a board in the Department of Health to promulgate water quality standards and regulations. The General Assembly passed the measure and created the Sanitary Water Board. The act granted the board only circumscribed power, but allowed for investigations and advisory. Its main function was to propose policies to be ratified elsewhere. The legislative intent charged the board with focusing on sewage disposal practices and working with neighboring states on problems of interstate character. Acid mine drainage was, however, again specifically exempted from possible restrictions, upholding its protection under state law.[37] Thus, although the creation of the board represented a milestone in stream pollution control, it possessed a major loophole.

Despite the board's limitations, another acid drainage lawsuit forced the state and its new board to address pollution issues more seriously. In 1923 the Pennsylvania Supreme Court rendered a decision in favor of the Pennsylvania Railroad against several small coal operators who had polluted a reservoir. This decision undermined the *Sanderson* decision doctrine by forcing the state to defend the interests of the commonwealth against a pollutant threatening the public interest.[38]

The Pennsylvania Railroad v Sagamore Coal et al.

At the turn of the century, the Pennsylvania Railroad combated damages to equipment caused by acid by constructing an independent water supply system. Completed in 1927, the system included thirty-six reservoirs along a 441-mile pipeline network. The Indian Creek watershed, some sixty-five miles southeast of Pittsburgh, became one of the first reservoir sites. Indian Creek also contained some low-grade bituminous coal deposits, which were mined commercially beginning just after the reservoir's 1906 construction. By 1920 coal production rose to a level where acidic discharges threatened the quality of the railroad's water supply and the company filed a legal complaint.

The railroad sued on the grounds that its water supply was corrupted, but also that the pollution damage involved a public nuisance. The company had deliberately sold water to regional water suppliers as far away as Pittsburgh in order to manufacture a case. Thus, the pollution potentially threatened the public health. Health authorities followed this line of reasoning, especially when pressured by local government officials such as Pittsburgh Mayor W. A. Magee concerned with the quality of municipal drinking water supplies. The railroad corporation also enlisted the aid of powerful state officials such as the Pennsylvania attorney general, who acted as a "party plaintiff" on behalf of the affected citizens.

In the Court of Common Pleas of Fayette County, trial Judge John Q. Van Swearingen denied the public interest link, claiming the railroad only enjoyed the rights of "an ordinary riparian owner." The Pennsylvania Railroad enjoyed no legal right to protection under Pennsylvania law. His decision reaffirmed the *Sanderson* one in that it supported the coal companies' "property right" to pollute.[39]

The Pennsylvania Supreme Court overturned the lower court ruling in September 1924. Justices concluded that the pollution created a public nuisance and that it could be enjoined since the public used the water. The opinion ruled that coal companies possessed "no right of any kind" to discharge acidic water into streams when the public made use of the water. The decision did not overturn the *Sanderson* doctrine, but it created a precedent for the state should public interests be compromised. With regard to the attorney general's involvement, the court ruled that the public had a right to prevent actions of property holders if their actions harmed a public good.

The state, according to the court, had a justifiable interest in the suit in defense of public interests. The decision supported the right of the state, through its agency, the Sanitary Water Board, to respond to citizen complaints, just as it had for the Pennsylvania Railroad. This faced Governor Pinchot and the Sanitary Water Board with a critical policy decision—how to defend the public's interest but not bring radical harm to a leading energy producing industry.

Following the Indian Creek decision, citizen complaints regarding water pollution and acid drainage in particular soared. In response, the Sanitary Water Board adopted a stream classification system modeled on one adopted by Massachusetts. Dividing streams into three classes, the system acknowledged grossly polluted waters and allowed for their use as sinks. The classification also attempted to improve less polluted streams and to protect pure streams. The A streams were clean streams, fit for human consumption. Class B streams carried pollution but could be rehabilitated through abatement programs. And class C waters were recognized as "so polluted that they cannot be used as sources of public water supplies, will not support fish life, and are not used for recreation."[40]

Policies developed in the early 1920s as a result of the creation of the board and the impact of the Indian Creek decision seem more incremental than major shifts. Pinchot devised a series of "cooperative agreements" with industrial polluters in an effort to find solutions. Cooperation symbolized Pinchot's conservationist mindset that government and industry together could solve environmental issues for society's benefit. Arrangements with leather tanners, pulp and paper mills, manufactured gas companies, and petroleum refiners produced some positive results. One such agreement involving by-product coke ovens reduced damaging effluents significantly and served as a model for other industries and states. Environmental historian Joel Tarr concludes that "Pennsylvania pioneered in the area of cooperative agreements . . . to achieve voluntary pollution reduction."[41]

The Izaak Walton League

In the 1920s pressures to resolve problems resulting from acid mine drainage emerged from a host of directions. Domestic and industrial water users forced the Pennsylvania state government, at the very minimum, to address the issue with a growing number of policies and tactics, none of which seemed to work effectively. The growing number of sportsmen in the state were especially discontented. Sportsmen wielded considerable clout and demanded more aggressive state actions against polluters. When those actions failed or seemed of little benefit, sportsmen pushed the question beyond the state's boundaries and onto the national stage.

The Izaak Walton League of America was the most powerful outdoors and conservationist organization in the United States during the 1920s and 1930s. With nearly 2,900 local chapters and over 200,000 members, the Waltons commanded wide political influence. The organization's magazine, *Outdoor America,* informed members on a number of relevant issues but served also as an excellent means to build support for environmental actions. The Waltons, who must be considered a conservationist group, served as a model for environmental organizations of the 1960s and 1970s.

In Pennsylvania, the organization was especially strong because of the population's phenomenal interest in hunting and fishing. For the Pennsylvania membership, acid drainage threatened habitat and served as a catalyst for promoting progressive government activities. Prominent among the state's membership was Connellsville, Pennsylvania native Kenneth Reid, who served as national director and editor of *Outdoor America*. In the latter capacity, Reid concluded early that the state pollution efforts offered few solutions and that the only means of solving water resource issues rested with a strong federal authority. Within this context, Reid argued and organized the lobbying of Congress for various programs and federal laws. As a native of western Pennsylvania, his foremost concern was the damage caused by acid mine discharges.[42]

To Reid and other proponents of federal pollution control, existing policies that rested on state authority did not work. Testifying before Congress, Reid argued that "the disgracefully polluted conditions of our streams throughout the land stands as mute evidence of the utter breakdown and failure of the present alleged system for their protection." He declared that the grim condition of the nation's waterways as described by research conducted by federal agencies such as the U.S. Geological Survey affirmed this judgment. The complexity of the problem, and the power of industrial interests like coal, prevented state regulations from developing effective policy. Only by centralizing authority, he asserted, could the states and nation hope to solve a growing national dilemma.[43]

Walton members did not speak of one mind on conservation issues. Chapters included men who shared enthusiasm for the outdoors, but tempered their wildlife concerns when they threatened to compromise economic issues. Still, the core of the organization generally supported federal programs and promoted the development of state-guided policies to clean rivers. The organization promoted several clean water bills with limited success. The original Water Pollution Control Act passed in 1939, but vetoed by Franklin Roosevelt, was the product of years of Walton lobbying. The 1948 act that finally became law was a watered-down version of their base proposal.

Lobbying for federal water legislation was the primary aim of the Walton League and Reid during the 1930s. Yet they approached the ultimate goal by supporting a number of important ancillary issues and programs. The Walton League championed the Civilian Conservation Corps and the Federal Mine Sealing project. Both programs functioned under the guise of New Deal work relief. Walton support of the Federal Mine Sealing Program linked the organization with a pollution abatement program of national importance.

Sealing of Abandoned Coal Mines

Sealing abandoned coal mines as a method to abate acid water pollution had been considered since at least the early 1920s. Prior to that, it had been used for other purposes such as sealing shafts and other openings as a safety measure. Bulkheads also served as underground dams to harness mine water and prevent it from flooding working areas; it also helped pumping systems by forming reservoirs. Efforts to extinguish mine fires also included sealing as well as attempts to block the infiltration of mine gases.[44]

In 1921 Congress briefly discussed mine sealing as a pollution control measure.[45] During the same period, several representatives of the coal industry considered the method to be a plan with "some hope." Mining corporations had been pressured for three decades to alleviate their discharges, and sealing offered a method of pollution control. It was especially attractive if paid for by government. The first mines sealed as a matter of government policy and as a pollution control measure were those in the Indian Creek area, ordered sealed in 1924 by the Pennsylvania Supreme Court as a means to prevent the further contamination of the Pennsylvania Railroad's reservoir. The sealed mines on Indian Creek unintentionally served a larger purpose as a laboratory for state health authorities and, in particular, the U.S. Bureau of Mines, which had a great interest in methods to reduce acid effluents.[46]

The U.S. Bureau of Mines studied mine sealing as a pollution abatement method in the 1920s. These investigations, along with the Public Health Service's examinations, considered a variety of alternatives. R. D. Leitch, associate chemical engineer working out of the bureau's Pittsburgh station, conducted the most significant studies of mine drainage. His early analysis indicated that the only solution to prevent stream pollution from coal mines rested with chemical neutralization. However, costs made neutralization a prohibitive solution. From his observation of mines that had been sealed for safety measures or by natural caving, Leitch commented that on several instances a reduced flow issued from the mine workings that appeared to be of higher quality than normally expected. Considering the cost associated with neutralization and industry reluctance, sealing became the focus of further study.[47]

Leitch advanced the mine sealing idea using basic chemical assumptions about the production of acid. The accepted theory of acid creation concluded that formation required three elements: iron pyrites, oxygen, and water. Therefore, if at least one of the elements could be removed from the process, the production of acid might be stopped or reduced. In field studies at Indian Creek and other sites, Leitch witnessed reduced acid levels and, in some cases, alkaline water issuing from blocked and flooded areas in active mines. Thus, Leitch claimed a twofold benefit from mine sealing, one for the operators and one for the environment: (1) sealing worked-out sections reduced pumping costs and substantially decreased the costs for operators by lessening the corrosive impact on pipes and pumps; and (2) as a pollution control measure, sealing materially reduced the acid entering nearby streams.[48]

At first glance mine sealing seemed an ideal solution. It offered an inexpensive and simple remedy to an expensive and complex problem. In theory, it saved the mines money while reducing pollution. However, the idea did not take into account human and natural geologic factors that eliminated any perceived benefits. For the time being, however, with the blessing of the Bureau of Mines, Leitch and several other engineers from the Pittsburgh station pursued the investigation and the promotion of a large-scale sealing program that especially targeted abandoned mines.

Water officials in the Ohio Valley states believed abandoned mine sealing to be an effective solution to the pollution problem, but did not want to or could not finance such an undertaking. The per-mine cost was normally small, but the total of thousands of abandoned mines and exposed outcroppings represented a major appropriation. In addition, individual states hesitated to launch projects on the grounds that if other states did not follow suit, overall benefits were limited and funds wasted. Pennsylvania, for example, requested that sealing on the Monongahela River should begin on the headwaters in West Virginia. Thus, the improvements achieved through a Pennsylvania sealing program would not be diminished by upstream effluents. West Virginia and Ohio tendered similar arguments at Pennsylvania.[49]

The mining industry supported the idea, but did not want to finance a sealing program. Since the target of such a project focused on abandoned properties, industry leaders refused responsibility for other people's "empty hole(s) in the ground."[50] The operators' position did not, however, reflect the fact that many of the mines eventually sealed were actually properties still in the control of existing companies. What their position did reflect, beyond a reluctance to spend company money for sealing, was the corporate inclination to avoid responsibility for their discharges and to allow the federal government to manage what at other times they had argued was a "local problem, best dealt with on the local level." Industry leaders became increasingly interested in the bureau's work, however, when analysis indicated that significant money could be saved in pumping and equipment cost. "The coal mining industry," wrote William P. Yant, the bureau's supervising chemist, "is actually becoming interested in their mine drainage problems and are looking to the Bureau for assistance." The industry considered this a problem for the government to manage and, like the state governments, looked to Washington for solutions.[51]

The initial federal program, which started under the National Industrial Recovery Act (NIRA), reflected the fact that stream purification was considered to be a worthwhile public work. To the Izaak Walton League, an energetic advocate of mine sealing, the NIRA presented "the opportunity of a lifetime for cleaning-up much unnecessary pollution," especially pouring from abandoned mines.[52] Regional newspapers endorsed the program as well, noting both the pollution control benefits and the unemployment relief. The *Pittsburgh Sun-Telegraph* characterized sealing as the ideal approach since it provided "a way of giving relief from an intolerable condition without interfering with our important coal mining industry. Indeed the coal operators should welcome it because it would tend to put an end to the reproach that is now being heaped upon them as stream polluters."[53]

In November 1933, after much lobbying by state political leaders and Izaak Walton League pressure in Washington, the mine sealing program was approved as a Civil Works Administration relief effort. This initial program had a limited time period of about three months, but it paid for sealing expenses in Pennsylvania, West Virginia, and Ohio.[54] Pennsylvania sealed the first mine under the program—an abandoned mine on Plum Creek near Universal, which had polluted the Allegheny River.[55]

In September 1935, the WPA allocated funds for further mine sealing. Before then, several of the states financed some projects as part of county relief measures. A few local chapters of the Izaak Walton League and other sportsmen's groups continued to survey the coal country for sealing sites, and in some cases worked on mine openings in an effort to prove the desirability of continued funding. In the meantime, Kenneth Reid and the Waltons recommenced the political battle for federal funding. Reid came close to realizing his "long-cherished dream of sealing abandoned coal mines" on three occasions.[56] But, due to administrative snarls, the program was put off until 1935 when Congress passed the Emergency Relief Appropriations Act and funneled public works monies to the recently created WPA. Between its initial funding and the program's termination in June 1938, the WPA disbursed $5,495,000, with approximately 90 percent charged as labor costs.[57]

In the first two years of the WPA program (1935–1937), sealing crews covered over 47,000 openings at 1,527 sites in four states: Pennsylvania, Ohio, West Virginia, and Kentucky. Openings included both portals and surface breaks. The number of openings varied per mine from one to several hundred. In one case, crews sealed 500 openings in a Pennsylvania mine. Of the total, Pennsylvania secured the most openings, with a reported 30,000 at 317 mines in twenty-two counties. In comparison, West Virginia sealed 500 mines and 3,600 openings. The other states involved, Maryland, Tennessee, Indiana, and Alabama, did not file reports. In those states, as sealing took place, it became apparent that the discharge of acid from abandoned mines was not as severe as the acid discharges from industrial plants and they continued only limited work under the program.[58]

The sealing temporarily produced the desired effect. In Pennsylvania, for example, the Evans mine in Beaver County had drained 75,000 gallons of water containing 800 pounds of acid daily. After air sealing, the drainage dropped to 10,000 gallons, yielding 85 pounds of acid. Also in Pennsylvania, before sealing, the Commerce No. 4 mine in Cambria County drained over 100,000 gallons of water loaded with 3,000 pounds of acid a day. In 1937, the flow dropped to 32,000 with only 200 pounds of acid.[59]

Estimates vary, but many observers suggest the reduction in acid amounted to over 80 percent in some minor drainages. In 1940 the U.S. Public Health Service estimated that the average residual load of acid on the main Ohio River measured 48 percent of what it was prior to the sealing project. On the Monongahela River, sealing reduced acid loads by 51 percent. On the Kiskiminetas River, a tributary of the Allegheny and the source of acidic water troubling the Pittsburgh water supply, reduction efficiency at abandoned mines achieved one of the highest levels with a decline of 78 percent.[60]

The federal mine sealing program exhausted WPA funds in June 1938. The state of Pennsylvania appropriated over $2.5 million following World War II to extend the work and to pay for research. Most public authorities up through the 1950s considered the project an unqualified success. The program had reduced acid concentrations in the waters of the Ohio Basin. It served as an excellent example of the benefits of federal cooperation with the states' efforts in water pollution control. During the mid to late 1930s, when Congress debated several water pollution control bills not primarily designed as work relief measures, mine sealing served as a political touchstone for the advocates of greater federal involvement.[61] Unfortunately, as ultimately became clear, sealing achieved its only intended success by providing work relief; it retained limited shelf life as a political contrivance and less as a sanitation technique.

Mine sealing did not work—it produced only temporary relief from the problems associated with acid drainage. A combination of primarily natural forces and human interaction doomed the project. Drift mines are essentially subsurface holes in the ground. Since they are located near the surface, the overburden and strata are unstable. The areas above mines are subject to subsidence over long periods of time. Thus, surface breaks continued at sites covered (sealed), and erosion of openings took place at irregular intervals. The sealed portals suffered from the same fate. Instability of the strata surrounding the seals broke down walls and allowed air and water to enter or water to escape the mines. Air seals in particular collapsed due to changes in air pressure. As the outside air pressure changed, the mines "breathed" to reconcile the difference. Over time, the pressure deteriorated the seals and allowed air to enter the mines freely and recommenced the oxidation of pyritic materials.[62]

In June 1946, the Pennsylvania Sanitary Water Board financed investigations into the effectiveness of mine sealing. The board established industrial fellowships at Pittsburgh's Mellon Institute for Industrial Research. The original and subsequent fellowships designed to study acid drainage problems and mine sealing continued until 1962. S. A. Braley, senior research fellow, concluded that mine sealing did not reduce the discharge of acid from drift mines since the control techniques could not diminish the oxygen content of the mine atmosphere. The only benefit surface waters derived from sealing materialized when surface water was prevented from entering a mine or when underground reservoirs were formed.[63]

As a policy measure, mine sealing served a broader purpose in the development of water pollution control. The program illustrated the positive benefits of federal research into water pollution problems. And it had been developed at the request of the states to the Bureau of Mines and the Public Health Service, thereby solidifying the argument for continued federal involvement. Conservation organizations, such as the Izaak Walton League, learned the value of lobbying for federally sponsored pollution abatement programs. Arguments for advanced federal activity beyond the application of work relief used mine sealing as an example of the need for the national government to undertake a more active role in environmental affairs.

⌒

The examination of acid mine drainage illustrates certain crucial points concerning the history of conservation, pollution policy, and environmentalism. The pollution resulted from the extraction of a vital industrial resource. Accepting the trade-off of stream degradation in return for economic prosperity was a somewhat easy choice in an era bent on increasing its wealth. Yet, as the nineteenth century came to a close, negative effects began to impinge heavily on the economic benefits for society.

A conservationist perspective suggests that water carried multiple "wise use" applications. The conveying of waste material was a "wise use" if applied scientific applications through treatment processes regenerated the resource for further domestic and industrial uses. Gifford Pinchot expressed this position more fully than anyone ever connected to progressive notions relating to the American landscape. But Pinchot's gubernatorial response came much too late in a situation where water degradation was backed by common law and legislative statutes. No conservationist balance could be achieved after decades of such unrestrained resource practices.

In the first decades of the twentieth century, the need for coal as a fuel and resulting poor water quality locked the Pittsburgh region into an economic and environmental dilemma. Threatening the fragile coal industry could destabilize the entire region's industrial economy. Yet living with the growing health and financial burden resulting from the extraction of the resource posed an increasing threat to the well-being of people and the quality of the environment. Even the starkest of economic realists had to question the value of unrestrained growth when confronted with disintegrating locomotive boilers, rotting water faucets, and the stench from thousands of decaying fish. Thus, twentieth-century water pollution policy emerged from the realization, suggested by many indicators, that something was seriously flawed in society's neglect of the environmental effects of industrial pollution.

Acid mine drainage was a major source of Pittsburgh's environmental degradation. The evolution of governmental action to deal with the issue illustrates how values can shift as pollution injures a variety of societal groups. This case also indicates how what was originally defined as a local and state problem can result in national action. Contemporary environmental policy and limits in regard to coal mining have sharply reduced the scope of the acid drainage problem. The pollutant, however, especially that flowing from abandoned mines, continues to pose a threat to Pittsburgh and Pennsylvania streams and rivers. We are thus again reminded of how resource and environment tradeoffs made in the past pose a continued burden for the environment.

How, When, and for Whom Was Smoke a Problem in Pittsburgh?

ANGELA GUGLIOTTA

IN THE LONG HISTORY of urban air pollution in the United States, no city is more prominent than Pittsburgh. Pittsburgh deserves its prominence because of its eighteenth-century head start and its dramatic mid-twentieth-century environmental transformation. Pittsburgh's smoke story, like the story of urban pollution generally, is often told in terms of problem and solution or crisis and response. In such narratives, coal smoke, fly-breeding garbage, or raw sewage entering waterways are taken as materially given preexistent problems. The question for historians becomes how such problems were successfully solved or why they were not solved sooner. Environmental historians must count these important questions among those that drive their interest in the field. Yet, there are advantages in broadening the range of questions. Narratives of solution seldom do justice to the mixed losses and benefits inherent in most historical outcomes. Similarly they make it easy to see heroes and villains where human motives and capacities are usually more ambiguous. Seeing pollution as a passive and self-contained condition requiring amelioration also closes off chances to learn how changing environmental attitudes express other important cultural changes and how pollution itself can be a force in shaping social geography, civic culture, and economic conditions. To ask questions about historical actors' perceptions of pollution is to step back from how problems were solved and to ask how, when, and for whom environmental circumstances become problems in the first place. This essay explores smoke in its many roles in Pittsburgh history before the Renaissance, examining how, when, and for whom it was a problem, as well as what it might have been when it was not.

Early Smoke Observations

Pittsburgh and its smoke were born together: bituminous coal was burned in the garrison at Fort Pitt in the 1750s and smoke from mine fires created a cloud over the small settlement in the 1760s. As a frontier settlement Pittsburgh's civic existence had to be argued for. Smoke was part of this argument—an advertisement for Pittsburgh's resource abundance and the industriousness of its population. Early observations of smoke appeared alongside, and were even sometimes embedded in, typical New World rhetoric about beauty and bounty. In 1786, Hugh Henry Brackenridge, an early booster, suggested the Forks as a suitable setting for the frolic of Greek river gods, nymphs, and satyrs, but also celebrated its abundant coal.[1] Four years earlier, John Bernard had described Pittsburgh as follows: "On approaching Pittsburgh we were struck with a peculiarity nowhere else to be observed in the States: a cloud of smoke hung over it in an exceedingly clear sky, recalling to me many choking recollections of London."[2] In 1807, Christian Schultz, who had praised the city's "charming" situation and natural advantages, wrote, "The first entry into Pittsburgh is not equally agreeable to every person, as the sulphurous vapour arising from the burning of coal is immediately perceptible."[3]

Since Pittsburgh was a new city, whose existence was dependent on the extrinsic advantages of proximity to military and settlement frontiers, it was from the beginning instrumentally valued. Dependent on commercial advantages over rival settlements, its existence was precarious. Although Pittsburgh manufacturers undersold eastern goods to the West, the city's economic success was far from predetermined.[4] Economic strength was Pittsburgh's justification for continued existence, and as such was built laboriously and guarded jealously. Throughout its history, Pittsburgh would play one set of economic advantages against the other. When its primacy as Western entrepôt was first threatened soon after the War of 1812, the city attempted to make up in manufacturing what it lost in trade.[5] The city's other geographic advantages made this alternative civic identity possible. Although the War of 1812 had provided a stimulus to manufacturing, its end, and the dumping of British goods on American markets, brought commercial decline. When the war ended, Pittsburgh was left to struggle with the difficulties of its extrinsically defined identity. Facing serious commercial rivalry by the 1820s, as Wheeling was chosen as the site at which the National Road would cross the Ohio River, Pittsburgh consolidated its manufacturing strength. This brought an intensification of air pollution, which was universally noted by travelers.[6] Environmental degradation seemed a well-justified sacrifice to a city threatened by such economic uncertainties.

Smoke — That "Single Word"

While smoke was celebrated in these early years as a sign of abundance and industry, it was also the subject of civic concern and environmental regulation. As early as 1804, coal smoke had become a local nuisance, as Pittsburgh burgess General Presley Neville complained to George Stevenson, the president of City Council: "The general dissatisfaction which prevails and the frequent complaints which are exhibited in consequence of the Coal Smoke from many buildings in the Borough particularly from Smithies and Blacksmith Shops, compels me to address you . . . not only the consequence of the place, but the peace and harmony of the inhabitants depend upon speedy measures being adopted to remedy this nuisance."[7] Local dissatisfaction with smoke was further expressed in chimney height ordinances from the city's founding in 1816. These complaints and restrictions, together with ordinances regulating coke ovens and railroad smoke by midcentury, all belie the assumption that smoke was universally acceptable in the early years.[8]

In 1868, prominent biographer James Parton, in his *Atlantic Monthly* feature on Pittsburgh, used smoke to highlight tensions among Pittsburgh's urban and frontier, manufacturing and commercial identities. Parton credited the city's extreme pollution by bituminous coal smoke for the manliness of its men and the absence of frivolity among its women. He linked masculinity with virtuous industry and the rejection of luxury, and femininity with the frivolous enjoyment of material goods, especially clothing and domestic furnishings. All "dainty and showy apparel [was] forbidden by the state of the atmosphere," as was "delicate upholstery within doors." No dandies could live in Pittsburgh because yellow kid gloves would not stay clean. Only "some very young girls, in flush times, when wages [were] high," could use pastel bonnet ribbons, but "ladies of standing and experience" would "never think of such extravagance" and wore "only the colors that harmonize[d] with the dingy livery of the place."[9]

For Parton, smoke determined civic identity as embodied in local customs centering around industry: Pittsburgh's entire material culture was shaped by labor through smoke. Smoke was labor's product—it enforced, for both men and women, a preference for industry over luxury, virtue over sin. The close association of virtue with frugality and the eschewal of domestic and environmental amenities made early attempts to oppose smoke on moral grounds difficult.

Yet beneath protestations that smoke was Pittsburgh's essence and jovial dismissals of the discomforts and drudgery it imposed, discontent with Pittsburgh's environmental conditions bubbled. James Parton laid bare some of the inconsistencies in the rhetoric of the industrial frontier when he discussed the health claims made for smoke in the context of Pittsburgh's beginning streetcar suburbanization:

He [the Pittsburgher] insists . . . that the smoke of bituminous coal kills malaria, and saves the eyesight . . . the smoke, so far from being an evil, is a blessing . . . and it destroys every property of the atmosphere that is hostile to life. . . . All this is comforting to the benevolent mind. Still more so is the fact, that the fashion of living a few miles out of the smoke is beginning to prevail among the people of Pittsburg [sic]. Villages are springing up as far as twenty miles away, to which the business men repair, when, in consequence of having inhaled the smoke all day, they feel able to bear the common country atmosphere through the night.[10]

Parton used his discussions of smoke, health, and suburbanization to point to tensions within the conception of Pittsburgh as a smoky and harmonious frontier republic of free and equal industrious producers.

By the 1860s and 1870s, smoke, in the dominant view, was regarded as summing up Pittsburgh's whole identity. Two years before Parton wrote, smoke was at issue as neighbors sued a brickmaker on a bucolic bluff overlooking the city of Allegheny, annexed by Pittsburgh in 1907, for nuisance. Both judicial language and contemporaneous newspaper stories point to entanglements of gender, class, luxury, and virtue. The Allegheny County Court of Common Pleas issued an injunction against the brickmaker, John Huckenstine, forbidding him to burn bituminous coal since it injured the orchards, crops, health, and comfort of his neighbor. Huckenstine appealed to the State Supreme Court. Coverage in the local press derided the plaintiffs with subtle sarcasm that contrasted their enjoyment of luxury with the defendant's engagement in industry. The *Pittsburgh Gazette Times* called the plaintiffs "wealthy property owners" living in "comfortable and costly houses" with grounds "beautified" by "money, taste and the skill of the landscape gardener." It accused these country gentlemen of seeking not just to abate smoke but to abate the brickyard industry itself.[11] In 1871, the Pennsylvania Supreme Court overturned the 1866 injunction. Justice J. Agnew echoed Parton in seeing Pittsburgh's entire civic identity as subsumed by smoke. That "single word" described "the characteristics of . . . [the] city, its kind of fuel, its business, the habits of its people and the industries which . . . [gave] it prosperity and wealth."[12]

An editorial from the *Pittsburgh Gazette* from the same year as Huckenstine's appeal minimized the value of domestic cleanliness and comfort. While half-seriously considering, and then dismissing, prospects for smoke abatement through steam heating from central plants, the editorial implicitly accepted smoke's domestic discomforts and labor burdens. The editorialist was unwilling to exchange the city's "hearth stones" where "the crickets perch[ed] themselves in piping out cheerful tunes" for a domestic life made labor-free by "no dirt, no coal smoke" and "no dust from fires."[13]

Smoke's impoverishment of material life supported strictures against consumption upheld within the Scotch-Irish Presbyterian culture of Pittsburgh's founding families. It reinforced local values of frontier primitiveness and masculine roughness. Expansion of industry was regarded as a necessity, and complaints about smoke were characterized as threatening sustenance. Desires to protect health, comfort, property, or domestic life were taken to be luxurious tastes of coddled and feminized elites. As smoke ordinances, nuisance suits, and suburbanization during this same period make clear, however, smoke was not univocally accepted in Pittsburgh even in these early years. Yet, only when cultural and material changes interacted to break traditional associations among smoke, material austerity, and the city's economic welfare would antismoke sentiment gain the upper hand.

Natural Gas and Civic Soul-Searching

By the 1870s and 1880s, Pittsburgh would face a number of jarring local transformations related to and reinforced by larger cultural changes in American society. In the second half of the nineteenth century railroads superseded rivers, steel overtook iron, and petroleum and natural gas suddenly stood alongside coal as Pittsburgh's chief mineral advantages. Even Pittsburgh's characteristic atmosphere would be briefly denatured by technology in the latter part of the period, as clean natural gas temporarily replaced smoky bituminous coal as the major fuel for the city between 1884 and 1892. During Pittsburgh's natural gas period values previously regarded as antithetical to industry came to be seen by both employers and skilled workers as supportive of it. Natural gas made better iron, steel, and glass than bituminous coal. Skilled workers writing in the *National Labor Tribune* connected product quality and improved working conditions with smoke-free air, and domestic environmental quality with besieged republican entitlements to a decent standard of living.[14]

With the depletion of the local natural gas supply in the early 1890s, Pittsburghers from many quarters lamented the return of smoky skies and reflected on the gains of the natural gas period. Real estate and retail had become powerful economic interests in the city as natural gas promoted new downtown building and the development of a central business district. Pittsburghers whose means allowed had moved to the suburbs in response to crowding in mixed-class districts of the old walking city, brought on by the explosive expansion of industry and the industrial workforce after midcentury. Industry also suburbanized during this period, in search of larger tracts of flat land and escape from traditional strongholds of working-class solidarity.[15] Suburban residents escaped the full impact of industrial suburbanization as long as the natural gas supply remained viable. With the demise of natural gas, suburban elites realized that they were vulnerable to smoke from their newly coal-burning industrial neighbors.

Local and national cultural changes interacted with material conditions to generate resistance to the return of smoke. Pittsburgh's tradition of provincialism and frontier exceptionalism had long been supported by prominent families' disdain for domestic consumption and the pursuit of leisure and the arts which might have given Pittsburgh a claim to high civic culture. Public leisure and consumption, to the extent that the schedule of heavy industry left room for them, were dominated by the working classes. With the fragmentation of the working class due to immigration, employer attacks on unions and shop-floor power, labor reformers' assaults on working-class leisure culture, and the seductive charms of machine politics, working-class dominance of Pittsburgh's culture gave way. While a core of skilled workers voiced republican demands for smoke reduction as part of their right to a competence, representative professionals and businessmen complained of the costs of smoke to retail merchants and its effects on Pittsburgh's new parks and architectural showpieces. Both demand for political rights and desire for capitalist profit now drove interest in smoke abatement. With the rise of a more assertive elite culture in Pittsburgh, provincialism and frontier exceptionalism were superceded by claims to participation in a wider national culture, which promoted universal civic and environmental standards.[16]

The end of the natural gas period engendered an era of civic soul-searching as both elites and skilled workers were determined to hold onto the gains made in the period. The rise of elite culture contemporaneous with natural gas allowed Pittsburghers to connect with a number of national movements that would shape attitudes toward smoke in the subsequent period. Prominent among them were municipal housekeeping, crusading journalism, and the rising power of retail merchants and of a nascent consumer culture. Each national movement, however, had a unique manifestation in Pittsburgh because of the city's parochial and frontier past and its domination by heavy industry. In each of these movements smoke took a different position relative to Pittsburgh's many other urban problems.

The founders of Pittsburgh's first organized antismoke movement embodied many of the local and national cultural changes of the years between the Civil War and the turn of the century. Pittsburgh's Ladies Health Protective Association (LHPA) was organized in 1889, on the model of a similar New York City group, to combat impure water, inadequate garbage disposal, and smoke.[17] The group's methods and motives were grounded in the long tradition of women's charitable efforts to protect the poor from environmental threats to health. Middle-class women's concern with health intensified after midcentury, as connections between the health of the poor and that of their own families were made palpable by the uneven expansion of municipal services to manage water and waste. Popular versions of zymotic and germ theories of disease emphasizing air and dust transmission led to increased suspicion of all municipal dirt.[18] The LHPA portrayed smoke as an enemy of health under this rubric. In this way it was able to protect itself from accusations of frivolity and effete sentimentality that had long dogged opposition to Pittsburgh smoke on aesthetic grounds. The LHPA cast opposition to smoke as the protection of a necessity of life rather than as an expression of an elite taste for luxury.

The LHPA spearheaded passage of a smoke ordinance in 1892, but this initial ordinance covered only residential suburbs and exempted mill districts. Over the next twenty-five years, as Pittsburgh's economy began to diversify and its domination by heavy industry was mitigated, antismoke forces gained momentum. Geographically broader ordinances were passed over the opposition of local politicians and industrialists, who argued a range of topics, from the need of some metal heating furnaces to make smoke at certain points in production to universal exemption from smoke restriction for iron and steel mills.[19]

In 1900, and more intensively in 1906, Pittsburgh newspaper crusaders targeted air pollution. Publishing, in the latter campaign, more than fifty antismoke articles in one six-month period, *The Pittsburgh Sun* complained of fine clothes and well-cared-for homes sullied by locomotive smoke and of "handsome French poodles" carrying Jones and Laughlin's red ore dust about houses on their paws.[20] The *Sun* linked ornate clothing to monetary value when it spoke of the "dainty white dresses . . . blackened by soot"— the clothing of thousands of pedestrians ruined by steam sand diggers working beneath the Seventh Street Bridge over which they crossed daily. The paper claimed that, "more clothing has been ruined than could be purchased with the monetary returns from the sand and gravel gathered at that point." Articles described "the New York man" characterizing "the Pittsburgh man" as an "easy mark" for having put up with smoke for so long and connected domestic cleanliness and consumption directly with the economic value of real estate. The paper claimed credit for inspiring city councilmen to develop a new, stronger antismoke ordinance, passed after some struggle in 1907.[21] Appeal to such values contrasted sharply with their denigration in the press and the courts of the 1860s and 1870s. By the 1900s Pittsburgh's trade organizations, especially the Pittsburgh Chamber of Commerce, strongly backed smoke regulation. Smoke no longer was synonymous with economic sustenance.

Pittsburgh as Dystopia and the Mellon Smoke Investigations

In these years Pittsburgh would be the subject of national attention for many urban problems, not just for its famous smoke. Between 1907 and 1914 the landmark sociological study the Pittsburgh Survey roundly criticized the city for its low level of social provision and organization in contrast to its high level of industrial efficiency.[22] In 1912, as the city was reeling from these attacks, *Life* ran a feature on Pittsburgh in which it pictured local millionaires carrying money bags filled in the city out of its smoky gloom and off to New York City where they proceeded to marry chorus girls bent on high living.[23] This image of the city captured recent cultural changes in a way that could make Pittsburghers long for James Parton's city of hardworking employers whose love of industry and of smoke kept them from the vices of conspicuous consumption.

While some members of local elites accepted such criticisms, most saw Pittsburgh's problems in a different order of priority than that identified by the Survey or by *Life*. Reform-minded businessmen and club women reacted defensively against the Pittsburgh Survey's socioeconomic recommendations but accepted and pursued many of its environmental ones. This is especially apparent in University of Pittsburgh economist J. T. Holdsworth's *Economic Survey of Pittsburgh,* commissioned by the Chamber of Commerce. For Holdsworth, smoke abatement was Pittsburgh's "first and fundamental need."[24] The Economic Survey recommended business investment in real estate and truck farming, rather than unionization, factory inspection, or abolition of the twelve-hour day, as the solutions to Pittsburgh's social ills. The Economic Survey managed to deflect attention from the needs of working-class men for better hours, wages, and working conditions by focusing on the effects of smoke on the health of women and children. It emphasized this domestic victimization even though working men's pneumonia death rates were the highest of any adult demographic group.[25] The Economic Survey proceeded under the assumption, which underwrote the smoke abatement movement in many manifestations, that reforms worth undertaking either exacted no cost or provided further money-making opportunities for business.

In 1911 the Mellon family, bankers already invested in oil and aluminum rather than iron and steel, founded an institute of industrial research at the University of Pittsburgh.[26] The goals of the Economic Survey would mix with the conflicting ideology of the Pittsburgh Survey in one of the new institute's inaugural studies: the Mellon Institute Smoke Investigation (MISI). The Mellons saw smoke abatement in Pittsburgh as a public-spirited twist on their own commercial goals and commissioned their staff of twenty-five full- and part-time investigators to examine all aspects of Pittsburgh's smoke problem. The institute marshaled the Progressive era's proudest weapons—scientific and social scientific authority—to attack Pittsburgh smoke, an old and previously intractable problem. With the best expertise that Mellon money could buy, the investigation took up, one by one, questions that had long been raised about how to justify viewing smoke as a problem, how to apportion responsibility for it, and how to systematically ameliorate it. The investigation would publish ten bulletins between 1911 and 1922 covering a wide variety of smoke-related concerns: a survey of the sources of smoke; of combustion and abatement equipment; and bulletins covering the effects of smoke on architecture, weather, vegetation, human health, psychology, and the economic life of the city.[27] Yet, in MISI, scientific expertise would prove to be a double-edged sword, as many of its studies yielded ambiguous results, especially with respect to measurement of progress in smoke abatement and the relationship of smoke to human health.

This is particularly evident in the difficulties faced by MISI investigators in the interpretation of the results of their "soot-fall studies," relevant both to matters of health and of progress. In 1912–1913, 1923–1924, and again in 1929–1930, investigators placed open outdoor collection containers around the city and measured the amount of particulate matter collected over a period of several months.[28] On the basis of these measurements researchers made a number of important claims. When the results of the first soot-fall study were available, health investigators tried to correlate them with both pneumonia and tuberculosis rates in the city. To their surprise, they found a strong correlation between soot-fall and neighborhood pneumonia rates but none between smoke and tuberculosis. In order to counter assumptions that it was poverty and not smoke that caused the elevated pneumonia rates in certain neighborhoods, investigators examined this correlation as well. Researchers were interested in showing that smoke was a problem for all of Pittsburgh's citizens, not just another accident of poverty that the populace at large could ignore. They claimed to find no significant correlation between soot-fall and poverty, as measured by population density. Yet neighborhoods with the highest soot-fall, and highest pneumonia rates, were generally in the top half of the population density ranking.[29] Different kinds of ambiguities, equally troubling to anti-air-pollution forces, would arise in the interpretation of subsequent soot-fall studies, as noted below.

The smoke investigation took up many of the issues raised in earlier debates about smoke. Issues of the economic cost of smoke and the relation of smoke and health were central. The Mellon Institute Smoke Investigation superimposed a new bacteriological interpretation on questions about the healthfulness or unhealthfulness of smoke that had been formulated in the nineteenth century under other disease theories. Did smoky air destroy organic poisons or kill germs? No more bacteria were found or grown in sooty media than in those not impregnated with soot.[30] New understandings of germ theory, widely held by the 1910s, showed that air per se was not a medium for the growth or transmission of bacteria.[31] Were Pittsburghers' "mottled lungs" dangerous to the health of their owners? The investigators concluded that "pulmonary anthracosis," called a "community disease" by MISI, actually promoted the formation of lesions that walled off bacteria and promoted healing in cases of tuberculosis. Yet smoky air was found to be a great contributor to Pittsburgh's number one killer, pneumonia.[32]

The MISI economic studies were central to the Mellon investigation, including its connection to Pittsburgh's changing civic consciousness. These studies attempted to calculate the cost of smoke to the city by surveying merchants and housewives about lost merchandise and excess work caused by Pittsburgh's soot burden. They emphasized both domestic comfort and consumption as goods to be preserved rather than as vices or expressions of frivolity. In this way, MISI's outlook accorded well with the cultural changes the city had undergone in the preceding forty years. The institute's emphasis on household labor and household budgets showed its connection to the social survey movement with which MISI's director, John O'Connor, had strong links.[33] The Mellon study identified commercial and real estate interests with domestic comfort and cleanliness and explored ambiguous connections between dirt and disease in an era in which germ theory and the New Public Health lessened suspicion of undifferentiated dirt.

Throughout the teens, MISI workers carried on a campaign of public education and support of the efforts of the office of smoke inspector. In these years Pittsburgh newspapers and on at least one occasion even the *New York Times,* declared that Pittsburgh was no longer America's smokiest city.[34] Proclamations of success also came from the publicity generated by MISI's soot-fall studies, which showed a decline in the amount of tarry soot falling on the city. Results were ambiguous at best, however, showing an increase in total solids precipitated between the 1912–1913 and the 1923–1924 surveys. The difficulties in interpreting soot-fall study results—in deciding what kind of matter to regard as significant—suggested deeper investigations into the composition of air pollution and turned attention of investigators away from visible smoke alone.[35]

Through the 1920s and 1930s Mellon-funded air pollution fellowships and pneumonia studies followed MISI's initial round of investigations. The conflict that surrounded these studies illustrates how difficult it was to take seriously environmental threats to health in an era of bacteriological hegemony and emphasis on contact transmission and curative medicine. Money intended for investigation of links between air pollution and pneumonia was diverted to work on Ralph Mellon's development of an antipneumonia serum.[36]

The De-emphasis of Environment and Health

Environmental reform in service of public health had long been a chief instrument of civic discipline. This orientation was most intense during the late nineteenth century and the Progressive era, just as Pittsburgh's smoke abatement movement had gotten underway. This situation had changed by the 1920s. The second and third decades of the twentieth century brought an attenuation of the centuries-long focus on strong relationships between environment and health. By this time, institutions of public health controlled certain circumscribed aspects of the environment—water and sewage—however imperfectly this was carried out in Pittsburgh.[37] Strong scientific justification was no longer available for broader environmental efforts. Without strong impetus for smoke abatement driven by a public health that saw a generally dirty environment as its chief enemy, smoke abatement lost a powerful justification. If abatement was to be promoted at all, it would have to be primarily on the basis of other arguments. Yet such arguments as were available were only intermittently applicable to Pittsburgh.

Economic arguments for Pittsburgh's future as dependent on retail, real estate, and the attractions of a pleasant domestic and cultural life were unnecessary during the wartime production boom. During World War I Pittsburgh's newly diversifying economy had been temporarily returned to its former state of extreme domination by heavy industry.[38] While smoke abatement interest and claims of smoke abatement success continued in the 1920s and 1930s, Mellon Institute's Herbert Meller sometimes complained of lack of interest and support among public health and engineering communities nationwide.[39] It is difficult to explain early claims to success in light of subsequent portrayals of Pittsburgh in these years as the foil against which the accomplishments of the Renaissance of the 1940s and 1950s were measured. The 1920s and the 1930s saw shifts away from on-site steam production and toward generation of electricity for power by central plants outside the city. These factors tended to reduce soot-fall within the city itself, since soot-fall was an aspect of air pollution likely to have its greatest effects near its source. A survey of the twenty-five largest U.S. cities concluded that Pittsburgh was less smoky than Cincinnati or St. Louis.[40] Pittsburgh's reputation as *the* smoky city was beginning to seem undeserved. Despite claims of environmental improvement through these years, writers and artists took Pittsburgh's smoky character as unique and artistically meaningful, both in their direct portrayals of it and in their musings about what both smoke and nature meant to the city.[41]

By the Great Depression smoke was once again linked with prosperity and with the city's precarious economic survival, identified by most Pittsburghers with the future of (now re-unionizing) heavy industries. Although Mellon Institute employed WPA workers between 1937 and 1940 to distribute "Smog and You" questionnaires to Pittsburghers and to carefully tabulate results, in 1939 Pittsburgh's Bureau of Smoke Regulation was closed.[42] In 1937 the new home of the Mellon Institute, the existing Temple of Science at Fifth and Dithridge, was dedicated. The interior of the new building well expressed the orientation of the family that would become the leaders in Pittsburgh's Renaissance. In the midst of hard times, the Mellons turned away from Pittsburgh's iron, steel, and smoke identity and toward the materials of which the nation's future would be built. The new

Mellon Institute's interior was lavishly decorated in Alcoa aluminum.[43] The Mellons, like larger and larger segments of Pittsburgh's elite since the 1880s, sought to raise their city out of a position of frontier and industrial exceptionalism and to the level of universal civic standards. This was, in a sense, a move beyond the instrumental and extractive values on which the city was founded.

Smoke Control and the Future of Pittsburgh

In the late 1930s, partially as a result of the renewed efforts at the Mellon Institute to re-awaken interest in smoke abatement, a new antismoke coalition formed in the city.[44] Yet, with World War II, Pittsburgh's economy was again thoroughly absorbed in heavy industrial production. During the war years, the Pittsburgh region alone produced more steel than Japan and Germany combined. Nonetheless, as elite leaders like the Mellons looked toward the city's return to its previous economic trajectory, they worried, as had the Chamber of Commerce at the turn of the century, about population loss, inadequate housing, and the difficulties of attracting and keeping corporate and commercial executives. They saw Pittsburgh's future not in its distinctive heavy industry but in economic, industrial, and commercial ventures as diversified as their own investments.[45] Pittsburgh's economic future, in their eyes, was linked to national and global ventures rather than to its coal, its rivers, its steel, or its industrial workforce—the factors for which it had been instrumentally valued since its frontier beginnings. These concerns sustained the smoke control efforts begun in the late 1930s and early 1940s which would culminate in the piecemeal implementation of the 1941 air pollution control ordinance, regarded as the cornerstone of Pittsburgh's Renaissance. Despite laudable attention to their city's intrinsic worth, elite transfer of instrumental valuation and capitalist investment to other products and other locales would spell eventual ruin for those most closely bound to Pittsburgh's distinctive industries—those who had been most willing to link their livelihoods with environmental sacrifice.[46] Smoke was regarded as a problem in Pittsburgh by diverse and shifting constituencies and for a variety of sometimes conflicting reasons. Yet it also bore other meanings as well. Individual complainants since the 1780s saw smoke as uncomfortable, unhealthy, and, perhaps, embarrassing. Still, between 1800 and the 1860s it was also an advertisement of the city's industrial potential, representing a worthwhile sacrifice to sustain Pittsburgh's continued economic development. In the early and mid-nineteenth century smoke embodied virtues of frugality and industry. Complaints about smoke were seen to threaten sustenance and express a vicious love of luxury. Yet, from the mid-nineteenth century on, smoke drove elites to move to the East End and later to abandon Pittsburgh for New York City. The technological and cultural changes of the 1870s and 1880s remade Pittsburgh's civic value system. The natural gas period broke the connection between smoke and industry as skilled metalworkers and their employers recognized dirty bituminous coal as an impediment to optimum metal production. Workers went further in insisting that coal smoke denied them their republican right to a competence. As the role of dirt in the city environment assumed increasing importance in public health efforts of the late nineteenth century, smoke could be targeted as a paradigmatic cause of disease. In addition, as Pittsburgh culture lost its provincialism, Pittsburghers began to feel as though they had been duped into accepting pollution that would not have been tolerated in other cities. They complained about the domination of the local economy by heavy industry, in which Pittsburghers had previously taken such pride. Rather than representing virtuous industry and frugality, Pittsburgh smoke, by the end of the nineteenth century, was a threat to domestic comfort, luxury goods, and real estate interests, which were seen as legitimate economic concerns.

Throughout the first half of the twentieth century abatement supporters struggled to maintain smoke's status as a problem worthy of the effort to find a solution. From the 1890s onward smoke also functioned as an acceptable outlet for elite reform energies. Smoke was a more tractable problem than the inadequate earnings, long hours, or lack of unionization for which Pittsburgh had been nationally criticized. Yet a many-pronged attack on smoke was difficult to sustain beyond the first decade of the twentieth century. Dominance of bacteriological models of disease made it increasingly difficult to fight smoke as an urgent threat to public health. Arguments from economic diversification as a means of civic survival were not consistently compelling, especially in light of claimed reductions in visible smoke. Nonetheless, fighting smoke became a way for elite Pittsburghers like the Mellons to abandon, in one sense, the instrumental and extractive approach to Pittsburgh for which generations of local elites had been criticized. It allowed them, however, to do so without abandoning the basic instrumentalist logic of capitalism: to improve Pittsburgh's environment and certain aspects of its economic future, while simultaneously turning away from Pittsburgh's oldest industries toward wider global investments. Smoke—for the Chamber of Commerce and for the Mellons— was not only a problem but an opportunity. It offered the chance to redeem their city's reputation, tarnished by many urban shortcomings, without abandoning the essential economic values that had created smoke and other urban problems in the first place.[47]

&

I have argued that moving beyond the narrative of problem and solution offers a better historical understanding of ways in which the environmental history and the social and cultural histories of particular places reciprocally shape one another. As we have seen in the discussion above, pollution and attitudes toward it both shaped and were shaped by Pittsburgh's cultural and social history. Social and cultural history formed environmental attitudes, and as a consequence, environmental conditions. Smoke was tolerated on the frontier more easily than elsewhere and the values of the city's Scotch-Irish founders deemphasized the worth of what smoke destroyed. As the dominance of working-class culture declined, local manufacturers, managers, and professionals became less provincial in their outlook and more willing to apply universal civic standards to Pittsburgh. Interests in economic diversification contributed to the eventual rejection of smoke. Conversely, environment influenced Pittsburgh's social and cultural history. Smoke extended the dominance of frontier values, keeping Pittsburgh rough, masculine, and primitive even after the days of Indian danger and keelboatmen had passed. Smoke helped Pittsburgh to maintain its status as a city of spectacle, notable in travelers' accounts after the spectacular qualities of the Belle Riviere had been obscured by it. Smoke's limitations on the enjoyment of civic culture worked with local ethnic and religious strictures to keep the city valued for profit potential rather than quality of life. It helped to shape locations of rich and poor neighborhoods, and to structure suburbanization. The absence of smoke in the natural gas period helped to create the city's central business district. The Chamber of Commerce worried, from the 1890s on, about smoke's influence on Pittsburgh's economy, inclining it strongly to heavy industry and limiting possibilities in light industry and trade.

Concern over smoke's limitation of local business opportunities persisted for the Mellons. Why this was a decisive motive remains an open question. Did the holding of diverse investments drive smoke cleanup or did desire to clean up smoke, to any extent, drive investment decisions? If more money was to be made in using other places instrumentally and extractively than in concerning themselves with Pittsburgh's future, should not the Mellons have simply "abandon[ed] it," as Frank Lloyd Wright suggested, and as Pittsburgh industrialists had been accused of doing for decades? Perhaps this is the juncture at which the power of cultural history should be acknowledged. The Mellons and other old Pittsburgh families wanted to rise above the sorts of accusations that had dogged local elites, and their own ancestors, for decades. It was neither material conditions alone nor national trends in economics or technology that gave the impetus to Pittsburgh's Renaissance—that allowed smoke to be seen as a problem by those with the power to solve it. It was, to a large degree, the history and ethos of this particular city.

Revisiting Donora, Pennsylvania's
1948 Air Pollution Disaster

LYNNE PAGE SNYDER

AN AIR POLLUTION disaster in southwestern Pennsylvania forged the link between air pollution and serious damage to health in the public's imagination, as well as among the residents of the Monongahela River Valley steel and smelter towns of Donora and Webster, where the disaster unfolded over the course of five days in late October 1948. During that time, a temperature inversion trapped cooled coal smoke and industrial effluent within the horseshoe bend of the river that enclosed the towns and the surrounding farmland, literally smothering the region's fourteen thousand inhabitants beneath a thick blanket of sulfur oxides, carbon monoxide, and heavy metal particulate. The disaster, or smog, as it came to be known, evoking the photochemical soup over the Los Angeles basin, has often been cited as a precursor and inspiration for federal air pollution legislation in the 1960s and 1970s and for the establishment of the U.S. Environmental Protection Agency in 1970. It is also cited as one of the landmark events that mobilized public sentiment in favor of federal regulation rather than continued state and local jurisdiction over polluters.[1]

This chapter considers Donora's place in the environmental history of western Pennsylvania as well as the history of environmental protection in the United States, as seen through the eyes of federal public health officials. While Donora's air pollution episode made an explicit connection between air pollution and health, it is also memorable for what it did not inspire, namely, meaningful engineering, legislative, or public health reforms to protect local residents from further harm related to environmental pollution. The events and actions that followed after the smog illustrate some of the key dynamics shaping the relationships between industry and the environment in the Pittsburgh region; that is, the importance of public-private partnerships in improving environmental quality, the weak role of the federal government in the environmental public health arena, and the key part played by grassroots organizations in framing the issues.

Timing played an important part in the creation of the Donora smog as a symbol in environmental and in public health affairs.[2] The smog occurred during a period of tremendous growth, both for the nation's economy and in the federal government's roster of domestic responsibilities. The smog also occurred during a transition in environmental affairs in the United States from early twentieth-century conservationism to the new social movement of environmentalism that would emerge in the 1960s.[3] A boom in the national economy after 1945 provided the material and rhetorical underpinnings of a smog explanation. Growth was the key word: in industrial development, in urban density, in population, and in a diffuse anxiety about growth itself. The Donora smog episode presented an opportunity to critique the cold war's pattern of economic growth and to condemn "technology out of control," the military-industrial complex and atomic weapons.[4] Locally, however, the issue did not slow or reverse economic growth but ensured that the Donora district would share in this national abundance. Local officials and civic leaders wanted modernization of Donora's mills and changes that would remove an immediate threat to health without jeopardizing an economic future.

In addition, public health itself was changing, and rapidly. As mortality rates from infectious and communicable disease declined, the focus of federal efforts was shifting from the more population-based approaches of earlier decades toward what health economists have termed a "supply-side" policy, to craft a national infrastructure of hospitals, biomedical laboratories, and trained professionals, all to meet an anticipated demand for health services. Despite the defeat of proposals for national health insurance in the 1930s and 1940s, the spread of third-party, workplace-based insurance promised to fuel this demand with private dollars.[5]

Many in the public health community believed that chronic disease was the central issue to address through these new federal programs and resources.[6] To them, the Donora smog was less meaningful as an immediate, catastrophic, industrial threat to public health and more significant as an "acute" outbreak of "chronic" ailments, disability, and premature deaths linked to lower level, long-term exposures to the vector of environmental pollution. The Donora smog accelerated public health officials' interest in using science to demonstrate the connections between air pollution and damage to human health. A generation of biomedical researchers began their careers inspired by Donora's disaster, building on previous knowledge about air pollution's damage to crops, livestock, and property, particularly from sulfur oxides and aerosolized particulates. Entrepreneurs among the U.S. Public Health Service (USPHS) engineering leadership tried to parlay their programs in water pollution control, industrial hygiene, and general sanitation, operated in collaboration with state health departments, into a part of this new national infrastructure.[7] Their efforts met with mixed success in the face of the health service's politically conservative, medically oriented bureaucracy during the 1950s. As a result, federal officials responding to Donora found themselves at a crossroads, attempting to pursue innovative fieldwork while accommodating local pressures that pitted jobs against health.

State health departments, especially California's, contested the transformation of Donora into an "acute" phase of a chronic disease rather than into a call for federal leadership and economic policies to prevent the threat of air pollution from industrial processes or products.[8] They challenged the federal government's "supply-side" approach to public health and, in particular, the Federal Air Pollution Control Act of 1955, predecessor of the 1963 Clean Air Act, which committed the Public Health Service to funding the production of scientific knowledge rather than regulatory programs, public works, or tax incentives for private sector pollution controls.[9] Municipal public health officials pressed the federal government to investigate their "little Donoras" and learn from regional and local experiences with air pollution. But postwar federal health policies, combined with the Public Health Service's lack of institutional clout and political timidity in the face of resistance from industrial polluters, meant little satisfaction for health departments and their local, urban political constituencies.[10] Donora's legacy as a "wake-up call" for research was fashioned from the scarred lungs and shortened lives of the residents of Donora and Webster.

The name "Donora" became a public relations appeal for the U.S. Congress to appropriate more funds for environmental public health, as well as a symbol of generalized public concern about the environment. To public health officials, it has been a reminder about paths not taken and battles lost in the forging of federal policies. As a result, many then and since have dismissed the smog's significance. In 1957, for example, USPHS air pollution program leader Dr. Harry Heimann received an invitation to speak on the upcoming tenth anniversary of the Donora smog.[11] Heimann had been the lead medical investigator during the 1949 Donora survey. At the time of the request, the USPHS was supporting one of its first research projects under the federal 1955 act, a multiple year contract with the University of Pittsburgh to evaluate the smog's longer-term impacts. Heimann refused the opportunity to deliver an address about Donora's smog, replying that he saw no reason to memorialize the event. The article that follows is an effort to challenge this dismissal, by adding a more accurate and nuanced story to the public record about Donora and its infamous air pollution.

"The Death-Dealing Smog over Donora, Pennsylvania": Industrial Air Pollution, Public Health Policy, and the Politics of Expertise, 1948–1949

A few days before Halloween, 1948, a heavy fog blanketed the Northeast and Midwest. Severe atmospheric conditions cloaked airports, slowed traffic to a crawl, dispatched people with respiratory ailments to the hospital for oxygen, and coated surfaces with a sticky film of muck. Pittsburgh survived the episode without daytime streetlights, a credit to a newly enforced smoke control ordinance and to the city's decreasing reliance upon soft coal fuel.[12] But thirty miles southeast of Pittsburgh, along the Monongahela River, the situation worsened critically for the steel town of Donora and its downwind neighbor, the city of Webster. On Saturday, October 30, seventeen people died in the space of twelve hours and thousands more were left gasping for breath. A day later, the suffocating conditions lifted as quickly and as mysteriously as they had descended.

In the years since 1948 the name "Donora" has become a legend in twentieth-century environmental history.[13] Internationally, it has symbolized the excesses of postwar economic growth visible in southern California's eye-stinging haze, from which the name for the disaster, the Donora smog, was coined. In the 1950s this interpretation spurred urban campaigns for smoke control ordinances. Among scientists, engineers, and physicians, the smog episode catalyzed a decade of work to understand the freshly perceived threat of air pollution to public health. In Washington, D.C., Congress and U.S. Public Health Service officials crafted new environmental policy in the form of provisions for research support, training, and technical assistance in the 1955 Clean Air Act.

But interpretations of the meanings of the smog have been based on descriptive accounts of the era. They do not analyze the historical influence of manufacturers upon public discussion about air pollution. In the case of the 1948 disaster, controversy over the role of a zinc smelter framed explanations about how air pollution threatened public health. As witnesses to three decades of environmental deterioration, many local residents blamed Donora's mill for the mass deaths and illnesses. Others fearful of losing their industrial jobs downplayed the linkage between smelter effluent and the smog. Zinc Works managers, lawyers, and the experts they retained emphasized the role of inclement weather and the region's hilly terrain in precipitating the disaster. A USPHS survey of the smog became an opportunity to mediate among a number of competing explanations.

Smog investigations, particularly the USPHS survey, expressed and reinforced beliefs about the economic dependency of Donora-area residents upon the Zinc Works. This was achieved in part by blaming weather and topography for concentrating pollution to a deadly level, rather than the Zinc Works for causing or disproportionately contributing to the smog. The choice of an epidemiological study laid a foundation for the development of new policy and bolstered arguments for urban smoke control ordinances. At the same time, an emphasis upon health-effects research helped protect the Zinc Works against liability for the disaster and supported continued operation of the mill at further risk to the community. In the context of regional history, a smog explanation that stressed weather and topography helped protect against the threat of litigation or a municipal ordinance with regulations so expensive that closure of the Zinc Works was its owners' preferred alternative.

"Worse than anything a steel mill belched forth": The Zinc Works at Donora

The zinc smelter at Donora sat on forty acres of land adjacent to the Monongahela River, in the basin of a valley created by four-hundred-foot cliffs and immediately upwind of the city of Webster. Controversy focused on whether the smog disaster was part of regional environmental deterioration attributed to the Zinc Works.

Atmospheric effluent derived from a series of five interrelated cycles of production at the Zinc Works. They included the roasting or oxidation of zinc-bearing ores to release sulfurous fumes, the agglomeration of the roasted ores with fuel, the smelting or reduction of the ore-fuel mixture into molten zinc, the reaction of roasting fumes with nitrogen oxides to form liquid sulfuric acid, and the reprocessing of gaseous and particulate wastes and heat trapped during production. Like other metallurgical plants in southwestern Pennsylvania, the Zinc Works relied upon gas and soft coal fuels. Combustion released sulfurous fumes, carbon monoxide, and carbon dioxide. Technologies unique to the Zinc Works poured a variety of heavy metal dusts and large amounts of carbon monoxide gas into the valley atmosphere.[14]

The Zinc Works' relationship to the environment reflected the economies of its World War I origins and the historical imprint of U.S. Steel upon the Pittsburgh-area landscape. During 1915 the American Steel & Wire Company, a U.S. Steel subsidiary, built the smelter to take advantage of wartime shortages. Zinc was an uncharacteristic investment for the corporation, given the traditions of product oversupply, narrow profit margins, and resistance to business consolidation in the smeltering industry. But the high price for metal compelled action. Pittsburgh was the center of domestic zinc consumption, and U.S. Steel subsidiaries were the largest single group of consumers. Company infrastructure offered access to fuel and raw materials, as well as proximity to rail and river transport. When U.S. Steel opened a by-product coking works in the neighboring town of Clairton in 1918, the Zinc Works gained a customer for the sulfuric acid generated as a by-product of smelting.

The valley location in Donora proved ill suited for dispersing the smelter's atmospheric effluent. In 1918 the American Steel & Wire Company paid off the first legal judgment against it for air pollution damage to health.[15] Beginning in the early 1920s, Webster landowners, tenants, and farmers sued for damages attributed to smelter effluent—the loss of crops, fruit orchards, livestock, and topsoil, and the destruction of fences and houses. At the height of the Great Depression, dozens of Webster families joined together in legal action against the Zinc Works, claiming air pollution damage to their health.

American Steel & Wire countered with protracted legal battles to discredit the claims. In addition, Zinc Works managers developed strategies to mitigate the smelter's environmental impacts. The company distributed limestone to area farmers for the purpose of neutralizing soil made infertile by acidity and attempted to adapt smelting furnaces to less smoky operation.[16] A weather station was established in 1926. Together with visual observations, weather forecasts may have served as the basis for regulating the level of smelter production, as was done at other smelters in agricultural areas. During the early 1920s the Zinc Works chemists began to measure levels of heavy metals and sulfurous fumes in local air. But regular sampling was discontinued in 1935 after it was observed that there was little correlation between measurements and the level of industrial activity.[17]

The design of the Zinc Works reflected past legal disputes over smelter smoke, as well as constraints, such as the valley location, dictated by the economics of affiliation with U.S. Steel. Large doses of dust-laden gases from the smelter furnaces were considered beyond remedy. But ore roaster effluent was filtered and reprocessed. Heavy metal dusts were collected using electrostatic devices originally designed for use in Montana copper smelters. Roaster fumes were converted into sulfuric acid by means of a process developed to end litigation against smelters in California and Tennessee. The process added a new type of air pollutant—nitrogen oxides—but realized profits from the industrial chemicals market. Another strategy developed at western smelters was the construction of chimneys up to 600 feet high to aid in the dispersion of effluent. Although Donora's Zinc Works was surrounded by ridges averaging 400 feet, mill stacks extended at most 150 feet.[18]

For decades before the 1948 smog, the local Zinc Works was, in the eyes of the public and often in the eyes of the law, a threat to public health with links to environmental deterioration. Local atmospheric conditions provided a colorful subject for author Thomas Bell, a former Zinc Works employee, who described the area in his novel about immigrant life near Pittsburgh:

Freshly charged, the zinc smelting furnaces, crawling with thousands of small flames, yellow, blue, green, filled the valley with smoke. Acrid and poisonous, worse than anything a steel mill belched forth, it penetrated everywhere, making automobile headlights necessary in Webster's streets, setting the river-boat pilots to cursing God, and destroying every living thing on the hills."[19]

"Mysterious, death-dealing smog": The Disaster

On Tuesday, October 26, 1948, the usual morning pall over Donora and Webster lingered after 10:00 A.M. It became more distinctive on Wednesday and did not burn off at all on Thursday. At noon on Friday, October 29, Zinc Works superintendent M. M. Neale checked the pattern of effluent diffusion from the mill's stacks and reported nothing out of the ordinary.[20]

By Friday evening, local residents were crowding into nearby hospitals and dozens of calls were made to the area's eight physicians. While fire department volunteers administered oxygen to those unable to breathe, Board of Health member Dr. William Rongaus led an ambulance by foot through darkened streets to ferry the dead and dying to hospitals or on to

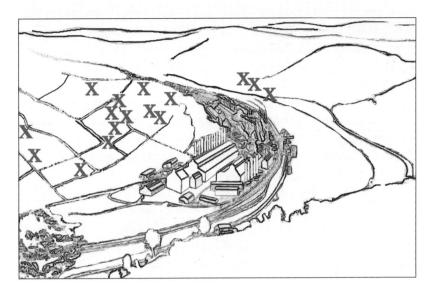

FIG. 4. Location of deaths in the Donora smog incident

a temporary morgue. On Rongaus's advice, those with chronic heart or respiratory ailments began to leave town late Friday evening, but before noon on Saturday, eleven people had died. Conditions had not improved by Saturday night, and with roads congested by smog and traffic, evacuation became impossible.[21]

As awareness of the disaster grew, the smog itself began to dissipate. Gossip columnist Walter Winchell broadcast news of Donora nationally on his radio show, bringing the horrifying scene to the nation as well as to local residents. After midnight, U.S. Steel's general counsel, Roger M. Blough, called Neale to order the smelter furnaces shut down at 6:00 A.M. Sunday morning. Before dawn, chemists under contract to the steel corporation arrived at the mill. Two industrial hygienists from the Pennsylvania Department of Health joined them to measure the atmospheric concentrations of sulfur compounds associated with smelters and with the combustion of soft coal fuel. By midday Sunday, rain had dispersed the smog, and a series of emergency meetings began in Donora. At the first one, the Board of Health reported nearly six hundred persons ill and twenty dead from asphyxiation in a population of approximately fourteen thousand.[22]

Accusations were fired squarely at the Zinc Works for what newspapers were calling an airborne poison or plague. Plant workers testified about the excessive use of reprocessed, smoky materials in smelter furnaces. Dr. Rongaus denounced air pollution from the Zinc Works as "just plain murder," noting that severe air pollution in neighboring towns had not caused a similar tragedy. The *Monessen Daily Independent,* a newspaper that served the city of Webster, drew parallels between decades of landscape deterioration and the smog. In a series of editorials, the editor of the *Independent* called for the mill to be renovated or removed to a desert area where its effluent would no longer threaten district residents. When Zinc Works managers insisted that the plant had operated without incident since 1915, Board of Health president Charles Stacey replied that three decades without modernization made the Zinc Works long overdue to go out of business.[23]

Others, including the chief chemist from Pittsburgh's smoke control bureau, argued that the smog was caused by the accumulation of effluent from many sources—domestic and commercial furnaces, locomotive engines, and industrial processes such as those at the Zinc Works. To them, the smog indicated the need for a local smoke control ordinance. For Pittsburgh and other industrial cities dependent upon soft coal fuel, ordinances were an integral part of economic revitalization efforts after World War II.[24]

The historical power of American Steel & Wire over the regional economy frustrated attempts to formulate a plan of action. Six of Donora's seven borough councilmen were United Steelworkers (USW) leaders. They feared that attempts to regulate the mill would result in the loss of industrial jobs. Pittsburgh's experiences showed that air pollution control and preservation of jobs were not contradictory goals. But passage of an effective ordinance would require the support of local industry, which in turn would depend upon proof that a serious problem existed. Donora's leaders expressed skepticism that the state health department would produce much more than a "whitewash" of the smog episode. The borough council voted to disregard state authority over public health and called for an investigation by the U.S. Public Health Service.[25] In a supporting letter to Pennsylvania's governor, a USW official explained "that protocol should not be permitted to stand in the way of protecting our workmen, their jobs, and the welfare of the community."[26]

At first, the U.S. Public Health Service rejected the request for an investigation. A top official characterized Donora's smog as a one-time "atmospheric freak" caused by the utter breakdown of atmospheric dilution out of the narrow valley. On Thursday a USPHS engineer toured the area with state officials and met with the borough council. At a press conference that afternoon, he announced his approval of state plans to manage the situation through a permanent series of air sampling stations and a warning system to curtail industry if concentrations of "indicator" pollutants exceeded recognized limits for health. With air quality samples available only after the Zinc Works had been closed, no evidence linked the mill to the smog. The federal engineer explained the smog in Donora as a matter of industrial air pollution, yet recommended that the Zinc Works reopen on the following Monday. To his supervisor, he noted that continued idling of the Zinc Works "would not necessarily prevent a repetition of the illnesses of the preceding weekend and might induce a false feeling of security."[27]

Dissatisfied with state and federal responses, Donora's borough council and the United Steelworkers created their own investigation. On Friday, USW founder Phil Murray mailed district leaders an offer of $10,000 for an "independent and unbiased" study of the disaster. The following evening the borough council voted to accept the USW grant and listened to a presentation from Dr. Clarence Mills, a medical school professor from Cincinnati. Mills argued that a health effects survey would establish a stronger basis for an ordinance, or damage claims against the Zinc Works, than attempts to sample air quality. The council adopted Mills's plans, using part of the grant to hire six housewives as canvassers and the borough assessor as coordinator to administer a questionnaire of Mills's design.[28]

Convincing the U.S. Public Health Service to Investigate the Smog

On November 9, the Zinc Works resumed limited production. The state's promise to monitor air quality was the only guarantee offered against recurrence. Their approach to air sampling revealed the widely shared belief that the Zinc Works was in some measure responsible for the smog. Monitoring sites formed a series of concentric circles about the Zinc Works. Readings were annotated with information about the number of active Zinc Works processes. Calculation of pollutant concentrations allowed comparison of outdoor conditions with levels in the confined spaces of factories and tunnels, for which provisional safety limits had been established. Donora resembled Los Angeles in that each lay in the bottom of "bowl-shaped" terrain subject to weather in which slow winds and stagnant air trapped hot effluent close to the ground. Given the uneven dispersion of pollutants, the levels recorded in measurements reflected the sampler's choice of location and timing. To translate samples of dust mass or fume volume into standard measures of concentration, state technicians collected information about wind speed and direction, humidity, temperature, and barometric pressure. Monitoring was an inexact science at best, one that state officials proposed as a prototype activity for a new Division of Industrial Air Pollution.[29]

The state's focus upon industrial sources was of the utmost concern to the Industrial Hygiene Foundation, a consortium of manufacturers who sponsored research through Pittsburgh's Mellon Institute. The foundation was organized in 1935 in response to public and congressional concern about the high incidence of silicosis and other work-related respiratory diseases. By sponsoring research, sometimes in collaboration with federal agencies, corporations cultivated expertise, legislation, and popular support for their policies. To foundation members the Donora smog demonstrated how quickly legal responsibility for workplaces might extend to include products "thrown out" into the atmosphere.[30]

Through the foundation, American Steel & Wire mobilized expertise to manage the Donora episode. A contract was arranged with an MIT meteorologist to analyze the role of weather in the smog's formation and destructiveness. Foundation engineer Wesley C. L. Hemeon spent the first week of November in a search for clues that included collecting filter sediment from home electronic air cleaners and air from tire inner tubes.[31] On the day that the Zinc Works resumed operations, Herneon proposed to American Steel & Wire managers that they request a health effects survey from the Public Health Service. Little evidence related the smelter directly to the smog. The documentation of health effects would be both time-consuming and costly. A federal survey would clarify the circumstances surrounding the disaster, while lending public credibility to the company's position that the Zinc Works had not caused the smog. In addition, Hemeon recommended that American Steel & Wire arrange for an industrial hygiene program and plans to control mill air pollution to "insure that the plant's operators would never again be suspected of responsibility for any illnesses that might occur in the future in the town of Donora."[32]

A week later, the company formally denied responsibility for the smog, blaming "an unprecedentedly heavy fog which blanketed the borough for five consecutive days."[33] At the same time, American Steel & Wire announced plans to investigate the smog and to prepare a courtroom defense. The contract went to a team at Cincinnati's Kettering Laboratory of Applied Physiology under the direction of Dr. Robert Kehoe. Kehoe and the Kettering lab provided the steel company with informal professional alliances with the USPHS and an experimental approach supportive of the claim that weather and terrain had caused the episode. Kehoe was a pioneering industrial physician who had built his reputation through consulting work for the alkylated lead additives industry.[34] He contributed a causal theory about the physiological impact of pollutants that would prove useful for establishing or dismissing legal claims of responsibility. According to Kehoe, pollutants were ubiquitous in the environment, growing more so during the previous half-century of industrialization; only sustained, highly concentrated exposures could cause permanent damage to the internal balance of materials which human bodies maintained.

Although each conducted their own smog study, the Commonwealth of Pennsylvania, Donora's then borough council, the United Steelworkers, and finally the American Steel & Wire Company called upon the USPHS for an investigation. At the foundation's annual meeting in mid-November, the Public Health Service announced a reversal of earlier policy. Its Division of Industrial Hygiene would use Donora and Webster for the first comprehensive survey of the health effects of air pollution. After this announcement, one USPHS official added that in recent history there was "no condition more terrifying" than the one engendered by the smog.[35] For the USPHS the Donora survey was a chance to develop a new program, adapting the methods of industrial hygiene to address the threat of air pollution believed to be imminent in postwar industrialization, urbanization, and population growth.

"All you need is a pair of reasonably good eyes":
The Social Shaping of Expertise About Smog

The experimental nature of the USPHS field survey was an uneasy accommodation of the contradictory agendas of regional, state, industrial, and federal interests. Attempts to deemphasize the contribution of the Zinc Works elicited the resistance of Webster residents, demonstrating powerfully how beliefs in local economic dependency influenced the development of smog explanations.

When the U.S. Surgeon General called Donora a giant "scientific test tube" for studying air pollution, borough council President John Duda responded by urging full cooperation with government researchers as the only way to restore the town's reputation.[36] Duda may have been referring to Dr. Mills's health effects survey for the borough. The results, released in late December, counted not hundreds but thousands made ill by the smog and revealed a marked underreporting of illness by the families of Zinc Works employees.[37]

Federal researchers sidestepped the issue of Zinc Works responsibility. The Division of Industrial Hygiene's approach reflected the political conservatism and limited jurisdiction of the USPHS. The federal government interpreted its role as support of state and local health departments rather than direct control over matters of public health and welfare. In addition, the division relied upon the permission of employers for access to workplaces, the sites and subjects of their research inquiries.[38]

Before the Donora smog, the Bureau of Mines in the Department of the Interior had been the primary agency for air pollution studies, which had focused on sources and their reduction through more efficient use of resources. In late 1948, Bureau of Mines Chief Louis McCabe was lead administrator for the first air pollution program in Los Angeles County. Until halted by the USPHS survey, the bureau's Pittsburgh office had been involved in a smog study of its own, one concerned with the role of Donora's Zinc Works. The USPHS survey took advantage of bureau resources, borrowing staff and technical support, but rejected collaboration with the Bureau of Mines.[39]

In the USPHS study, air quality sampling and weather modeling became the environmental counterparts to the search for health effects. These techniques replaced visual observations of effluent diffusion and local accounts that ascribed historical environmental change to the Zinc Works. Unlike Bureau of Mines investigations, air quality sampling was conducted not to check the efficiency of furnaces but to compare pollutant levels with safety limits established for workplaces. The USPHS choice of sampling locations reflected its interest in how a variety of sources affected air quality. In contrast to the state's air sampling points, which ringed the Zinc Works, federal researchers collected samples around residential, commercial, and industrial areas both under and above the valley's walls.[40]

The USPHS approach to epidemiology further deemphasized local concern about the Zinc Works. In early December 1948, USPHS physicians and nurses duplicated the borough's door-to-door survey. Press releases emphasized the confidentiality of the survey's random sampling method to discourage what one official reported to be a common experience for interviewers: "Many of the residents, fearful of the wrath of the plant in which they worked—which, of course, everyone was blaming informally at that point—actually minimized the illnesses they had suffered during the smog. Others, who were more angry than afraid, made the most of their illnesses and probably exaggerated." In addition, sanitary engineers assessed housing stock and water quality, veterinarians interviewed pet owners and dairy farmers, and negotiations began for the exhuming of the bodies of smog victims for autopsy.[41]

Federal adoption of air sampling, weather modeling, and epidemiology, rather than a focus upon the Zinc Works, roused downwind residents to action. Frustrated by what *Monessen Daily Independent* editorials called "the boondoggling spirit in which the whole business is being undertaken," residents from Webster and area farms began meeting in sessions organized by local restaurateur Abe Celapino. The group called itself the Webster Society for Better Living and adopted the credo "Clean Air and

Green Grass!" Critical of American Steel & Wire's influence over Donora's government, society officials mobilized to press for a local smoke control ordinance. They drew support from the work of Dr. Mills, whose analysis of the borough's health effects survey had estranged him from further public investigations. In early February 1949, Mills issued a round of press releases that named the Zinc Works as the source of a lethal agent layered over the valley during the smog. He observed that Donora was quickly becoming a ghost town as a result of fear about a smog recurrence.[42]

Like borough council president Duda, Webster Society president Abe Celapino urged residents to become involved with federal epidemiology, but in the hopes of honing, rather than dulling, a focus upon the Zinc Works. Society members queried farmers about past litigation, wrote the State Department of Agriculture about replanting Webster's sandy hillsides, and organized an outing for free chest x-rays. After the society learned of plans to temporarily resume full production at the Zinc Works to demonstrate the mill incapable of causing smog, members petitioned the USPHS to make reenactment public and add a "test smog" to their investigation.[43]

American Steel & Wire agreed to a two-week "test smog" period late in April 1949, transforming the Webster Society's request into a hotly contested, new notion of Donora's environment as a laboratory for explaining smog.[44] The Commonwealth of Pennsylvania, the USPHS, Dr. Mills, and the Kettering Laboratory observed the simulated return to presmog operating conditions. Public Health Service engineers sampled air quality during the test period to compare estimated pollutant concentrations with those computed for the period of curtailed production. If the Zinc Works had been responsible for the disaster, hazardous concentrations would be expected and would aid in the diagnosis of health effects. Yet borough, state, and federal authorities argued that without a replay of extreme weather conditions, the test period presented no threat to public health.

Webster Society leaders found the test smog to be too successful. After the first day, the society called upon parents to keep their children indoors and began cataloguing dozens of health complaints. A state legislator mourned the fact that a smoke control bill pending in the state assembly had not passed "in time for a committee to be on hand to witness the Donora tests." But the USPHS declined comment on the significance of the test and denied receiving notice of health complaints. Based upon their visual observations of effluent and reports from workers, Dr. Mills and society leaders doubted that American Steel & Wire had truly restored the operations of the preceding fall. Damage from the Zinc Works, according to the *Monessen Daily Independent,* was "something no scientific investigation is necessary to prove. All you need is a pair of reasonably good eyes."[45]

Convincing American Steel & Wire to Take Action

The test smog demonstrated both the strength of public belief in Zinc Works responsibility and the validity of American Steel & Wire Company's belief that available methods would not implicate the Zinc Works. In the wake of corporate apprehension about liability, Dr. Robert Kehoe advocated research services as a cost-effective investment not only toward a courtroom defense, but also toward the expense of regulation, municipal or otherwise, believed to be imminent.[46]

Before the Donora smog, neither manufacturers nor public health professionals considered air pollution an urgent issue.[47] At the annual meeting of the Smoke Prevention Association in May 1949, a leading industrial physician and consultant to insurance companies dismissed air pollution as a threat, except "on rare occasions [when] Mother Nature has played us false."[48] That same day, Dr. Kehoe suggested to American Steel & Wire a program of voluntary research such as that which had allowed the lead additives industry to continue potentially hazardous operations. Beyond its usefulness in preempting regulations he considered ill advised, Kehoe explained that research addressed: "The crux of the problem is the cost of control. Control is possible in most cases now, but the cost is exorbitant—not from the standpoint of employee or public protection, where the control unit safeguards health, but from the standpoint of what the unit does in a mechanical sense."[49]

Kehoe's approach was laid out in his laboratory's contractual work at Donora. Kettering researchers, like the USPHS, used air quality sampling to complement a health effects survey. Mill workers, rather than community residents, served as research subjects in accordance with Kehoe's theory that permanent damage from industrial poisons would first be seen in the more highly concentrated exposures of the workplace. In air quality sampling, emphasis was placed upon the role of weather and terrain as mechanisms to concentrate pollutants to a deadly level. While the state's air sampling points ringed the Zinc Works and federal technicians varied air sampling by source, Kettering's were arrayed along the valley's contours, well beneath the ridges suspected of having trapped the effluent. The main recommendation for control matched that advocated by the state. To "nip a dangerous situation in the bud," Kettering recommended that American Steel & Wire regulate Zinc Works production according to the capacity of the local atmosphere to disperse effluent, gauged by means of a series of air quality monitoring and a weather forecasting service.[50]

Kettering's focus on health effects reflected American Steel & Wire's interest in avoiding liability rather than supporting a new municipal smoke control ordinance. Dr. Mills and the Webster Society proposed legislation similar to that in Pittsburgh, which was based on the use of research to reduce the cost of air pollution controls. Pittsburgh industrial leaders had themselves led reform efforts, winning countywide legislation in the spring of 1949. The Allegheny County ordinance mandated research, a strategy that moved the issue of air pollution beyond previous common law and statutory remedies to a matter of industrial policy. U.S. Steel and other area manufacturers moved quickly to establish research projects through the American Iron and Steel Institute.[51]

Allegheny County civic elites saw air pollution as an integral problem for economic revitalization. In contrast, Donora's economy was captive to a single employer, American Steel & Wire. While the company had expanded the wire-making part of its complex in Donora during World War II, most construction and modernization in the 1940s occurred outside of the Pittsburgh region. As well, the Zinc Works was reaching the end of its operating lifetime. In neighboring Burkettsville, Pennsylvania, the mill's technological sister plant closed in 1947. Plans to replace the Zinc Works' furnaces with less smoky, more resource-efficient processes had been prepared in September 1948, only to be laid aside as economically unfeasible weeks before the smog episode.[52]

Webster Society leaders denied that their calls for an ordinance meant support for closing the plant. But the steel company offered few alternatives. When American Steel & Wire president Clifford Hood met with Webster Society officials in late August 1949, he agreed that "acrid, white smoke" from the Zinc Works was a nuisance. If redesigned smelter furnace appliances did not help, he acknowledged, the company would be forced either to operate permanently and unprofitably on a schedule of curtailed production or to shut down entirely.[53]

The potential expense of air pollution control was an issue beyond the scope of USPHS efforts. A focus on health effects rather than sources allowed the politically cautious agency to avoid the issue of possible calls for regulating local industry. A shift from source-based to health-based standards for air quality did not diminish the prospect of enormous costs to modify production or to dismantle obsolescent mills. Would corporations like American Steel & Wire be held liable for costs as far as would be practicable to improve the efficiency of resource use? Or would manufacturers be held liable for the public health costs of air pollution, irrespective of expense, to ensure that processes did not damage health?

Reinterpreting the 1948 Smog

When the USPHS released its findings in mid-October 1949, the report's inconclusive results bore out the working assumptions of Zinc Works managers and the Industrial Hygiene Foundation. Air quality sampling, weather modeling, and the test smog did not pin responsibility for the smog upon the Zinc Works. Pollutant levels estimated from measurements taken during the test smog had not exceeded workplace safety limits. Like the borough council's initial survey, the federal report confirmed that almost half of the area's residents had described themselves as affected by the smog. The deadly outcome of the episode was attributed to a combination of fumes from a variety of sources, inclement weather, and preexisting respiratory and heart disease. The U.S. Surgeon General cited the inconclusive results of the survey as an argument for federally sponsored research into newly outlined uncertainties of meteorology, atmospheric chemistry, and the physiology of health effects.[54]

In press releases and professional journals, Dr. Mills protested the federal approach to environmental analysis. He argued that air quality measurements were too crude a basis for discussion of the question of Zinc Works responsibility. Air samples did not, for example, detect the enormous quantities of nitrogen oxides and carbon monoxide released from the Zinc Works and presumed to be trapped within the valley during the smog. Mills proposed working from a model of regional environment drawn from an early description of Pittsburgh, known as "hell with the lid clamped on." Simple multiplication of Zinc Works effluent rates by time, divided by the volume of air trapped within the valley, gave figures far above workplace limits for a number of industrial poisons. Although Mills did not account for atmospheric chemical reactions known at that time, his criticism remained valid: weather measurements recorded by the USPHS for translating sample data into concentrations were often useless, "influenced by buildings, steep hills, trees, and other obstacles," and had themselves been estimated from weather models.[55]

Both the Kettering and the USPHS teams worked from a model of the regional environment similar to the one described by Mills. One federal researcher described Donora and Webster as residing within a tunnel shaped by valley cliffs, with "blind-alley appendages cut by hilly terrain."[56] Weather and topography became indicators for concern, rather than the eroded hillsides and damaged vegetation downwind of the Zinc Works. Public Health Service lead investigator Dr. H. H. Schrenk described weather in the Donora district as "analogous to the ventilation of a plant or a vehicular tunnel" and held the unpredictable characteristics of this ventilation system responsible for the smog. At the First National Air Pollution Symposium held in November 1949 in southern California, Kehoe described Donora "not [as] an industrial accident but [as] the victim of uniquely severe and enduring weather."[57]

The USPHS report effectively relieved Zinc Works managers of responsibility for the smog. The study disappointed those who had delayed filing legal claims in the belief that federal investigators would confirm the involvement of the mills. In the fall of 1949, dozens of area residents filed damage suits against the American Steel & Wire Company for the smog and for long-term property damage. In response, American Steel & Wire asserted its initial explanation: the smog was an act of God.[58]

Although the USPHS, the state, and Kettering concurred in denying Zinc Works responsibility, each proposed a warning system that tied weather forecasting and air quality sampling to cutbacks in mill production, as well as the permanent curtailing of production. Donora Borough officials accepted the situation as a compromise to preserve the local economy.[59] If the Zinc Works' effluent had contributed to the disaster, dependence upon this warning system left Donora and Webster at continued risk of another deadly smog. Since the mid-1930s, Zinc Works chemists had made little use of atmospheric monitoring after field studies indicated that readings did not correlate with mill production levels.[60] And the MIT meteorologist's report to the steel company concluded that weather conditions like those of late October 1948 could be predicted to occur every ten to fifteen years, perhaps even twice in the same month.[61]

⌐

Within the public health community and among federal policymakers, the Donora smog catalyzed a new approach to air pollution. In terms of policy: "The air pollution episode at Donora, Pa. in 1948 stimulated the first flow of legislative proposals at the Federal level in 1949 . . . the Donora episode was fixed in the rhetoric of nearly all proponents of Federal action, and the first Federal action was clearly along the lines of determining air pollution's health effects through sponsorship of appropriate research."[62] The USPHS approach to interpreting the smog fostered the symbolic use of the disaster as a warning sign regarding postwar economic growth rather than for the threat of economic decline that faced residents of communities like Donora and Webster.

The federal survey of Donora marked a new era for federal policy. It articulated a shift from program emphasis on source-based research to a focus on health effects research as a basis for policy making.[63] This shift held the potential to improve air quality by holding manufacturers to health-based standards more stringent than earlier ones based upon improving efficiency of resource use. But local fear of job loss transformed an innovative policy into an opportunity to shift attention away from a significant contributor to regional air pollution.

For the town of Donora and the city of Webster, smog investigations expressed and reinforced beliefs about the historical power of the United States Steel Corporation over the regional economy. Despite the threat of a second disaster, the Zinc Works remained open until a dramatic fall in metal prices early in 1957.[64] Newspaper coverage of its closing recited a litany which would become familiar to Pittsburgh-area residents: imports; underpriced local products, which had become uncompetitive due to the technological obsolescence of mills; the shifting of markets; and adversarial relations between management, labor, and the federal government.[65] No mention was made of Donora's historic role in inspiring a public health approach to air pollution codified into federal law in 1955. News of the closing created sorrow over the loss of jobs and relief for those who agreed with a *Monessen Daily Independent* editorial that: "[T]he Zinc Works may have cost the valley more jobs than it ever supplied, and the cost to the Donora-Webster area in terms of general community welfare is probably incalculable. We hope the people of the Valley, particularly those in the Donora vicinity, will not receive the United States Steel announcement about the Zinc Works with hand-wringing despondency. We think there is definitely a silver lining to this cloud."[66]

Strategies for Clean Air

The Pittsburgh and Allegheny County
Smoke Control Movements, 1940–1960

SHERIE R. MERSHON

and JOEL A. TARR

BETWEEN 1940 AND 1960, the city of Pittsburgh and Allegheny County experienced a major transformation in terms of their air quality—to a large extent, heavy smoke was eliminated from the atmosphere. How this feat was accomplished after smoke control advocates had, over the years, managed only sporadic improvements is a complex story, involving issues of public policy and public-private cooperation, active protests by women's and civic groups, and major shifts in fuel type and combustion technology. This chapter will consider the smoke control movement in both the city of Pittsburgh and Allegheny County. While there were a number of similarities at these two jurisdictional levels in terms of the participating individuals and institutions, there were also substantial differences in the targets of control and strategies of regulation. As will be considered, a definitive solution to the Pittsburgh region's smoke problem, but not to its broader air pollution problem, was formed during these years.

Smoke Control in the City of Pittsburgh

The years from 1940 to 1960 are critical in Pittsburgh environmental history from several perspectives. From the perspective of urban environmental changes that improved the quality of life for local residents, however, smoke control must be accorded first rank. For it was during these two decades that major changes in fuel supply, technology, and policy freed the city of its historical smoke burden. While the story is often presented as one of a triumph of the public/private coalition that brought about the Pittsburgh Renaissance, other critical dimensions need to be explored. This essay will focus upon the decision-making processes involved in formulating and implementing local public policy in regard to smoke, as well as the effects of the policy on various groups within the city.

Pittsburgh's success in eliminating dense smoke from its atmosphere in the immediate post–World War II period was a result of two interactive factors: (1) major changes in the fuels and/or combustion technology used by a majority of Pittsburgh householders, commercial firms, railroads, and some manufacturing industries; and (2) a municipal smoke control policy that required domestic consumers, industries, and transportation companies to change their fuel type and/or combustion equipment. The policy was originally based on the expectation that domestic consumers would meet clean air standards by using smokeless coal and/or smokeless heating equipment that burned regular bituminous coal. From approximately 1945 to 1950, however, over half the households in Pittsburgh shifted their fuel from bituminous coal to natural gas (see table 1). This change also required the retrofitting or replacement of existing combustion equipment. While other cities also moved from coal to natural gas or oil as domestic fuel, no other city in the nation experienced such a rapid rate of change.

Table 1. Fuel Change in Eight Cities, 1940–1950

City	Coal %		Natural Gas %		Fuel Oil %	
	1940	1950	1940	1950	1940	1950
Chicago	85.1	62	2.21	15	10.53	18.28
Cincinnati	89	45.9	7.75	46.1	0.9	5.01
Cleveland	86.9	47.7	11.03	48.7	0.53	1.64
Columbus	84.4	50.8	12.78	46.1	0.21	1.87
Louisville	89.1	52.8	8.36	41.1	0.51	4.43
Milwaukee	89.7	67.4	0.9	11.4	6.8	18.2
Pittsburgh	81	31.6	17.45	66	0.08	0.28
St. Louis	92.7	56.6	1.87	22.6	3.29	17.19

Pre–Smoke Control Pittsburgh

The problem of smoke pollution in Pittsburgh resulted from a conjunction of urbanization, industrialization, topography, and the availability at low cost of large sources of high-volatile bituminous coal. While air pollution is not only a problem of cities, it is normally more critical under urban conditions because of population density and increased economic activity. As Lawrence Tilly has observed, the "metropolis is a dependent ecosystem . . . [and] all ecosystems require a continuous supply of energy to power their activities." In Pittsburgh, this source of energy—bituminous coal— served for domestic and commercial heating purposes, for processing raw materials and manufacturing goods, and for fueling railroad locomotives. Heavy coal usage and local topographical and climatic factors that often produced temperature inversions combined to give Pittsburgh its enduring reputation as the "smoky city."[1]

To a large extent, in spite of various regulations, the smoke control movement failed to abate the smoke nuisance appreciably during the late nineteenth and early twentieth centuries.[2] In the 1920s and 1930s, therefore, smoke and fuel researchers and regulators set about to redefine the problem. There was general agreement among them that industries and railroads had made advances in the reduction of dense smoke. These improvements had been achieved through technological and fuel improvements, care in firing methods, and cooperation with municipal inspectors. Smoke investigators now believed that the smoke problem persisted because of a failure to control domestic furnaces, since "the amount of black smoke produced by a pound of coal is greatest when fired in a domestic furnace and that domestic smoke is dirtier and far more harmful than industrial smoke."[3]

Domestic furnaces in Pittsburgh had not been regulated for several reasons, the most important of which were the political and administrative problems involved in controlling the heating habits of a multitude of householders. In 1940, there were 175,163 dwellings in the city, of which 141,788 burned coal and 30,507 consumed natural gas; 53,388 of the coal burners had no central heating plant and used stoves to heat their homes. Smoke regulators lacked an effective administrative mechanism to control domestic smoke without employing hundreds of smoke inspectors. Politically, the issue was difficult because control threatened to impose higher costs for capital equipment and fuel on householders. And because of a historical equation between smoke and prosperity in Pittsburgh and other industrial cities, it was difficult to develop a public consensus for stringent controls.[4] In short, the problem was one of devising a strategy to change individual fuel-use behavior in the name of the collective social goal of clean air.

Organizing the Smoke Control Campaign

Smoke control was not a popular subject in a city scarred by the Depression; clear skies suggested closed factories, unemployed workers, and hard times for the many local businesses that were linked to the coal industry. As a sign of its belief that smoke equaled prosperity, in 1939 the Pittsburgh City Council had eliminated the Bureau of Smoke Regulation. "You'll never get elected again," said one politician to a member of the City Council who supported antismoke legislation. "Don't you know, the poor people, they don't want smoke control. It's going to cost them more money."[5] Many working-class people shared these opinions. Although they found smoke a nuisance, they were concerned that smoke control would threaten their livelihoods. Pittsburgh, therefore, appeared to be inhospitable to the passage of substantive legislation to limit smoke emissions from industries or homes.

Changing this situation required a campaign to convince the public that the benefits of smoke regulation would outweigh the costs. This campaign actually began in 1936 when a group of individuals secured a grant from the federal Works Progress Administration to do a survey of the impacts of smoke pollution on the community. The survey updated the reports of the important Mellon Smoke Investigations of 1912–1914 and provided the basis for a renewal of interest in smoke control. The Civic Club of Allegheny County and the Pittsburgh Chamber of Commerce, which were concerned with the city's image and feared that dirty air would cause population and industrial loss, played an important role.[6] Historically, antismoke drives led by such voluntary organizations had never been effective. However, by 1940–1941 two key distinguishing elements had emerged: the active involvement of three key individuals who cooperated with the voluntary organizations but who represented other critical elements in the decision-making field; and the example of St. Louis, a city that appeared to have solved its smoke problem.

The critical individuals were Abraham Wolk, a lawyer and City Council member; Edward T. Leech, the editor of the city's most influential newspaper, the *Pittsburgh Press;* and Dr. I. Hope Alexander, director of the Pittsburgh Department of Public Health. Wolk, described by a colleague as a "monomaniac" on smoke control, likely became involved in the campaign because of the effect of the smoke on his asthmatic son's health. He organized the political coalition necessary for passage of a new smoke ordinance and convinced Mayor Cornelius D. Scully, who was up for reelection in 1941, to support the legislation. Leech, a crusading editor, furnished critical media leadership, using his paper "like a war club" to advance smoke control. And Alexander, a physician, made smoke control into a public health crusade, emphasizing the damage that smoke was doing to the lungs and health of all Pittsburghers, regardless of class.[7]

St. Louis was also an industrial center dependent on bituminous coal. While Pittsburgh had been faltering in its fight against smoke during the 1930s, St. Louis was taking steps toward smoke control. Raymond R. Tucker, a combustion engineer who had headed the Department of Mechanical Engineering at Washington University of St. Louis, played the most important role. In 1934, he was appointed secretary to the mayor with instructions to devise a strategy to "clarify the air." Tucker realized that the method by which St. Louis and other cities had solved their water pollution problem—filtration at the source—furnished a model that could also be applied to the air. That is, if water could be rendered potable by removing impurities before distribution, then the air could be cleansed by controlling the quality of the fuel before consumption. "Smokeless air" would result from a law that required the burning of "smokeless" fuel or the use of smokeless equipment. Tucker fought an uphill battle attempting to secure legislation, and in April 1940, after a heating season characterized by heavy smoke palls, the St. Louis Board of Aldermen finally approved an ordinance requiring the use of smokeless fuel or smokeless mechanical equipment by fuel consumers, including homeowners. The essential control mechanism was city licensing of fuel dealers in order to control the quality of fuel at the source. The first test of the ordinance in the 1940–1941 heating season correlated with a series of smokeless days that city officials attributed to the new law.[8]

In February 1941, the *Pittsburgh Press* began a concerted series of articles and editorials pointing to St. Louis's success as evidence that Pittsburgh could also achieve clean air. Particularly effective in mobilizing opinion were photographs of a smoke-darkened St. Louis street before smoke regulation and the same street sunlit after the regulatory ordinance was implemented. Egged on by the *Press,* readers, especially irate housewives, bombarded Mayor Scully with over two hundred letters a day demanding action. During February, two delegations of Pittsburghers visited St. Louis. The first was led by Dr. Alexander and included several members of the Civic Club's Smoke Elimination Committee. The second was composed of members of the City Council who visited St. Louis on a "civic pilgrimage" to examine the administrative machinery of smoke control and assess its political viability. While some council members raised questions about the impact of smoke control on coal miners and on the poor, most returned convinced of its technical feasibility although concerned about its political practicality.[9]

The media—newspapers and the radio—were essential in generating a positive public attitude. Leech's *Pittsburgh Press* and the *Pittsburgh Post-Gazette* were the leaders in advocating a smoke control ordinance. Leech bombarded the public with editorials and articles about the evils of smoke and the advantages of control. Investigative reporter Gilbert Love, to whom Leech assigned the role of "knowledgeable community informant," translated medical information and technical reports into concise, informative articles. The editorial cartoonist Cy Hungerford accompanied Love's reporting with a series of penetrating antismoke cartoons.[10] Articles detailed the costs of smoke to the city in terms of high cleaning expenses and damage to health, property, and vegetation. Pittsburgh experienced a number of extremely smoggy days during the 1940–1941 winter, accentuating the urgency of the issue. The *Press* played on the adverse atmospheric conditions by publishing photographs contrasting city air quality with that in the suburbs. Letters to the editor calling for smoke control were published almost daily, although there was also a smattering of letters expressing concern that smoke control would cause a loss of jobs.[11]

The Mayor's Commission for the Elimination of Smoke

The antismoke campaign attempted to win support from all organized groups within the community, as reflected in the membership of the Mayor's Commission for the Elimination of Smoke, appointed on February 18, 1941. Mayor Scully declared that "Pittsburgh must, in the interest of its economy, its reputation and the health of its citizens, curb the smoke and smog which has made this season, and many others before it, the winter of our discontent."[12] The commission was chaired by Councilman Wolk and included Dr. Alexander; A. K. Oliver, chairman of the board of the Pittsburgh Coal Company, the district's largest coal company; H. Marie Dermitt, secretary of the Civic Club and a founding member of the 1913 Smoke and Dust Abatement League; Leech of the *Pittsburgh Press;* Ralph C. Fletcher, research director of the Federation of Social Agencies; William N. Duff, chairman of the Smoke Abatement Committee of the Chamber of Commerce; Patrick T. Fagan, president, District 5 of the United Mine Workers; Mrs. H. K. Breckenridge, a "prominent" club woman; and Mrs. W. C. Ridge, member of the Pittsburgh Board of Education. The commission thus comprised representatives of business, labor, government, the media, the health professions, and voluntary civic and welfare associations. The appointment of three women reflected the campaign leadership's perception of their importance in achieving smoke control. In addition to

Nature and the city juxtaposed: Schenley Park and Oakland, 2002. The Cathedral of Learning of the University of Pittsburgh is on the right. Photo by Joel A. Tarr.

George Westinghouse surveys a tableau of his most famous inventions. Westinghouse Pond, Schenley Park, 2003. Photo by Joel A. Tarr.

Pittsburgh, ca. 1902, viewed from Mount Washington. *Source:* Carnegie Library of Pittsburgh.

The integrated steel mills lined the banks of the Monongahela River for many miles, lighting up the nighttime sky. This is the Pittsburgh Steel Company's Monessen Works in 1956, about thirty miles from Pittsburgh. *Source:* Library and Archives Division, Historical Society of Western Pennsylvania, Pittsburgh, Pa.

The Pittsburgh works of the Jones & Laughlin Iron and Steel Corporation, 1947. These facilities spanned both sides of the Monongahela River within the Pittsburgh city boundaries, with the blast furnaces on the north bank and the open hearth furnaces on the south bank. *Source:* Standard Oil Collection, Carnegie Library of Pittsburgh.

The Pitcairn rail yards, 1951. Photo by W. Terry Stuart and used with permission.

Mine patch homes perched over a slag heap, ca. 1920. *Source:* Carnegie Library of Pittsburgh. Photo by John Collier.

Houses perched on the sides of the hills, 1935. The sewer building activity in this picture illustrates that these hillside homes were initially built without sewers and depended on privy vaults. *Source:* Pittsburgh City Photographer Collection, Archives Service Center, University of Pittsburgh.

The Monongahela Incline, ca. 1900. Beginning in 1870, inclines, powered by steam engines, furnished access to some of the city's hilltop neighborhoods. *Source:* Carnegie Library of Pittsburgh.

Some homes could only be reached by stairways, often constructed of wood. Photo by Joel A. Tarr, 2002.

St. Pierre's Ravine, with Schenley Park in the background and the Carnegie Library and Museum of Natural History to the left. The city filled in the ravine in 1913–1914 to provide a grander entrance to Schenley Park but today it is occupied by a parking lot. New plans have been made, however, to restore it as a park and natural area. *Source:* Carnegie Library of Pittsburgh

Washington's Landing on Herr's Island. New development on an industrial brownfield. The forty-two-acre island, located in the Allegheny River about two miles from the Pittsburgh Point, combines private housing, light commercial development, and public recreational space. Photo by Joel A. Tarr.

BRIDGE OVER THE MONONGAHELA RIVER, PITTSBURG, PENN.

This 1854 picture illustrates the importance of the rivers and river commerce. The smoke plumes also indicate the pride taken in the city's productivity. The bridge in the background is the suspension bridge John Roebling built in 1846 on the piers of the city's first bridge, the deck of which burned in the Great Fire of 1845. (Note the spelling "Pittsburg" in the picture's title.) *Source:* Carnegie Library of Pittsburgh.

The Monongahela wharf, 1932. A busy location for commerce and passenger traffic in the nineteenth century, by the 1920s it had been transformed into a parking lot for automobiles. Notice the cobblestones that had formerly served to hold the bank so that horses and wagons could unload river steamers. The bridge is the Wabash Bridge, which no longer stands. *Source:* Pittsburgh City Photographer Collection, Archives Service Center, University of Pittsburgh.

Coal barges on the Monongahela River (a "floating coal vein") in front of U.S. Steel's Clairton Coke Works ca. 1950. *Source:* Library and Archives Division, Historical Society of Western Pennsylvania, Pittsburgh, Pa.

The 1936 flood. Parts of downtown Pittsburgh were under twelve feet of water. Eight flood control dams now prevent floods of this severity. *Source:* Library and Archives Division, Historical Society of Western Pennsylvania, Pittsburgh, Pa.

Homes in Junction Hollow, Oakland section of Pittsburgh, 1912. Notice the open sewers covered with wood planking. *Source:* Pittsburgh City Photographer Collection, Archives Service Center, University of Pittsburgh.

Privy vaults were widely used throughout the city well into the twentieth century. The picture is of row houses in the Woods Run section of Pittsburgh, 1921. Note the water pump close to the privy on the right. *Source:* Pittsburgh City Photographer Collection, Archives Service Center, University of Pittsburgh.

Sewer pipes discharged sewer overflow into local creeks as well as the rivers. This picture is from 1926 and shows a location in the Allegheny Cemetery. *Source:* Pittsburgh City Photographer Collection, Archives Service Center, University of Pittsburgh.

Pumping oil seepage into the Monongahela River, 1950, before sewage treatment. *Source:* Carnegie Library of Pittsburgh. Photo by Clyde Hare.

Untreated sewage from the city's combined sewer system is still discharged from overflow pipes into the rivers on wet weather days. Photo by Joel A. Tarr.

Warnings about wet weather combined sewer overflows and possible dry weather flows into area rivers were posted in 2003 because of heightened sensitivity to the problem. This sign is on the Monogahela riverfront trail abutting the "Waterfront" development that occupies the former U.S. Steel mill site in Homestead. Photo by Joel A. Tarr.

Smoke from the Shoenberger Iron Works in the Strip District, 1906. *Source:* Carnegie Library of Pittsburgh.

"Among the Coke Furnaces of Pennsylvania," *Harper's Weekly,* January 30, 1886. Thousands of beehive coke ovens were scattered over southwestern Pennsylvania well into the twentieth century. They presented a fiery sight at night. *Source:* Carnegie Library of Pittsburgh.

Before smoke control and the arrival of natural gas in the city, the downtown was often shrouded in heavy smoke during the daylight hours. This picture was taken at the intersection of Liberty and Fifth Avenues, winter, ca. 1940, at 10:40 in the morning. *Source:* Smoke Control Lantern Slide Collection, ca. 1940–1950, Archives Service Center, University of Pittsburgh.

Women and women's groups played an important role over the decades in trying to achieve smoke control. Here women march in the downtown in 1946 with masks on their faces to dramatize that smoke was bad for people's health. *Source:* Carnegie Library of Pittsburgh.

Advertising for smoke control, 1946. *Source:* Library and Archives Division, Historical Society of Western Pennsylvania, Pittsburgh, Pa.

After the burden of smoke was reduced, a number of buildings in the downtown were cleaned. This picture from ca. 1950 shows the contrast between the Gulf Building, which had been cleaned, and the Koppers Building, which had not been. *Source:* Library and Archives Division, Historical Society of Western Pennsylvania, Pittsburgh, Pa.

A gob pile of coal mine wastes. Image courtesy of Eugene Levy Collection, Carnegie Mellon University Libraries, Special Collections.

A municipal dump for garbage and an associated pig farm, Reserve Township, 1937. Open garbage dumps and pig farms were widely used to dispose of solid wastes into the 1950s. *Source:* Allegheny County Health Department.

Pouring slag. Although not a Nine Mile Run photo, this was typical of the slag dumping practices in the valley. *Source:* G. W. Josephson, F. Sillers Jr., and D. G. Runner, *Iron Blast-Furnace Slag: Production, Processing, Properties, and Uses,* Bulletin 479, Bureau of Mines (Washington, D.C.: GPO, 1949).

The Nine Mile Run Valley in 1921, before slag dumping. *Source:* Citizens' Committee on City Plan, *Parks Report* (Pittsburgh: Citizens' Committee on City Plan, 1923).

The slag mountain in Nine Mile Run overshadowing homes in the neighborhood of Duck Hollow. Photo by Joel A. Tarr, 1998.

Culverting Nine Mile Run. *Source:* Pittsburgh City Photographer Collection, Archives Service Center, University of Pittsburgh.

New urbanism type homes in Summerset (summer 2002), the housing development built on the Nine Mile Run slag heap. Photo by Joel A. Tarr.

these members, a technical advisory subcommittee was appointed to the commission. The role of the technical subcommittee was to present recommendations concerning control of particular sources of smoke such as railroads and metallurgical companies to the commission and to gather information on questions such as the availability of smokeless fuel and smokeless equipment.[13]

While the commission was holding its hearings, the Civic Club and the League of Women Voters conducted a countywide campaign of public arousal and education, employing a network of voluntary associations that could both communicate information about the benefits of smoke control and serve as a political pressure group. While voluntary organizations of all types were represented in the network, women's groups were the most numerous. As homemakers, women of all classes knew how much extra cleaning smoke necessitated, with the burden falling most severely on working-class women who lived close to the mills. Middle-class and upper-class women in the Civic Club and the League of Women Voters coordinated luncheons and lectures and provided speakers to interested groups.[14]

The Smoke Elimination Commission held twelve closed meetings and four public meetings. John P. Robin, executive secretary to the mayor, noted that the purpose of the public meetings was to "get across to the public something which . . . still needs more hammering,—the need for smoke control. . . . It gives the papers and the Commission a show. It gives the people a chance to be part of [the] . . . meetings."[15] The first three public meetings were carefully orchestrated for maximum impact, including the testimony of ten local physicians concerning the negative health effects of smoke; impassioned complaints by women's club representatives about the negative impacts of smoke on women and on family life; and the testimony of householders and other fuel users about the advantages of mechanical stokers and processed coal.[16] The fourth public meeting was called at the request of the Western Pennsylvania Coal Operators Association and was intended to present the coal industry's point of view.

The commission's closed meetings served to provide information on policy-relevant questions. Early in the proceedings, a consensus emerged among the members that smoke should be eliminated, not just abated. Surprisingly, there was also consensus that households and commercial firms rather than large industries contributed the most to the smoke nuisance. Finally, there was agreement that the policy adopted should not damage any Pittsburgh industry by reducing coal production or imposing excessive compliance costs. The commission members recognized that smoke control would entail costs, but they still believed that the right policy could achieve smoke elimination without creating undue hardships to individuals or to industry. As Wolk noted early in the commission's proceedings, "We want to make this city smokeless without hurting anybody."[17]

A smoke control policy based on smokeless fuels and mechanical equipment, however, could potentially burden coal miners and low-income consumers more than other groups. The Steel City Industrial Union Council—which represented over 100,000 CIO members in Allegheny County, including the United Mine Workers (UMW)—had unanimously endorsed the principle of smoke control early in March. A UMW representative sat on the commission to watch over the miners' interests and those of labor in general. During the hearings he often asked questions about fuel costs and possible job losses by miners, but he appeared to agree that smoke control would not substantially impact mine employment since the need for smokeless coal would actually result in the mining of larger amounts of bituminous.[18]

The issue of how the poor would pay for higher fuel costs or for new combustion equipment was frequently discussed. Mayor Scully noted to the commission that "our problem is a psychological propaganda problem to keep somebody from attacking the program . . . on the theory that it's going to hurt the little fellow and do great harm to people who are underprivileged."[19] Generally the commission members, including the labor representative, agreed that smoke control would bring more benefits than costs to the working class because they were most exposed to smoke pollution at work and at home. But specific mechanisms for aiding the poor were seldom discussed aside from a possible delay in implementing the law for domestic consumers until cheap and adequate supplies of smokeless coal were available. While both a subsidy plan and a revolving fund were briefly mentioned as options, the commission never pursued them.[20]

Numerous technical questions confronted the commission, and the members depended upon their technical subcommittee and the testimony of experts from the relevant industries for advice. The technical subcommittee reports, presented in May, dealt with domestic combustion technology and coal consumption and with the control of smoke and dust from railroads, steamboats, and stationary and metallurgical sources. The subcommittee recommended that the domestic fuel supply be regulated so that householders would have to use either smokeless fuel or smokeless equipment. However, to insure the availability of adequate supplies of both fuel and equipment, they suggested that enforcement against domestic consumers be delayed for at least three years until after the commercial and industrial sectors had complied with the law. The long delay was necessary not only to secure compliance by the nondomestic sectors, but also to permit the construction of plants to produce smokeless fuel.[21]

The coal industry was especially concerned about getting its views before the commission and the public. Under pressure from cleaner competing fuels such as oil and natural gas, as well as from antismoke campaigns in other cities, coal producers worried about the loss of a critical market. The Western Pennsylvania Coal Operators Association, representing seventy-six firms that produced over 80 percent of the region's coal, created its own smoke committee to investigate the problem. In mid-May, at the same time that the commission's technical subcommittee was making its recommendations, the association requested a special public hearing to present their smoke committee's report.[22]

The coal operators took the position that it was "in the long range interest of coal producers—and coal users—to help find a way by which smokeless and efficient heating can be economically obtained." They argued, however, that a smoke control policy based on the use of processed coal was "wishful thinking," since they doubted that the capital required for developing the industry could be obtained. The coal producers feared that such a policy would result in cleaner fuels, such as natural gas or oil or low-volatile coal, capturing the Pittsburgh domestic market with severe harm to the local coal industry, the unemployment of over two thousand Allegheny County miners, and higher consumer fuel prices.

The Coal Operators Association proposed the adoption of "improved" equipment for the smokeless combustion of bituminous coal as an alternative to the use of processed coal or other smokeless fuels. The industry was supporting research and development of such equipment at Bituminous Coal Research, the Battelle Memorial Institute, and various universities. In order to allow time for the commercial development of this technology, the coal producers asked that smoke control be implemented in a series of stages, with industry first and domestic consumers last. In this manner, clean air would be attained without destroying the markets for western Pennsylvania bituminous.[23]

The Commission's Report and the Passage of the Ordinance

At the conclusion of the commission's hearings, John P. Robin of the mayor's office and Gilbert Love of the *Pittsburgh Press* prepared a final report to the mayor. All members of the commission, including the coal industry and labor representatives, signed the report. It listed the names of two hundred voluntary organizations, including fifty-six women's clubs, twenty-four business organizations, and many labor and civic groups as supporters. The report concluded that eliminating smoke from Pittsburgh's air was feasible and argued that doing so would "bring about a new era of growth, prosperity and well-being." Clean air would ostensibly improve living conditions, halt suburban migration, attract light industry, and create new industrial activity and employment, especially in the area of coal-based processed fuels. These benefits would result from a policy requiring the use of smokeless fuels and/or smokeless mechanical equipment. The report dismissed the Coal Operators Association's concerns that such a policy would negatively affect the coal industry and maintained that requiring the burning of smokeless fuels would actually increase regional coal production: "Pittsburgh might well become the location of a new coal processing industry, selling its products not only in this city and the suburbs . . . , but in distant communities."[24] Commission member A. K. Oliver, chairman of the board of Pittsburgh's largest coal company, accepted this possibility and signed the final report.

The commission also argued that "the smoke elimination plan would impose little or no additional burden on the low-income groups of the city."[25] Smokeless fuel might cost more than high-volatile bituminous, the report acknowledged, but it would produce more heat. In addition, the commission predicted that many low-income families would purchase new smokeless stoves when their present equipment wore out, making possible a return to cheap high-volatile fuel. In order to control the price and quality of smokeless fuel, the commission recommended the creation of a fuel consumer's council that would protect low-income residents against short weights and other fraud and help extend their fuel dollar. John P. Bussarello, the UMW representative, signed the report, indicating that the unions were willing to accept the position that smoke control would not place undue burdens on the miners or the working class.

The enforcement procedures recommended by the commission rested on the concept of controlling smoke at the source. Over a staged two-year period, all fuel users would have to either burn smokeless fuels or adopt smokeless mechanical equipment. The timetable for implementation was as follows:

1. Industries, office buildings, hotels, apartment houses, and commercial establishments by October 1, 1941

2. Railroads by October 1, 1942

3. Domestic users and all other fuel consumers by October 1, 1943

Specific standards governing the emission of dense smoke as defined by indexes on the Ringelmann Chart were issued for different classes of users. In addition to smoke, the suggested ordinance provided for regulation of other air pollutants such as fly ash, noxious acids, gases, and fumes.[26]

The commission recommended the creation of a Bureau of Smoke Prevention headed by a "qualified engineer" and housed in the Department of Health. Permits would be required for new installations and reconstruction of existing heating plants, and the superintendent could impose fines and seal equipment that violated the law. A five-member board would hear appeals. Ultimately, the report maintained, public opinion would determine if the city would become smoke-free: "Public cooperation is the vital ingredient of any civic improvement, and the bureau of smoke prevention by mobilizing the force of public determination will be able to see to it that the law will be enforced right up to the hilt." Chairman Wolk introduced the proposed ordinance in the City Council. Railroad and steamboat interests and the Jones & Laughlin Steel Corporation attempted to secure modifications of certain provisions, but were unsuccessful. Early in July 1941, the council voted eight to one to approve the smoke ordinance. Edward Leonard, a councilman active in labor circles, cast the only dissenting vote, protesting that the ordinance would be detrimental to both the poor and industry.[27]

Several factors explain the success of the smoke control advocates in obtaining the legislation. St. Louis's example was critical because it demonstrated that smoke control could be a reality in an industrial city. Through effective media use and a citywide network of voluntary organizations, the campaign managers were able to convince most Pittsburghers that the benefits of smoke control would outweigh the costs. Opposition to the proposed law was uncoordinated and fragmented, while organized labor and the coal industry, which could have combined to block the ordinance, were co-opted by the argument that smoke control would stimulate a new processed coal industry. The power of the antismoke coalition was most clearly revealed in the lack of serious political debate in City Council over the smoke ordinance. All significant power groups within the city either supported the measure or remained neutral toward its passage.

Implementing the Pittsburgh Smoke Control Program

The 1941 Smoke Control Ordinance included three stages of implementation. Stages one and two, directed primarily against industries, commercial establishments, and railroads, were implemented as planned. However, the Bureau of Smoke Prevention limited its enforcement of the law during the war. Dr. Sumner B. Ely, the head of the bureau, stated that industry and the railroads were doing their best to meet the standards under wartime conditions and stressed the need for cooperation and understanding in seeking compliance. The smoke inspectors, he maintained, should supply "advice and assistance" rather than playing the role of policemen. The original implementation date for domestic consumers—October 1, 1943—was waived, with the agreement that full enforcement would begin six months after the war's end.[28]

The intense focus on productivity, the limited regulation of industry and railroads, and the lack of controls over domestic heating equipment resulted in very poor Pittsburgh air quality during the war. The city suffered a number of severe smoke palls, requiring that downtown streetlights be turned on at midday.[29] The need for strict enforcement of the Smoke Control Ordinance during the postwar period appeared all the more urgent to the antismoke forces. The most critical implementation issue continued to be enforcement against domestic consumers. To maintain the impetus that had resulted in the ordinance's passage, the Civic Club created a new organization—the United Smoke Council (USC), consisting of eighty allied organizations from Pittsburgh and Allegheny County. The council's slogan was "Now More than Ever," and it organized three committees: one to study the availability of new smoke-elimination devices and smokeless fuels; a second to aid the smoke bureau in enforcement; and a third to encourage antismoke laws throughout the county. The USC focused upon public educational efforts about the continued need for smoke control. M. Jay Ream, who chaired the Civic Club's Smoke Elimination Committee, was appointed its first head.[30]

A second important civic association that entered the field of smoke control was the Allegheny Conference on Community Development (ACCD), formed in 1943. The ACCD had as its mission the development of "an over all community improvement program" for Pittsburgh. Primarily concerned with the economic revitalization of the central business district and the region, it viewed environmental improvements like smoke control as essential to community rejuvenation. The ACCD was vital to the smoke control campaign because of the concentrated corporate power that it represented. Its key sponsor, Richard King Mellon, exercised vast economic might through his leadership of the Mellon banking interests and linked corporations such as Gulf Oil, Koppers Coke, and Pittsburgh Consolidation Coal. Mellon indicated his interest in smoke control in 1943 in response to a request for help from the USC's Ream, noting that it was an issue with which his father had been concerned. He suggested that Ream make contact with the officials at the ACCD, and a merger between the two groups became a reality at the end of 1945.[31]

The merger of the USC with the ACCD was important because it supplied the USC with funding, access to professional and technical staff, and

the backing of powerful corporate leaders. It also integrated the single-is-
sue focus of smoke control into a larger campaign for urban improvement.
The USC, with its wide net of community organizations, enlarged the
scope of the ACCD program and increased public support. Thus, the two
organizations joined to provide the bureaucratic structure and planning
essential for policy implementation.[32]

High-level political support remained a crucial ingredient. In the
spring of 1945, David Lawrence was elected mayor of Pittsburgh and made
it clear that he favored smoke control. As the chair of the Allegheny
County Democratic Committee, Lawrence was concerned with strength-
ening his party's hold on the city. In a move often described as politically
courageous, he allied himself with the Republican-dominated ACCD's
agenda for civic reconstruction, including a commitment to implement the
smoke control law at an early date. Lawrence later explained that although
this decision displeased many Pittsburgh Democrats, he "resisted all pressure and temptation to ease up and take it slowly."[33]

Setting an effective implementation date for residential smoke control
depended on the accuracy of the available technical information. The most
important questions still concerned the availability and costs of low-volatile fuel and mechanical equipment. In addition, the effects of the law on
the coal industry and upon working-class users remained major issues. The
ACCD hired C. K. Harvey, an engineering consultant, to study these problems and make recommendations. The coal companies again initiated
their own study group under the auspices of the newly formed Western
Pennsylvania Conference on Air Pollution.

In his report to the ACCD, Harvey concluded that while there would
not be sufficient smokeless equipment to permit the use of high-volatile
coal by October 1, 1946, adequate supplies of low-volatile fuels would be
available from central Pennsylvania mines. He asserted that although
500,000 tons of coal would need to be imported, this amount was only 3
percent of the county's production and would not discernibly affect either
the coal companies or labor. In a separate letter to Ream, Harvey repeated
the argument made in the 1941 Smoke Elimination Commission report that
the demand for low-volatile coal would stimulate the creation of a processed fuel industry based on local bituminous.[34]

In regard to the impact of the policy on consumers, Harvey also reit-
erated the claim that the higher heating value of smokeless coal might
conceivably lower "the average fuel bill." By using smokeless coal in their
present equipment, he added, consumers would be able to salvage the "recovery life" of their furnaces before converting to smokeless equipment.
"Thus," he noted, "the Ordinance can be put into effect without further

delay and with a minimum of capital investment and cost." Harvey argued that delaying implementation until smokeless equipment was widely available would be an error because "the public may become discouraged and lose its present enthusiasm for smoke pollution abatement."[35]

Satisfied with the accuracy of the Harvey report, the ACCD Executive Committee acted on February 25 to approve an October 1, 1946 effective date for enforcing the smoke control law against domestic users. Within several weeks, however, members of the ACCD's Smoke Abatement Technical Committee raised questions concerning the accuracy of Harvey's claim that adequate supplies of smokeless coal would be available to meet domestic needs. Simultaneously, committee president George Love and vice president J. D. Morrow of Pittsburgh Consolidation Coal requested a special meeting of the ACCD Executive Committee to present the bituminous coal producers' arguments for a delay.[36]

The coal producers argued that it would be a mistake to implement the smoke control law on October 1, 1946, because of inadequate smokeless coal supplies. Enforcement, they warned, would cause great hardship throughout the city and should be postponed until smokeless stoves and furnaces were available. The underlying concern of the coal industry was that enforcement of smoke control without the availability of technology to burn local bituminous coal smokelessly would drive consumers to cleaner fuels. "Coal producers," said the technical report of the Western Pennsylvania Conference on Air Pollution, were "opposed to smoke not only from the civic or humanitarian standpoint, but because it results in dissatisfaction with their product." If Pittsburgh acted, the report continued, other cities would follow, affecting thousands of miners and workers in related industries. The end result would be "the progressive crippling and possible destruction of a large segment of the Western Pennsylvania bituminous coal industry."[37]

The conflicting data presented by the two technical committees led to an ACCD-brokered compromise. The enforcement date against domestic users would be delayed one year to October 1, 1947. Strict enforcement against industrial and commercial coal consumers, institutions, and apartment houses, however, would begin on October 1, 1946. The ACCD, the Coal Operators Association, and the city agreed to cooperate in maintaining public interest in smoke abatement. Although some members of the USC opposed the revision, the Executive Committee of the ACCD approved it unanimously. This outcome was understandable, since Arthur B. Van Buskirk, Mellon's representative on the Executive Committee, was instrumental in shaping the compromise. Mayor Lawrence also indicated his agreement.[38]

In late April, the City Council held hearings on revisions to the smoke ordinance providing for the new implementation date. Representatives of the ACCD and the USC presented a petition outlining the agreement reached earlier between the ACCD, the Coal Operators Association, and the city; it was signed by the leaders of various civic and labor groups. Officials of several coal corporations, the Retail Coal Merchants Association, the UMW, the Teamsters, and the General Laborer's Union all made statements appealing for delay. Presentations by engineers from the coal companies and Bituminous Coal Research provided technical information confirming the shortage of low-volatile fuel and smokeless equipment. The League of Women Voters and several women's clubs, the Board of Trade of the Squirrel Hill Chamber of Commerce, and several disaffected USC members were the only voices calling for retention of the original date. On April 29, 1946, the Pittsburgh City Council unanimously passed the amended ordinance.[39]

Enforcement and Response to the Smoke Control Ordinance

With the passage of the ordinance secured, the ACCD and the United Smoke Council, in coordination with the Pittsburgh Bureau of Smoke Prevention and the Lawrence administration, proceeded with efforts to insure effective implementation. By requiring domestic users either to install smokeless equipment or to use smokeless fuels, the Bureau of Smoke Prevention aimed at altering the behavior of consumers in heating their homes. Householders could choose among several alternatives in order to meet the law's requirements: purchase smokeless combustion equipment that would permit the continued use of high-volatile fuels; switch to alternative fuels such as natural gas or oil; or use smokeless coal in existing stoves and furnaces. Because the third option required the least capital outlay, most low-income households preferred it. From the perspective of enforcement, however, this alternative posed the most difficulties.

There were approximately 100,000 homes using hand-fired coal-burning stoves and furnaces in Pittsburgh, including about 69,000 that depended on small coal stoves for cooking as well as heating. To enforce against the individual domestic consumer was an impossible task for the Bureau of Smoke Prevention's twelve inspectors. The bureau solved this problem by copying St. Louis's approach of focusing on the coal distribution yards (approximately thirty) and the coal truckers. It forbade yards to sell high-volatile coal for use in hand-fired equipment and truckers to deliver it. Truckers hauling coal in the city had to be licensed and have license numbers painted on the side of their trucks for easy identification. Those caught hauling illegal—"bootleg"—high-volatile coal were subject to fines, as were dealers who made illegal sales.[40]

The winter of 1947–1948 was critical for the new statute, and the dire predictions of the law's critics were partially borne out. Smokeless fuel supplies proved inadequate, prices were inflated (smokeless coal was usually at least 25 percent costlier than high-volatile bituminous), and dealers sold inferior grades of coal. Because of unfamiliarity with the characteristics of low-volatile coal, as well as the sale of low-grade mixtures, many residents had serious problems obtaining sufficient heat. Complaints about the law poured into city hall, newspaper offices, and radio stations, and several city council members attempted to have it suspended. "Undoubtedly," an important city official later admitted, "some very real difficulties were imposed on many people . . . perhaps if we had waited a year, it could have been done smoothly and with less inconvenience and cost and hardship to some people."[41]

The ordinance fell hardest on poor families, since fuel costs composed a larger percentage of their budget than those of higher income groups and because of their fuel-buying habits.[42] Working-class people commonly used older, inefficient stoves for heating and cooking, and they purchased their coal by the week in bushel lots from itinerant truckers because they had neither the cash nor the storage space to buy larger amounts. While there had been considerable discussion in both the 1941 and 1946 hearings about special considerations for the working class, cash subsidies were provided only for public-assistance recipients.[43] The Bureau of Smoke Prevention attempted to educate low-income consumers as to the proper measures of firing smokeless coal rather than fining people for smoke violations. In 1948, for instance, only fifteen persons were summoned before magistrates for smoke violations, as compared with 250 trucker violations. As one lawyer involved in the coal trade noted, the inspectors "deliberately went real easy on the smoke in poor neighborhoods and thought that they would get rid of that by eliminating the trucking of illegal fuel rather than by moving against poor Mrs. Murphy."[44]

Despite the many difficulties with fuel supply, the heating season of 1947–1948 showed a considerable improvement in air quality compared to previous years. An unusually mild winter aided in reducing the smoke palls. "Pittsburgh Is Cleaner" reported the *Pittsburgh Press* on February 21—the worst smogs were gone, homes were cleaner, and white shirts did not develop black rings around the collars. In statistical terms, Pittsburgh received 39 percent more of the available sunshine in the winter of 1947–1948 compared with 1946–1947; the hours of "moderate" and "heavy" smoke decreased approximately 50 percent during the same period; and dust-fall measurements also showed a slight decline as compared with 1938–1939. The USC boasted in a publication entitled, "The New Look in Pittsburgh," that Pittsburgh was losing its reputation as "the Smoky City." During the next few years, heavy smoke nearly disappeared from the Pittsburgh atmosphere. In 1955, for instance, the Bureau of Smoke Prevention reported only 10 hours of "heavy" smoke and 113 hours of "moderate" smoke as compared with 298 hours of "heavy" smoke and 1,005 hours of "moderate" smoke in 1946.[45]

In its 1951 report, the Bureau of Smoke Prevention calculated the total savings from smoke control as $26,808,000, or $41 per capita for improvements in "greater cleanliness." This included savings on cleaning expenses, reduced building depreciation, laundry bills, injury to vegetation, and fuel costs. In addition, the bureau observed that domestic consumers would save from improved fuel combustion caused by the installation of "more efficient burning equipment."[46] Finally, the report noted that without successful smoke control, many other civic improvements underway in Pittsburgh during the immediate postwar years would not have taken place.

Because of the visible improvement in air quality, public opinion shifted from limited to strong approval of the law. Public opinion surveys taken by a local advertising agency before and after the winter of 1947–1948 showed marked increases in favorable views. A poll in the summer of 1947 reported that 63.2 percent of those questioned favored smoke control. A follow-up poll in August 1948 showed 75 percent in favor. There were positive changes across all income levels, including low-income groups. Of the respondents in 1948, 32 percent said they found conditions "much better" in terms of the amount of smoke and dirt in Pittsburgh; 40 percent found conditions "somewhat better"; 22 percent found them "about the same"; and 2 percent found them "worse." The high approval rate for the ordinance is noteworthy given that 57 percent of those using fuel other than natural gas (mostly low-volatile processed coal) complained about the fuel, usually in regard to price. The public-opinion data are fragmentary and incomplete, but they suggest that many Pittsburghers were prepared to pay higher prices for environmental quality.[47]

The Shift to Natural Gas

Improvements in Pittsburgh air quality following the full implementation of the Smoke Control Ordinance in 1947–1948 did not necessarily result from the types of fuel and equipment substitutions that local policy makers had originally projected. In 1941, and also to an extent in 1946–1947, those involved in formulating and implementing the ordinance assumed that coal would remain the city's dominant domestic heating fuel for some time. Natural gas and oil were more expensive than coal through World War II, and supplies were erratic. "Lower cost to consumers and availability at all times," noted the Bureau of Mines in 1943, "are the principal factors favoring the use of coal."[48] Reliance upon smokeless coal produced from local bituminous or the use of equipment permitting smokeless combustion of bituminous would produce clean air. This strategy protected the interests of the local coal industry and coal miners. Repeated assurances by policy makers that the smoke problem could be solved without damaging the coal industry were intended to secure the acquiescence of the industry and the UMW in the law's passage and implementation.[49]

While low-volatile and processed coal (Disco) and smokeless coal-burning equipment did play a role in reducing smoke in 1947–1948, they steadily declined in significance thereafter. Low-priced natural gas, furnished by pipelines from the Southwest and stored in underground storage pools, increasingly became the dominant fuel used for Pittsburgh domestic heating.[50] The rates of change for the city are striking. In 1940, 81 percent of Pittsburgh households burned coal and 17.4 percent used natural gas (from Appalachian fields); by 1950, the figures were 31.6 percent for coal and 66 percent for natural gas. This shift entailed a change in fuel type and combustion equipment by almost half of all city households, most of which took place after 1945.[51]

The switch to natural gas in Pittsburgh would undoubtedly have occurred without the smoke control law because of price and convenience factors. Union contracts calling for higher wages and improved working conditions drove coal prices upward in 1947–1949, while numerous strikes caused supply difficulties.[52] Coal thus lost the advantages of lower cost and constant availability that had caused the Bureau of Mines in 1943 to predict its continued supremacy over competing fuels. Moreover, heating with gas rather than coal was much more convenient. The data reviewed here, however, also suggest that the Pittsburgh Smoke Control Ordinance accelerated the rate of change. Price and supply factors were operative in other cities as well as Pittsburgh, but in no other city in the nation was the rate of fuel change so rapid.[53] The evidence suggests that the coal producers and miners were correct that the smoke control law would hasten the loss of their domestic markets and their jobs, although even they did not anticipate the rapidity of the change.[54]

Industry and Smoke Control in Allegheny County, 1946–1959

The slogan that "smoke knows no boundaries" was a fixture of the campaign against smoke during the 1940s. Because airborne pollutants dispersed readily over a wide geographical area, steps that the city of Pittsburgh or any other single municipality took to regulate them could easily be nullified if neighboring localities did not impose similar controls. Awareness of the need for a regional approach led the USC, the ACCD, and other private civic organizations to seek a smoke control ordinance for all of Allegheny County, even though substantial political obstacles stood in the way.[55]

Many of the difficulties were rooted in the fact that heavy industry, mining, and railroads were located primarily outside the city. Although Pittsburgh contained a majority of all Allegheny County manufacturing establishments in 1947, with a few exceptions these central-city plants were relatively small.[56] The vast mills and factories owned by Pittsburgh's dominant industrial firms were generally located elsewhere, in satellite mill towns such as Homestead, East Pittsburgh, and Neville Island. Numerous working coal mines existed in rural and suburban areas of the county, while sprawling railroad freight yards and repair shops nestled in the river valleys. The scale and scope of these industrial facilities differentiated countywide smoke control from the problems that had earlier challenged city policy makers. Whereas regulating pollutants from household furnaces and commercial sources had been the primary tasks in the city, regulating industrial effluents emerged as the key issue in the drive for a county law.

Concerns about industrial pollution affected the political dynamics of the Allegheny County clean air campaign in two vital ways. First, large industrial corporations had a much greater stake in countywide smoke control than they had in the 1941 city ordinance. County legislation would have a more direct, substantial impact upon their business operations, obliging them to alter their core production processes or invest in costly pollution abatement equipment. Steelmakers, for example, would come under pressure to reduce the volume of ore dust from their furnaces. Coal companies faced possible restrictions on the disposal of wastes from mining operations because these wastes, known as gob piles, frequently caught fire and spread plumes of smoke across the landscape. Confronted with a potentially sweeping expansion of governmental control over their internal affairs, corporate managers had potent incentives to organize in defense of their specific interests and to take an active role in shaping the county's regulatory authority.

Railroad Smoke Control

Regulating railroad smoke emissions was a major issue of contention in both the city and the county. The railroad industry, which already had a long history of conflict with local governments over pollution problems, was determined to maintain control over its operations. Railroad executives detested the city ordinance, which, in their view, imposed unrealistic limits on the amount of dense smoke that locomotives could emit. They feared that separate, incompatible city and county laws would hamper regional railroad operations.[57] Most important, the potential costs of reducing smoke pollution alarmed them. Many rail lines experienced declining profitability in the late 1940s due to inflation and rising competition from motor vehicles. Under these circumstances, the expenses of retrofitting steam locomotives with smoke-abating devices or switching to cleaner diesel-electric locomotives were problematic. Furthermore, many railroads that served Pittsburgh obtained a large share of their freight revenue from coal hauling and were thus wary of any measure that might further decrease local coal production and consumption.[58]

The railroads attracted popular disfavor because they had used their political influence to win an exemption from a 1943 state enabling law that empowered Allegheny County to regulate smoke from all other sources. This loophole infuriated county residents, who regarded it as a flagrant violation of the principles of fairness and shared sacrifice upon which any workable ordinance should be based. Commissioner John J. Kane, the most powerful elected politician at the county level, realized that the public demanded an end to the railroad exemption. He urged smoke control advocates to concentrate on persuading the Pennsylvania legislature to abolish it.[59]

Railroad regulation thus became the focal point of an intense political struggle. On one side stood the railroads, whose aversion to smoke control epitomized the apprehensions that many industries felt about the costs of clearing the air. On the other side stood the preponderance of public opinion and some thirty vocal civic organizations that depicted smoke abatement as essential to the future well-being of the entire metropolitan area. Business-sponsored associations such as the ACCD, which had some sympathy with both positions, faced a difficult challenge. They had to ensure that railroads were regulated, but they sought to do so without ignoring the economic issues that the railroad executives had raised.

On March 3, 1947, two state legislators—a Republican and a Democrat—introduced into the Pennsylvania House of Representatives a bill that would give the Allegheny County Commissioners jurisdiction over railroad smoke. Known as the Fleming-Barrett Bill, this measure reflected a carefully crafted political strategy masterminded by the ACCD. It was one element of the "Pittsburgh Package," a set of ten proposals aimed at increasing the capacity of the city and county governments to address postwar urban issues. Working closely with state and local politicians, the ACCD had forged a bipartisan consensus behind the entire program. ACCD officers and the County Commissioners had also consulted with railroad executives, who had orally pledged to refrain from any overt criticism. The idea was to secure the repeal of the railroad exemption as part of a larger urban improvement campaign and then to work out the details of how the county would exercise its newfound power later.[60]

The railroads, however, reneged on their promises and threw the future of the Fleming-Barrett Bill into doubt. At a March 18, 1947, committee hearing in the House of Representatives, just after Executive Director Park Martin of the ACCD had stated that the railroads had taken no position on the measure, an assistant general manager of the Pennsylvania Railroad (PRR) contradicted him by proclaiming that the PRR was in fact opposed. It quickly became clear that the PRR served as the leader of several railroads that had joined in a lobbying campaign to thwart or at least weaken any new smoke control regulations pertaining to their industry.

A persistent story entrenched in Pittsburgh folklore holds that the financier Richard King Mellon, who was widely recognized as the leader of the Pittsburgh business community, defused the railroad opposition with one confidential telephone call. Invoking his power as a director of the PRR and as the holder of controlling interests in numerous corporations that shipped their products on that railroad, Mellon allegedly contacted Martin Clements, the PRR's president, and demanded that all resistance to the Fleming-Barrett Bill cease immediately. Clements ostensibly complied. This account has some basis in fact; Mellon publicly endorsed all the Pittsburgh Package bills, and there is no reason to doubt that he interceded with the PRR management on behalf of the Fleming-Barrett legislation.[61]

However, a singular focus on Mellon's role obscures a much broader public-private effort to counteract the railroads' political influence. Smoke control advocates in Pittsburgh organized a multifaceted counterattack designed to shame the railroads into backing down. The USC dispatched emergency notices to its supporters, imploring them to telephone or write to legislators on behalf of the Fleming-Barrett Bill. Mellon and the ACCD urged corporate executives to bring peer pressure to bear on the railroads; several, including Benjamin F. Fairless, the president of U.S. Steel, conspicuously did so.[62] Crucial support came from key political leaders such as Mayor Lawrence, Commissioner Kane, and Governor James Duff. The daily Pittsburgh newspapers kept up a steady flow of publicity that criticized the railroads' position and framed the conflict as one of special interests versus the common good.[63]

Finding themselves politically isolated, representatives of four major railroads met with representatives of the ACCD, the USC, and the Chamber of Commerce and arranged a truce. On March 24, 1947, these firms announced that they would drop their opposition to the Fleming-Barrett Bill. The local civic associations, in exchange, pledged to work for a "reasonable and practical" county ordinance that would address the railroad executives' substantive concerns. On May 9, 1947, Governor Duff signed the bill into law.[64] Allegheny County now possessed all the legal power that it needed to develop a comprehensive ordinance that would cover all sources of smoke. The policy debate accordingly shifted back to the local level, to the task of deciding upon the precise content of that ordinance.

Creating a System of Industrial Self-Governance: The 1949 Ordinance

In the wake of the acrimonious railroad battle, both the business community and the County Commissioners were determined to avoid further open conflicts over air pollution policy. They sought to establish a cooperative, nonadversarial method for setting and implementing the new rules. The policy formulation process that the county adopted between 1947 and 1949 reflected these priorities by relying upon intensive negotiations among business, civic, and governmental officials that tailored the law to the particular circumstances of various industries. This process often amounted to delegating public rule making and enforcement authority to officials of private corporations, who then monitored their own compliance.[65] Through such public-private cooperation, the stakeholders hoped to obtain significantly cleaner air without imposing excessive costs upon business firms or deterring industrial activity in Allegheny County.

The county's approach to reducing air pollution paralleled that of the city in some respects. Like the city, the county maintained that airborne pollutants had to be controlled at their points of origin and that the controls must apply to all industrial, commercial, and residential sources. As city officials had done in 1941, the County Commissioners solicited input from diverse stakeholder groups. The seventeen-member Allegheny County Smoke Abatement Advisory Committee, formed in September 1947 to draft the Smoke Control Ordinance, included representatives of industry, organized labor, and academic and civic organizations. Dr. Edward R. Weidlein, who was both the executive director of the Mellon Institute of Industrial Research and the chair of the ACCD, headed this committee.[66]

However, the role of businesspeople in defining technical standards and timetables for regulating industrial pollutants was far greater in the county than in the city. Weidlein established four subcommittees—Steel, Railroads, Heating and Power Plants, and Miscellaneous Industries—to determine strategies for correcting the pollution problems associated with specific industrial activities. Each subcommittee was chaired by a senior executive of a major local corporation; for example, Charles R. Cox, president of the Carnegie-Illinois division of U.S. Steel, led the Steel Subcommittee, while Curtis M. Yohe, president of the Pittsburgh & Lake Erie Railroad, headed the Railroads Subcommittee. Corporate managers and engineers staffed the subcommittees, providing data and giving technical advice.[67] These business and professional appointees performed the vast bulk of the work involved in crafting the industrial provisions of the county Smoke Control Ordinance.

Not surprisingly, the draft legislation that emerged after eighteen months of arduous subcommittee meetings at the Mellon Institute was respectful of industry viewpoints and markedly less strict than the 1941 city law had been. Although proclaiming that "the production or emission of dense smoke within the County of Allegheny is prohibited," the text contained a maze of qualifications, exemptions, and delays that limited the force of that prohibition.[68] It contemplated a gradual reduction of smoke, ash, and dust over the span of a decade while limiting the compliance costs placed upon corporations.

The section on railroads exemplified this philosophy. Responding to the railroads' demands for "reasonableness," the draft language made more generous allowances for locomotive smoke and ash than the city did. City law permitted a locomotive to generate dense smoke for only one minute per hour; in contrast, the Advisory Committee's proposed county law permitted dense smoke for up to four minutes per hour while a locomotive was being readied for use and for up to one minute in any fifteen-minute period while a locomotive was in use. The proposal also set only a five-year target, not a fixed requirement, for reducing the amount of fly ash generated by railroad equipment.

Other industrial facilities received similar sympathetic treatment. Existing iron-puddling furnaces and cement kilns, for instance, were given five years to conform to restrictions on smoke and dust output, while towboat operators had three years to comply. Some industries—especially the region's economic backbones, steel and coal—did not have to meet any specific performance standards for air pollution. By-product coke ovens and open-hearth furnaces faced no limitations other than a general stipulation that they "incorporate those means of controlling emissions of smoke and fly ash which have been proven to be economically practical."[69] Existing blast furnaces were required only to have gas cleaning devices installed within ten years.

These exemptions often reflected the claims of industry experts that no suitable technologies existed to deal with certain pollution problems. To cover such cases, the draft ordinance included a mandate for corporations to conduct research and experiment with possible solutions. All steel companies that operated open-hearth furnaces or Bessemer converters in Allegheny County, for instance, had to participate in a research program. A similar provision applied to coal producers, who agreed to pool their resources in a joint effort to find ways of preventing and suppressing gob pile fires.

The Advisory Committee as a whole deferred to the technical expertise of its four subcommittees and accepted their recommendations. In December 1948, the committee turned its findings over to the County Commissioners. Its final document contained not only detailed industrial provisions but also general regulations governing the operation and inspection of all "fuel-burning equipment" in commercial, residential, and industrial settings and mandating fines or equipment shutdowns for law violations. The draft ordinance also envisioned postponing the application of smoke control to private homes. Mindful of the city's difficult early experiences with obtaining clean-burning fuels, and sensitive to the political value of making industry go first, the Advisory Committee suggested that householders remain exempt until 1953. On May 17, 1949, the County Commissioners adopted the Advisory Committee draft with only a few slight changes. The Smoke Control ordinance of Allegheny County became effective on June 1, 1949.[70]

Implementation of the law rested upon the same principles of public-private cooperation and industrial self-governance that had marked the work of the Advisory Committee. The new Allegheny County Bureau of Smoke Control was incapable of monitoring and enforcing air pollution restrictions on its own. Its staff, which initially consisted of only five inspectors—fewer than the city employed—and a handful of supervisors and clerks, could not effectively patrol the entire county while at the same time keeping up with permit applications. Given its limited resources, the complexity of many industrial pollution issues, and the vagueness of some sections of the 1949 law, the bureau had little choice but to rely on the voluntary cooperation of the firms that it regulated. Indeed, some industries, such as the railroads and certain steel companies, conducted their own inspections and informed the county of their findings.[71]

Such informal collaboration was also the conscious preference of both the regulators and corporate officials. Thomas C. Wurts, the engineer who served as the first director of the Bureau of Smoke Control, noted in 1951 that his agency referred to its field staff as "combustion instructors" rather than "smoke inspectors" in order to project a nonconfrontational image.

Business-sponsored civic organizations assisted by providing informal channels of communication between regulators and businesspeople. The most important of these channels ran through the USC, which sponsored regular meetings at the engineers' club of Western Pennsylvania for the purpose of helping to bring industrial transgressors to terms. Representatives of the council, the city and county governments, and the offending corporations met in the privacy of the engineers' club dining room to air complaints and work out compliance agreements. Such arrangements facilitated the discreet handling of reported violations, "with a minimum of trouble making and legal action," throughout the 1950s.[72]

Impacts of the County Statute, 1949–1960

The system of business-government cooperation that the 1949 Smoke Control Ordinance institutionalized brought mixed results. Many industrial and commercial firms strove to comply with the law; others procrastinated or encountered difficulties that they could not readily surmount. Over the course of a decade, air quality in the Pittsburgh area improved, but this progress always coexisted with failures that cast doubt upon the efficacy of the ordinance and upon the political principles that it embodied.

No methods for systematically measuring the level of air pollution across Allegheny County existed in the 1950s; analysts depended on visual observations and anecdotal reports. The evidence that they compiled indicated that the air was generally becoming cleaner. Dense smoke and heavy sootfalls became rare in most sections of the county, and vegetation began to return to formerly barren hillsides. Changes in technology and fuel use accounted for most of the visible improvements. Like their counterparts in the city, corporations and individuals in suburban and rural areas reduced pollution by substituting cleaner-burning fuels in place of bituminous coal and by installing mechanical devices to limit the formation of smoke and ash. Most of these changes had begun well before 1949, so that the county Smoke Control Ordinance had the principal effect of accelerating preexisting trends.

The railroads met their legal obligations primarily by phasing in diesel-electric locomotives as quickly as they could afford to do so. By January 1953, diesels accounted for 79 percent of all locomotives operating in the county, and several local connecting railroads had become completely diesel. By 1958, steam engines had vanished entirely from local service, thus removing a major source of dense smoke, ash, and public ire.[73]

Other industrial and commercial enterprises likewise found that upgrading their heating and power-generating systems, adopting clean-burning fuels, and adding scrubbing or dust-collecting devices to their stacks yielded both cleaner air and economic benefits. U.S. Steel con-structed new boilers at two of its largest mills and also began capturing and reusing valuable blast furnace gases and iron ore dust. Many firms switched to natural gas, a choice that became easier as the region's leading gas suppliers steadily enlarged their transmission networks and increased gas storage capacity. The booming postwar economy facilitated these tech-nological shifts; during the late 1940s and the 1950s, firms often incorpo-rated smoke control measures into broader programs of plant expansion and modernization.[74]

As the notorious smogs that had long sullied the reputation of the city diminished, local business and civic leaders portrayed smoke control as a triumph for Pittsburgh and took pride in their contributions to it. They posited a symbiotic relationship between a cleaner urban environment and the long-term prosperity of the region. Park Martin of the ACCD asserted in 1953 that quality-of-life concerns such as clean air had come to equal or outweigh factors such as tax rates in determining business location deci-sions. Explaining that "an active, progressive, well-governed community will win out in competition for new industry over backward, unprogressive communities," he hailed smoke abatement as an essential precondition for attracting new investment to the Pittsburgh area.[75] The fact that the imple-mentation of local smoke-control laws coincided with a period of indus-trial growth seemed to demonstrate that smoke abatement was compat-ible with a vibrant economy.

However, not every industrial pollution issue had a technological solu-tion in which community welfare and corporate social responsibility coin-cided with economic self-interest. The mandatory research programs that were supposed to deal with hard cases met with only modest success dur-ing the 1950s. Although business-sponsored experimentation led to several advances, including improved techniques for extinguishing gob pile fires and scrubbing blast furnace gases, several pressing problems remained unresolved.[76] The most glaring failures lay in the steel industry's inability to find comprehensive methods of lowering emissions from open-hearth furnaces and by-product coke plants. Promising technologies, such as the use of electrostatic precipitators to capture metallic dust from open hearths, were often expensive enough that firms balked at installing them.[77] Moreover, certain forms of air pollution lay beyond the scope of the 1949 county ordinance. Language in both the underlying state-enabling legislation and the text of the ordinance itself suggested that the county had power only to regulate "smoke," interpreted to mean visible particu-late matter. Fumes, gases, and odors fell outside the boundaries of this definition, so that the county—unlike the city—had no legal authority to regulate invisible pollutants. Thus, when fume-laden air settled over the Monongahela Valley in October 1954 and damaged hundreds of homes, the Bureau of Smoke Control took no official action on the grounds that it lacked jurisdiction over the substances that had caused the havoc.[78]

High levels of industrial air pollution thus remained a serious concern in some areas of Allegheny County, particularly in the Monongahela Valley and the Ohio Valley where steelmaking was concentrated. These populous areas did not receive the vaunted benefits of clean air. "Hot spots"— industrial plants that inspired recurrent complaints about smoke, dust, and fumes—continued to trouble regulators and the public throughout the 1950s. Prominent offenders included various U.S. Steel plants in the Monongahela Valley, the expanding Pittsburgh Coke & Chemical Company operations on Neville Island, and the Jones & Laughlin Pittsburgh Works.[79]

Over time, rising public discontent with the relatively slow pace of change translated into a critique of the regulatory strategy that the County Commissioners had adopted. Suspicions multiplied concerning lax enforcement and complaints that relations between the regulators and the regulated industries had become too cozy. In 1955, the ACCD Executive Committee expressed unease about "a feeling in some quarters that the county smoke enforcement program was not as effective as it should be."[80] By 1957, Director Wurts of the Bureau of Smoke Control was openly admitting and denouncing the existence of persistent noncompliance with the 1949 ordinance.[81] Technical and legal constraints, a weak bureaucracy, and dependence upon the willingness of industry to police itself had combined to limit the law's effectiveness.

Toward the end of the decade, some observers began to call for a major overhaul of local air pollution policy. One possible step was to consolidate the enforcement powers of the city and the county—a change that became virtually inevitable after the city surrendered its public health regulatory powers to the newly formed Allegheny County Health Department in 1957. The move toward consolidation stirred controversy. City officials hesitated to yield control of their program, which they rightly believed to be broader and more stringently monitored than the county's, while the county Bureau of Smoke Control resisted any move that might disrupt its amicable relationships with the business community. The County Commissioners finally resolved the matter by setting up a new Citizens Advisory Committee in 1959 to draft a single new ordinance that would cover both Pittsburgh and the rest of the county. Chaired by Charles H. Weaver, the vice president for atomic research at Westinghouse Electric, this body—like its 1947 predecessor—was firmly dominated by corporate executives and technical experts.[82]

Other voices argued that reform should go much further because the principles of industrial self-regulation and cooperation between government and industry had failed. The leading proponent of this view was the Allegheny County Citizens against Air Pollution (ACCAAP), a grassroots organization that had grown out of neighborhood protests against persistent smoke and dust problems in the Monongahela Valley. Denouncing local officials for treating industrial polluters too leniently, the members of this group claimed that both the existing county law and the alternative version that the Citizens Advisory Committee had under consideration gave private corporations too much control over public policy. The ACCAAP revived the potent populist charge of favoritism toward big business, attacking the exemptions and long phase-in periods that the county had granted to various industries.[83]

Such ideas were not yet widely shared, but they suggested a shift in public attitudes and indicated the limitations of the locally based, consensus-seeking approach that had dominated environmental reform in Pittsburgh during the immediate postwar era. The 1949 Allegheny County Smoke Control Ordinance had resulted from an effort to strike a balance between rising public expectations for a clean environment on the one hand, and persistent public and business concerns about intrusive government regulation and compliance costs on the other. By 1960, that effort had begun to founder on criticism that its results had not been far-reaching enough.

⌒

The accomplishment of smoke control in Pittsburgh must be viewed as a major environmental achievement. However, whether atmospheric smoke would eventually have disappeared without the passage and implementation of the city and county smoke regulations is also a major question. In retrospect, the answer is yes, since ultimately it was the arrival of cheap, clean, and abundant natural gas in the region that led to the elimination of smoke-producing coal as a major element of heating fuel. This development was unanticipated. The local ordinances, however, deserve credit for accelerating the movement toward the adoption of cleaner-burning fuels.

Within the city, smoke control created equity issues as well as accelerated fuel and technology change. Because it required switching to a higher-priced fuel and/or investing in new capital equipment, the Smoke Control Ordinance generated financial problems that fell most heavily upon low-income residents. Coal miners also suffered a loss of jobs because of reductions in coal consumption. While aware of these potential problems, policy makers who formulated the terms of the ordinance and made decisions about implementation never seriously considered subsidy mechanisms to cushion impacts on the working class. They assumed that the public and private benefits that would result from smoke control would overshadow costs and inequities.

Smoke-free air, accomplished through a combination of municipal policy and fuel and technology changes, yielded a number of public and private gains. The aesthetic benefits were obvious, including more sunshine and a reduction in dirt and grime, while the cleaner air undoubtedly brought health improvements. Smoke elimination was also extremely important as a preliminary step toward the urban renewal program known as the Pittsburgh Renaissance that reshaped the city after World War II. Without smoke abatement, this municipal overhaul would not have taken place. The smoke control movement thus became an important element in the postwar modernization of Pittsburgh.

The picture of Allegheny County smoke control differs somewhat from the situation in the central city. Industries and railroads were particularly responsible for the county's air quality problems, with domestic sources playing a less important role. Due to the political power of these economic interests, regulatory authorities were reluctant to demand major changes to produce cleaner air. Rather than follow a command and control approach, the county Bureau of Smoke Control used a collaborative, consultative philosophy, trusting that industry would gradually reform itself. Some industries did, but others did not, thus exposing the weaknesses of the cooperative approach in an industrial region. In the final analysis, it is clear that in the absence of strong external sanctions, the major Allegheny County industries—particularly steel and railroads—would only adopt new and cleaner technologies when such improvements brought clear economic benefits. It is also clear that many air pollution problems exceeded the narrow scope of the 1949 county ordinance. Thus, the metropolitan area as a whole would have to await stronger air pollution legislation to attain a level of clean air that went beyond the elimination of visible smoke.

Slag in the Park

ANDREW S. MCELWAINE

WHILE MUCH OF THE focus of Pittsburgh environmental history has been on pollution of the air and the water and on efforts to restore these essential environmental goods, the land has also suffered from abuse. Throughout the Pittsburgh region the land has served as the depository for wastes of various sorts, including steel mill slag, coal mine debris, ashes, manufactured gas plant refuse, and garbage and other domestic effluents. These wastes have historically marked the landscape in the form of huge slag mountains, gob piles, filled in wetlands, altered riverbanks, and open garbage dumps. They have provided visible evidence that environmental values had been subordinated to those of material production.

In this context, this chapter will focus on the destruction of one of Pittsburgh's major landed amenities—the valley of Nine Mile Run—through its use as a dump for slag from area iron and steel manufacturers. Slag, a by-product of iron and steel production, was dumped in the open throughout western Pennsylvania.[1] The pile in question covers 238 acres along a creek known as Nine Mile Run in Pittsburgh's East End; it extends along the valley from the Squirrel Hill Tunnel to the Monongahela River shore. For over ninety years the southern end of the site has represented the largest stretch of open riverfront land in the city. During the first three decades of the twentieth century,

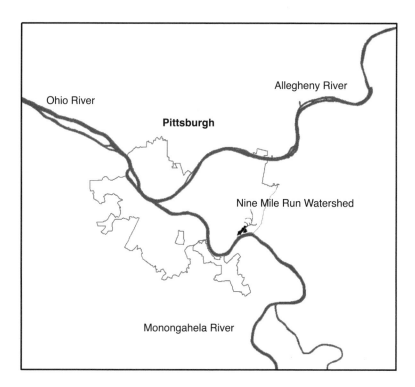

FIG. 5. The Nine Mile Run watershed

Pittsburgh elites and progressives attempted but failed to conserve this area for public use as a park. In the next seven decades, however, its use as a slag dump transformed it into a gruesome moonscape, buried under as much as 120 feet of industrial by-products and wastes. At the century's end, however, another effort began to restore the run and make the site available for public use for purposes of housing and creation of a green corridor. As a new draft of this land's history is now being prepared, the time is ripe to reconsider the previous drafts, and to draw some conclusions from the journey this parcel of land has experienced.

City Growth and the Absence of Landed Amenities

Throughout the nineteenth century, population increases and industrial expansion applied increasing pressure on Pittsburgh's environment. The second half of the century, especially, saw extraordinary growth—natural increase and immigration expanded the city's population from 50,000 in 1860 to over 300,000 in 1900. Pittsburgh was becoming one of the largest cities in America. In the same period the city expanded its land area from a little over one square mile to over thirty. After 1907, when neighboring Allegheny City was annexed, Pittsburgh approached a half million residents. For over a hundred years, however, the city grew without any significant land use or environmental regulation or management. The result was an admixture of industrial, commercial, and residential uses crammed into each section of Pittsburgh and surrounding communities. Streets and essential services were likewise mismatched to the needs of the landscape and there was little notion of land use controls.[2]

Landed amenities were as hard to find in nineteenth-century Pittsburgh as clean air and clean water. Aside from one small plot, the city lacked parks completely. Near the end of the century, however, Pittsburgh Public Works Director Edward Bigelow, inspired by Central Park and the parks movement in other American cities, made it a priority to establish parks in Pittsburgh's middle-class and elite residential areas. In 1889 he acquired three hundred acres as a donation from Mary Schenley to form the basis for Schenley Park in the city's Oakland and Squirrel Hill neighborhoods and purchased the land for Highland Park in the East End. In addition, in the early twentieth century, Progressive reformers and women's clubs led the way in creation of several "recreation parks" in the neighborhoods. Most of the city's densely congested working-class areas, however, remained devoid of any open space.[3]

The 1890s and early twentieth century saw the beginning of a reaction against Pittsburgh's polluted environment as the city's professional and business elites moved toward reforming urban conditions. Their philosophy largely involved a nascent urban environmentalism that sought both voluntary controls on and rational planning for the Pittsburgh landscape. The attempt of urban elites to impose their own will onto the landscape, however, relied upon moral suasion and rational behavior; the political and economic system of industrial America was not particularly responsive to either. Turn-of-the-century Pittsburgh spawned a Civic Club, an Engineers' Society, a Chamber of Commerce, and other civic organizations devoted to urban improvement. These organizations sought an efficient city freed of the burdens of smoke, sewage, traffic, and dilapidation. In the case of the Civic Club, the effort went beyond aesthetics and involved a moral issue: a dirty environment, it was believed, led to crime and immorality. The effort was in part informed by landscape designer Frederick Law Olmsted Sr.'s belief that a healthy atmosphere and environment would directly improve the well-being of urban residents. By providing a healthy and attractive city, with recreation and open space, many of the city's professionals believed that working-class pathologies could be ameliorated.

While improving conditions, the process could also serve the professional and business classes' paternalism and self-interest.[4]

Frederick Law Olmsted Jr. and His Vision for Nine Mile Run Valley

Nine Mile Run was an important element in a larger strategy to bring parks and recreation to the city and upgrade the quality of the urban environment. The valley was one of Pittsburgh's more remarkable landscapes and largest undisturbed areas. It represented Pittsburgh's last remaining public access point to the Monongahela River, since industry had already seized the rest of the waterfront. Located in the city's East End and running north to south, it drained a 6.7 square mile watershed and traversed a steep slope on its southerly course to the river. A variety of communities, including Wilkinsburg, Homewood, Edgewood, and Squirrel Hill surrounded it. For much of the nineteenth century it was of little note, a community of small landowners several miles from the core of Pittsburgh. Photographs from the early 1920s show a lush valley with little development. Uses in the late nineteenth century included a salt mine, a few natural gas wells, several farms and houses, and a small golf course.[5]

Progressive land use advocates for open space and land use controls in Pittsburgh targeted Nine Mile Run for preservation in the early twentieth century. They had three options at their disposal. The first and most direct was to acquire the land for a park and add it to the city's growing park infrastructure. The second was to create a city plan, implement strict zoning, and prevent intrusions into sites such as Nine Mile Run. The third was to let the market take its course. The latter, which was essentially a default, took place, and protected open space in Pittsburgh remained limited to four parks and a smattering of playgrounds.

The struggle for open space in Pittsburgh was part of a much larger effort to exert control over the degradation of the region's air, land, and water. Here the region's turn-of-the-century elites attempted to use the same public policy tools that had failed in the case of sewage treatment and smoke control. In 1909, George Guthrie, a reform mayor and one of the few Democrats elected in the early twentieth century, appointed a Civic Commission to deal with the deteriorating urban landscape. Its mandate was broad but its powers nonexistent. Nevertheless, it represented one of Pittsburgh's first attempts at environmental improvement through a public-private partnership.

The Pittsburgh Civic Commission was made up of the city's top business and professional leaders. Notably lacking was the metals industry. The group interpreted its mandate as one of urban planning and reform, encompassing rail, water, and street systems, public lands and buildings, sewage, control over development, smoke abatement, building codes, and further studies. In sum, the initial desire of the commission was nothing less than a comprehensive city plan with a broad regulatory mandate overseen by impartial representatives such as those on the commission itself. Frederick Law Olmsted Jr., the son of the great landscape designer and architect, was engaged to assist the commission's members in their deliberations. Unfortunately for the commission, Mayor Guthrie left office in 1909 and was replaced by Republican William Magee, nephew of longtime mayor Christopher Magee. Magee had little use for the planning body.[6]

The commission's work grew out of, but failed to embrace the findings of, the Pittsburgh Survey (1909–1914), sponsored by the Russell Sage Foundation.[7] The Survey, an independent review of the city's urban conditions, had documented Pittsburgh's deplorable environmental and social conditions. The commission, however, quickly set aside the Survey's social agenda and instead focused on environmental issues. The Pittsburgh Survey had recommended better working conditions, more sanitary housing, and economic improvement for the region's workers. Representing newer, more professionalized businesses, the Civic Commission's members had no tolerance for the favoritism and patronage of the old machine of Chris Magee. They also had little tolerance for major social changes; they looked to changes in urban systems to gradually bring about social reform. Half the commission's members appeared in the Blue Book, the city's social register; a quarter of the members were lawyers, and over a third were businessmen. Guthrie added four workers, but they were greatly outnumbered. As wealthy residents of the East End, the commission's members strongly embraced the paternalism of the larger reform movement.

The Civic Commission's primary project was its plan for the city, prepared by Frederick Law Olmsted Jr. Olmsted's report, completed in 1910 and published in 1911, was among the commission's better efforts. He recommended a new system of downtown roads and conservation of Pittsburgh's steep slopes. He attempted a comprehensive city plan including improvements in the riverfront, rail links, and street changes. He was also the first to recognize the value of Nine Mile Run:

Perhaps the most striking opportunity noted for a large park is the valley of Nine Mile Run. Its long meadows of varying width would make ideal playfields; the stream, when it is freed from sewage, will be an attractive and interesting element in the landscape; the wooded slopes on either side give ample opportunity for enjoyment of the forest, for shaded walks and cool resting places; and above all it is not far from a large working population in Hazelwood, Homestead, Rankin, Swissvale, Edgewood, Wilkinsburg, Brushton, and Homewood; and yet it is so excluded by its high wooded banks that the close proximity of urban development can hardly be imagined. If taken for park purposes, the entire valley from the top of one bank to the top of the other should be included, for upon the preservation of these wooded banks depends much of the real value of the park.[8]

Magee's administration, however, largely ignored Olmsted's recommendations, except in regard to improving downtown traffic circulation. Magee embraced planning insofar as it dealt with improving transportation and commerce; the explosion of automobile traffic in the downtown business district made improvement imperative. The rest of Olmsted's recommendations—conserving steep slopes and purchasing Nine Mile Run in particular—were ignored. The failure was significant. Olmsted's vision would have provided a variety of open space and aesthetic improvements to the region. Instead, Magee promoted a $10 million bond issue for infrastructure that did not provide for open space, smoke control, or sewer treatment.

The Civic Commission refused to endorse Magee's proposal and urged that the bond issue be defeated. But the bond issue won handily and the Civic Commission faded away. The proposal to purchase the Nine Mile Run valley also faded, but one questions whether Nine Mile Run could have been acquired in this period. Olmsted, for instance, did not aggressively pursue the matter. Having filed his report, he left Pittsburgh and took no active role in the development of the region. Having proposed a park, he left it to his clients on the commission to follow up. The Civic Commission clearly would have preferred that Magee's bond issue provide conservation funding, including the preservation of Nine Mile Run, but the fight over Magee's bonds also seemed to devolve into a grudge match between the commission and Magee. Retaining open space was lost in this fight.[9]

The effort to acquire Nine Mile Run was also subordinated to the city's need for new playgrounds. The Civic Club of Allegheny County, which was also dominated by Blue Book members, sought active recreation rather than open space, and managed to out-compete the Civic Commission's recommendations for scarce city funds. Playground reformers believed that while parks provided passive enjoyment and might satisfy Olmsted's conception of the park as a source of relief for urban tensions, organized playgrounds fulfilled the more important role of socializing children to modern urban society and preparing them for citizenship. The city proceeded to issue bonds throughout the 1910s for playgrounds and to maintain the four existing parks, but no effort was made to acquire Nine Mile Run.[10]

Although Magee disregarded most of Olmsted's recommendations, he did provide support for creation of a Pittsburgh Department of City Planning, the formation of which the state legislature authorized in 1911. The department promptly came up with an action plan that included a review of the road system, an investigation of river improvements, enhancement of public buildings and lands including parks, adequate water supply, smoke abatement, and intergovernmental relations. In sum, it was almost everything the Civic Commission had asked for. Once again, however, advocates for rational use of the landscape were disappointed. The legislature and the City Council gave the department little actual power. Planning was advisory and the department staff and the Planning Commission that oversaw it had no regulatory authority. Nonetheless, in 1912 the Department of City Planning began work on a comprehensive city plan.

In 1913, the Department of City Planning boasted eight staff people, but during World War I its small staff was all but eliminated in a cost-cutting move. No comprehensive plan ever emerged and no new parks were created. Similarly, Magee established a Bureau of Recreation to promote playgrounds, but its professional manager resigned after only two years and little was accomplished. The professional bureaucracy that the community elite had hoped would bring effective government to Pittsburgh collapsed in a few years. Whether it would have been up to the challenge of managing Pittsburgh's diverse needs was never tested.[11]

Nevertheless, planning may have been the most effective remaining means of protecting open space such as Nine Mile Run. As it became increasingly apparent that the Magee administration was not willing to expend funds on land acquisition, land use restrictions became Nine Mile Run's only hope. Indeed, park acquisition was such a low priority that when the H. J. Heinz family offered to donate their East End home and landscaped grounds for a park, the gift was refused because of the maintenance costs. Frick Park, based on the estate of coke and steel baron Henry Clay Frick, had been accepted as a gift only a few years before, and the city was struggling to keep up its existing infrastructure, even though much of it had been donated.[12]

The Citizen's Committee on City Plan's Vision for Nine Mile Run

In 1916, New York City had adopted zoning and Pittsburgh leaders saw it as a model. Zoning did not exist in Pittsburgh prior to 1923. The landscape was at the mercy of whoever happened to own it at any time, and Progressives found the situation increasingly intolerable. On October 26, 1918, Richard B. Mellon and two of his associates invited industrial and civic leaders to meet at Mellon Bank. Mellon, the son of Judge Thomas Mellon and brother of Andrew Mellon, was chief executive officer of Mellon Bank and the financier for much of the region's business activity. The other two were Charles Armstrong, head of Armstrong Cork Company, and James Hailman, the engineer at the City Planning Commission. Fifteen individuals attended the meeting and heard Mellon and Armstrong urge them to discuss city planning and the need for action "to secure for the city the benefits of scientific planning such as is now being applied elsewhere in order to control its proper development, both industrially and socially." The group voted to form a citizens' committee on planning. The involvement of a dominant business figure such as R. B. Mellon clearly had a significant impact on the process.

The Citizens' Committee on City Plan (CCCP) was formed with Armstrong as president and Mellon as vice president. The second meeting was set for November 27. The invitation read, "The object of the organization is the creation of a city plan for Pittsburgh and the development of city planning in all its aspects in the Pittsburgh district. The formation of such a volunteer committee is in line with similar action in the other large cities of the country and is considered not only the best, but practically the only way to secure for Pittsburgh the benefits of scientific and comprehensive City planning, leading to systematic progress along predetermined lines."[13]

The new effort was significant. Six task forces were created to study a range of urban problems in depth. A newsletter, *Progress,* was begun. George Ketchum, a well-known public relations executive, took control of outreach and assembled an eleven-thousand-person mailing list. The several reports amounted to a comprehensive city plan. Although the demographics of the CCCP were similar to that of the Civic Commission—predominantly prominent professionals and business managers—the number and volume of participants was impressive. Frederick Bigger, an architect and planner, served as the professional staff of the committee. The size and economic clout of the committee quickly won major and wide support. Magee, still in office, wisely decided not to cross the committee but instead endorsed its program.[14]

The committee's subcommittee on recreation issued its parks report in 1923. The subcommittee was made up of William H. Robinson of the H. J. Heinz Company, H. Marie Dermit of the Allegheny County Civic Club, James Hailman of the City Planning Department, Grant Hubley of the Oil Well Supply Company, Edgar J. Kaufmann of the downtown department store, Herbert May of the May Drug Company, and Arthur Pierce of Cutler-Hammer Manufacturers. It was a group representing the service industry and the region's civic leadership. No representative of heavy industry was on the committee; instead it was made up of representatives of light manufacturing, of processing, of the retail trades, and of professionals. It was a group that would promote environmental improvement in the region, but not back any extreme measures. Howard Heinz, the thirty-six-year-old chairman of the H. J. Heinz Company, served on the board of the larger committee and worked through Robinson to ensure a strong report. There is no record of dissent from the other members of the panel.[15]

The report harshly criticized the existing method of allocating parks and recreation in the city. They found that recreation was heavily tilted toward the wealthiest communities while working districts lacked access to open space. They also deplored the lack of available land for waterside parks. The subcommittee noted that in the whole Monongahela River valley only Nine Mile Run was adequate as a location for a waterfront park. All the others were foreclosed because of rail, road, or industrial activities at the water line. Most significant for this article, the CCCP Parks Committee recommended that Nine Mile Run be made into an active waterside attraction. The subcommittee dramatically changed the more passive attributes that Olmsted had suggested for the site and recommended a botanical garden, athletic field, camp and picnic grounds, tennis courts, a theater, and a lake with a small beach.

These recommendations reflected the beliefs of subcommittee members that parks should contribute to the overall physical and moral health of the community rather than having any intrinsic value. The subcommittee also hoped that such a recreation-oriented park would offset the undesirable elements of commercial recreation such as were provided at Kennywood Amusement Park, located across the Monongahela River in West Mifflin. Apparently the committee members felt that the latter activities attracted undesirable characters and did not lead to moral improvement. Instead, the committee argued that an investment in so-called healthy recreation was also an investment in public health, contentment, and efficiency.[16]

Historian Roy Lubove dismissed the work of the CCCP with much the same disdain he held for the Civic Commission. For Lubove, both were

made up of business and professional elites who sought bureaucratic ratio-
nalization instead of fundamental change. Yet, there were important dis-
tinctions between the two entities. Much of the Civic Commission's work
was disregarded and the commission itself lacked a following. The CCCP
was much broader and operated with its own professional staff led by
Frederick Bigger, and had induced the city government to endorse its
efforts. Mayor William Magee, a fierce opponent of the Civic Commission,
embraced the committee's work. The committee naively assumed, however, that Nine Mile Run could be acquired and protected, recommending
that public funds be made available for the acquisition. As events would
show, however, time had already run out.[17]

The only other element of the Citizens' Committee's work that
affected Nine Mile Run was its emphasis on zoning and planning. The
committee's recommendations, published in 1923 and adopted by the City
Council, included separate zoning for heavy and light industrial, commercial and low-density and high-density residential areas, as well as limited
building heights in certain zones. The resulting act divided the city's real
estate community and professional elites.[18] The banking and real estate
interests had done well by Pittsburgh's haphazard development styles,
which allowed buyers and sellers to work without regard for the landscape
and free of community oversight or restriction. For the East End residents
of the committee, however, the operations of the free market endangered
not only the physical health of the community, but also its future as a place
to do business. Those who held to the first draft of Pittsburgh's history—
that of unparalleled economic opportunity from rugged individualism—
clashed directly with progressives seeking to place limits on economic use
of natural resources.

The Citizens' Committee members were clearly concerned that further unregulated regional deterioration would drive residents and business
away. Their opponents brought in heavy ammunition to counter them.
United States Senator David Reed testified against the zoning ordinance on
behalf of the banking community and claimed the city's police power
could only be applied for reasons of safety, health, and general welfare, and
not for general civic beauty. "Beauty may be desirable, but liberty is more
so," said Reed. "Neither the City Council nor the state legislature can exercise police powers for aesthetic reasons." The Department of City Planning staff responded that the ordinance carefully avoided aesthetic zoning,
and conceded that it was not authorized. Thus, the zoning advocates were
forced to argue that zoning was not an aesthetic issue but a control of nuisances. This severely limited their ability to keep industrial activity out of
the Nine Mile Run valley.[19]

Moreover, the proposed ordinance was riddled with holes. It gave broad amendatory and variance powers to the City Council, the Planning Department, and to the new Zoning Board of Adjustment. According to the Pittsburgh Regional Planning Association's own published history, where parks and playgrounds were concerned the Citizens' Committee could be little more than a gadfly. It became clear by the late 1920s that the plan was not going to be followed. Frederick Bigger in exasperation noted that "therein lies our community stupidity, for piecemeal planning leads us nowhere."[20] The committee's own newsletter, *Progress,* later complained that "the right of the individual property holder to market his property is superior to the right of the community to control development."[21] All 238 acres of Nine Mile Run valley were zoned residential. The protection that zoning provided, however, came much too late.

The Duquesne Slag Products Company of Pittsburgh had purchased ninety-four acres in Nine Mile Run in September 1922, before enactment of the zoning ordinance, with the intent of disposing waste slag produced in the iron-making process. The Duquesne Company was established in 1906 to dispose of slag primarily from the Jones & Laughlin mills in Pittsburgh and the U.S. Steel Homestead Works in Rankin. By locating their disposal operations so close to the major mills, Duquesne Slag's transportation costs were low, and they were able to gain substantial steel industry business. Jones & Laughlin Steel, in particular, took advantage of the lower price. Although there is no evidence that Duquesne Slag was influenced by the pending zoning decision, it is possible that it made the purchase in order to preempt protective legislation. By making the original purchase, industry was now grandfathered in the valley and Duquesne Slag dominated it for the next seventy years. Located within a few miles of the nation's largest steel mills, Duquesne Slag's Nine Mile Run site gave them a competitive advantage over other disposal companies. Indeed, the company would have the Jones & Laughlin disposal account for the next half-century.[22]

The Citizens' Committee took notice of Duquesne Slag's presence in the Nine Mile Run valley, writing that the use of the valley for industrial purposes would be a mistake and that its natural value far outweighed its value to industry.[23] Like the Civic Commission before it, however, the Citizens' Committee was unwilling to move beyond advocacy toward implementing its proposals directly. The founding of the Western Pennsylvania Conservancy, a voluntary organization devoted to land acquisition for public conservation purposes, was a decade away, and no private effort materialized to buy up the valley for conservation. Nor was there an active lobbying effort for the committee's parks recommendations. As had happened with the zoning ordinance, the committee appeared to expect city government to pick up its recommendations and implement them without a fight. Moreover, the committee made so many recommendations—six volumes worth in all—that it did not have the resources to oversee the implementation of such a broad agenda. Nine Mile Run's acquisition fell by the wayside.

On a more fundamental level, public-private partnerships such as the Citizens' Committee were divorced from the wards and neighborhoods that made up the backbone of Pittsburgh's politics. Despite its newsletter and public relations work, the committee lacked the following needed to enact lasting reform while the Progressive elites who made up the committee eschewed such electioneering. Instead, they relied on persuasion and publicity, which did not reach the larger polity. The committee's successors, including the Allegheny Conference on Community Development, faced a similar tension between elite programs centered on the central business district, and the aspirations of neighborhood and community-based organizations.

Duquesne Slag did not purchase the entire valley at once. Beginning on the western slope and progressing eastward, the company made purchases slowly over forty years, from 1922 to 1962. By doing so, the company avoided controversy for some time. Because Duquesne Slag owned property in the Nine Mile Run valley prior to the creation of zoning, their industrial use of what was zoned residential land was deemed a "non-conforming use" and allowed to proceed. Indeed, there was no significant effort to prevent the creation of the slag pile. Incredibly, Duquesne Slag continued to claim a "non-conforming use" for every additional parcel of land they purchased, even though those lands were zoned residential and were not part of the original ninety-four acres acquired in 1922.[24]

According to Duquesne Slag, dumping began in 1922. The company used heavy equipment to remove metallics from the slag after dumping—probably large magnets—in order to sell any scrap that might have been mixed in with the slag. The company kept an employee on site to check the slag as it came in—by barge and by rail—to ensure that it did not contain other wastes. However, over the years, other types of wastes, including fly ash and abandoned cars, were dumped in Nine Mile Run, probably surreptitiously. The slag pile was built up in the center, but tapered off as it approached residential areas. The slag was watered as it was dumped in order to reduce some of the dust, and the location of the major dumping grounds in a valley reduced the residential areas exposed to the noise. The earliest dumping was clustered on approximately half of the original ninety-four acres, the remainder being unsuitable land. The slag pile grew quickly. Aerial photographs of Nine Mile Run show a slag pile twenty to twenty-five feet in height in 1937, covering the northern and western portions of the property.[25]

The Failure to Protect Neighborhood Environments: The Case of Swisshelm Park

As the slag pile expanded beyond its early boundaries, it ran into a hailstorm of opposition from surrounding neighborhoods. These community activists operated, however, without any connection to the reform agenda of the city's professional and business leadership. The link between business professionals and community organizations was never made and remains a weakness in the region's development agenda to this day.

While the Allegheny Conference and the city government were launching the Pittsburgh Renaissance in 1945 with a mission of environmental improvement and modernization of the city's infrastructure, Duquesne Slag Products Company was purchasing more land in the Nine Mile Run valley. Their total holdings increased to nearly two hundred acres, and the slag pile expanded along with the purchases. Throughout the Second World War, according to residents of the area, three shifts a day worked unloading slag. A rail spur had been built directly into the valley to facilitate disposal, with as many as twenty trains a days carrying between 185 and 200 tons of hot slag each dumping their cargo. At the same time, the Squirrel Hill and Swisshelm Park neighborhoods expanded, bringing more and more people into the general vicinity of the slag pile. The result was politically combustible.[26]

Swisshelm Park is a once rural community in the easternmost section of Pittsburgh that had become a middle-class residential area. It bordered Nine Mile Run on its southeastern corner. As the slag pile advanced eastward, noise and dust pervaded the community. In 1937, citizens of the neighborhood incorporated the Swisshelm Park Civic Association. One of the main concerns of the association, if not its main concern, was noise and dust from the slag operations. In 1936, the citizens of the area petitioned the Henry Clay Frick estate and the city to purchase the northeastern portion of the valley for inclusion in Frick Park in order to ensure that the slag pile would not extend to Swisshelm Park, but with no success. The Civic Association continued the effort and formally petitioned the city for the purchase. Not surprisingly, the requests were rebuffed for lack of funds.[27]

Beginning in 1942, the Civic Association engaged in what at first were friendly, and then more strident, protests against Duquesne Slag's noise levels. Duquesne Slag rejected the complaints, noting that increasing population in the area was bringing more and more people onto the perimeter of their property, and implying that the homeowners should have known they were moving next to an active industrial site. That Duquesne Slag had only recently acquired much of the property in question was not mentioned. In 1946, after letters to the company produced unsatisfactory results, the Civic Association appealed to the Board of Zoning Adjustment, complaining that the noise levels were in violation of the area's residential zoning.

In January 1947, the Board of Zoning Adjustment rejected the association's complaint, noting that Duquesne Slag's use of the site was a nonconforming use by virtue of their preexisting ownership. That the activity in question was taking place well outside of the original 1922 land purchase did not affect the board's decision. The association protested that the noise levels were inappropriate regardless of zoning, but the board's staff declined to reconsider the matter, referring the association to the courts. The board's cavalier dismissal of the association's complaint and appeal are remarkable in that they refused to give any consideration to the association's position or to investigate the matter. The association's complaint included a protest against blasting and use of heavy equipment at odd hours. The board merely noted that the operation in question had been going on for some time, including a period prior to the enactment of zoning, and that therefore the issue was outside of their jurisdiction.[28]

In 1950, Duquesne Slag decided to end rail disposal of slag and instead shift entirely to barges. Rail rates had been increasing and barge transport was a more inexpensive means of moving the waste materials. At first, the company began to build a wharf without any notice to the city and without a permit. As the Civic Association raised questions, however, Duquesne Slag decided to request a change in the area's zoning. To construct a wharf, loading docks, and to increase truck traffic in the area, management decided to attempt to have a portion of Nine Mile Run deemed industrial. The company asked the Zoning Board of Adjustments to rezone the portion of Nine Mile Run fronting the Monongahela River. The board quickly approved the request and forwarded it to City Council for final action. A quick hearing was called at which community members strongly objected to the change, noting that it would leave the southern end of the valley open to any industrial use Duquesne Slag or a future owner might deem appropriate. In addition, residents complained of the truck traffic, noise, and nuisance of the slag operation. Moreover, they formally objected to Duquesne Slag's use of a residential area for industrial purposes. Nonetheless, City Council scheduled final action on the bill for May 29.[29]

On May 28, the Swisshelm Park Civic Association called an emergency meeting to formulate a strategy. They resolved to seek a postponement of the council's action in order to marshal their forces and to appear in large numbers during the City Council hearings. The association resolved to take direct action to prevent rezoning.[30] On May 29, 1950, several dozen members of the Civic Association appeared before City Council and objected to passage of the rezoning ordinance. Surprised by the number of opponents, council pushed back the date of final passage by a week and called another hearing.

On June 5, 1950, Duquesne Slag Products backpedaled and sought to make concessions. They offered to build a footbridge over the areas of heaviest truck activity, to minimize noise, to oil the road to prevent dust, and to otherwise quiet its operations. They also agreed to cease all rail operations in the area—although this was already their intention, given the cost of rail transport. The company also indicated that it wanted to fill in the slag pile. When asked how long this might take, the company's attorney estimated the time at less than a decade. Swisshelm Park's witnesses instead demanded that council turn down the legislation and disallow further use of the site for slag disposal. Their proposal fell on deaf ears. Councilmen Weir and Fagan repeatedly noted that they were powerless to stop the slag disposal operation and stated that the company had a right to dump on its land regardless of past zoning. The council quietly enacted the rezoning bill in July.[31]

Duquesne Slag kept none of its promises. In 1954 the Swisshelm Park Civic Association petitioned City Council again, noting that noise, dust, and improper use of residential land threatened their property values and possibly their health. On March 29, another hearing was called. Duquesne Slag protested that they had kept their promises, but had not constructed a footbridge over their truck route on the grounds that few pedestrians ever ventured into the valley. Members of the association testified that City Council should not permit further use of residential land for industrial purposes. They noted that Duquesne Slag was dumping on over ninety acres of land outside of their original 1922 purchase and that the land was zoned residential. Moreover, the association testified that the company had built a scrap metal recovery facility on-site without a permit. This new operation was located outside the original lands of Duquesne Slag and was clearly not subject to a nonconforming use exemption. Jack Buncher of the Buncher Company, a contractor managing the scrap recovery operation, stated bluntly that interference in the slag and scrap operation would threaten the survival of Jones & Laughlin Steel Company and with it the city's economic health. Rather than taking action, council referred the matter to the city solicitor's office for a legal opinion. On February 14, 1955, nearly a year later, the city solicitor filed a brief report that acquiesced in Duquesne Slag's fait accompli. Ignoring the case built by Swisshelm Park, the solicitor noted that if Duquesne Slag shut down now, an eyesore would be created and that continued filling of the slag pile would be beneficial. On that basis, the dumping could continue. With that, the city government let the matter drop.[32]

Frustrated by the city's inability to protect their interests, Swisshelm Park retained the law firm of Thorp, Reed, and Armstrong to pursue legal action. After sending letters to Duquesne Slag and meeting with representatives of the company, attorney Frank Gaffney advised the association against any further action. Enjoining Duquesne Slag, wrote Gaffney, would require questionable legal proceedings at great cost to the association's small treasury. Thorp, Reed, and Armstrong, however, had a conflict of interest. The firm represented Allegheny Asphalt, a company doing business with Duquesne Slag and which had previously been sued by residents of Second Avenue in Hazelwood, along with Duquesne Slag, for nuisances in that neighborhood. Thorp, Reed, and Armstrong never disclosed this conflict; Thomas Horrocks of Swisshelm Park discovered it in 1956 and brought it to the law firm's attention. The association ended its relationship with Thorp, Reed, and Armstrong, but never had its day in court.[33]

In 1958 the city of Pittsburgh enacted a new zoning statute. Duquesne Slag Products succeeded in having the entire Nine Mile Run valley zoned "S"—special use—a level of zoning which allowed their operations to continue. The 1958 rezoning mooted the Swisshelm Park Civic Association's zoning case against the company. The association protested the change and urged that the land remain a residential zone, but met with the same indifference from City Council as before. Nevertheless, the association continued to monitor the site carefully, filing repeated nuisance and zoning complaints against Duquesne Slag for the next twenty years. Although the group was an annoyance to Duquesne Slag in that period, no substantive action to change company policy occurred. The city government's administrative functions had completely and utterly failed to protect the Nine Mile Run valley, and the association's private law firm was too heavily conflicted to represent the community's interests. The last slag was dumped on the site around 1972; by then, approximately seventeen million cubic yards of slag filled the valley nearly from end to end.[34]

Fulfilling the Vision

During the 1980s, several plans for the development of Nine Mile Run were made. In 1982, for instance, the Department of City Planning explored the possibilities for residential and light industrial development, but could not attract a developer. In 1987, J. J. Gumberg, a shopping center developer, obtained an option to buy the site and proposed to build a shopping and office center on it. Citizens from nearby residential areas, however, objected to highway construction related to the Gumberg plan and were able to block development. Finally, in October 1995, after a private developer had constructed a block of upper-income housing (Rosemont) close to the edge of the slag heap, thus confirming the viability of residential housing at that site, the city of Pittsburgh purchased the 238-acre location for $3.8 million.[35] The city selected Cooper, Robertson & Partners, a landscape development firm, to prepare a master plan to begin the transformation of Nine Mile Run into a residential complex and an associated greenway.[36]

The Cooper, Robertson plan was imaginative in many ways, providing for an innovative urban neighborhood oriented toward pedestrian uses, landscape remediation, and steep slope modification and vegetation. But it recommended culverting the uncovered part of the stream in order to provide a land bridge connecting both sides of the site. This plan to bury the stream was reviewed and questioned by a group of faculty at Carnegie Mellon University who secured funding from the Heinz Family Foundation to prepare an alternative plan that focused on restoring the stream as an essential element of the public space within the development. That plan, with an outline of how to restore the stream, coupled with the untenable costs of moving slag, resulted in the Cooper, Robertson plans' modification to include an open stream channel as a feature of the greenway running through the property.

The Cooper, Robertson master plan accepted by the city for the site envisioned an extension of Frick Park through the slag to the Monongahela River and construction of mixed-income housing. Community involvement in the city's design and management of the site was strikingly different in regard to past actions at the site. Public meetings on both the design of the housing and the extension of Frick Park were held. An important public-private partnership involving local groups and including the Swisshelm Park Civic Association, the Squirrel Hill Urban Coalition, the developer, the city, and a team of experts from Carnegie Mellon University and the University of Pittsburgh, was formed to guide development. Leadership in housing and landscaping design was undertaken by Summerset Land Development Associates, a partnership of the development groups and the Commonwealth of Pennsylvania, the city of Pittsburgh, the Urban Redevelopment Authority of Pittsburgh, and Equitable Gas Company. Changes were made to the size and the scope of the housing development in order to reduce the concerns of surrounding communities about traffic and potentially health-threatening dust concerns. The site was graded with careful monitoring of airborne dust. The developer proceeded to level the slag hills and piles, cover them with fill and topsoil, lay out streets, and construct model houses on the site. When completed, the site will include 710 single-family homes, townhouses, and luxury apartments set in three interconnected neighborhoods. The new development, known as Summerset at Frick Park, has been chosen as one of the Department of Energy's national flagship communities in its Building America / PATH partnership.[37]

Carnegie Mellon University's Studio for Creative Inquiry provided leadership on the greenway (public space) plan, along with the Pittsburgh Department of City Planning, 3 Rivers Wet Weather Inc., and the Pennsylvania Department of Environmental Protection. The greenway includes a mile-and-a-half-long greenway trail, which connects the Monongahela River, Frick Park, and the communities of Edgewood, Swissvale, Wilkinsburg, and Pittsburgh. The trail emerges from the wooded Frick Park with a restored stream-channel and wetlands and then passes under a major street (Commercial Avenue) and along the newly vegetated slag slopes before ending where Nine Mile Run meets the Monongahela River. The sewer problems affecting water quality in the stream, originally identified by Frederick Olmsted Jr., will finally be addressed. The stream will be restored to a natural meander within its original floodplain, with the U.S. Army Corps of Engineers constructing a wetlands to absorb wet weather storm surges. A meadow will be turned into a soccer and baseball field with an adjacent parking lot.

The city is now in the process of recreating aspects of Olmsted's and Bigger's vision at Nine Mile Run, but one has to carefully reconsider what has passed before. The failure of civic leadership and community-based organizations to cooperate, even to communicate, in the face of the disaster at Nine Mile Run is obvious. The paternalism of the Civic Commission and Citizens' Committee may have made such cooperation impossible. Thereafter, the Allegheny Conference and the Pittsburgh Renaissance for the most part ignored the area in favor of the central business district. Swisshelm Park, as a neighborhood, lacked the resources and the clout to affect the outcome at Nine Mile Run. Whether collaboration among the city's professional and business leaders and its neighborhoods might have changed the outcome is a tantalizing "what if." The complicity of the city of Pittsburgh in the destruction of Nine Mile Run is significant. The Zoning Board of Adjustment and the city solicitor ignored their own ordinances and procedures in favor of Duquesne Slag's operations. The mayor's office ignored repeated requests from civic leaders to buy the valley and protect it. The need of the steel industry for cheap disposal sites took precedence over community health and the interests of future generations.

Whatever the failures and weaknesses of the neighborhoods and the Progressive-era environmental reformers, they do not excuse the lack of leadership in the city. As Roy Lubove points out, Progressive reformers were elites with little public support. The coalition favoring environmental improvement did not seek broader political and social intervention that might have overcome Magee's opposition to open space or have prevented Duquesne Slag from doing damage to the valley. Bureaucratic management, in the end, was not able—and often did not try—to stem the sea of waste and pollution that was enveloping Pittsburgh and the industrial heart of America. Community groups without the backing of civic leadership could do little but complain.

Of the variables involved in the decision to turn Pittsburgh's most promising park site with river access into a slag pile, some were endemic to the city. These included a tradition of decentralized decision making that made it difficult to impose the community's will on the landscape. Other variables were less parochial and might include the unwillingness of government to intervene in the modification of the landscape, the lack of power and resources available to bureaucratic professionals in the city and in civic institutions, the weakness of neighborhood groups in large cities, and the business community's inability to police itself. These variables effectively undermined public-private partnerships in their effort to prevent the loss of irreplaceable landscapes such as Nine Mile Run. Moreover, they point to the weakness of such partnerships in the early to mid-twentieth century: lacking political power and economic resources, they were no match for heavy industry.

Beyond Celebration

Pittsburgh and Its Region in the Environmental Era— Notes by a Participant Observer

SAMUEL P. HAYS

IN THE EARLY 1970s when I began inquiries into modern environmental affairs I decided that they should include state and local as well as national activities. But I also found that this line of study faced a major roadblock. Each state and locality seemed to be convinced that its own environmental actions were superior to those of others, and around this self-satisfaction each had erected a climate of celebration of its environmental virtues that seemed to differ markedly from observations of its environmental circumstances. Hence, I wanted to find some way of exploring both environmental practices and environmental images, what people did as well as what they professed to believe.[1]

I readily found that Pittsburgh was a useful case study. The city's main activists in shaping its self-images, such as the media and the city's institutional leaders, were eager to define Pittsburgh's accomplishments in "cleaning up" the city's air to reflect a major change from its smoky past; yet daily around me there was evidence of considerable resistance from the city's industries to air pollution programs and a tendency of its most vocal leaders to backtrack on what the city had purportedly accomplished. At the same time, I observed few efforts among those leaders to establish continuing improvement in air quality as one of the community's main objectives. Here was a typical case, which I encountered in examining many such state and community environmental circumstances, of a vast difference between celebration and practice.[2]

The observations about Pittsburgh presented here are derived from forty years of "participant observation" of the city and region's environmental affairs. This includes my presence at innumerable meetings, participation in conferences, conversations with many individuals, public lectures presented in a variety of civic venues, papers prepared for presentation in administrative and legislative forums, environmental courses taught at the University of Pittsburgh, and assistance to a variety of groups in their attempts to understand and cope with environmental circumstances. While some of these experiences were documented, many were not but serve as accumulated personal experiences which contributed to the development of general impressions about the city's environmental affairs. Over the years this combination of participation and observation generated a picture of an environmental culture distinctive to the Pittsburgh region and forms an important source for this essay.

At the same time as I was involved in Pittsburgh environmental affairs, I came to think and write about national environmental activities through the accumulation of documentary evidence derived from many sources. These also helped to shape a concept of environmental culture in comparative terms involving the varied levels and elements of environmental culture in different cities, states, and regions. This perspective suggested an examination of how Pittsburgh was similar or different from other geographical areas in terms of its environmental culture. That mode of thinking plays an important role in this essay as a method for identifying more precisely the city's distinctive environmental characteristics. Thus this essay is a combination of my personal experience as a "participant observer" of the city's environmental affairs and comparative analysis within a broad framework.

Pittsburgh's Environmental Circumstance

Two interrelated sets of environmental circumstances are basic to this venture in urban environmental history: the natural environment surrounding the city and the region that generated either inspiration or resignation, and the level of environmental culture displayed by its people and its institutions. One involves the region's natural assets and physical environmental characteristics. The other involves the region's human environmental assets, its environmental institutions, the role of environmental affairs in its media, its government, its educational focus, and its search for environmental knowledge and understanding—in short, the range of factors that combine to form its human environmental culture. As I proceeded in the role of "participant observer" in the environmental affairs of the city, region, and state I was continually seeking answers enabling me to trace and identify these themes.

The stimulating, even inspirational role of positive natural environmental assets are an integral part of environmental engagement in many places: the Sierra Nevadas in California, the Adirondacks in New York, the Chesapeake or San Francisco Bays, the North Country of the Great Lakes, the southern Appalachians, or the massive wetlands of the South. Over the years such amenities have helped to define the environmental meaning of many a region. That definition has been sharpened when such amenities have been organized into formally designated natural assets such as national or state parks, forests, wildlife refuges, or "natural areas." These have brought to the region not only visibility but professional skills associated with their management that add a critical mass of environmental skills and leadership resources and they have served as magnets for public interest and visitation.

The Pittsburgh region possesses few such marked environmental assets and has a history that has given little emphasis to those that do exist. The state's demography is defined largely by two major metropolitan centers in its southeast and its southwest, and a large, relatively forested, and rural area in between which has aroused little attention from its urban centers. To most of the urban inhabitants the state's north and interior are relatively unknown. The North-Central Highlands above Interstate 80, for example, has as large an area of public lands and a similar balance of public and private lands as the Adirondacks in New York. In fact, the early interest in establishing a Pennsylvania state forest system drew heavily for its inspiration on the Adirondack example. But while the Adirondacks played a major role in defining the natural environmental context of New York state environmental activity, the Pennsylvania North-Central Highlands have not.[3]

Pennsylvania has few nationally managed natural environmental assets. There is only one national natural park, associated with the middle and upper Delaware Rivers, and only two small wildlife refuges. It has a number of national historic sites which provide some focus with their associated natural areas, but whose natural values are rarely emphasized. The state park system includes a number of units in western Pennsylvania that are known as recreational assets, but have not yet evolved into a regionwide system of natural assets and play only a limited role in the environmental lives of people in the region. And the Allegheny National Forest remains for most Pittsburghers a largely unknown area "up north" that comes into their vision only occasionally.

Pittsburgh's own environment has long suffered from environmental degradation because of its industrial history—for instance, the massive acidic water pollution arising from coal mining, which still renders many of its streams an environmental liability rather than an asset, and air pollution from coal burning and the steel mills, which have left a legacy of soil degradation. One regional asset is its extensive city and county park systems, though the city parks have experienced cycles of care and neglect. The recent creation of the Pittsburgh Parks Conservancy provides a new focus on the city parks, although thus far the organization seems to be more concerned with physical rehabilitation of structures in the city's parks than with using the parks to inspire the community around natural values.[4] The county parks, however, remain in mediocre condition. The legacy of this industrial past has prompted the region to be self-conscious and apologetic of its environmental limitations.

Closely associated, and perhaps in causal tandem, with the region's lack of positive environmental assets is a limited level of environmental culture. While there were a number of significant past cases of environment initiative, many of these have not advanced or have moved only sporadically. Decision makers often seem to be relatively apathetic in incorporating environmental objectives into regional thinking and action about present and future community values. This is in contrast to vigorous emphasis on other realms of civic enterprise such as sports, arts and culture, medical and educational resources, and job growth and development.

A sharper sense of this can be identified and explored through comparative analysis of the environmental activities and achievements of other states, regions, and cities. City comparisons are difficult because of a lack of comparative data, but some will be made along specialized categories later in the chapter. State comparisons, however, are possible, and here Pennsylvania comes out at about the middle: at the low end of a range of urbanized states in the East, the North, and the Pacific Coast, and at the upper end of more rural, Southern, and mountain states in regard to environmental programs and assets. Long-term analysis of environmental voting patterns in Congress place Pennsylvania elected representatives at a similar middle level.[5]

Such observations can also be made at a regional level, showing the general level of support for environmental objectives as reflected in economic, media, educational, and professional institutions. Environmental culture includes the vigor and liveliness of public participation in environmental organizations and affairs; the extent of the environmental curriculum in secondary and higher education; the quality of its newspaper reporting and observations; and the degree to which the public leaders of a city and region define present community circumstances and future goals in environmental terms. This culture also includes how governments spend their resources, especially what they borrow funds to finance; the sources within the community from which they draw their environmental advisors and leaders; the degree to which both private and public leaders establish themselves as vigorous advocates of environmental progress as a basis for shaping the community's future; the level of popular interest in environmental self-education; and the degree to which those who dominate the scientific work in community institutions see their role as supporting environmental progress rather than restraining it.[6]

As this analysis of Pittsburgh's environmental context proceeds, we shall be focusing not just on the region's wider environmental circumstances, but also on the state and evolution of its environmental culture. But first we establish a setting for such a focus through a brief overall foray into the region's environmental history.

Pittsburgh's Recent Environmental History: A Brief Sketch

The high point in post–World War II environmental activity in the Pittsburgh region came in the late 1960s and early 1970s. It was marked by the expansion of the state parks system led by Maurice Goddard, in which the Western Pennsylvania Conservancy played a significant role by brokering the acquisition of most of the western Pennsylvania state parks. We now consider these as major past accomplishments. This initiative, however, has long since ended, and the state park system has added no new acreage since 1970. Pennsylvania is one of six states who have less state park acreage in 2000 than in 1970.[7] While the Conservancy looks back to this time in listing its accomplishments, its own work in acquiring large blocks of forested environmental amenities came to a halt with the fiasco of the Presidential Oil Tract. This event led to such opposition to the Conservancy's land acquisition policy in the northwestern part of the state and in the state legislature that the Conservancy's future role may be confined to only limited land acquisitions.[8]

These years surrounding 1970 were also marked by significant state and local action, which often dovetailed in air and water pollution matters.[9] Pittsburgh lawmakers in the state legislature played an important role in both sets of issues, and Republican Governor Raymond Schaeffer was an especially important figure in pressing the state's new environmental policy and program. Extremely noteworthy were the combined role of water quality and surface mine reclamation legislation that were deeply significant for southwestern Pennsylvania with its heavy involvement in coal mining. The problem here was the enormous environmental degradation that had been brought to the region by the coal industry. Many of the region's streams—half of the stream mileage is a reasonable figure—were so polluted with acid mine drainage that they were unusable as sources of industrial water, potable drinking water, or aquatic habitat. The legislation was well crafted—water should be made cleaner but, more important, strip mines would have to be reclaimed by restoring the overburden and providing a new vegetative cover. With time the required cover was enhanced in ways ranging from simply planting a few trees to restoring the entire plant community to its original quality and flora.

The new program, however, fulfilled only a limited amount of its promise. The coal industry fought its implications, which gave rise to a new federal surface mine control act in 1977 that was crafted not to mimic the Pennsylvania program but to enable that program to become effective under the pressures of the industry to demolish it.[10] As time went on, however, the administration of the combined requirements of state and national legislation were also stymied by the industry. The industry would post a bond to finance state-sponsored reclamation if it had not done the reclamation itself, but the bond required did not keep pace with inflation, and hence the need greatly exceeded the resources. Unreclaimed coal lands were the order of the day. Pressure from citizen groups on the Department of Environmental Resources and its successor, the Department of Environmental Protection, led to little improvement, and the lawsuits which they brought to the issue lingered without results over the years. The environmental degradation from coal mining in the region remains a major regional environmental liability. A similar story could be told for the oil and gas drilling industry.

The early 1970s also held great promise for improving the air quality of the Pittsburgh region. Considerable strides toward that objective had been made earlier, less by the role of government through ordinances and more by the decisions of homeowners and commercial establishments to shift from coal to natural gas as a fuel. These developments occurred in the latter part of the 1940s and greatly reduced smoke and soot. By the end of the 1960s the major source of air pollution problems had shifted from home and commercial heating to industrial sources, especially the utility and steel industries. This new phase of the history of air pollution in Pittsburgh involved a combination of county ordinance, state law, and the federal Clean Air Act of 1970; together they brought a new initiative to efforts to improve regional air quality. The Pittsburgh Chamber of Commerce, however, strenuously opposed the local ordinance and the state law and regulations, but the United Steelworkers of America and the recently formed citizen's organization, the Group against Smog and Pollution (GASP), provided strong support.[11]

But this vigorous activity came to a close by the end of the 1970s. Political support at the level of the County Commissioners declined, and the County Health Department became more of a compliance agency to implement federal requirements rather than forging and implementing the county's own measures in a progressive fashion. This change was underscored when Duquesne Light, which had played a major role in the earlier era by installing sulfur-dioxide "scrubber" technology on two of its Allegheny County power plants at Elrama and Phillips, declined to install them on its third plant at Cheswick despite earlier agreements to do so. The Allegheny County Health Department approved this change. Industry became a much more dominant influence in air pollution matters and the County Commissioners and the health department both became far more inclined to protect industry from advanced control requirements than to foster them.

Resistance to federal air pollution control initiatives was even more evident in the debates over new Environmental Protection Agency (EPA) efforts to control ozone arising from both automobile and utility emissions. On these issues the overwhelming interest of the region's political and economic leaders in job growth and development persuaded them to focus on "compliance" with federal requirements rather than pursue progressive air quality improvement. The most dramatic issue of the 1990s was their firm opposition to the proposed EPA inspection and maintenance program for automobiles. In a series of events, Pittsburgh and its region demonstrated how sharply it had declined from its support of air quality improvement in the 1970s.[12] Recent evidence of this decline was the proposal, firmly backed by the new county executive, Jim Roddy, to merge the county's air pollution control program with that of the state, thus ending the potential ability of the county to exercise leadership in a progressive program to improve air quality. Such an action would define the county's program more firmly as one of compliance with objectives set elsewhere rather than community initiative and leadership.

Perhaps the most readily visible symbol of the decline in environmental affairs in the state, and by implication in the region since those heady days of the early 1970s, was the fate of the so-called environmental rights amendment to the state constitution that Pennsylvania voters approved in 1970. This provided a strong statement of the "right" of Pennsylvanians to enjoy clean air, clean water, and a natural environment, a statement that often conveys to people in the state an image of Pennsylvania's environmental culture. But in a massive turnabout from the days in which that amendment was passed, the commonwealth courts ruled that the amendment was not "self-enforcing," that it had no force or effect unless and until the legislature passed enabling legislation. It was not even interpreted so as to require an "environmental impact analysis" similar to that in federal law.[13]

Of equal importance in the state's frustrated environmental objectives was the quiet erosion of the project to develop an "environmental master plan." This was mandated in the statute establishing the new Department of Environmental Resources, and a number of task forces were formed to focus on specific aspects of the state's environment. Considerable optimism was expressed that the plan would provide guidance for a progressive state environmental program. Two closely related proposals were for a state natural area program and a state natural history survey, similar to those in Ohio and Illinois, that would give focus to the state's natural assets and establish a firm basis for future policies devoted to natural areas.[14] Over the course of the 1970s working groups related to these proposals within the department seemed to provide some enthusiasm for continuing the momentum of the early part of the decade. But these efforts languished and few of the resulting ideas were turned into policy; within several years they were all but forgotten.

Pittsburgh's Environmental Self-Image

Despite the limited level of its environmental culture, and perhaps because of it, the city and the region have sought to perpetuate a myth of vigorous levels of environmental achievement. This appears to be a common characteristic of many a city, region, and state, but the contrast between professed myth and achievement is especially marked in Pittsburgh. I will therefore identify several instances of community mythology in order to establish their role in obscuring the community's limited level of environmental culture.

One such myth is the community's record on reducing air pollution.[15] Through a combination of leadership from Mayor David Lawrence and banker and civic leader Richard King Mellon, so the argument goes, the city government took up the task of reforming the "smoky city" in an action that reflects, still to this day, the city's environmental commitment. From such action the city's air pollution was greatly reduced. Many an analysis of Pittsburgh's recent urban history recounts those events with great pride.

The record is otherwise. The city's smoke was greatly reduced after World War II, less by the role of government through local ordinances and more by the decisions of homeowners to switch from coal to natural gas and by railroad adoption of diesel-electric locomotives. The major sources of heavy smoke came from coal burning in homes and in locomotives. The ordinance which the city council adopted was intended to follow the St. Louis example of requiring that only "smokeless solid fuel" ("processed" coal), which burned far more cleanly, be sold in the city. Implementation of the ordinance, however, was postponed during World War II and did not come into effect until October 1947. Over the same period of time, pipelines were constructed which carried natural gas from the Texas gas fields to the northeast, and homeowners quickly took up this new source of heat. It was slightly more expensive than coal, but far cleaner and much easier for homeowners to use; by 1950 approximately 65 percent of homeowners used the cleaner fuel. The switch in fuel by locomotives from coal to diesel was well underway over the same period of time, and while it might well have been that Richard King Mellon helped to persuade the railroads to speed up that transition, it was due far more to the economic advance of new fuels and new locomotive engines than to any act of city or county government (see Mershon and Tarr, this volume).[16]

If one takes the longer view, the more pervasive conclusion is that progressive steps in improving air quality after the initial drive to control smoke came about from a variety of influences, including some from county political leaders and mobilization of public sentiment and some from the United Steelworkers, who held the nation's first citizen air pollution conference in Washington, D.C., in 1969 and played an important role in persuading Governor Raymond Schaeffer to adopt more stringent air quality standards. Combined, these influences won out over the stubborn resistance of the city's Chamber of Commerce and other representatives of industry.

Over the years since then, progress in cleaner air has come primarily from action at the federal level in which the Group against Smog and Pollution (GASP), has played a crucial role at the local level. At the present time, small gains have been made along the route of cleaner air, but at the same time new recruits have been added to the environmental opposition. This was most notable after the federal Clean Air Act of 1990 when the American Automobile Association of Southwestern Pennsylvania took up the leadership in mobilizing its troops and the auto repair shops of the region against EPA's proposed inspection and maintenance program. The rather remarkable role of GASP as a relatively small but technically knowledgeable and determined group of citizens to move continually for progressive air quality improvement is well known among national citizen clean air groups. It is one of the few such environmental groups distinctive to the Pittsburgh region that is well respected beyond the community.[17]

An equally exaggerated world of achievement has risen around the figure of Rachel Carson, whose past is affirmed in the region through the Rachel Carson Homestead, a center for nature education; the Rachel Carson Institute at Chatham College where she earned her college degree; and through annual events in which her role in the nation's environmental affairs is celebrated. In various venues at the time of her birthday speakers regularly praise her association with the city and the region. The state even named the office building which houses its Department of Environmental Protection the Rachel Carson building. Such efforts continually call up positive associations with the environmental cause and give the region a self-identity that exudes a feeling of self-satisfaction.

This symbolic identification with a regional hero, however, fails to observe that Rachel Carson is one of the most tragic figures of modern environmental affairs. For while she was eminently successful in establishing a general sense of the environmental role of toxic chemicals, the control she sought of those chemicals has been one of the greatest failures of modern environmental policy. The personal tragedy of Rachel Carson—to be so revered and yet so completely ignored in public policy—was perpetuated in Pittsburgh in a variety of venues. Among them was the almost complete absence within the city of attempts to implement her major objective of seeking to reduce the level of toxic chemicals to which humans and the environment were exposed. This included coverage of relevant public policies in the media, the activities of nature centers such as the Rachel Carson Homestead and Beechwood Farms, the Pittsburgh Science Center, and the curriculum of colleges and universities.[18]

Carson was deeply attuned to the policy issues, and yet those in Pittsburgh that seek to celebrate her name also avoid association with activities which defined her role in the nation's public affairs. The current debate over the implementation of the 1996 federal Food Safety and Protection Act, for example, the modern venue for pesticide issues dealing with human health, includes no serious advocate for the act in the Pittsburgh region.[19] The personal tragedy of Rachel Carson, that the celebration of her life runs in tandem with such a massive failure of public discussion of policies she espoused, is a major example of the striking gap between environmental self-congratulation and practice in Pittsburgh.

Pittsburgh's State of Environmental Culture

The relatively low level of environmental culture which the Pittsburgh region has displayed over the past few decades, and continues to display, can be tracked through several of the region's institutions: (1) citizen organizations that define and advance environmental objectives; (2) media that chart positive environmental directions in comparison with similar directions in economic development, sports, arts, travel, and tourism; (3) education at primary and secondary levels and especially in higher education; (4) community leadership which might or might not chart new stages in environmental progress; and (5) bookstores where shelves of books deal with public environmental issues.

Citizen Organizations and the Media

The infrastructure of Pittsburgh citizens' environmental organizations, despite several decades of their existence, remains rather limited in comparison with other regions. The individual organizations can be counted almost on one hand: the Group against Smog and Pollution (GASP), Clean Water Action, the Citizen's Coal Project, and the Sierra Club. Of these, Clean Water Action and the Sierra Club are branches of national organizations that have state chapters as well as local groups and draw much of their resources in public affairs from that larger affiliation. Two local citizen organizations, GASP and the Citizen's Coal Project, have maintained a sustained and independent presence in the region for many years with some national recognition. In more recent years the Allegheny Defense Project, based at Clarion, Pennsylvania, but with a Pittsburgh branch, has been able to establish a forum for citizen action pertaining to the Allegheny National Forest. And, more recently, the organization Penn's Future, a statewide group, has also established a Pittsburgh staff person and office.

While these organizations have been able to establish an independent presence in Pittsburgh, others have not. For many years Pittsburgh maintained an affiliate of the American Lung Association, a major advocate on the national scene for continually improved air quality programs. But this local branch, which originated as a tuberculosis association in the form of a fund-raising Easter Seal League, refused to work with GASP on programs to curb air pollution and, in fact, publicly opposed efforts in the mid and late 1990s to advance national pollution control measures. These tendencies led the Pittsburgh American Lung Association to dissociate itself from the national association and to become an entirely separate organization stressing lung diseases not associated with air pollution.

The regional branch of the National Audubon Society, in sharp contrast with many branches elsewhere, has usually declined to participate in actions to foster public policies advanced by the national society. On occasion it joined with other public-issue-oriented organizations in the Pittsburgh region, most notably when a network of Pittsburgh organizations drew together to support the Alaska Lands Act. Since the 1970s the regional Audubon Society has preoccupied itself with the development of its nature center, Beechwood Farms, and its environmental education program for children. It has declined to participate in public issues, even to the extent of being unwilling to join in defense of the national endangered species program.

A somewhat similar fate befell efforts to establish a local presence for the National Wildlife Federation. In the mid-1980s the state Wildlife Federation sought to install a staff member in Pittsburgh, but attempts to provide financial support through door-to-door canvassing were not sufficient to continue the program beyond a short period of time. Again in the late 1990s, the National Wildlife Federation made serious inquiries in Pittsburgh toward establishing one of their regional resource centers, but concluded that interest and potential support were insufficient. The failure to develop a vigorous issue presence in Pittsburgh in the case of both the Audubon Society and the National Wildlife Federation meant that the resources of the national organizations were not available to advance a citizens' environmental presence in the city.

Efforts to bring these individual independent citizens' organizations together into a network that could establish more effective visibility on the city and regional scene have had only sporadic success. The very first such effort, the Allegheny County Environmental Coalition of the early 1970s, got off to a rocky start because of financial dependence on business sources of funding, which limited its independence. Over the years the celebration of Earth Day brought organizations together, but often the network was so broad that it prevented a clear focus on public environmental issues. In addition, reliance on support from business firms greatly restricted the ability to express a clear environmental message.[20] Recent celebrations at the Frick Nature Center, however, have been sponsored by independent environmental organizations and have been free of dependence on business corporations; they have attracted numerous groups, suggesting the potential for a wider city environmental movement.[21]

Pittsburgh's mass media has not made up for this limited level of citizen environmental organization. While it provided an average amount of both news coverage and editorial comment, it seldom included environmental objectives amid its numerous attempts to define the city's goals and ambitions. While environmental affairs occupied a persistent niche in its general outlook on what was important to the city, its assessment of environmental objectives in civic affairs failed to reach a level similar to the focus on sports, arts and culture, entertainment, and especially economic development.[22] Radio and television reporting about the environment was almost nonexistent, and only the newspapers provided any environmental information to the general public. In the 1970s, when water quality and strip mine reclamation took the spotlight, outdoor recreation and sports writers were prominent, although coverage was usually confined to local and state affairs. In the 1970s and early 1980s the most effective writer was Ralph Haurwitz of the *Pittsburgh Press;* when that paper was folded into the *Pittsburgh Post-Gazette,* Don Hopey developed into the region's most reliable environmental reporter. Coverage of national environmental affairs was far more limited and often dependent on stories from national papers such as the *New York Times* and the *Washington Post.*[23] The local papers shared the limitations of the national news services in their inability to go beyond momentary events to display an understanding of underlying environmental circumstances. Unfortunately, these limitations of the media drew no protest from a public desiring more extensive and reliable sources of information.[24]

While the city's newspapers often took more favorable environmental positions in their editorial pages than was reflected in their news reporting, they seldom commented on the region's environmental circumstances in statements about the region's state of well-being. The annual assessments of the past year and the coming year by the *Pittsburgh Post-Gazette,* for instance, included little about environmental affairs, except, perhaps, the well-worn story about how the city had "cleaned up" air pollution. Equally noticeable was the absence of environmental considerations in the comparative "benchmarks" or urban analyses, which the *Post-Gazette* popularized in the 1990s. The paper did espouse outdoor recreation, such as hiking/biking trails, as an amenity to keep young talented people in the city and to attract new migrants. However, the context was a desire to invigorate the "new economy," not emphasize environmental values.

Sports, culture and the arts, and tourism all loomed large amid advocacy for the "new economy" to replace the old economy of iron and steel and extractive industry. There were many features on such subjects, and major construction efforts to foster this side of the city's present and future were well supported. But one could not detect in the press's agenda concern with larger environmental thinking or activities. The work of the Western Pennsylvania Conservancy in acquiring land for conservation purposes was duly noted, but rarely was mentioned in the annual accounts of the region's civic assets. While the city's rivers were "rediscovered" by the media, they were thought of largely as places where new development would replace the old, and rarely were thought of as a striking opportunity for natural amenity open space that might be as distinctive to visitors and potential residents as the dramatic vista on exiting the Fort Pitt Tunnel from the west. Clearly, environmental amenities are not included in the core of regional values, and one can only conclude that the city and region's environmental potential does not rank high in the minds of those who shape the media's efforts to influence the region's civic aspirations.

Education and Knowledge

Environmental affairs opened up vast new vistas of knowledge; they identified major realms of the unknown which remained untapped as sources of understanding of how the world worked and about the impact of humans on natural conditions and processes. Educational institutions of all kinds were called upon to modify their resources and learning opportunities from the beginning levels of the school system to the outer reaches of higher education. In addition, however, since environmental affairs engaged citizens of all walks of life and at ages beyond formal schooling, it also led to demands for new discoveries into the only barely known environmental world, new ways of learning, new access to knowledge, and new ways of applying knowledge. Much of a community's level of environmental culture was reflected in the way in which its institutions responded to these new opportunities and demands.

At the elementary and secondary school levels, environmental education became the major arena in which younger students were exposed to environmental knowledge. Nature centers became an important focal point of these activities, and in Pittsburgh, Beechwood Farms, managed by the local Audubon Society, is most significant. Its programs are developed in close cooperation with environmental education programs in the schools and give overwhelming stress to nature education. In similar fashion, the Frick Environmental Center in the city's Frick Park is providing educational opportunities for school students, and, in the 1990s, the Rachel Carson Homestead, a relatively new player in the nature center world, began to develop a third regional focal point for nature-oriented environmental education.[25]

Given the size of the population of Pittsburgh and its region, however, its environmental educational resources are relatively limited in number, and far smaller than in many comparable cities. Moreover, while all seem to enjoy positive support in the region's media, civic leaders make no attempt to assess their adequacy in comparison with other cities or to establish them as major assets for the region's future. The centers limit their programs primarily to nature education, and while all give some attention to matters such as recycling and solar energy, few stray beyond these limits to provide education about public environmental issues. And while they provide opportunities for adults to enjoy the outdoors through passive nature observation and walking, they do not also offer educational opportunities in the wider range of public environmental issues.

The public school curriculum provides more extensive opportunities for environmental education for young people. While there are state legislative requirements for environmental education, and these have led to organized activity among teachers on behalf of programs to implement those requirements, these rarely surface in public life beyond the more limited confines of the schools. When they do, they frequently are presented in the media in terms of the controversies that they arouse. A continual problem confronting environmental education teachers is the limited financial support for their programs and the lack of curriculum materials. Regulated industries frequently seek to fill this vacuum by developing their own versions of classroom materials, often providing public visibility. In the 1970s, for instance, the nuclear industry distributed free material that extolled the virtues of nuclear power as a clean source of energy, with special emphasis on the schools around the nuclear power plant at Shippingport, west of Pittsburgh. The coal industry provided similar materials in the 1970s and 1980s, and sought to include them in the state-sponsored environmental education program. In the 1990s the hardwood timber industry, with strong support from the state's forest management agency, the Bureau of Forestry, sought to shape a state-mandated environmental education forest curriculum.[26] All of these efforts became controversial, some more publicized than others, and all indicated the degree to which regulated industries often seek to bend environmental education to their policy objectives.

In the curriculum of the region's colleges and universities, environmental education plays an insignificant role. While environmental affairs enters the research and professional realms of those institutions, it rarely penetrates the undergraduate level of liberal arts education. Active student interest in environmental affairs is limited, and is often confined to campus-based environmental programs such as recycling and energy conservation rather than issue-based curricula. Much of what occurs arises from the activities of individual faculty with environmental interests who persuade their departments to offer environmental courses in economics, geography, political science, sociology, or history, but these have had limited support within their institutions and none of the institutions of higher education in the city or the region take up environmental studies as an institutional commitment.[27]

The University of Pittsburgh had an active environmental program in the 1970s and 1980s. While there was no formal major in environmental studies, students could form their own interdisciplinary major from environmental courses in various departments under the guidance of an advisor; each year, for almost a decade, six to ten students did so.[28] But the program suffered a severe blow when the university abolished the Geography Department; in addition, faculty with environmental interests in other departments were not replaced, and their courses were discontinued after their departure. An effort to arouse faculty interest through interdepartmental gatherings seemed to hold some promise, but after several meetings it became clear that most members, as well as the university, were more interested in projects that would bring in research funding rather than in allocating funds to build up faculty environmental resources in a planned manner.[29]

Most of the environmentally based programs at the University of Pittsburgh and regional institutions focus on the technical and engineering aspects of federal and state programs to implement pollution control requirements or develop "green" technology.[30] Institutions visualized the opportunity to provide technical training for employment in industry, consulting firms, and government that had come into being when public environmental programs in air and water pollution and waste disposal materialized. But these rarely extended to curricula that would give equal attention to environmental courses in the social sciences or the humanities with the thought that public environmental issues were as deeply involved in environmental subjects as in technical applications.[31]

Two institutions, Carnegie Mellon University and Chatham College, played their own distinctive roles in environmental higher education in the Pittsburgh region. Carnegie Mellon's interest in environmental affairs grew out of its faculty's professional and technical resources which expanded to include public policy concerns. Perhaps its most distinctive bailiwick is its Department of Engineering and Public Policy, strongly linked with the Department of Civil and Environmental Engineering. Several faculty have played prominent roles in national public environmental affairs and made research contributions to environmental issues. Resources were also provided to provide a broader curriculum in environmental matters, such as environmental history and environmental decision making. Technical and engineering affairs, however, formed the primary emphasis. Yet the Carnegie Mellon graduate program, largely because of the interest of selected faculty members, was distinctive in its contribution to the city's meager programs in environmental graduate training. Environmental affairs, more broadly considered, however, did not take on an independent impetus and direction and one might well attribute this to the limited role of the liberal arts in a predominantly technical and engineering institution.[32]

The role of Chatham College in environmental education took a quite different twist, one that sought to emphasize the institutional role not just in undergraduate education but public education beyond the classroom. In the last decade of the twentieth century, Chatham sought to capitalize on the fact that Rachel Carson was one of its most famous graduates by establishing the Rachel Carson Institute, which was to house a variety of environmental activities. The most significant of these turned out to be a series of short courses for the general public in a range of environmental subjects, most of which were confined to the more general context of ecological or natural history education, with scanty attention to public issues. They were intended to create a cadre of adults with a beginning knowledge of natural history who might then be useful as volunteers in environmental affairs, and this would lead to a certificate on completion of the short course. But by the beginning of the new century the Rachel Carson Institute had not yet lived up to its promise.[33] Limited financial commitment from the college had led to a limited program with serious turnovers in leadership; its future contribution to environmental affairs in the Pittsburgh region remained quite problematical.[34]

The adult education program of the Rachel Carson Institute identified a significant component of environmental education that was less formal and more geared to the popular side of environmental knowledge. Public engagement in environmental affairs led to a widely shared desire to know more about "how the environment works." Many an issue which aroused public interest involved a search for knowledge to help cope with the problem. It led to library research, to seeking knowledge and advice from university "experts," to subscribing to magazines and reading books, and to surfing the Internet. Most of this was action-based in that it was shaped and aroused by a desire to "do something" or, as the phrase went, "make a difference," but also by the knowledge that the problem had a factual component within which it had to be understood and addressed. As they became aware of the wider environmental world upon entering higher education, many young people were caught up in this search for knowledge and looked upon their experience in higher education as an opportunity to acquire it. Or, as adults, they sought out institutions of higher education where they could become better informed about environmental affairs.

Many institutions of higher education looked upon this desire for environmental knowledge as an opportunity, but the Pittsburgh colleges and universities did not and at times seemed to look upon these knowledge opportunities of environmental affairs as circumstances to be avoided rather than taken up.[35] At the University of Pittsburgh, for example, while the administration responded to its own student clientele by engaging in recycling and energy conservation, it looked with skepticism upon student involvement in public issues as something to be avoided. Its most publicized venture was when it refused to approve a Nader-style public interest research group on the Pitt campus which would have been funded through a student activity fee contributed by those students who wished to support the venture. At the same time, while some universities elsewhere sought to make their facilities available to environmental public interest groups composed of adults through their adult education or "extension" programs, Pittsburgh institutions of higher education did not do so. While this appeared to have some connection to the fear of disapproval from the industries subject to environmental regulation on which they drew heavily for support, it appeared to be as much motivated by the tendency in higher education to move education from the realm of "real world" affairs to the ivory tower of academic life.

These limited contributions to popular education also were characteristic of some of the city's prominent civic institutions, such as the Phipps Conservatory, the National Aviary, the Pittsburgh Zoo, and the Natural History section of the Carnegie, as well as the more recently established Carnegie Science Center. While one can detect some environmental components in the programs of each of these institutions as they reach out to the public, they are more frequently devoted to the early education of children rather than to the education of adults in public policy.[36]

These failures of the region's educational institutions to respond in more than minimal fashion to the new world of environmental knowledge could be traced in its most immediate circumstances to the policies of institutional administrators and policy makers. But in a wider sense they reflect the relative indifference to environmental affairs in the community at large.

I have been especially interested in the availability of books on environmental affairs in bookstores as an indicator of a region's environmental culture. Over the years I have visited a number of bookstores in cities across the nation always with an eye to observing the books on the shelves dealing with environmental issues. I have often discussed with the store's purchasing staff the factors that determine their selection of books. Invariably, their decision is based on a judgment on the staff's part of what the public in that community wishes to read. This seemed to confirm observations of the limited number of environmental books on the shelves of

Pittsburgh bookstores. I have over the years frequently browsed the shelves of the University of Pittsburgh bookstore. Books on environmental issues there declined markedly over the years after a burst of activity in the early and mid-1970s; the category under which they were located shifted from "environment" or "ecology" to a more general category of "science" or "public affairs." In contrast, locally owned bookstores in two smaller places that I frequent (Traverse City, Michigan, and Boulder, Colorado) have a much more extensive collection of environmental issue books on their shelves than the Pittsburgh stores, an indicator of a much higher level of environmental culture of those regions.

Environmental Restraint and Opposition

The relatively modest level of environmental culture in Pittsburgh and the region provided an opportunity for those of the environmental opposition who counseled restraint on environmental objectives to exercise considerable, even dominant, influence in the region's environmental affairs. Opponents sought to exercise influence over citizen organizations by providing financial support and by redefining environmental objectives away from public issues that were controversial and toward often superficial "green" activities, mostly quite trivial and devoted more to image building rather than to concrete results. They continually sought to place the regulated industry in a positive light through publicity and symbol-building activities. The effect was to obscure those citizen organizations and issues that called for more vigorous public environmental action. This tended to replace effective environmental initiatives with milder ideas and actions, to limit resources devoted to higher levels of environmental quality, and to enhance the images of their development objectives.

In the late 1960s and early 1970s, for instance, Allegheny County was hospitable to the newly formulated environmental programs of the time. Most notably, the county's air pollution ordinance seemed to be in sync with innovations at both the state and federal levels. One of the more visible signs of this was the decision by Duquesne Light to install sulfur-dioxide "scrubbers" on two of its three electric generation plants in the county, the Philipps and Elrama plants upwind of the city. This was in line with state objectives, as Pennsylvania was one of the few states to require old power plants to reduce emissions in contrast with the federal law that pertained only to new generating facilities. These efforts occurred despite opposition from the county's business community which, represented by the Chamber of Commerce, turned out in force to object to them.[37]

The "energy crisis" of the mid-1970s, however, gave rise to one of the first serious efforts on the part of the regulated industry to establish a stronger political position in regional environmental affairs. Spearheaded by the nuclear industry, Americans for Energy Independence (AEI) had a nationwide agenda but was based in Pittsburgh. Its efforts targeted the Pittsburgh region because the group apparently felt that there was little fear of a possible countermove from a weak citizens' environmental community. While the energy issues of the day gave rise to considerable action for an "energy efficiency" strategy on the part of the citizens' environmental community, AEI took on a far less effective program of simply keeping tires well inflated and car engines well tuned. The AEI program dominated the Pittsburgh scene, largely because of the vacuum created by the absence of an alternative program, and marked the Pittsburgh region more firmly as a place of limited and even nonexistent citizen action.[38]

In the 1970s the steel industry retained a dominant place in the region's economic and political leadership, but due to its declining role in the region's economy and GASP's successful effort to publicize its pollution responsibility for coke oven emissions and poor water quality in the Monongahela River, its influence was somewhat neutralized. As the steel industry withdrew from the region's production it also withdrew from a dominant position in its environmental politics. In turn, the Duquesne Light Company assumed an increasingly dominant position in the region's environmental affairs. While it was joined by several other business firms in the region, such as the Giant Eagle grocery chain, its main ally in these efforts was a newcomer on the Pittsburgh scene, the Pennsylvania Environmental Council (PEC). Established initially in the early 1970s in Philadelphia, the PEC opened a regional office and began to undertake western Pennsylvania projects; soon it was working in tandem with Duquesne Light to establish a dominant environmental position in the region.

The Pennsylvania Environmental Council played a distinctive but complex role in the state's environmental affairs, and now in southwestern Pennsylvania.[39] Organized in the early 1970s, the PEC, while adopting a name similar to several other state environmental councils, was top-down in organization and distanced from citizen's advisory groups. Its board was chosen to represent three constituencies—industry, labor, and environmental professionals, both public and private.[40] Its stated goal was to work out differences among those constituencies before taking a position, and in doing so it was frequently at odds with citizen advocacy groups throughout the state. As a result, the two were more than suspicious of each other, since citizen groups found that when push came to shove in an environmental battle, the PEC would frequently compromise with the opposition, and in so doing proved to be more than friendly with the regulated industry. The Pennsylvania Environmental Council was well liked by successive gubernatorial administrations and usually chosen by them for advice in contrast with state citizen environmental organizations. While regulated industries did not necessarily fully support PEC's politics, they frequently found them preferable to those of the citizen environmental community.[41] On the whole, one could well argue that PEC's ambiguous role played an important part in frustrating and limiting the development of an effective genuine citizen environmental movement in the state, which lagged far behind those of other states, such as in nearby West Virginia.[42]

When the PEC established its regional office in Pittsburgh it almost immediately gained as much credibility with the region's economic and political leadership as it held at the state level in Harrisburg. Because it would not make "waves" by engaging in public debate over environmental issues and thereby embarrass either governmental officials or industry leaders, it was much preferred to those few more active and more truly citizen groups in the city. As such a "safe" environmental organization, it soon found a common ground with Duquesne Light in attempting to define the region's environmental affairs. Its most publicized public component was the Three Rivers Environmental Awards, jointly sponsored by the PEC and Duquesne Light. In providing a series of awards for environmental activities, these events exercised a major influence in communicating to other institutional leaders what sorts of environmental activities and groups were acceptable and what were not. Rarely did those associated with policy-active citizen environmental organizations receive recognition, and most such awards were given to those who did not engage in contesting public issues or identifying sources of environmental inaction or opposition.

In the 1990s these efforts to define and influence the region's environmental affairs were redirected as a result of the emerging interest in redefining the city's and region's economy towards the "new technology," with a major emphasis on computer/electronic-based business ventures: how to attract people with such skills to the city; how to prevent people with such skills from seeking jobs elsewhere. This new thrust had two major consequences for regional environmental politics. First, it gave considerable emphasis to the region's recreational resources, and especially outdoor recreation, thought to be of vast importance in attracting young, technically trained workers. Simultaneously, the nation's interest in hiking and biking trails and especially in converting old railroad rights-of-way into such trails expanded in the Pittsburgh region. Public funds from both national and state sources provided support. The Western Pennsylvania Conservancy had taken the initial lead in the 1970s in acquiring an old right of way along the Youghigheny River between Ohiopyle and Confluence as part of its general interest in obtaining conservation lands in the Laurel Highlands. Now this was greatly expanded into a regionwide system of rails/trails that seemed to evolve in sync with the promotion of the new technology-based economy. Leaders from diverse institutions joined the bandwagon of rails to trails.[43]

The second environmental impact of the new economy was to give added impetus to the environmental involvement of the university professional community. One case was a local attempt to develop a Pittsburgh-based "relative-risk" project sponsored by the Environmental Protection Agency that focused on citizen efforts to think through both the scientific issues and public values involved in trade-offs in environmental policies. This cooperative venture between the Allegheny County Health Department and several professionals at Carnegie Mellon University came to a quiet end after much publicity and several meetings because of ineffective leadership, inadequate funding, and minimal public participation. The contrast with a variety of successful state and local relative-risk projects elsewhere was striking.[44]

The involvement of professionals at both Carnegie Mellon and the University of Pittsburgh in the Pittsburgh Technology Council, which sought to give a larger twist to the role of environmental affairs in the "new technology" of the city and the region, was also important. This project sought to identify the environmental conditions required by the new technology to bring into the Pittsburgh scene environmental activities in other cities connected with their "new economies."[45] Such efforts, however, seemed to be more indirect in regard to environmental values than direct, and to nibble around the edges of environmental policy through the image of the "green" city rather than to focus on well-defined urban environmental objectives.[46]

A second venture, a so-called computer "Green Map" as part of an international Green Map program featuring "green areas" in cities around the world, was an even more ambitious undertaking. Its first version combined a selected few environmental assets confined primarily to outdoor recreation facilities and emphasized "tourist destinations" that had little environmental content. Later editions expanded the coverage to include a wide range of geographical locations that subordinated even further distinctive regional environmental or ecological sites. A marked feature of the Pittsburgh Green Map was a list of relevant regional environmental organizations, but the list did not include any of the region's citizen-based groups.[47] One could conclude that the Green Map project of the Technology Council was another significant example of the desire of Pittsburgh leaders to "celebrate" a grossly exaggerated environmental presence amid an exceptionally weak record of environmental performance.[48]

During the same recent period several brownfield renewal projects have incorporated environmental objectives. These include the redevelopment of Herr's Island from an industrial blighted area to a residential and recreational community (Washington's Landing), the transformation of Nine Mile Run so that the stream once projected to be culverted is now planned as a watershed environmental amenity in a new residential development located on an old slag heap (Summerset), and the redevelopment of the Monongahela shoreline from a center for steel mills to "new economy" buildings with considerable open space (the Pittsburgh Technology Center). All are quite different in their environmental quality than the previous industrial structures. Such cases of environmental improvement, however, have not yet evolved into a firm and clear advocacy of regional environmental objectives that is coordinate rather than subordinate to developmental objectives in such affairs as sports, arts and culture, education, and the new economy.

⌒

Pittsburgh is not alone in the limited level of its environmental culture, since it shares its environmental characteristics with many regions of the country, especially in the South and the western Midwest. Here also the remnants and traditions of the old economy and the traditional culture organized around activities of an earlier time still dominate. Some are marked by the persistence of older agrarian values and others by the heavy industries of the old factory belt, often referred to as the Rustbelt. Pittsburgh and its immediate region provide an especially useful and focused example of the continuing power of that legacy and an inability to advance much beyond it. Despite almost four decades of environmental activity in the nation as a whole there has not yet developed in this region a vigorous voice to define regional environmental aspirations, to describe circumstances, set goals, determine progress toward those goals, and give support to those who seek to advance the region's environmental culture. At the beginning of the twenty-first century the region remains in an environmental lethargy which has remained relatively unchanged since the momentary outburst of activity around thirty years before. While occasionally new initiatives appear on the scene they have made little dent in that continuing lack of emphasis on environmental goals and progress. On all sides one hears much from advocates of the "future" in economic development, sports, arts and culture, health and medicine, and education, but about the region's environmental future there is only a relative silence.

Afterword

JOEL A. TARR

THE INTRODUCTION TO this book began with a series of observations made by various commentators about Pittsburgh during the years of the city's heyday as an industrial center. The city they describe was filled with environmental horrors: the air dismal and dark due to persistent heavy smoke, the hillsides barren of vegetation, the valleys filled with slag, and the rivers and streams polluted with sewage and industrial wastes. Other commentators, however, were intrigued by the power of the "industrial aesthetic" that dominated the landscape—the huge mills casting tongues of fire into the sky, hills dotted with the red eyes of coke furnaces, rivers serving as "floating coal veins," and long cars of trains threading their tracks along the riverbanks and through the valleys and filling the air with the shriek of their whistles and smoke from their boilers.

Today articles about Pittsburgh appearing in national journals like the *National Geographic* and the *New York Times Sunday Magazine,* the travel sections of newspapers throughout the nation as well as local magazines and newspapers, various types of booster literature, and a large number of websites, all stress the natural beauty of the city and its environment: clean air, fishing and boating on the rivers, bicycle trails, park renewal, lush vegetation, and the restoration of urban streams. Delegations of urban planners and politicians from around the world visit the city to appreciate and comprehend its Renaissance and, more recently, the redevelopment of inner city brownfields into places for residences, shopping, and research and development. Pittsburgh and its region, astonishingly, is becoming a destination for green tourism, and memories of the dark industrial city are disappearing fast.

One must ask, however, just as the earlier image had its mirror opposite, whether the same might be true of today's portrayal of Pittsburgh as a metropolis growing ever greener and moving toward sustainability. This is not an easy question to answer, even though Pittsburgh is a city obsessed with measures of comparability between it and its urban rivals. Strong critics of the city's tendency to celebrate past accomplishments but show only limited dedication to new environmental goals, such as Samuel P. Hays in this volume, note the restricted environmental infrastructure and failure of the city's educational and other institutions to strive toward major environmental advances. The constraints on the protection of the environment are also reflected in the region's tendency to sprawl into the metropolitan area's green periphery rather than protecting this valuable part of its heritage, to contemplate usurping valuable riverfront land for a high-speed expressway, and to tolerate industrial violators of air pollution statutes.

A regional "report card," therefore, would have to acknowledge that while many gains have been made in the last half-century, obstacles still remain to Pittsburgh's reaching a new level of environmental excellence. Some of these hurdles are a result of the massive problems left by extensive industrialization and deindustrialization, while others are a consequence of the city and the region's past focus on problem solving that emphasized immediate and short-term goals without considering long-term consequences. A striking example of this is the region's present concern with combined sewer overflow problems. The southwestern Pennsylvania region has 755 combined sewer overflow points that discharge mixed rainwater and raw sewage into the rivers during wet weather, causing serious pollution problems; the city of Pittsburgh itself has more overflow points than any other city in the nation. The continued existence of such a system reflects the unfortunate consequences of path dependency in regard to an older form of sewer system, resistance to attempts by regulatory bodies to force system replacement, the region's governmental fragmentation that impedes unified action to solve environmental problems, and the inability of past leadership to convince the population to make hard choices about water pollution issues.[1]

So what might the future bring from an environmental perspective and is the past a possible guide to enlightenment? The various chapters of this book have taken the reader on a guided tour of a selected number of themes in Pittsburgh environmental history and these have clearly illustrated the environmental degradation that took place as well as both the successful and unsuccessful efforts at remediation. Ironically, it has been the region's recent deindustrialization with consequent economic dislocations that has produced substantial improvements in air and water quality and land rehabilitation. Decision making in the city has often been top-down, strongly influenced by the positions of various elites and corporations, although elites themselves have frequently been divided over actions to improve the environment. From an environmental justice perspective, the working class, immigrant groups, and African Americans have often borne the heaviest burdens from the pollution of the air, water, and land. These inequities were frequently a result of inferior or nonexistent municipal services, but also resulted because working-class living areas were located close to places of employment, especially iron and steel mills, that were heavy environmental polluters.

If the history is any guide to the future, it suggests that Pittsburgh will continue to make environmental gains, especially in terms of constructing a green infrastructure such as bike trails, improving its parks, and reclaiming its riverbanks. Further gains, however, will have to overcome challenges from factors such as the region's legacy of governmental fragmentation, tension between economic development and the protection of environmental goods, and a lack of leadership with strong environmental goals. If these limitations could be overcome, change and improvement may advance faster than anticipated, with Pittsburgh setting the pace as one of the nation's leading green metropolises. Hopefully, accompanying future change will be a further exploration of Pittsburgh environmental history and the study of major issues still not investigated.[2] Knowledge of its history can help Pittsburgh advance along the road to environmental improvement without forgetting its past.

A Continuation of the Walk in a Pittsburgh Park

The hot day is over—the first day of summer—and the park again beckons with its promise of green shade. It provides an oasis from the heat reflected from the stone buildings and concrete and asphalt pathways of the city. Outside my office on the long, sloping, grass-covered hill I can see youngsters flying a large white model airplane, causing it to glide far further than I thought possible. Students sit on the hill underneath the trees, reading, embracing, or just contemplating the green foliage and hills beyond. Couples walk hand in hand. Dogs romp on the hill, happy to be free from the tether of the leash. Bike riders pump up the inclines or glide down the slopes, their machines occasionally leaping from the road. Beyond, buildings of different shapes and sizes loom—church steeples, museums, university structures, and a towering Cathedral of Learning—emphasizing that nature and the city coexist and even border and overlap each other, both providing sustenance in different ways for the urban population.

NOTES

Introduction

1. Barbara Judd, "Edward M. Bigelow: Creator of Pittsburgh's Arcadian Parks," *The Western Pennsylvania Historical Magazine* 58 (January 1975): 53–67.

2. Francis G. Couvares, *The Remaking of Pittsburgh: Class and Culture in an Industrializing City, 1877–1919* (Albany: SUNY Press, 1984), 107–8.

3. For an insightful discussion of these issues, see Matthew Gandy, *Concrete and Clay: Reworking Nature in New York City* (Cambridge: MIT Press, 2002).

4. The Parton, Glazier, and Duffus quotations can be found in Roy Lubove, ed., *Pittsburgh* (New York: New Viewpoints, 1976). The Spencer quotation is from Joseph Frazier Wall, *Andrew Carnegie,* 2d ed. (Pittsburgh: University of Pittsburgh Press, 1989), 386.

5. For a recent review of the literature, see Joel A. Tarr, "Urban History and Environmental History in the United States: Complementary and Overlapping Fields," in *Environmental Problems in European Cities of the Nineteenth and Twentieth Century,* ed. Christoph Bernhardt (New York: Waxmann, 2001), 25–39; also available at http://www2.hnet.msu.edu/~environ/historiography/usurban.htm.

6. Donald Worster, "Transformations of the Earth: Toward an Agroecological Perspective in History," *Journal of American History* 76 (March 1990): 1087–1106.

7. See, for instance, Christine Meisner Rosen and Joel Arthur Tarr, eds., "The Environment and the City," a special issue of the *Journal of Urban History* 20 (May 1994): 299–434, and the references in Tarr, "Urban History and Environmental History in the United States."

8. Andrew Hurley, ed., *Common Fields: An Environmental History of St. Louis* (Saint Louis, Mo.: Missouri Historical Society, 1997); Craig E. Colten, ed., *Transforming New Orleans and Its Environs: Centuries of Change* (Pittsburgh: University of Pittsburgh Press, 2000); and Char Miller, ed., *On the Border: An Environmental History of San Antonio* (Pittsburgh: University of Pittsburgh Press, 2001).

9. For a recent discussion of the building of these forts in the context of the war between the French and British empires, see Fred Anderson, *Crucible of War: The Seven Years' War and the Fate of Empire in British North America, 1754–1766* (New York: Vintage Books, 2000). The British initially built Fort Prince George in 1754 at the Point.

10. Basic Pittsburgh data is available from many websites. For instance, see the website for Pittsburgh City Planning at *http://www.city.pittsburgh.pa.us/cp/*.

11. David Cuff et al., eds., *The Atlas of Pennsylvania* (Philadelphia: Temple University Press, 1989), 52–67.

12. See William D. Pearson and B. Juanelle Pearson, "Fishes of the Ohio River," *Ohio Journal of Science* 89, no. 5 (1989): 181–87. The Pearsons report that of the 159 Ohio River species identified, humans had introduced 14. The revived health of the river ecology is reflected by the fact that of the 52 fish species that had been present in 1818, only one is no longer found in the river.

13. *Atlas of Pennsylvania*, 58–67; Joseph F. Merritt, *Mammals of Pennsylvania* (Pittsburgh: University of Pittsburgh Press for Carnegie Museum of Natural History, 1987).

14. Paul A. W. Wallace, *Indians in Pennsylvania* (Harrisburg: Pennsylvania Historical and Museum Commission, 1993).

15. There is no recent comprehensive history of Pittsburgh. See, however, Samuel P. Hays, ed., *City at the Point: Essays in the Social History of Pittsburgh* (Pittsburgh: University of Pittsburgh Press, 1989).

16. Nicholas Casner, "Polluter versus Polluter: The Pennsylvania Railroad and the Manufacturing of Pollution Policies in the 1920s," *Journal of Policy History* 11 (spring 1999): 179–200.

17. See, for instance, Andrew Hurley, *Class, Race, and Industrial Pollution in Gary, Indiana, 1945–1980* (Chapel Hill: University of North Carolina Press, 1995). The journal *Environmental History* devoted its April 2000 issue to the theme of environmental justice in the city.

The Interaction of Natural and Built Environments in the Pittsburgh Landscape

1. See Ben Marsh and Peirce Lewis, "Landforms and Human Habitat," in *A Geography of Pennsylvania*, ed. E. Willard Miller (University Park: The Pennsylvania State University Press, 1995), 17–43; David Cuff et al., eds., *The Atlas of Pennsylvania* (Philadelphia: Temple University Press, 1989), 11–33. For a description of such a journey in the 1840s, see Jack D. Warren, ed., "A Young Woman's Vision of Western Pennsylvania: The Diary of Mary Ann Corwin, 1842–1843," *Pittsburgh History* 75 (summer 1992): 91–107.

2. Henry Leighton, *The Geology of Pittsburgh and Its Environs* (Pittsburgh: The Carnegie Institute, 1927).

3. Ibid., 37–43.

4. Fred Anderson, *Crucible of War: The Seven Years' War and the Fate of Empire in British North America, 1754–1766* (New York: Vintage, 2000), 18–24. See also Richard White, *The Middle Ground: Indians, Empires, and Republics in the Great Lakes Region, 1650–1815* (New York: Cambridge University Press, 1991), and Daniel K. Richter, *The Ordeal of the Longhouse: The Peoples of the Iroquois League in the Era of European Colonization* (Chapel Hill: University of North Carolina Press, 1992).

5. Solon J. Buck and Elizabeth Hawthorn Buck, *The Planting of Civilization in Western Pennsylvania* (Pittsburgh: University of Pittsburgh Press, 1939), 19–45.

6. See ibid., 19–45.

7. John Melish, *Travels in the United States of America* (Philadelphia: 1812), as excerpted in John W. Harpster, ed., *Crossroads: Descriptions of Western Pennsylvania, 1720–1829* (Pittsburgh: University of Pittsburgh Press, 1938), 251; Jennifer Ford,

"Landscape and Material Life in Southwestern Pennsylvania, 1798–1838" (Ph.D. diss., University of Pittsburgh, 2001).

8. Paul A. Chew, *Southwestern Pennsylvania Painters: Collections of the Westmoreland Museum of Art* (Greensburg, Pa.: Westmoreland Museum of Art, 1989). See, for instance, the following paintings: Eugene A. Poole, *River Landscape with Cows;* Jasper Lawman, *Trout Stream Landscape;* and William Coventry Wall, *River Scene at Sunset.*

9. Rina C. Youngner, "Paintings and Graphic Images of Industry in Nineteenth Century Pittsburgh: A Study of the Relationship between Art and Industry," 2 vols. (Ph.D. diss., University of Pittsburgh, 1991), 1:4.

10. Verna L. Cowin, *Pittsburgh Archaeological Resources and National Register Survey* (Pittsburgh: Carnegie Museum of Natural History, 1985); and Leland D. Baldwin, *Pittsburgh: The Story of a City, 1750–1865* (Pittsburgh: University of Pittsburgh Press, 1937).

11. Essay by Russel Errett in *Magazine of Western History* 7 (1887): 33–44, as quoted in Harpster, *Crossroads,* 287–88.

12. For early manufacturing in Pittsburgh, see George Thurston, *Pittsburgh as It Is* (Pittsburgh: W. S. Haven, 1857); Catherine Reiser, *Pittsburgh's Commercial Development: 1800–1850* (Harrisburg: Pennsylvania Historical and Museum Commission, 1951); for iron and steel, see John N. Ingham, *Making Iron and Steel: Independent Mills in Pittsburgh, 1820–1920* (Columbus: Ohio State University Press, 1991), 21–46; and for coal, see Howard N. Eavenson, *The First Century and a Quarter of American Coal Industry* (Pittsburgh: Privately printed, 1942), 155–204.

13. Rina Youngner and Emily Hetzel, "The Artist Looks at Industrial Pittsburgh, 1836–1993," catalog, University of Pittsburgh Art Gallery, June 3–30, 1993; Youngner, "Paintings and Graphic Images of Industry," 74.

14. Youngner, "Paintings and Graphic Images of Industry," 144 202. See, for instance, G. F. Muller, "The City of Pittsburgh," *Harper's New Monthly Magazine* 62, no. 367 (1882): 49–68.

15. John R. Stilgoe, *Metropolitan Corridor: Railroads and the American Scene* (New Haven: Yale University Press, 1983), 81. See also David E. Nye, ed., *Technologies of Landscape: From Reaping to Recycling* (Amherst: University of Massachusetts Press, 1999).

16. For a discussion of the siting and development of these mills, see Kenneth Warren, *The American Steel Industry, 1850–1970: A Geographical Interpretation* (Oxford: Clarendon Press, 1973).

17. Laurie Graham, *Singing the City: The Bonds of Home in an Industrial Landscape* (Pittsburgh: University of Pittsburgh Press, 1998), 35. "Weird spectacle" quote from Reuben Gold Thwaites, *Afloat on the Ohio: An Historical Pilgrimage of a Thousand Miles in a Skiff from Redstone to Cairo* (Chicago: Way and Williams, 1897), as quoted in Dan Hughes Fuller, "Roughing It on the River: Reuben Gold Thwaites in Western Pennsylvania," *Pittsburgh History* 79 (1996): 116.

18. "There are squares of great foundries, streets of machine-shops and locomotive-works and engine-making establishments, besides huge shops that send wrought-iron and steel bridges into the world." Noted in Muller, "The City of Pittsburgh," 62–63.

19. Quote from Stilgoe, *Metropolitan Corridor,* 78; see also 96–97. George H. Thurston was a famous Pittsburgh booster who wrote a number of fact-filled

books about the city in the nineteenth century. See, for instance, his *Pittsburgh and Allegheny in the Centennial Year* (Pittsburgh: W. W. Anderson, 1876), which contains chapters on the different industries. See also David Demarest and Eugene Levy, "Visualizing the Industrial Landscape: The Photographers of Pittsburgh's Westinghouse Air Brake Company, 1900–1960," *Pittsburgh History* 77 (spring 1994): 4–21.

20. Quoted in Joel A. Tarr, "The Pittsburgh Survey as an Environmental Statement," in Maurine W. Greenwald and Margo Anderson, eds., *Pittsburgh Surveyed: Social Science and Social Reform in the Early Twentieth Century* (Pittsburgh: University of Pittsburgh Press, 1996), 172.

21. Some of the best discussions and images of the railroad landscape are in the illustrated volumes written by amateur railroad historians. See, for instance, Ken Kobus and Jack Consoli, *The Pennsy in the Steel City: 150 Years of the Pennsylvania Railroad in Pittsburgh* (Kutztown, Pa.: Kutztown Publishing Co., 1996), and *The Pennsylvania Railroad's Golden Triangle: Main Line Panorama in the Pittsburgh Area* (Pittsburgh: Pennsylvania Railroad Technical & Historical Society, 1998); also Howard V. Worley Jr. and William N. Poellot Jr., *The Pittsburgh & West Virginia Railway* (Halifax, Pa.: Witheirs Publishing, 1989). For a more detailed discussion of the effects of the railroad on the region, see David Hounshell, Mark Samber, and Joel Tarr, "Economic Impact of Rail Transportation in Western Pennsylvania, a Report to the National Park Service" (Pittsburgh: Department of History, Carnegie Mellon University, August 1993).

22. Engineers' Society of Western Pennsylvania, *Pittsburgh* (Pittsburgh: Cramer Printing & Publishing Co., 1930), 113–19.

23. See the photograph in Stefan Lorant, *Pittsburgh: The Story of an American City* (Lenox, Mass.: Author's Edition, 1988), 264.

24. For the Pitcairn Yard, see "PRR-Pitcairn Yard," available at http://www.trainweb.org/horseshoecurve-nrhs/Pitcairn.htm; for the Conway Yard, see "Conway Yard," available at http://home.swbell.net/jwacht/ambridge/id53.htm.

25. See Sherie R. Mershon and Joel A. Tarr, "Strategies for Clean Air: The Pittsburgh and Allegheny County Smoke Control Movements, 1940–1960," this volume.

26. Willard Glazier, "The Great Furnace of America," quoted in Roy Lubove, ed., *Pittsburgh* (New York: Franklin Watts, 1976).

27. *Coal and Coke Resource Analysis: Western Pennsylvania and Northern West Virginia* (Washington: America's Industrial Heritage Project, Department of the Interior, 1992), appendix A, 77; and Carmen DiCiccio, *Coal and Coke in Pennsylvania* (Harrisburg: Pennsylvania Historical and Museum Commission, 1996), 37.

28. Kenneth Warren, *Wealth, Waste, and Alienation: Growth and Decline in the Connellsville Coke Industry* (Pittsburgh: University of Pittsburgh Press, 2001), 221–28.

29. DiCiccio, *Coal and Coke in Pennsylvania*, 113–14.

30. Around the houses, companies sometimes built wooden picket fences that were whitewashed, and encouraged tenants to plant vegetable and flower gardens. "Garden" competitions were often held in the towns. Margaret M. Mulrooney, *A Legacy of Coal: The Coal Company Towns of Southwestern Pennsylvania* (Washington: America's Industrial Heritage Project, Department of the Interior, 1989), 9–29; DiCiccio, ibid., 89–95; *Coal and Coke Resource Analysis*, 47–49.

31. David Demarest and Eugene Levy, "Touring the Coke Region," *Pittsburgh History* 74 (fall 1991): 105–8.

32. Warren, *Wealth, Waste, and Alienation,* 11–24.

33. Jones & Laughlin broke from this pattern by constructing a major beehive installation (1,504 ovens) within the Pittsburgh neighborhood of Hazelwood between 1898 and 1903. See William L. Affelder, "Jones & Laughlin's Coke Plant," *Mines and Minerals* 29 (December 1908): 195–99.

34. John A. Enman, "Connellsville Coke: Catalyst and Victim of Change," in *The Early Coke Worker,* ed. Dennis F. Brestensky (Connellsville, Pa.: Southwestern Pennsylvania Heritage Commission, 1994), 2–29.

35. Muriel Earley Sheppard, *Cloud by Day: The Story of Coal and Coke and People* (Chapel Hill: University of North Carolina Press, 1947), 2. For a discussion of some of the environmental effects of coke production in beehive ovens, see Warren, *Wealth, Waste, and Alienation,* 221–28; Joel A. Tarr, *The Search for the Ultimate Sink: Urban Pollution in Historical Perspective* (Akron: University of Akron Press, 1996), 388–93.

36. Warren, *Wealth, Waste, and Alienation,* 195–203.

37. M. Camp and C. B. Francis, *The Making, Shaping and Treating of Steel,* 4th ed. (Pittsburgh: Carnegie Steel Co., 1919), 101–29.

38. For environmental problems caused by by-product coking, see Tarr, *Search for the Ultimate Sink,* 385–412; Charles O. Jones, *Clean Air: The Policies and Politics of Pollution Control* (Pittsburgh: University of Pittsburgh Press, 1975).

39. Joel A. Tarr, "The Plume Is Gone, but We Can't Forget Hazelwood," *Pittsburgh Post-Gazette,* May 27, 1998, A-13.

40. Cowin, *Pittsburgh Archaeological Resources,* passim, and Reiser, *Pittsburgh's Commercial Development,* 124–40.

41. Leland R. Johnson, *The Headwaters District: A History of the Pittsburgh District, U.S. Army Corps of Engineers* (Pittsburgh: U.S. Army Engineer District, 1979).

42. Edward K. Muller, "The Legacy of Industrial Rivers," *Pittsburgh History* 72 (1992): 64–75.

43. See Joel A. Tarr, "Infrastructure and City-Building in the Nineteenth and Twentieth Centuries," in *City at the Point: Essays on the Social History of Pittsburgh,* ed. Samuel P. Hays (Pittsburgh: University of Pittsburgh Press, 1989), 213–39.

44. Quoted in Albert W. Atwood, "Pittsburgh: Workshop of the Titans," *The National Geographic Magazine* 96 (July 1949): 117.

45. Clay McShane and Joel A. Tarr, "The Centrality of the Horse in the Nineteenth-Century American City," in *The Making of Urban America,* 2d ed., ed. Raymond A. Mohl (Wilmington, Del.: SR Book, 1997), 12–23. The electric streetcar, however, was not pollution free. Its demands for electricity contributed to the smoke burden produced by electrical generating plants.

46. Joel A. Tarr, *Transportation Innovation and Changing Spatial Patterns in Pittsburgh, 1850–1934* (Chicago: Public Works Historical Society, 1978), 6–21.

47. For a discussion of this issue, see Richard Pinkham, "Stream Restoration and Daylighting: Opportunities in the Pittsburgh Region," in *Three Rivers Second Nature Project Reports: Phase II 2001, Monongahela River Valley,* ed. Tim Collins (Pittsburgh: Studio for Creative Inquiry, June 2002).

48. Among the major culverted streams flowing into the Allegheny River were

Negley Run, Haights Run, Cemetery Run, and Two Mile Run in the city's eastern end. On the city's North Side, Jack's Run, Butcher's Run, and Spring Garden Run, also flowing into the Allegheny, were culverted. Flowing into the Monongahela River from the city's eastern section were Soho Run and Four Mile Run, fully culverted, and parts of Nine Mile Run, partially culverted.

49. See Warren, "A Young Woman's Vision of Western Pennsylvania," 99, 105. Interestingly, Corwin made this observation in 1843 on the westward leg of her trip from Philadelphia to Cincinnati. When she had passed through Pittsburgh going west in 1842, she noted that it was "the very dirtiest city that I ever saw in all my life, and as noisy as it can well be."

50. *The City of Pittsburgh and Its Public Works* (Pittsburgh, 1916), 21; and Frederick Law Olmsted Jr., *Pittsburgh: Main Thoroughfares and the Down Town District* (Pittsburgh: Pittsburgh Civic Commission, 1911), 93.

51. Olmsted, *Main Thoroughfares*, 109–10.

52. Cowin, *Pittsburgh Archaeological Resources*, 73–74.

53. Steven J. Hoffman, "The Saga of Pittsburgh's Liberty Tubes: Geographical Partisanship on the Urban Fringe," *Pittsburgh History* 75 (1992): 128–41.

54. For images of Pittsburgh's downtown landscape, see Carnegie Library of Pittsburgh, "Photos and Scenes of Pittsburgh"; available at http://www.carnegielibrary.org/subject/pgh/photos.shtml.

55. *Digest of the General Ordinances and Laws of the City of Pittsburgh* (Pittsburgh, 1938), 475; *The City of Pittsburgh and Its Public Works*, 29–31; Charles M. Reppert, "Recent Retaining Wall Practice," *Proceedings, Engineers Society of Western Pennsylvania* 26 (1910): 316–17.

56. Joseph G. Armstrong, "Annual Report of the Department of Public Works," *Annual Reports of the Executive Departments of the City of Pittsburgh* (1912): 6.

57. *City of Pittsburgh and Its Public Works*, 26–28.

58. John Bodnar, Roger Simon, and Michael P. Weber, *Lives of Their Own: Blacks, Italians, and Poles in Pittsburgh, 1900–1960* (Champaign: University of Illinois Press, 1983), 153–80.

59. H. L. Mencken, "The Libio for the Ugly," *Prejudices: Sixth Series* (New York: 1927), 187–93.

60. Tarr, *Transportation Innovation*, 10. See also "Pittsburgh Inclines Tribute"; available at http://members.tripod.com/riid/inclines.html.

61. Information on steps supplied to the editor by Robert D. Regan, Pittsburgh, Pa. See also "'Steptrek' Raises Profile of Pittsburgh's 700 Hillside Stairways," *Pittsburgh Post-Gazette*, March 22, 2000. For the burden imposed by steps, see F. Elisabeth Crowell, "Painter's Row: The Company House," in Paul U. Kellogg, ed., *The Pittsburgh District: Civic Frontage*, a volume in The Pittsburgh Survey (New York: Survey Associates, Inc. 1914), 132–33; S. J. Kleinberg, *The Shadow of the Mills: Working-Class Families in Pittsburgh, 1870–1907* (Pittsburgh: University of Pittsburgh Press, 1989), 90.

62. Florence Larrabee Lattimore, "Skunk Hollow: The Squatter's House," in Kellogg, *The Pittsburgh District: Civic Frontage*, 124–30; James Zanella, "From the *Paesi d'Italia* to the Village of Larimer: A Study of Pittsburgh's Forgotten Little Italy, 1920–1950" (University of Pittsburgh, 2001, unpublished paper), 5.

63. "Rapid Transit for Pittsburgh: A Discussion," *Proceedings, Engineers Society of Western Pennsylvania* 25 (1909): 468.

64. Ralph Brem, "341-Foot Stone-Arch Bridge Buried Near Proposed Research Park," *The Pittsburgh Press*, June 16, 1963.

65. Olmsted, *Main Thoroughfares*, 101–6; Barry Hannegan, "Schenley Plaza— Place of Dreams," *PHLF News*, no. 144 (1996): 10–15.

66. Jessie Welles to Allen T. Burns, letter, February 1, 1910, in Papers of Frederick Law Olmsted, Manuscript Division, Library of Congress, Washington, D.C., Reel 200.

67. Kellogg, *The Pittsburgh District: Civic Frontage*, 44–45.

68. For Pittsburgh bridges, see Walter C. Kidney, *Pittsburgh's Bridges: Architecture and Engineering* (Pittsburgh: Pittsburgh History & Landmarks Foundation, 1999); also, "Bridges and Tunnels of Allegheny County and Pittsburgh, Pa."; available at http://pghbridges.com/.

69. *The City of Pittsburgh and Its Public Works*, 38.

70. See Kidney, *Pittsburgh's Bridges*, 130, for the Monongahela Connecting Bridge. On land bridges, see Engineers' Society of Western Pennsylvania, *Pittsburgh*, 129–33.

71. Robert J. Gangewere, *The Bridges of Pittsburgh and Allegheny County* (Pittsburgh: Carnegie Library of Pittsburgh, 2001), 4.

72. Tarr, "The Pittsburgh Survey as an Environmental Statement," 170–89.

73. John F. Bauman and Edward K. Muller, "The Olmsteds in Pittsburgh: Part II, Shaping the Progressive City," *Pittsburgh History* 76 (1993–1994): 191–205.

74. "Annual Report, Department of Public Works," *Annual Reports of the Executive Departments of the City Pittsburgh, 1913*, 396, quoted in Roy Lubove, "City Beautiful, City Banal: Design Advocacy and Historic Preservation in Pittsburgh," *Pittsburgh History* 75 (1992): 30.

75. Kristin Szylvian Bailey, "Fighting 'Civic Smallpox': The Civic Club of Allegheny County's Campaign for Billboard Regulation, 1896–1917," *Western Pennsylvania Historical Magazine* 70 (1987): 3–28.

76. Olmsted, *Main Thoroughfares*, 106–12; and "Annual Report of the Department of Public Works: City Planning Commission," *Annual Reports of the Executive Departments of the City Pittsburgh: The City of Pittsburgh, 1913*, 108.

77. M. Graham Netting, *Fifty Years of the Western Pennsylvania Conservancy: The Early Years* (Pittsburgh: The Western Pennsylvania Conservancy, 1982), 67–68.

78. Bauman and Muller, "The Olmsteds in Pittsburgh: Part II," passim; and Roy Lubove, *Twentieth-Century Pittsburgh: Government, Business, and Environmental Change* (New York: John Wiley & Sons, 1969), 87–105.

79. Lubove, *Twentieth-Century Pittsburgh*, 63–78, 106–41; Sherie R. Mershon, "Corporate Social Responsibility and Urban Revitalization: The Allegheny Conference on Community Development, 1943–1968" (Ph.D. diss., Department of History, Carnegie Mellon University, 2000); Robert C. Alberts, *The Shaping of the Point: Pittsburgh's Renaissance Park* (Pittsburgh: University of Pittsburgh Press, 1980).

80. Lubove, *Twentieth-Century Pittsburgh*, 142–77.

81. Roy Lubove, *Twentieth-Century Pittsburgh: The Post-Steel Era* (Pittsburgh: University of Pittsburgh Press, 1996), 57–85; Shelby Stewman and Joel A. Tarr, "Four Decades of Public-Private Partnerships in Pittsburgh," in *Public-Private*

Partnership in American Cities, ed. R. Scott Fosler and Renee A. Berger (New York: Lexington Books, 1982), 95–99.

82. For the collapse of the regional steel industry and its impacts, see John P. Hoerr, *And the Wolf Finally Came: The Decline of the American Steel Industry* (Pittsburgh: University of Pittsburgh Press, 1988); William Serrin, *Homestead: The Glory and Tragedy of an American Steel Town* (New York: Times Books, 1992); and Judith Modell, with photographs by Charlee Brodsky, *A Town Without Steel: Envisioning Homestead* (Pittsburgh: University of Pittsburgh Press, 1998).

83. The Steel Industry Heritage Corporation has played an active role in attempting to preserve structures, artifacts, and records relating to the steel industry region. See, for example, Jan Ackerman, "Steel Industry Preserved"; available at http://www.riversofsteel.com/articles/postgazette39.asp.

84. For case studies of these brownfield sites and their redevelopment, see the web site of the CMU Brownfield Center; available at http://www.ce.cmu.edu/Brownfields/.

85. These developments are mostly reported in the newspapers. See, for example, Eve Modzelewski, "Rolling on the Rivers," *Pittsburgh Post Gazette,* August 5, 2001; Tom Barnes, "Task Force Lays Out Grand Plan for Riverfronts," *Pittsburgh Post Gazette,* October 23, 2001; and Tom Barnes and Dan Fitzpatrick, "Renaissance III," *Pittsburgh Post Gazette,* March 22, 1998.

86. See for example, Roxanne Sherbeck, "We're Rolling on the Rivers," *Pittsburgh Post Gazette,* September 17, 2000.

87. Pennsylvania Economy League, *Southwestern Pennsylvania Water and Sewer Infrastructure Report* (Pittsburgh, 2002), 18.

River City

1. There are 90.5 miles of rivers and 2,024 miles of streams in Allegheny County alone.

2. Henry Leighton, *The Geology of Pittsburgh and Its Environs: A Popular Account of the General Geological Features of the Region* (Pittsburgh: Carnegie Institute Press, 1927), 2. Southwestern Pennsylvania is part of the larger physiographical region known as the Appalachian Plateau, which extends from southern New York to northern Georgia and Alabama.

3. Edward K. Muller, "The Point," in *Geographical Snapshots of North America,* ed. Donald G. Janelle (New York: The Guilford Press, 1992), 231–34.

4. Solon J. Buck and Elizabeth Hawthorn Buck, *The Planting of Civilization in Western Pennsylvania* (Pittsburgh: University of Pittsburgh Press, 1939), 19–66.

5. Walter O'Meara, *Guns at the Forks* (Pittsburgh: University of Pittsburgh Press, 1965); and Fred Anderson, *Crucible of War: The Seven Years' War and the Fate of Empire in British North America, 1754–1766* (New York: Alfred A. Knopf, 2000).

6. Leland D. Baldwin, *Pittsburgh: The Story of a City, 1750–1865* (Pittsburgh: University of Pittsburgh Press, 1937), 76–84.

7. James E. Vance Jr., *This Scene of Man: The Role and Structure of the City in the Geography of Western Civilization* (New York: Harper & Row Publishers, 1977), 265–69.

8. Baldwin, *Pittsburgh,* 103; John W. Reps, *Town Planning in Frontier America* (Princeton, N.J.: Princeton University Press, 1969), 261–66.

9. Catherine Elizabeth Reiser, *Pittsburgh's Commercial Development, 1800–1850* (Harrisburg, Pa.: Pennsylvania Historical and Museum Commission, 1951); and Richard C. Wade, *The Urban Frontier: Pioneer Life in Early Pittsburgh, Cincinnati, Lexington, Louisville, and St. Louis* (Chicago: The University of Chicago Press, 1959), 39–46.

10. Reiser, *Commercial Development*, 45–51.

11. Ibid., 53–68.

12. John J. Kudlik, "Locks, Dams, Steamboats, and Monongahela River Navigation," in *Contextual Essays on the Monongahela River Navigation System* (Huntingdon, Pa.: Heberling Associates, Inc., 1999), 70–86.

13. Shera A. Moxley, "From Rivers to Lakes: Engineering Pittsburgh's Three Rivers," a report (Pittsburgh, Pa: The Studio for Creative Inquiry, Carnegie Mellon University, 2001), 4–9; and Leland D. Baldwin, *The Keelboat Age on Western Waters* (Pittsburgh: University of Pittsburgh Press, 1941), 56–84.

14. Leland R. Johnson, *The Headwaters District: A History of the Pittsburgh District, U.S. Army Corps of Engineers* (Pittsburgh, Pa.: U.S. Army Engineer District, 1979), 63–100.

15. Reiser, *Commercial Development*, 85–111.

16. *Pittsburgh Gazette,* May 18, 1838, as quoted in ibid.,133. For evidence of intense pressure of activity on the wharf, see "An Ordinance to Prevent Obstructions and Nuisances in Water Street," September 10, 1816, in *Ordinances of the City of Pittsburgh* (Pittsburgh: City of Pittsburgh, 1828), 78–79.

17. Verna L. Cowin, *Pittsburgh Archaeological Resources & National Register Survey* (Pittsburgh, Pa.: Carnegie Museum of Natural History, 1985); Baldwin, *Pittsburgh,* 241–47.

18. Joel A. Tarr, "Infrastructure and City-Building in the Nineteenth and Twentieth Centuries," in *City at the Point: Essays on the Social History of Pittsburgh,* ed. Samuel P. Hays (Pittsburgh: University of Pittsburgh Press, 1989), 222–25.

19. Ibid., 216–17; and R. Jay Gangewere, "Bridges to the City," *Carnegie Magazine* (July/August 1993): 24–35.

20. *Pittsburgh: Souvenir of the Spring Meeting of the American Society of Mechanical Engineers,* (Pittsburgh: ASME, 1928), 58–70; and Robert J. Gangewere, *The Bridges of Pittsburgh and Allegheny County* (Pittsburgh: Carnegie Library of Pittsburgh, 2001), 12.

21. Gerald M. Kuncio, "Golden Age in the City of Bridges," *Western Pennsylvania History* 82 (summer 1999): 58–73.

22. Tarr, "Infrastructure and City Building," 246–47; Walter C. Kidney, *Pittsburgh Bridges: Architecture and Engineering* (Pittsburgh: Pittsburgh History & Landmarks Foundation, 1999), 141–42; and Frederick Law Olmsted Jr., *Pittsburgh Main Thoroughfares and the Down Town District: Improvements Necessary to Meet the City's Present and Future Needs, a Report* (Pittsburgh: Pittsburgh Civic Commission, 1910), 133–65.

23. Michael Koryak, "River Reborn," report of the U.S. Army Corps of Engineers, Pittsburgh District (May 1990), 5; and Daniel F. Jackson, *Aquatic-Life Resources of the Ohio River: Section I, Historical Notes on Fish Fauna* (Cincinnati, Ohio: Ohio River Valley Sanitation Commission), 10.

24. Henry Oliver Evans, *Iron Pioneer: Henry W. Oliver, 1840–1904* (New York: E. P. Dutton & Company, 1942), 6–7.

25. John J. Kudlik, "You Couldn't Keep an Iron Man Down: Rowing in Nineteenth Century Pittsburgh," *Pittsburgh History* 73 (summer 1990): 51–63.

26. Scott C. Martin, *Killing Time: Leisure and Culture in Southwestern Pennsylvania, 1800–1850* (Pittsburgh, Pa.: University of Pittsburgh Press, 1995), 28–29, 111, 121, 124; and Joel A. Tarr and Denise DiPasquale, "The Mill Town in the Industrial City: Pittsburgh's Hazelwood," *Urbanism Past and Present* 7 (winter / spring 1981): 1–14.

27. Glenn Porter and Harold C. Livesay, *Merchants and Manufacturers: Studies in the Changing Structure of Nineteenth-Century Marketing* (Baltimore, Md.: The Johns Hopkins University Press, 1971), 65–69; and David H. Wollman and Donald R. Inman, *Portraits in Steel: An Illustrated History of Jones & Laughlin Steel Corporation* (Kent, Ohio: The Kent State University Press, 1999), 8–20.

28. Valerie S. Grash, *The Commercial Skyscrapers of Pittsburgh Industrialists and Financiers, 1885–1932* (Ph.D. diss., The Pennsylvania State University, 1998).

29. John N. Ingham, *Making Iron and Steel: Independent Mills in Pittsburgh, 1820–1920* (Columbus: Ohio State University Press, 1991), 47–95.

30. *Pittsburgh* (1928), 46–57.

31. Johnson, *The Headwaters District*, 146.

32. Ibid., 114–73; Moxley, *From Rivers to Lakes*, 20–27.

33. Edward K. Muller, "Industrial Suburbs and the Growth of Metropolitan Pittsburgh," *Journal of Historical Geography* 27 (spring 2000): 58–73.

34. Charles C. Plummer and David McGeary, *Physical Geology*, 5th ed. (Dubuque, Iowa: William C. Brown Publishers, 1991), chap. 10; and Tom L. McKnight, *Physical Geography*, 5th ed. (England Cliffs, N.J.: Prentice Hall, 1996), chap. 16.

35. Vagel Keller, "Anatomy of a Brownfield" (Department of History, Carnegie Mellon University, 1999, photocopy), 3. Today, history buffs familiar with pictures of the sloping ground where Pinkerton detectives tried to land near the pump house at the Homestead Works in 1892, are confronted with a vertical drop of more than twenty feet to the river over a cement bulkhead.

36. Michael Koryak, "Wetland Regulation in Appalachia," in *Symposium on Wetlands of the Unglaciated Region* (Morgantown, W.Va.: West Virginia University, 1982), 237; and the website "Watershed Atlas of the Monongahela and Allegheny Rivers," Resource Center (Pennsylvania Environment Council); available at www.watershedatlas.org.

37. Evans, *Iron Pioneer*, 7–8.

38. *Report of Flood Commission of Pittsburgh, Penna.* (Pittsburgh, Pa.: Flood Commission of Pittsburgh, Penna., 1912), 11–15 and appendix 1.

39. Roland M. Smith, "The Politics of Pittsburgh Flood Control, 1908–1936," 2 parts, *Pennsylvania History* 42 (January 1975): 5–24 and 44 (January 1977): 3–24.

40. Letitia C. Langord, *Urban Waterways: Public Access and the Public Trust* (Ph.D. diss., University of Pittsburgh, 1977), 203.

41. Kenneth J. Heineman, "The Changing Face of Schenley Park," *Pittsburgh History* 72 (fall 1989): 117.

42. Edward K. Muller, "The Legacy of Industrial Rivers," *Pittsburgh History* 72 (summer 1972): 64–75; and Kudlik, "You Couldn't Keep an Iron Man Down," 61–62.

43. Roy Lubove, *Twentieth-Century Pittsburgh*, vol. 1, *Government, Business, and*

Environmental Change (New York: John Wiley & Sons, 1969), 106–41; Shelby Stewman and Joel A. Tarr, "Four Decades of Public-Private Partnerships in Pittsburgh," in *Public-Private Partnerships in American Cities*, ed. R. Scott Fosler and Renee A. Berger (Lexington, Mass.: D. C. Heath & Co., 1982), 59–127; and John F. Bauman and Edward K. Muller, "The Planning Technician as Urban Visionary: Frederick Bigger and American Planning, 1915–1954," *The Journal of Planning History* 1 (May 2002): 124–53.

44. Langord, *Urban Waterways*, 208–11.

45. Olmsted, *Pittsburgh: Main Thoroughfares*, 19–28; John F. Bauman and Edward K. Muller, "The Olmsteds in Pittsburgh: Part II, Shaping the Progressive City," *Pittsburgh History* 76 (winter 1993/1994): 191–205; and Lubove, *Twentieth-Century Pittsburgh*, 87–105.

46. Roy Lubove, *Twentieth-Century Pittsburgh*, vol. 2, *The Post-Steel Era* (Pittsburgh, Pa.: University of Pittsburgh Press, 1996), 368.

47. The only sports fans to experience this distinctive Pittsburgh sight were those watching events on television, which flashed pictures of the Point from overhead blimps. Most professional sports fans of the 1970s could identify Pittsburgh's Point even if they had never been to the city. The original plan for the stadium did provide an open end to take in the view, but it would have increased the construction costs. Instead, a round, completely closed stadium was built. Information is based on a conversation with Robert B. Pease, former executive director of the Urban Redevelopment Authority of Pittsburgh and former executive director of the Allegheny Conference on Community Development.

48. Edward K. Muller, "Pittsburgh's Waterfront Lands," a final report to the Urban Redevelopment Authority, Pittsburgh, Pa., 1983; Muller, "The Legacy of Industrial Rivers," 71–74; and Langord, *Urban Waterways*, 207.

49. The rivers will continue to move bulk cargo in vast quantities for years to come, and the Army Corps of Engineers is in the midst of a massive improvement of the old locks and dams on the upper Ohio and Monongahela Rivers. The port of Pittsburgh encompasses a combined two hundred miles of the three rivers. See Port of Pittsburgh website and Christine H. O'Toole, "Rollin' on the Rivers: The Region's Proud Heritage Continues as the Country's Busiest Inland Port," *Pittsburgh Magazine* (October 2000): 144–49.

50. Michael Koryak, "The Impact of Above Grade Sewerline Crossings on the Distribution and Abundance of Fishes in Recovering Small Urban Streams of the Upper Ohio River Valley," *Journal of Freshwater Ecology* 16 (2001): 591–92.

51. Kathleen Knauer and Tim Collins, "Water Quality: Phase I, Executive Summary–Year 2000," a report (Pittsburgh, Pa.: The Studio for Creative Inquiry, Carnegie-Mellon University, 2001), 7–14; Kellie Fenton, "Improvement in Water Quality: An Examination of the Pollution of Pittsburgh's Rivers, 1940–Present" (Pittsburgh, Pa.: Carnegie Mellon University, 1999, typescript); and Don Hopey and Jeffrey Cohan, "Sewage Problems Run Deep in Region," *Pittsburgh Post Gazette*, July 14, 2002.

52. For an overview of the general situation of redevelopment, see Lubove, *Twentieth-Century Pittsburgh*, vol. 2.

53. Ibid., 201–7.

54. R. Jay Gangewere, "The Three Rivers Heritage Trail," *The Carnegie Magazine* 60 (March/April 1991): 22–30.

55. See, for example, "Task Force Lays Out Grand Plan for Riverfronts," *Pittsburgh Post-Gazette,* October 23, 2001.

56. Early in the 1990s, for example, city officials and transportation planners considered splitting a new expressway in half and putting one direction on the southern shore of the Mon River and the other direction on the northern shore—in effect, making both shores inaccessible.

Critical Decisions in Pittsburgh Water and Wastewater Treatment

1. For a comprehensive study of these issues on a national level, see Martin V. Melosi, *The Sanitary City: Urban Infrastructure in America from Colonial Times to the Present* (Baltimore: Johns Hopkins University Press, 2000); for Pittsburgh infrastructure development, see Joel A. Tarr, "Infrastructure and City-Building in the Nineteenth and Twentieth Centuries," in *City at the Point,* ed. Samuel P. Hays (Pittsburgh: University of Pittsburgh Press, 1989), 213–64.

2. Richard C. Wade, *The Urban Frontier: The Rise of Western Cities, 1790–1830* (Cambridge, Mass.: Harvard University Press, 1959), 95; Catherine E. Reiser, *Pittsburgh's Commercial Development, 1800–1850* (Harrisburg: Pennsylvania Historical and Museum Commission, 1951), 129; Leland D. Baldwin, *Pittsburgh: The Story of a City* (Pittsburgh: University of Pittsburgh Press, 1938), 156; and Charles D. Jacobson and Joel A. Tarr, "No Single Path: Ownership and Financing of Infrastructure in the Nineteenth and Twentieth Centuries," in *Infrastructure Delivery: Private Initiative and the Public Good,* ed. Ashoka Mody (Washington, D.C.: The World Bank, 1996), 1–35.

3. Richard A. Sabol, "Public Works in Pittsburgh Prior to the Establishment of the Department of Public Works" (Department of History, Carnegie Mellon University, 1980, research paper), 5; Frank Kern, "History of Pittsburgh Water Works, 1821–1842" (Department of History, Carnegie Mellon University, 1982, research paper), 1–4; and Wade, *Urban Frontier,* 292.

4. Kern, "History of Pittsburgh Water Works," 6; Wade, *Urban Frontier,* 296; and Sabor, "Public Works in Pittsburgh," 5. The initial cost was $40,000.

5. Erwin E. Lanpher and C. F. Drake, *City of Pittsburgh: Its Water Works and Typhoid Fever Statistics* (Pittsburgh: City of Pittsburgh, 1930), 23–25; *Report of the Filtration Commission of the City of Pittsburgh, Pennsylvania* (January 1899), 73–74, 94–96.

6. James H. Thompson, "A Financial History of the City of Pittsburgh, 1816–1910" (Ph.D. diss., University of Pittsburgh, 1948), 44–45; Paul Studenski and Herman E. Kross, *Financial History of the United States* (New York: McGraw-Hill, 1952), 13.

7. City of Pittsburgh, "Report on the Recent Outbreak of Diphtheria in Pittsburgh," *Annual Report of the Department of Health* (Pittsburgh,1878); "Pittsburgh in 1880," in U.S. Department of the Interior, Census Office, *Tenth Census of the United States, 1880, Report of the Social Statistics of Cities,* vol. 1 of 2 [George E. Waring Jr., comp.], (Washington: GPO, 1887), 866; and Clayton R. Koppes and William P. Norris, "Ethnicity, Class, and Mortality in the Industrial City: A Case Study of Typhoid Fever in Pittsburgh, 1890–1910," *Journal of Urban History* 2 (May 1985): 269–75.

8. Susan J. Kleinberg, *The Shadow of the Mills: Working-Class Families in Pittsburgh, 1870–1907* (Pittsburgh: University of Pittsburgh Press, 1989), 87–93; Robin L. Einhorn, *Property Rules: Political Economy in Chicago, 1833–1872* (Chicago: University of Chicago Press, 1991), 104.

9. Charles Davis, in discussion following Geo. H. Browne, "A Few of Pittsburgh's Sewers," *Transactions Engineers' Society of Western Pennsylvania* 1 (January 1880–June 1882): 229; Terry F. Yosie, "Retrospective Analysis of Water Supply and Wastewater Policies in Pittsburgh, 1800–1959" (Doctor of Arts diss., Carnegie Mellon University, 1981), 14–16, 48–49, henceforth cited as Yosie, "Pittsburgh Water Supply and Wastewater Policies."

10. Before the availability of piped-in water Americans had used various sources, such as cisterns, wells, and local ponds, to provide a household water supply. See Maureen Ogle, *All the Necessary Conveniences: American Household Plumbing, 1840–1890* (Baltimore: Johns Hopkins University Press, 1996).

11. Yosie, "Pittsburgh Water Supply and Wastewater Policies," 49.

12. Jacqueline Corn, "Municipal Organization for Public Health in Pittsburgh, 1851–1895" (Doctor of Arts diss., Carnegie Mellon University, 1972), 15–16; John Duffy, "The Impact of Asiatic Cholera on Pittsburgh, Wheeling, and Charleston," *Western Pennsylvania Historical Magazine* 47 (July 1964): 205, 208–9.

13. Browne, "A Few of Pittsburgh's Sewers," and Davis discussion, in Browne, 214–49.

14. J. H. McClelland, "Dangers to Health in Suburban Districts," *Fifth Annual Report of the State Board of Health* (Harrisburg, Pa., 1891), 390–91; *Annual Report of the Pittsburgh Board of Health, 1890* (Pittsburgh, 1891), 69.

15. Joel A. Tarr, "The Separate vs. Combined Sewer Problem: A Case Study in Urban Technology Design Choice," *Journal of Urban History* 5 (May 1979): 308–9; Brown, "A Few of Pittsburgh's Sewers," 219–21.

16. Jon A. Peterson, "The Impact of Sanitary Reform upon American Urban Planning," *Journal of Social History* 13 (fall 1979): 84–89.

17. During the 1880s the Board of Health attempted to force scavenger firms to utilize the "odorless excavator" technology to clean cesspools. See Yosie, "Pittsburgh Water Supply and Wastewater Policies," 104–8.

18. The Street Acts, passed by the city councils in 1887–1889, provided that street and lateral sewer improvements would be made on the petition of one-third of the abutting property owners in a neighborhood. All abutters, however, would be assessed for improvements. In 1891 the State Supreme Court declared these acts unconstitutional. See Thompson, "Financial History," 178–79; Yosie, "Pittsburgh Water Supply and Wastewater Policies," 112–13.

19. *Fourth Annual Report of the State Department of Health* (Harrisburg, Pa., 1911), 1476; Koppes and Norris, "Ethnicity, Class, and Mortality in the Industrial City," 266.

20. Koppes and Norris, "Ethnicity, Class, and Mortality in the Industrial City," 270–75.

21. Quoted in Nancy Tomes, *The Gospel of Germs: Men, Women, and the Microbe in American Life* (Cambridge: Harvard University Press, 1998), 189–90.

22. Quoted in Koppes and Norris, "Ethnicity, Class, and Mortality," 271. For a study of a similar situation in Pittsburgh's neighboring city of Allegheny, see

Bruce W. Jordan, "The Allegheny City Water Works, 1840–1907," *Western Pennsylvania Historical Magazine* 70 (January 1987): 29–52. Pittsburgh annexed Allegheny in 1907.

23. *Report of the Joint Commission of the Chamber of Commerce of Pittsburgh, Engineer's Society of Western Pennsylvania, Allegheny County Medical Society, and Iron City Microscopical Society* (Pittsburgh, 1894).

24. James O. Handy to Allen Hazen, Allen Hazen Papers (Cambridge, Mass.: Massachusetts Institute of Technology Archives). The Citizen's League, "an organization of public-spirited young men," provided the funding. See James Otis Handy, "Story of the Efforts Which Led to the Purification of the Water-Supply of Pittsburgh, and to the Elimination of Typhoid Fever from that Cause," *Proceedings of the Engineers' Society of Western Pennsylvania* 43 (February 1927–January 1928): 182–85.

25. Draft copies of the report are located in the Allen Hazen Papers, MIT Archives. *Report of the Filtration Commission of the City of Pittsburgh, Pennsylvania* (Pittsburgh, January 1899), C.C. no. 406); Mark J. Tierno, "The Search for Pure Water in Pittsburgh: The Urban Response to Water Pollution, 1893–1914," *Western Pennsylvania Historical Magazine* 60 (January 1977): 23–36.

26. Handy, "Story of the Efforts," 189–90. Handy noted that Bigelow "was absolutely consistent in his disbelief in the contamination of the water-supply; therefore, in his opinion, there was no need to purify it. He accused us of infidelity to the business interests of our city in questioning the purity of our water-supply."

27. *Pittsburgh Dispatch,* February 7, 1899; May 23, 1899; August 1, 1901; August 7, 1901; November 12, 1901; and December 12, 1901; C. E. Drake, "Statistics of Typhoid Fever in Pittsburgh," in *City of Pittsburgh, Its Water Works* (Pittsburgh, 1931), 29–38; Tierno, "The Search for Pure Water in Pittsburgh," 35–36. For an enlightening discussion of the differential effects of sewers and water filtration in Pittsburgh, see chapter 3, "Sewers: When, Where, and to What Effect?" in Werner Troesken, *Water, Race, and Disease* (Cambridge, Mass.: MIT Press, forthcoming).

28. Frank E. Wing, "Thirty-Five Years of Typhoid," in *The Pittsburgh District: Civic Frontage, the Pittsburgh Survey,* ed. Paul Underwood Kellogg (New York, 1914), 63–86. In November 1908, as part of the Pittsburgh Civic Exhibit held in the Carnegie Institute, a 250-foot frieze containing silhouettes of 622 persons who had died from typhoid fever in the city the previous year was exhibited.

29. Colleen K. O'Toole, *The Search for Purity: A Retrospective Policy Analysis of the Decision to Chlorinate Cincinnati's Public Water Supply, 1890–1920* (New York: Garland Publishing, 1990), 67–76.

30. Michael P. McCarthy, *Typhoid and the Politics of Public Health in Nineteenth-Century Philadelphia* (Philadelphia: American Philosophical Society, 1987). See also Carolyn G. Shapiro-Shapin, "Filtering the City's Image: Progressivism, Local Control, and the St. Louis Water Supply, 1890–1906," *Bulletin of the History of Medicine* 54 (July 1999): 397–412. The St. Louis situation was complicated by the fear of threats to the city's water supply from the Chicago Sanitary and Ship Canal. For a study of a city that chose not to filter its water but rather to rely on upcountry sources, see Fern L. Nesson, *Great Waters: A History of Boston's Water Supply* (Hanover, N.H.: University Press of New England, 1983).

31. The importance of the issue of technological choice was highlighted for the authors by Michael Blackhurst in "Pittsburgh and Typhoid Fever—1883–1908" (Pittsburgh, Carnegie Mellon University, 1999, research paper); Yosie, "Pittsburgh Water Supply and Wastewater Policies," 128–29; Steven J. Diner, *A Very Different Age: Americans of the Progressive Era* (New York: Hill & Wang, 1998), 176–208.

32. See, for example, Pittsburgh Chamber of Commerce, *Sewage Disposal for Pittsburgh* (Pittsburgh, 1907); G. Soper, "The Sanitary Engineering Problems of Water Supply and Sewage Disposal in New York City," *Science* 25 (1907): 601–5 and *Committee on Pollution of State Waters, Protest against the Bronx River Valley Sewer* (New York, 1907); Merchants Association of New York, *The Battle of the Microbes: Nature's Fight for Pure Water* (New York, 1908); and "The Unusual Prevalence of Typhoid Fever in 1903 and 1904," *Engineering News* 51 (1904): 129–30.

33. F. H. Snow, "Administration of Pennsylvania Laws Respecting Stream Pollution," *Proceedings of the Engineers' Society of Western Pennsylvania* 23 (1907): 266–83.

34. "Sewage Pollution of Water Supplies," *Engineering Record* 48 (1909): 117.

35. "The Greater Pittsburgh Sewerage and Sewage Purification Orders," *Engineering News* 63 (1910): 179–80; "Pittsburgh Sewage Purification Orders," ibid., 70–71; "The Sewerage Problem of Greater Pittsburgh," *Engineering Record* 61 (1910): 183–84; see also G. Gregory, "A Study in Local Decision Making: Pittsburgh and Sewage Treatment," *Western Pennsylvania Historical Magazine* 57 (1974): 25–42.

36. "The Most Important Sewerage and Sewage Disposal Report Made in the United States," *Engineering Record* 65 (1912): 209–12; "Pittsburgh Sewage Disposal Reports," *Engineering News* 67 (1912): 398–402.

37. N. S. Sprague, superintendent, Bureau of Construction, to Jos. G. Armstrong, director, Pittsburgh Department of Public Works, "Letter of Transmittal," February 9, 1912, 9, copy in Allen Hazen Papers, MIT Archives.

38. "The Most Important Sewerage and Sewage," *Engineering Record* 65 (1912): 400–401.

39. "The Pittsburg [sic] Sewage Purification Order: Letters from Commissioner Dixon and May Magee," *Engineering News* 67 (1912): 548–52.

40. N. S. Sprague, superintendent of the Pittsburgh Bureau of Construction, noted, "Practical sanitation means the greatest good for the greatest number, and would it not be a better policy to conserve the public funds and apply them to other sanitary measures which would produce far greater results." See Sprague to Armstrong, "Letter of Transmittal," 8–9.

41. "The Pollution of Streams," *Engineering Record* 60 (1909): 157–59; Melosi, *The Sanitary City*, 111–16.

42. For an enlightening discussion of these choices in the Connecticut River, see John T. Cumbler, *Reasonable Use: The People, the Environment, and the State, New England 1790–1930* (New York: Oxford, 2000), 131–60.

43. W. L. Stevenson, "Pennsylvania Sanitary Water Board: Powers, Duties, and Policies," *Engineering News-Record* 91 (October 25, 1923): 684–85; T. Saville, "Administrative Control of Water Pollution," *Transactions, American Institute of Chemical Engineers* 27 (1931): 74–77.

44. E. A. Holbrook, "Pollution of Pittsburgh's Rivers," *The Pennsylvania Engineer* 1 (October 1936): 12. In 1934, 14.8 percent of Pittsburgh households and

22.2 percent of the households in Allegheny County outside of the city were not connected to sewers. *Real Property Inventory of Allegheny County* (Pittsburgh: Bureau of Business Research, University of Pittsburgh, 1937).

45. Kenneth A. Reid, "We Can't Afford Pollution," *Pennsylvania Angler* 6 (February 1937): 4; Nicholas Casner, "Polluter versus Polluter: The Pennsylvania Railroad and the Manufacturing of Pollution Policies in the 1920s," *Journal of Policy History* 11 (1999): 179–200

46. *Pennsylvania Legislative Journal*, April 28, 1937; May 5, 1937, 3621; May 19, 1937, 4833; May 21, 1937, 5368–73; May 24, 1937, 5590–91; May 25, 1937, 5757, 5791–92; and June 2, 1937, 6608–9, 6567–68. See also D. E. Davis, "Planning for Pollution Control at Pittsburgh, Pennsylvania," *Proceedings American Society of Civil Engineers* 64 (1938): 51–56, and Davis, "A Solution for the Problem at Pittsburgh," *Civil Engineering* 7 (January 1937): 5. Some authorities had argued that the mine acid neutralized bacterial wastes. For a discussion of the problem of mine acid, see Casner essay, this volume.

47. F. Eugene Reader, "Financing Municipal Sewage Treatment Facilities in Pennsylvania by Use of Municipal Authorities," *Dickinson Law Review* 58 (1954): 335–36; "Municipal Authority Act," Act No. 191, June 28, 1935, *Laws of the General Assembly of the Commonwealth of Pennsylvania* (Harrisburg, 1935); "Municipal Authorities Act of 1945," Act No. 164, May 2, 1945 (Harrisburg, 1945).

48. General Committee on Sewage of the Municipalities of Allegheny County, *Report Concerning Treatment and Disposal* (Pittsburgh, 1939), 9–33.

49. *Biennial Report of the Pennsylvania Department of Health for the Period June 1, 1942, to May 31, 1944* (Harrisburg, 1944), 51 (hereafter referred to as *Biennial Report*); ibid., June 1, 1944, to May 31, 1946, 45; and J. C. Graul, "Pennsylvania's Clean Stream Program," *Public Works* 80 (February 1940): 28

50. Yosie, "Pittsburgh Water Supply and Wastewater Policies," 359–62.

51. See the essays in Samuel P. Hays, "Part IV: Environmental Politics since World War II," *Explorations in Environmental History: Essays by Samuel P. Hays* (University of Pittsburgh Press, 1998).

52. Field tests conducted by the Pennsylvania Department of Health showed that the dissolved oxygen level at many river locations was below the minimum level necessary for the maintenance of aquatic life. In 1943, the U.S. Public Health Service study of the Ohio River showed that the organic waste load reaching the Ohio River from Pittsburgh and its suburbs had a population equivalent of 1,334,300. In addition, there were 1,032,000 tons per year of acid waste. U.S.P.H.S., *Report of the Ohio River Committee*, House Document no. 265, 78th Congress, 1st session, August 27, 1943 (Washington, D.C.: GPO, 1944), 1273; General Committee on Sewage of the Municipalities of Allegheny County, *Report Concerning Treatment and Disposal*, 14–15; *Report of the Ohio River Committee*, House Document no. 265, 78th Congress, 1st session, August 27, 1943 (Washington, D.C.: GPO, 1944), 1273; and Ivan G. Hosack, "Public Health in Pittsburgh: Analysis-Progress-Recommendations, 1930–40" (Pittsburgh: General Health Council of Allegheny County, 1941), 78.

53. See Roy Lubove, *Twentieth-Century Pittsburgh* (New York, 1969), 108–41.

54. *Pittsburgh Press*, June 19, July 16, and December 19, 1945.

55. *Pittsburgh Press*, July 1, 16, 1945.

56. "Municipal Authorities Act Abatement of Stream Pollution," *Allegheny*

Conference Digest 1 (July 1945): 6; Park Martin, "Narrative of the Allegheny Conference on Community Development and the Pittsburgh Renaissance, 1943–1958" (Pittsburgh, 1964, photocopy), 35; John F. Laboon, *Chronological Highlights of the History of the Allegheny County Sanitary Authority*, vol. 1 of 2 (Pittsburgh: 1973), 1–2.

57. *Pittsburgh Press*, June 19, July 1, Sept. 9, 1945; and Laboon, *Chronological Highlights*, 1:1–2.

58. Martin, *Narrative of the ACCD*, 5; Laboon, *Chronological Highlights*, 1:1– 2.

59. Laboon, *Chronological Highlights*, 1:5.

60. Ibid., 1:7–8, 10.

61. Ibid., 1:10–11.

62. For a biography of Lawrence, see Michael P. Weber, *Don't Call Me Boss: David L. Lawrence, Pittsburgh's Renaissance Mayor* (Pittsburgh: University of Pittsburgh Press, 1988).

63. Yosie, "Pittsburgh Water Supply and Wastewater Policies," 382–83, 389–91; *Pittsburgh Press*, April 17, June 9, 14, 1949.

64. Yosie, "Pittsburgh Water Supply and Wastewater Policies," 383–93.

65. "Pittsburgh Digs Deep for Cleaner Streams," *Greater Pittsburgh* (August 1959), 11; John F. Laboon, "Controlled Submergence of Pittsburgh's Deep Sewers," *Proceedings American Society of Civil Engineers*, Sanitary Engineering Division (July 1958); "Concentrated Sludge: The Laboon Process," *Engineering News-Record* 147 (October 11, 1951): 30–32; and John C. Miller, "Sludge Flotation by the Laboon Process: McKees Rocks Sewage Treatment Plant" (Master's thesis, University of Pittsburgh, 1948).

66. In 1960 these municipalities sued in Common Pleas Court claiming that ALCOSAN had violated state law by charging them a higher service fee than other Authority members. In 1965, however, the judge dismissed the case. See Yosie, "Pittsburgh Water Supply and Wastewater Policies," 398; *Pittsburgh Press*, August 3, 1949. Some communities, such as Duquesne and West Mifflin, resisted joining ALCOSAN, while Penn Hills did not join until compelled to by the EPA in 1995. They were motivated by several reasons, including the so-called "hazard of centralization" and a desire to build and control their own disposal plants. According to Laboon, some town officials anticipated financial and patronage gains from controlling their own sewage treatment facilities. See Laboon, *Chronological Highlights*, 1:74, 115, and interview with John Laboon, 1978.

67. "Preserving Our Water Resources—ALCOSAN's Area-wide Approach to Sewage Disposal Saves Dollars," *Pennsylvania Economy League Newsletter* (October 1960).

68. "Allegheny County Sanitary Authority: Progress Report," January 1, 1958, 8.

69. The Authority attempted to acquire various water companies in the Pittsburgh area to simplify service-billing procedures through the reading of household water meters, but opposition from Mayor Lawrence, two of the county commissioners, and the ACCD blocked the plan. See Laboon, *Chronological Highlights*, 1:17–56.

70. Laboon, *Chronological Highlights*, 1:45–47, 50, 77–78; vol. 2, appendix 1.

71. Ibid., 1:80–81; *Pittsburgh Press*, October 10, 17, 195; Laboon, *Chronological Highlights*, 1:80–83.

72. Laboon, *Chronological Highlights,* 1:26–27; David L. Cowell, "Sewer Rentals Based on Water Consumption," *Pennsylvania Department of Internal Affairs Bulletin* 19 (September 1951): 14–16.

73. *Pittsburgh Press,* August 13, 1953.

74. Ibid., August 2, 13, 1953; March 24, 1954; October 12, 1955; John F. Laboon, "$100 Million Loan Finances the Allegheny County Sewage Works," *Wastes Engineering* 26 (December 1953): 650; Laboon, *Chronological Highlights,* 1:85. The Mellon interests reversed an earlier decision to avoid financial involvement with the agency because the bank came to see the loan to the Sanitary Authority as a profitable business investment.

75. Laboon, *Chronological Highlights,* 1:86–116; *Report of the Allegheny County Sanitary Authority* (Pittsburgh, 1958, 1960), 13, 30.

76. See Melosi, *The Sanitary City,* 8–14, for a discussion of path-dependency in regard to water and sewer systems.

77. See *Investing in Clean Water: A Report from the Southwestern Pennsylvania Water and Sewer Infrastructure Project Steering Committee* (Pittsburgh, 2002). In 2002, The National Academy of Sciences / National Research Council appointed a "Committee on Water Quality Improvement for The Pittsburgh Region" to study the problem and come up with recommendations. See Don Hopey, "National Experts to Study Region's Sewer Problems," *Pittsburgh Post-Gazette,* May 17, 2002.

Acid Mine Drainage and Pittsburgh's Water Quality

1. Howard N. Eavenson, *The First Century and a Quarter of the American Coal Industry* (Baltimore: Waverly Press, 1942), 166.

2. Andrew B. Crichton, "Disposal of Drainage from Coal Mines," *Proceedings of American Society of Civil Engineers* 53 (1927): 1656–66.

3. For a fuller treatment of the history of acid mine drainage, see Nicholas A. Casner, "Acid Water: A History of Coal Mine Pollution in Western Pennsylvania, 1880–1950" (Ph.D. diss., Carnegie Mellon University, 1994).

4. Andrew B. Crichton, "Mine-Drainage Stream Pollution," *Transactions of the American Institute of Mining and Metallurgical Engineers* 69 (1923): 442.

5. Robert L. P. Kleinmann, "Acid Mine Drainage in the United States," paper on file, U.S. Bureau of Mines, Pittsburgh Research Center.

6. U.S. Congress, House, Committee on Public Works, *Acid Mine Drainage: A Report,* 87th Cong., 2d sess., 1962, 13–18.

7. Don C. Jones, "Acid Mine Drainage—Its Control Reduces Stream Pollution," *Mechanization* 15 (October 1951): 85–88, 91. Pennsylvania Act of August 23, 1965, P.L. 372, act no. 194.

8. Eavenson, *The First Century,* 156.

9. James B. Lackey, "The Flora and Fauna of Surface Waters Polluted by Acid Mine Drainage," *Public Health Reports* 53 (August 26, 1938) 1499–1507.

10. Thomas P. Roberts, "Acids in the Monongahela River," *Proceedings of the Engineers' Society of Western Pennsylvania* 27 (1911): 384. See also R. D. Leitch, "A General Review of United States Bureau of Mines Stream Pollution Investigations," Research Investigation 3098, April 1931, 5; and William D. Pearson and Juanelle B. Pearson, "Fishes of the Ohio River," *Ohio Journal of Science* 89 (1989): 181–87.

11. Roberts, "Acids in the Monongahela," 378.

12. City of Pittsburgh, *Report of the Filtration Commission* (January 1899), 33–34; J. A. Mohr, "Acid in the Monongahela River Water," *Proceedings of the Engineers' Society of Western Pennsylvania* 17 (1901): 237.

13. U.S. Public Health Service, "A Study of the Pollution and Purification of the Ohio River," *Public Health Bulletin No. 143* (July 1924), 166.

14. Mark J. Tierno, "The Search for Pure Water in Pittsburgh: The Urban Response to Water Pollution, 1893–1914," *Western Pennsylvania Historical Magazine* 60 (January 1977): 23–36.

15. Samuel James Lewis, "Quality of Water in the Upper Ohio River Basin and at Erie, Pa.," *Water Supply and Irrigation Paper No. 161,* United States Geological Survey (Washington, D.C.: GPO, 1906), 51.

16. Tierno, "The Search for Pure Water," 35–36.

17. Joel A. Tarr, "Searching for a Sink for an Industrial Waste," in *The Search for the Ultimate Sink: Urban Pollution in Historical Perspective* (Akron, Ohio: The University of Akron Press, 1996), 396–97.

18. Roberts, "Acids in the Monongahela," 413–15.

19. E. C. Trax, "A New Raw Water Supply for the City of McKeesport, Pennsylvania," *Journal of the American Water Works Association* 3 (1916): 947–58.

20. Lewis, "Quality of Water," 50–51.

21. Alexander Potter, "The Design, Construction, and Operation of the New Water Softening and Filtration Plant at McKeesport, Pa.," *Journal of Engineers' Society of Pennsylvania* 1 (1909): 163–217.

22. Trax, "A New Raw Water," 948–49.

23. Theodore Tonnele, "The River, Well, and Spring Waters of McKeesport, Pa., and Vicinity," *Proceedings of the Engineers' Society of Western Pennsylvania* 10 (1894): 28. See also U.S. Public Health Service, "A Study of Pollution and Purification of the Ohio River," *Public Health Bulletin No. 143* (Washington, D.C.: GPO, 1924).

24. S. J. Kleinberg, *The Shadow of the Mills: Working-Class Families in Pittsburgh, 1870–1907* (Pittsburgh: University of Pittsburgh Press, 1989), 214–15.

25. Crichton, "Mine-Drainage Stream Pollution," 438.

26. R. V. Norris, "The Unwatering of Mines in the Anthracite Region," *The Engineering Magazine* 34 (1907): 160–61.

27. On pH level, see Kermit L. Herndon, "A Survey of the Mine Drainage in the West Fork River Basin," *West Virginia University College of Engineering Bulletin* (May 1931): 115–45; on pitting in iron, see Edwin M. Chance, "Use of Mine Water as Boiler Feed," *Coal Age* 11 (1917): 600–601.

28. On acidic sludge, see Andrew B. Crichton, "Stream Pollution and Coal Mining," *Mining Congress Journal* 12 (1926): 419; on expenses, see Crichton, "Disposal of Drainage from Coal Mines," *Proceedings of American Society of Civil Engineers* 53 (1927): 1664.

29. Young, "Pollution of River Water," 216. On the National Tube Company's treatment plant, see Potter, "The Design," 166.

30. R. C. Bardwell, "Water Treatment for Railway Systems," *Water Works and Sewage* 80 (January 1933): 9; Young, "Pollution of River Water," 216.

31. Bardwell, "Water Treatment," 13; Crichton, "Disposal of Drainage," 1334; Roberts, "Acids in the Monongahela," 383.

32. Roberts, "Acids in the Monongahela," 405–10.

33. Act of April 22, 1905, Pa. P.L. 260 (repealed 1937).

34. *The Pennsylvania Coal Company v Sanderson and Wife*, 113 Pa. 126, 149–57.

35. Curtis H. Lindley, *A Treatise on the American Law Relating to Mines and Mineral Lands*, vol. 3, 3d ed. (San Francisco: Brancroft-Whitney Co., 1914), 2040–49.

36. *McCune v Pittsburgh & Baltimore Coal*, 238 Pa. 83. For greater analysis of the *Sanderson* case, see Timothy R. Watson and Loel R. Burcat, "Legal Aspects of Pennsylvania Water Management," in Shymal K. Majumdar, *Water Resources in Pennsylvania: Availability, Quality, and Management* (Philadelphia: The Pennsylvania Academy of Science, 1990), 220–25.

37. Robert Broughton, Thomas A. Koza, and Gary F. Selway, "Acid Mine Drainage and the Pennsylvania Courts," *Duquesne Law Review* 11 (1973): 504. See also Abel Wolman, "State Responsibility in Stream Pollution Abatement," *Industrial and Engineering Chemistry* 39 (1947): 562.

38. The Pennsylvania Railroad case and the Sanitary Water Board relations are discussed in more detail in Nicholas Casner, "Polluter versus Polluter: The Pennsylvania Railroad and the Manufacturing of Pollution Policies in the 1920s," *Journal of Policy History* 11 (spring 1999): 179–200.

39. Court of Common Pleas of Fayette County, Uniontown, Pennsylvania: case in equity no. 1023, the Mountain Water Supply Company, the Dunbar Water Supply Company, and the *Pennsylvania Railroad et al., Appellants, v Sagamore Coal Co. et al.*, 281 Pa. 233, 12–98.

40. W. L. Stevenson, chief engineer, Sanitary Water Board of Pennsylvania, "The Powers, Duties and Policies of the Sanitary Water Board of the Common-wealth of Pennsylvania," Papers of Gifford Pinchot, Library of Congress, file 1535, "Governor's Papers."

41. Tarr, "Searching for a Sink for an Industrial Waste," 385–411.

42. The role of the Izaak Walton League is discussed in greater detail in Nicholas Casner, "Angler Activist: Kenneth Reid, the Izaak Walton League, and the Crusade for Federal Water Pollution Control," *Pennsylvania History* 66 (autumn 1999): 535–53.

43. U.S. Congress, Water Pollution Control Hearings, Committee on *S. 1691: A Bill to Prevent the Pollution of Navigable Waters of the United States and other Purposes*, 67th Cong., March 1939, 71.

44. John W. Foreman, "Deep Mine Sealing," paper on file, U.S. Bureau of Mines Library, Acid Mine Drainage files, n.d.

45. U.S. Congress, House, Committee on Rivers and Harbors, *Hearings: The Pollution of Navigable Waters*, 67th Cong., H. R. 8783, 1921, 87.

46. R. R. Sayers, W. P. Yant, and R. D. Leitch, "General Review of United States Bureau of Mines Stream Pollution Investigations," *American Institute of Mining and Metallurgical Engineers* 94 (1931): 144. See also the Records of the U.S. Public Health Service, National Archives RG 90, General Correspondence Files, 1924–1935, and Records of the U.S. Bureau of Mines, National Archives RG 70, General Correspondence files, 1933—Mine Sealing.

47. R. D. Leitch, "Observations on Acid Mine Drainage in Western Pennsylvania," *The Mining Congress Journal* 14 (1928): 835.

48. R. D. Leitch and W. P. Yant, "Sealing Old Workings: Prevents Acid Formation and Saves Pipes and Streams," *Coal Age* 35 (February 1930): 78–80.

49. Bureau of Mines records, "Confidential Memorandum" to Y. P. Yant, supervising chemist, from R. D. Leitch, dated November 24, 1933.

50. E. A. Holbrook, "Pollution of Pittsburgh's Rivers," *The Pennsylvania Engineer* (October 1936): 12–13, 19.

51. Bureau of Mines Records, letter to M. C. Fielder, chief engineer, from William Yant, dated August 13, 1936.

52. Bureau of Mines Records, "Sealing Abandoned Coal Mines and Preventing the Spread of Mine Pollution," Izaak Walton League memo, n.d.

53. See editorial, "Sealing Abandoned Mines!" *Pittsburgh Sun-Telegraph,* October 6, 1933.

54. U.S. Congress, House, "Acid Mine Drainage," *A Report Prepared for the Committee on Public Works,* 87th Cong., 2d sess., 1962.

55. "First Mine Sealed under CWA Program," *Pittsburgh Post-Gazette,* December 22, 1933.

56. Kenneth A. Reid, "Sealing Abandoned Coal Mines," *The National Waltonian* (February 1935): 4–5, 16.

57. U.S. Congress, "Acid Mine Drainage," 13.

58. "Stream Pollution Checked by Cooperative Program," *The American City* 52 (September 1937): 101–3, and "Mine Sealing Reduces Acid Pollution of Streams in the Ohio Basin," *Coal Mining* 14 (1937): 6–7; "Mine-Sealing Program to Reduce Acid Pollution in Streams," *Engineering News-Record* (January 9, 1936), 42.

59. "Stream Pollution Checked," 102–3.

60. U.S. Congress, House, "Ohio River Pollution Control," *Report of the Ohio River Committee for the U.S. Public Health Service,* H. Doc. 266, part 2, 1944, 193.

61. On state funding, see Don C. Jones, "Acid Mine Drainage: Its Control Reduces Stream Pollution," *Mechanization* 15 (October 1951): 85–88, 91; on water pollution control bills, see U.S. Congress, Senate, *Hearings before the Committee on Commerce,* 76th Cong., 1st sess., March 1939, 7–10.

62. Willard W. Hodge, "Waste Disposal in the Coal Mining Industry," *Mellon Institute Report,* located at Bureau of Mines Records, Office of Surface Mining, Pittsburgh.

63. S. A. Braley, Summary report on Commonwealth of Pennsylvania Department of Health Industrial Fellowship, nos. 1–7, August 1946–December 1953. See also Braley, *Special Report on Evaluation of Mine Sealing,* for the Coal Industry Advisory Committee to the Ohio River Water Sanitation Commission, Research Project no. 370–78 (February 1962).

How, When, and for Whom Was Smoke a Problem in Pittsburgh?

1. Hugh Henry Brackenridge, "Brackenridge's Account of Pittsburgh in 1786," from *Pittsburgh as Seen by Early Travelers: Descriptions by Those Who Visited It from 1783 to 1818,* cited in the *Monthly Bulletin of the Carnegie Library of Pittsburgh* (April 1902–June 1906): 289–90, 334–35.

2. John Duffy, "Smoke, Smog and Health in Early Pittsburgh," *The Western Pennsylvania Historical Magazine* 45 (June 1962): 95.

3. Christian Schultz, "Extract from Schultz's Travels," from *Pittsburgh as Seen by Early Travelers: Descriptions by Those Who Visited It from 1783 to 1818,* cited in the *Monthly Bulletin of the Carnegie Library of Pittsburgh* (April 1902–June 1906): 180.

4. Richard C. Wade, *The Urban Frontier: Pioneer Life in Early Pittsburgh, Cincinnati, Lexington, Louisville, and St. Louis* (Chicago: University of Chicago Press, 1959), 322–27.

5. Leland Baldwin, *Pittsburgh: The Story of a City, 1750–1865* (Pittsburgh: University of Pittsburgh Press, 1937), 184–200.

6. Many other travelers also commented on Pittsburgh's smoke. See ibid., 157–58, and Duffy, "Smoke, Smog and Health in Early Pittsburgh," 95.

7. Quoted in John J. O'Connor, "The History of the Smoke Nuisance and of Smoke Abatement in Pittsburgh," *Industrial World* (March 24, 1913): 352.

8. *Ordinances of the City of Pittsburgh* (Pittsburgh: Johnston and Stockton, 1828), 117; Resolution of November 29, 1830, Historical Society of Western Pennsylvania, Select and Common Council Records (1806–1938) MSS # 46, box 3, folder 3, "Joint Committees, 1830–1837"; "An Ordinance Relating to Brick Kilns and Coke Ovens and Burning Brick and Coke," Select and Common Council Records (1806–1938) MSS # 46, box 3, folder 4; *Ordinances of the Select and Common Councils of the City of Pittsburgh*, 21 (Allegheny Valley Railroad, 1856), 49 (Pittsburgh and Steubenville Railroad, 1856, orig. ord. 1852); *Digest of the Acts of Assembly: The Codified Ordinance of the City of Pittsburgh* 169 (Pittsburgh and Connellsville Railroad, 1858, orig. ord. 1853).

9. James Parton, "Pittsburg," *Atlantic Monthly* 21 (January 1868): 17–19.

10. Ibid., 20, 22.

11. See Glenn Britton, "Boosters and Kickers: Allegheny Smoke and Defining the Public Good," paper presented at the Eastern Historical Geography Association, Pittsburgh, September 25–28, 1997; *Pittsburgh Gazette-Times*, July 11, 1871.

12. Huckenstine's appeal, 70 Pa. 102; Christine Rosen, "Differing Perceptions of the Value of Pollution Abatement across Time and Place: Balancing Doctrine in Pollution Nuisance Law, 1840–1906," *Law and History Review* 11 (1993): 303–81, discusses the shift in balancing doctrine of Pennsylvania judges from concerns about "the human discomfort caused by pollution" before 1860, to "confined themselves to assessing the value of alleviating pecuniary damages to property" (379).

13. *Pittsburgh Gazette*, October 27, 1871.

14. "Steps of Much Needed Progress," *National Labor Tribune* (hereafter *NLT*), March 28, 1891; "A Pittsburgh Outrage," *NLT*, November 9, 1889. The *NLT* published more than fifty articles between 1888 and 1893 on the prospects of Pittsburgh's natural gas supply and the possible substitution of cleaner fuels for coal. The paper's writers unanimously opposed the return to use of raw bituminous in the mills because of its negative effects on product quality, working conditions, and the external environment.

15. For views of Pittsburgh social and labor in this period, see Francis G. Couvares, *The Remaking of Pittsburgh: Class and Culture in an Industrializing City, 1877–1919* (Albany: State University of New York Press, 1984); Paul Krause, *The Battle for Homestead, 1880–1892: Politics, Culture, and Steel* (Pittsburgh: University of Pittsburgh Press, 1992); and S. J. Kleinberg, *The Shadow of the Mills: Working-Class Families in Pittsburgh, 1870–1907* (Pittsburgh: University of Pittsburgh Press, 1989).

16. See Couvares, *The Remaking of Pittsburgh*, for cultural transformations. For discussions of the working-class conceptions of "a competence," see Krause, *The Battle for Homestead*, 9–10.

17. Robert Dale Grinder chronicles these developments in "'From Insurgency to Efficiency': The Smoke Abatement Campaign in Pittsburgh before World War I," *Western Pennsylvania Historical Magazine* 61 (1978): 187–202. My interpretation of the economic meanings of smoke in this period and of the rise and fall of women's separatist antismoke activism in Pittsburgh differs sharply from his.

18. See Nancy Tomes, "The Private Side of Public Health: Sanitary Science, Domestic Hygiene and the Germ Theory, 1870–1900," *Bulletin of the History of Medicine* 64 (1990): 509–39, and Maureen Ogle, *All the Modern Conveniences: American Household Plumbing, 1840–1890* (Baltimore, Md.: Johns Hopkins University Press, 1996).

19. The 1892 ordinance was first debated in Pittsburgh's Select and Common Councils on March 14, 1892, but was not passed until May of that year. The March debate included clear evidence of the council members' desires to protect heavy industry from smoke restriction. "The Anti-Smoke Movement: Councils Discussed It Yesterday to Little Purpose," *Pittsburgh Times*, March 15, 1892; "Important City Measures," *Pittsburgh Press*, March 16, 1892; "Dense Smoke to Stop with New Law," *Pittsburgh Sun*, July 18, 1906; and "Glad You're after the Horrid Smoke Pests," *Pittsburgh Sun*, July 20, 1906.

20. Other papers, the *Pittsburgh Gazette-Times*, *Pittsburg* [sic] *Daily Dispatch*, and the *Pittsburgh Post* together published more than twenty articles on smoke between June and November 1906.

21. "Clothing Is Ruined by Sand Digger—Thousands of Persons Risk Health and Property in Crossing Seventh Street Bridge," *Pittsburgh Sun*, July 9, 1906; "An Anti-Smoke Ordinance Is Demanded at Once," ibid., June 22, 1906; and "Abatement to Be Offered Monday—Councilman C. D. Tilbury Will Call upon City Attorney Rodgers to Draw Up an Ordinance," ibid., July 23, 1906.

22. Paul Underwood Kellog, ed., *The Pittsburgh Survey* (New York: Survey Associates Inc., Russell Sage Foundation, 1909–1914); see also Maurine W. Greenwald and Margo Anderson, eds., *Pittsburgh Surveyed: Social Science and Social Reform in the Early Twentieth Century* (Pittsburgh: University of Pittsburgh Press, 1996).

23. *Life,* May 16, 1912.

24. John F. Bauman and Margaret Spratt, "The Pittsburgh Survey and Urban Planning," in Greenwald and Anderson, *Pittsburgh Surveyed,* 153–69; J. T. Holdsworth, *Report of the Economic Survey of Pittsburgh* (Pittsburgh: n.p., 1912).

25. Kleinberg, *The Shadow of the Mills,* 98.

26. John W. Servos, "Changing Partners: The Mellon Institute, Private Industry and the Federal Patron," *Technology and Culture* 35 (April 1994): 221–57. The Mellons also held major investments in Consolidated Coal.

27. *Mellon Institute of Industrial Research and School of Specific Industries Smoke Investigation* (Pittsburgh: University of Pittsburgh, 1912–1922), includes *Bulletin No. 1*, "Outline of the Smoke Investigation" (1912); *Bulletin No. 2*, Elwood H. McClelland, "Bibliography of Smoke and Smoke Prevention" (1913); *Bulletin No. 3*, J. E. Wallace Wallin, "Psychological Aspects of the Problem of Atmospheric Smoke Pollution" (1913); *Bulletin No. 4*, John J. O'Connor Jr., "The Economic Cost of the Smoke Nuisance to Pittsburgh" (1913); *Bulletin No. 5*, Herbert H. Kimball, "The Meteorological Aspect of the Smoke Problem" (1913); *Bulletin No. 6*, Raymond D. Benner, "Papers on the Effect of Smoke on Building Materials"

(1913); *Bulletin No. 7*, J. F. Clevenger, "The Effect of the Soot in Smoke on Vegetation" (1913); *Bulletin No. 8*, A. A. Straub, "Some Engineering Phases of Pittsburgh's Smoke Problem" (1914); *Bulletin No. 9*, Oskar Klotz and William Charles White, eds., "Papers on the Influence of Smoke on Health" (1914); *Bulletin No. 10*, Robert James McKay, "Recent Progress in Smoke Abatement and Fuel Technology in England" (1922).

28. "Pittsburgh Air Found Cleaner," *Pittsburgh Press*, March 20, 1930; H. B. Meller, "The Facts About Our Soot and Dust," *The Pittsburgh Record*, 1930.

29. William Charles White and C. H. Marcy, "A Study in the Influence of Varying Densities of City Smoke on Mortality from Pneumonia and Tuberculosis," 155–63, cited in Klotz and White, *Bulletin No. 9*.

30. W. L. Holman, "The Bacteriology of Soot," 104–22, cited in ibid.

31. Nancy Tomes, *Gospel of Germs: Men, Women, and the Microbe in American Life* (Cambridge, Mass.: Harvard University Press, 1998), 95–96.

32. See the papers in Klotz and White, *Bulletin No. 9*.

33. E. B. Lee, "The Effect of Smoke on the Interior of Buildings," in Benner, *Bulletin No. 6*, 50; O'Connor, *Bulletin No. 4*, 13–18, 23–24. The emphasis on household budgets mirrors that in Margaret F. Byington, *Homestead: The Households of a Mill Town* (1910). O'Connor corresponded with Paul Kellogg, and the work of MISI was reviewed in *The Survey* magazine. See "Industrial Research: Pittsburgh," *The Survey* 27, no. 7 (May 18, 1912): 313. Alice Hamilton, "Fatigue: Smoke: Motherhood and Other Equally Varied Factors Which Turn the World's Work into a Problem of Life and Health," *The Survey* 29, no. 2 (November 2, 1912): 152–54.

34. In 1916, smoke inspector Henderson used United States Weather Bureau "Smoky Day" statistics to claim a 46 percent reduction in smoke since 1912 despite continuing rapid increases in the consumption of bituminous coal. National acknowledgment of improvements in Pittsburgh's air was common by the 1920s. "Pittsburgh Model of Spotlessness," *Pittsburgh Gazette Times*, December 7, 1922, quotes the *Cleveland Plain Dealer* as recognizing Pittsburgh's 80 percent reduction in smoke and as proclaiming to its readers, "What Pittsburgh has done Cleveland intends to do." The article "King Smoke Losing Grip on Pittsburgh, Research Reveals: Tar Content Removal Is Great, Inquiry Shows: City's Record Beats London," *Pittsburgh Post*, October 1, 1924, ranked London ahead of Pittsburgh in air pollution. The article, "Pittsburgh and Collars," *New York Times*, October 21, 1927, also reported that Pittsburgh was less smoky than London. *Literary Digest* reported in the same year that St. Louis was dirtier than Pittsburgh; see "The Smokiest Cities," *Literary Digest*, April 24, 1927. "Pittsburgh No Longer Smokiest City in U.S.," *Pittsburgh Sun-Telegraph*, April 31, 1928, claimed Pittsburgh was no smokier than New York City.

35. H. B. Meller, "The Facts About Our Soot and Dust," *The Pittsburgh Record*, 1930; H. B. Meller, "Clean Air, an Achievable Asset," *Journal of the Franklin Institute* 217 (June 1934): 709–28; H. B. Meller, "What Is Ahead in Smoke Abatement?" *Chemical and Metallurgical Engineering* 38 (September 1931), n.p.; and H. B. Meller, "Smoke Abatement, Its Effects and Its Limitations," *Mechanical Engineering*, November 1926, 1275–83.

36. David Rosner and Gerald Markowitz, *Deadly Dust: Silicosis and the Politics of Occupational Disease in Twentieth Century America* (Princeton, N.J.: Princeton University Press, 1991), 17–23. See Ralph Mellon, "A Brief Outline of Research

Activities on the Pneumonia Fund," April 1, 1933, for a summary of these activities.

37. Kleinberg, *The Shadow of the Mills.*

38. For discussion of smoke increases nationwide during World War I, see David Stradling, *Smokestacks and Progressives: Environmentalists, Engineers and Air Quality in America, 1881–1951* (Baltimore: Johns Hopkins University Press, 1999), 147–50.

39. Letter of September 22, 1933, from H. B. Meller and L. B. Sisson to Dr. H. J. Rose of Mellon Institute, complaining that "our studies showed us that the physicians of the nation were not exercising leadership in the struggle against air pollution"; Meller, "Need of Medical Cooperation in the Problem of Smoke Abatement" (paper presented at the New York Academy of Medicine, November 6, 1933). Both in Archives of Industrial Society (AIS), University of Pittsburgh, Mellon Institute of Industrial Research, 83.7, ser. 1, box 2, FF 26. H. B.

40. H. B. Meller, "Pittsburgh and Clean Air," *Industrial and Engineering Chemistry,* August 1931; "Progress against Smoke," *Pittsburgh Post-Gazette,* January 16, 1934, claimed that St. Louis and Cincinnati had "more dust particles per square foot" than Pittsburgh.

41. See Frances Lester Warner, "The Pittsburgh Owl," Pennsylvania Department 113th Annual Meeting, Supreme Council 33 D.E.G.A.A.S.R. Freemasonry, Pittsburgh, 1925; Eleanor Graham, "Pittsburgh 1932," Pennsylvania Department, Carnegie Library of Pittsburgh; available at http://www.carnegielibrary.org/exhibit/pgh32.html; Haniel Long, "How Pittsburgh Returned to the Jungle," *The Nation,* June 20, 1923. While several painters and printmakers, notably Aaron Gorson and Joseph Stella, had taken Pittsburgh's industry as subject for several decades, the 1920s through the 1940s saw increased photographic concentration on Pittsburgh's smoke. See especially the photographs of Hew Charles Torrance, Charles K. Archer, and Margaret Bourke-White. See also Rina C. Youngner, "Paintings and Graphic Images of Industry in Nineteenth Century Pittsburgh: A Study of the Relationship between Art and Industry" (Ph.D. diss., University of Pittsburgh, 1991).

42. "Air Pollution, City of Pittsburgh, Pennsylvania: Study and Analysis by Works Progress Administration 12–8–37 to 1–22–39 and Works Projects Administration 7–18–39 to 8–14–40," AIS.

43. Self-conscious use of symbolism in the design of the building is evident in documents published by the institute.

44. For an account of this period, see Joel Tarr and Bill Lamperes, "Changing Fuel Use Behaviors and Energy Transitions: The Pittsburgh Smoke Control Movement, 1940–1950," *Journal of Social History* 14 (summer 1981): 561–68.

45. The Mellon interests' investment patterns show that their futures were not bound primarily to the industries that made Pittsburgh synonymous with smoke.

46. David L. Rosenberg, "Did the Collapse of Basic Industry Really Take the Allegheny Conference by Surprise?" *In Pittsburgh,* March 21–29, 1990, 18, makes a similar argument about the meaning, in the context of Pittsburgh's eventual deindustrialization, of local elites' historically selective application of planning energy to environmental rather than socioeconomic problems. However, see Roy Lubove, *Twentieth-Century Pittsburgh,* vol. 2, *The Post-Steel Era* (Pittsburgh: University of Pittsburgh Press, 1996), 17–18, for a different perspective.

47. Roy Lubove, *Twentieth-Century Pittsburgh*, vol. 1, *Government, Business, and Environmental Change* (Pittsburgh: University of Pittsburgh Press, 1994), 106–15, emphasizes business leaders' interest in creating a hospitable environment for executives and their families in order to maintain Pittsburgh as a site for corporate headquarters.

Revisiting Donora, Pennsylvania's 1948 Air Pollution Disaster

1. Lynne Page Snyder, "'The Death-Dealing Smog over Donora, Pennsylvania': Industrial Air Pollution, Public Health, and Federal Policy, 1915–1963" (Ph.D. diss., University of Pennsylvania, 1994).

2. *Congressional Record*, 88th Cong., 1st sess., 19 Nov., 1963, 109, pt.17, 22329. On the importance of timing in the public perception of environmental public health issues, see Christopher Hamlin, "Environmental Sensibility in Edinburgh, 1839–1946: The 'Fetid Irrigation' Controversy," *Journal of Urban History* 20 (May 1994): 311–13, 332–34.

3. Samuel P. Hays, "From Conservation to Environment: Environmental Politics in the United States since World War Two," *Environmental Review* 6 (fall 1982): 14–41. On the history of air pollution in the twentieth century, see David Stradling, *Smokestacks and Progressives: Environmentalists, Engineers, and Air Quality in America, 1881–1951* (Baltimore, Md.: The Johns Hopkins University Press, 1999).

4. On environmental history during this time period, see Richard N. L. Andrews, *Managing the Environment, Managing Ourselves: A History of American Environmental Policy* (New Haven, Conn.: Yale University Press, 1999), 154–254; Robert Gottlieb, *Forcing the Spring: The Transformation of the American Environmental Movement* (Washington, D.C.: Island Press, 1993), 308–9. On critiques of technology that emerged during the cold war, see Thomas P. Hughes, "Counterculture and Momentum," *American Genesis: A Century of Invention and Technological Enthusiasm, 1870–1970* (New York: Viking Press, 1989), 443–72. On atomic imagery during the era, see Paul Boyer, *By the Bomb's Early Light* (New York: Pantheon, 1985).

5. Daniel M. Fox, *Health Policies, Health Politics* (Princeton: Princeton University Press, 1986). On the shape of federal public health policy beginning in the 1940s, see Rosemary A. Stevens, *In Sickness and in Wealth* (New York: Basic Books, 1989), 200–26; Paul Starr, *The Social Transformation of American Medicine* (New York: Basic Books, 1982), 266–378.

6. Discussion in this paragraph is based on the following sources: Elizabeth Fee, "The Origins and Development of Public Health in the United States," in *Influences of Public Health*, vol.1, *Oxford Textbook of Public Health*, 2d ed., ed. Walter W. Holland, Roger Detels, and George Knox (New York: Oxford University Press, 1991), 3–22; Daniel M. Fox, *Power and Illness* (Berkeley and Los Angeles: University of California Press, 1993).

7. Snyder, "'The Death-Dealing Smog.'"

8. On air pollution policy during this time period, see Scott H. Dewey, *Don't Breathe the Air: Air Pollution and U.S. Environmental Politics, 1945–1970* (College Station: Texas A & M University Press, 2000).

9. On the appeal of the health research orientation, see Shawn Bernstein, "The

Rise of Air Pollution Control as a National Political Issue" (Ph.D. diss., Columbia University, 1986), 221–22.

10. J. Clarence Davies III and Barbara S. Davies, *The Politics of Pollution*, 2d ed. (Indianapolis: Pegasus/Bobbs-Merrill, 1975), 27–32.

11. Memorandum, Harry Heimann to chief, Air Pollution Medical Program, 13 March 1958, U.S. Public Health Service, Record Group 90, 63A108, box 6, folder "meetings—Second Intl. Congress on AP. ap57" (College Park, Md.: National Archives and Records Administration).

12. "Fog in Fifth Day," *Pittsburgh Press* (hereafter referred to as *Press*), October 30, 1948, 1; "Fog Crowds Hospitals," *Monessen Daily Independent* (hereafter cited as *MDI*), October 29, 1948, 1, 2; Joel Tarr and Bill Lamperes, "Changing Fuel Use Behavior and Energy Transitions: The Pittsburgh Smoke Control Movement, 1940–1950," *Journal of Social History* 14 (summer 1981): 561–88; "The Smoke Law Passes Its Hardest Test," *Press*, November 2, 1948, 10.

13. See, for example, Gladwin Hill, introduction to U.S. Public Health Service, *Air Pollution in Donora: An Analysis of the Extreme Effects of Smog* (Elmsford, N.Y.: Maxwell Reprint Company, 1970); Edward Lawless, "The Donora Air Pollution Episode," in *Technology and Social Shock*, ed. Edward Lawless (New Brunswick, N.J.: Rutgers University Press, 1977), 217–25.

14. See "American Steel & Wire Company: Donora Zinc Works," undated pamphlet [1947], author's collection; T. N. Harris, "New Sulphuric Acid Plant," *Metallurgical and Chemical Engineering* 15 (September 15, 1916): 316, 318; W. R. Ingalls, "The Donora Zinc Works," *Engineering and Mining Journal* 102 (October 7, 1916): 648–54. Quotation in heading from Thomas Bell, *Out of This Furnace* (1941; reprint, Pittsburgh: University of Pittsburgh Press, 1976), 356.

15. On litigation surrounding air pollution from the Donora Zinc Works, see, for example, "*Burkhardt et al. v American Steel & Wire Company, Appellant*," *Pennsylvania Superior Court Reports* 74 (1921): 437–44; Supreme Court of Pennsylvania, Western District, "Brief for Appellant: *Anna Procz v the American Steel & Wire Corporation of New Jersey*," *Pennsylvania Decisions* 318, no. 395 (1935): 1434a; and "Fumes from Donora Mill Often an Issue in Court," *Pittsburgh Sun-Telegraph* (hereafter cited as *PST*), November 2, 1948, 3.

16. On air and soil monitoring and experiments to modify manufacturing technologies, see [Reed, Smith, Shaw, & McClay], "Donora Smog Cases: Evidence of Foreseeability," March 3, 1951, box 5, Robert Arthur Kehoe papers, Cincinnati Medical Heritage Center, University of Cincinnati Medical Center, Cincinnati, Ohio (hereafter RAK); U.S. District Court for the Western District of Pennsylvania, "*Alice A. DeVore et al. v American Steel & Wire Company*, Answers to Interrogatories," no. 8080 civil action, RG 21, Records of the U.S. District Court, National Archives Mid-Atlantic Region, Philadelphia, Pennsylvania (hereinafter cited as NAMA); Robert E. Swain, "Smoke and Fume Investigations," *Industrial and Engineering Chemistry* 41, no. 11 (November 1949): 2386.

17. J. K. Miller, "Bibliography of Data on Air Pollution at Donora," appendix A to [Reed, Smith, Shaw, & McClay], "Donora Smog Cases: Evidence of Foreseeability," March 3,1951, RAK.

18. [Reed, Smith, Shaw & McClay], "Donora Smog Cases: Evidence of Foreseeability," March 3, 1951, RAK; Donald MacMillan, "A History of the Struggle to

Abate Air Pollution from Copper Smelters of the Far West, 1885–1933" (Ph.D. diss., University of Montana, 1973); Robert E. Swain, "Smoke and Fume Investigations," *Industrial and Engineering Chemistry* 41, no. 11 (November 1949): 2384–88; Ligon Johnson, "The History and Legal Phases of the Smoke Problem," *Metallurgical and Chemical Engineering* 16, no. 4 (February 15, 1917): 200–204.

19. Bell, *Out of This Furnace*, 356–57.

20. [Reed, Smith, Shaw, & McClay], "Donora Smog Cases: Evidence of Foreseeability," March 3, 1951, RAK; quote used in heading is from James W. Ross, "Donora Smog Deaths Rise to 20," *Pittsburgh Post-Gazette* (hereafter referred to as *PG*), November 1, 1948, 1.

21. Berton Roueche, "The Fog," chap. 3 in *The Medical Detectives*, vol. 2 (1950; reprint, New York: Pocket Books, 1986), 46–47.

22. Information in this paragraph drawn from [Reed, Smith, Shaw, & McClay], "Donora Smog Cases: Evidence of Foreseeability," March 3, 1951, RAK papers; "Donora Fog Samples Tested to Learn How 19 Met Death," *Press*, November 1, 1948, 1, 2; Commonwealth of Pennsylvania, Department of Health (hereafter cited as Pa. Dept. of Health), Bureau of Industrial Hygiene, "Report of Investigation," RAK; Sam Schreiner Jr., "Donora Asks U.S. Probe of Smog Deaths," *PST*, November 2, 1948, 1, 3; "Causes of Deaths Sought as Smog Lifts at Donora," *PG*, November 2, 1948, 1, 2.

23. "19 Persons Die Here as Result of Smog," *Donora Herald-American* (hereafter cited as *DHA*), November 1, 1948, 1; "Donora Doctor Gives Version of Smog Deaths," *MDI*, November 1, 1948, 1, 2; "Editorial: Zinc Fumes Spread Ruin Miles around Donora," *MDI*, November 1, 1948, 4; "Editorial: A Blight on the Valley," *MDI*, November 2,1948, 4; "Editorial: A Valley Problem," *MDI*, November 3, 1948, 4; "Start Probes of Donora Smog Deaths: Boro's Council Meets," *MDI*, November 2, 1948, 1, 2; James W. Ross, "Donora Smog Deaths Rise to 20," *PG*, November 1, 1948, 1; "20 Dead in Smog," *New York Times* (hereafter cited as *NYT*), November 1, 1948, 1, 12.

24. "Donora Fog Samples Tested to Learn How 19 Met Death," *Press*, November 1, 1948, 1, 2; "Health Director Warns of Pneumonia Epidemic Here as Result of Smog," *DHA*, November 2, 1948, 1. On the Pittsburgh Renaissance and smoke control, see Joel A. Tarr and Bill C. Lampres, "Changing Fuel Use Behavior and Energy Transitions: The Pittsburgh Smoke Control Movement, 1940–1950," *Journal of Social History* 14 (summer 1981): 561–88.

25. "Zinc Works Gets Permission to Resume Monday," *MDI*, November 5, 1948, 1, 2. At the time of the smog, 950 persons worked at Donora's zinc smelter and almost 2,500 were employed at the adjacent steel and wire mills. The term is Board of Health president Charles Stacey's. "Special Session Held to Accept Financial Grant from Steelworkers," *DHA*, November 8, 1948, 1; Donora Asks U.S. Inquiry," *NYT*, November 3, 1948, 37; "Donora Asks U.S. Probe of Smog Deaths," *PST*, November 2, 1948, 1, 3.

26. David J. McDonald to James Duff, 4 November 1948, file 13, marked "DO-DZ, May 1, 1947 to May 1949 correspondence," box 50, David J. McDonald papers, United Steelworkers of America Archives, Historical Collections and Labor Archives, Pattee Library, The Pennsylvania State University, University Park, Pa. (hereafter cited as HCLA).

27. Both Donora's mayor and Pennsylvania's Department of Health had called upon the USPHS for assistance on Saturday, October 30, and had been refused. Duncan A. Holaday (sanitary engineer) to chief, Industrial Hygiene Division, November 16, 1948, folder 542.1 (1956), PHS; Tony Smith, "Atmospheric Freak Blamed by Chemist for Smog Tragedy," *Press,* November 3, 1948; Duncan A. Holaday (sanitary engineer) to chief, Industrial Hygiene Division, November 16, 1948, folder 542.1 (1956), PHS; Holaday to chief, November 16, 1948, PHS; Pa. Dept. of Health, "Progress Report on Investigations as to Causes of Donora Disaster," Donora subject files, RG190, James H. Duff papers, Pennsylvania Historical & Museum Commission Archives, Harrisburg, Pa. (hereinafter JHD); Paul F. Ellis, "Donora Becomes Laboratory for Scientific Study of Fumes," *DHA,* November 4, 1948, 9.

28. "Steel Union Offers $10,000 to Probe Smog," *Press,* November 5, 1948, 1, 10; "Donora to Accept United Steelworkers Aid," *MDI,* November 6, 1948, 1, 3; "See Donora as 'Laboratory' as Smog Inquiries Are Discussed," *MDI,* November 8, 1948, 1, 2; "Council Appoints Investigating Group," *DHA,* November 10, 1948, 1, 8; U. S. District Court for the Western District of Pennsylvania, "*Norman C. King Jr. et al. v American Steel & Wire Company.* Deposition of Dr. Clarence A. Mills," no. 8086 civil action, NAMA.

29. "Editorial: They'd Better Be Sure," *MDI,* November 6, 1948, 4; Pa. Dept. of Health, "Progress Report on Investigation as to Causes of Donora Disaster," [November 12, 1948], JHD. The new division was developed in response to the large number of manufacturing communities that had requested their own field surveys. See Joseph Shilen, "The Donora Disaster," *Industrial Medicine* (February 1949): 72.

30. David Rosner and Gerald Markowitz, *Deadly Dust: Silicosis and the Politics of Occupational Disease in Twentieth-Century America* (Princeton, N.J.: Princeton University Press, 1991), 106–9; Martin Cherniak, *The Hawk's Nest Incident: America's Worst Industrial Disaster* (New Haven, Conn.: Yale University Press, 1986); H. C. Willett, "The Meteorological Conditions as a Possible Factor Affecting Health Statistics at Donora, Pennsylvania" (Cambridge, Mass., 1950), RAK.

31. "Donora Smog Probers Hunt Air Filters," *PG,* December 13, 1948, 9.

32. W. C. L. Hemeon and John McMahon, "Final Report on the Donora Smog to American Steel and Wire Company," August 19, 1949, RAK.

33. "Zinc Plant Studying Fatal Smog," *PST,* November 16, 1948, 3; "A Message to Our Employees and Neighbors in Donora," *DHA,* November 16, 1948, 3, "Zinc Plant Denies Smog Death Blame," *Press,* November 16, 1948, 1, 14.

34. On Kehoe, see William F. Ashe, "Robert Arthur Kehoe, MD," *Archives of Environmental Health* 13 (August 1966): 138–42; David Rosner and Gerald Markowitz, "'A Gift of God'?: The Public Health Controversy over Leaded Gasoline during the 1920s," reprinted in *Dying for Work: Workers' Safety and Health in Twentieth Century America* (Bloomington: Indiana University Press, 1985), 121–39.

35. "Federal Experts Will Study Smog," *NYT,* November 19, 1948, 55; "Donora Smog to Get Full U.S. Probe," *PG,* November 19, 1948, 21.

36. "All-Out U.S. Health Survey to Be Conducted in Donora," *Press,* January 7, 1949, 1, 10; "Editorial: Let's Cooperate," *DHA,* January 12, 1949, 4. Quotation in heading from "Editorial: A Weak Defense," *MDI,* November 18, 1948, 4.

37. "Survey Is Launched in Donora," *MDI*, December 8, 1948, 1.

38. On the USPHS Division of Industrial Hygiene, see Henry Doyle, *The Federal Industrial Hygiene Agency* (Washington, D.C., 1975), 7, 10–11, 15–23. On USPHS policy during the 1940s and 1950s, see Fitzhugh Mullen, *Plagues and Politics* (New York: Basic Books, 1989), 82–131.

39. The Bureau of Mines had been involved in smelter pollution studies in the West. On the Bureau of Mines work in Donora, see O. C. Ralston (U.S. Bureau of Mines, Washington, D.C.) to R. C. Buehl (Bureau of Mines, Pittsburgh), November 1, 1948; Buehl to Ralston, November 5, 1948; Ralston to Buehl, November 9,1948, all in BM; L. B. Berger et al., "Occurrence of a Toxic Fog at Donora, Pennsylvania, October, 1948," RAK.

40. H. H. Schrenk, Harry Heimann, George D. Clayton, W. M. Gafafer, and Harry Wexler, *Air Pollution in Donora: Epidemiology of the Unusual Smog Episode of October 1948, Preliminary Report,* Public Health Bulletin No. 306 (Washington, D.C.: GPO, 1949), 113–15.

41. For the USPHS survey, see "Steelworkers Pick U.S. Public Health Service for Donora Probe," *MDI*, November 18, 1948, 1, 18; "Survey Is Set on Donora's Smog Deaths," *PG*, November 24, 1948, 15; "U.S. Opens Probe in Donora," *PST*, December 1, 1948, 3; "House Survey Underway in Smog Probe," *DHA*, December 8, 1948, 1; "U.S. Health Service Opens Probe of Donora Smog," *PG*, January 11, 1949, 15; Schrenk et al., *Air Pollution in Donora*, 3–4, 6–10, 54–77, 128; James G. Townsend, "Investigation of the Smog Incident in Donora, Pa., and Vicinity," *American Journal of Public Health* 40 (February 1950): 185.

42. "Editorial: More Surveys," *MDI*, January 12, 1949, 4. On Mills, see "Investigator Gives Final Smog Data," *DHA*, February 3, 1949, 1, 8; "Stiff Law Urged to Prevent New Smog Disaster," *Press*, February 3, 1949.

43. "Webster Forms Group to Fight Pollution," *MDI*, February 10, 1949, 1; "Webster Group Asks Zinc Mill to Operate Same as During Recent Smog Here," *DHA*, February 17, 1949, 1; "Sadtler Addresses Group in Webster," *DHA*, March 28, 1949, 1.

44. "Zinc Works to Operate Fully to Aid Probers," *MDI*, March 8, 1949, 1; "Donora Planning Smog to Run Test," *PST*, March 23, 1949, 1; "Urges Evacuation of Smog Victims for Test Period," *DHA*, April 1, 1949, 1; "Donora's Deadly Smog to Be Simulated—Safely," *PG*, April 13, 1949.

45. "Smog Rally Asks School Evacuation," *MDI*, April 19, 1949; "Wind Gives Relief to Webster," *MDI*, April 20, 1949, 1, 6; "Ills Laid to Smog in Donora," *PST*, April 19, 1949, 1, 2; "Ten Leave Webster as Zinc Works Operation Goes into Third Day," *DHA*, April 20, 1949; "Senate Passes Resolution for Study of Smoke," *MDI*, April 23, 1949, 1; "Editorial: A Weak Defense," *MDI*, November 18, 1949, 4.

46. Robert A. Kehoe to Harvey Jordan (American Steel & Wire Company), May 24, 1949, RAK.

47. In an article about the 1930 air pollution disaster over Belgium's industrialized Meuse Valley, industrial hygienist Philip Drinker commented that "Our stacks emit the same gases as did the Belgium, but fortunately, so meteorologists tell us, we have no districts in which there is even a reasonable chance of such a catastrophe taking place." See "Atmospheric Pollution," *Industrial and Engineering Chemistry* 31 (November 1939): 1318.

48. A. J. Lanza, "Health Aspects of Air Pollution" (paper presented at the 42nd

Annual Meeting of the Smoke Prevention Association of America, May 23–27, 1949).

49. Robert A. Kehoe to Harvey Jordan (American Steel & Wire Company), May 24, 1949, RAK.

50. William F. Ashe (Kettering) to Robert A. Kehoe [December 3, 1948?], RAK; Kettering Laboratory for Applied Physiology, "An Investigation of the Donora Disaster," RAK; Lester B. Roberts to American Steel & Wire Company, December 22, 1948, RAK.

51. On the Allegheny County ordinance, see Mershon and Tarr essay in this volume.

52. William T. Hogan, *Economic History of the Iron and Steel Industry in the U.S.*, vol. 3, part 5 (Lexington, Mass.: Lexington Books/D.C. Heath, 1971), 892, 1205–7; [Reed, Smith, Shaw, & McClay], "Donora Smog Cases: Evidence of Foreseeability," March 3, 1951, RAK.

53. "Webster Group, American Steel & Wire Heads in Congenial First Confab," *DHA*, July 22, 1949, 1; "Smoke Catcher of New Design Planned for Zinc Works to Cut Air Pollution," *DHA*, July 25, 1949, 1.

54. Schrenk et al, *Air Pollution in Donora*, 115–25, 161–64; "News of the Week," *Chemical and Engineering News*, October 24, 1949.

55. Clarence A. Mills, *Air Pollution and Community Health* (Boston: Christopher Publishing House, 1954), 64–69; Schrenk et al, *Air Pollution in Donora*, 115.

56. Ibid., 140.

57. H. H. Schrenk, "The Chemistry of Smog," *Industrial Hygiene Foundation Transactions Bulletin* 15 (1950): 12, 55–56; Robert A. Kehoe, "Air Pollution and Community Health," in Stanford Research Institute, *Proceedings of the First National Air Pollution Symposium* (Los Angeles, 1949), 115–20.

58. "$560,000 Donora Death Suits Filed," *Press*, September 8,1949, 1; "Relatives of Smog Dead Sue American Steel & Wire Company," *DHA*, September 9, 1949, 1, 4; "Death Smog 'Act of God,' Says Steel Company," *DHA*, September 29, 1949, 1.

59. Schrenk et al., *Air Pollution in Donora*, 165; "Editorial: God Didn't Do It," *MDI*, October 1, 1949, 4.

60. It appears that neither public officials nor Kettering researchers knew about American Steel & Wire's conclusion about air quality sampling. See J. K. Miller, "Bibliography of Data on Air Pollution at Donora," appendix A to [Reed, Smith, Shaw, & McClay], "Donora Smog Cases: Evidence of Foreseeability," March 3, 1951, RAK.

61. Schrenk et al., *Air Pollution in Donora*, 147.

62. Robert G. Dyck, "The Evolution of Federal Air Pollution Control, 1948–1967" (Ph.D. diss., University of Pittsburgh, 1971), 217.

63. Samuel P. Hays with Barbara D. Hays, *Beauty, Health, and Permanence* (New York: Cambridge University Press, 1987), 13–39.

64. "Zinc Works Here Retired After 42 Years' Service," *DHA*, July 9, 1957, 1; "An Editorial . . . Donora 'In Step' as Times Change," *DHA*, July 15, 1957, 1; "Phase Out at Donora Works: Foreign Competition, Shifting of Markets Responsible for the Shutdown of Operations," *U.S. Steel News* (April 1966): 16–17.

65. See John Hoerr, *And the Wolf Finally Came* (Pittsburgh: University of Pittsburgh Press, 1988); David Houston, "When Will We Ever Learn: The Lesson of Steel," *Pittsburgh History* 72 (winter 1989): 46–52.

66. "Editorial: The Valley and Its No. 1 Problem," *MDI*, July 9, 1957, 4. In a 1967 Los Angeles radio interview, Donora Mayor Al Delsandro characterized his community's attitude toward the events of 1948 and 1949: "we don't like to talk about the smog here in Donora, we think it's an unpleasant episode. We're reconstructing the community and we're doing pretty well now and we look for a good future. So the smog episode, very frankly, we'd like to forget and the world won't let us." Al Wiman, *A Breath of Death: The Fatality Factor of Smog* (North Hollywood, Calif.: Flamingo Press, 1967), 8.

Strategies for Clean Air

1. Lawrence Tilly, "Metropolis as Ecosystem," in *An Urban World*, ed. Charles Tilly (Boston: Little Brown, 1974), 466–73. For a review of nineteenth-century comments about Pittsburgh smoke, see John O'Connor Jr., "The History of the Smoke Nuisance and of Smoke Abatement in Pittsburgh," *Industrial World* 47, part 1 (March 24, 1913): 353–54. See Cliff I. Davidson, "Air Pollution in Pittsburgh: A Historical Perspective," *Journal of the Air Pollution Control Association* 29 (October 1979): 1035–41, for an attempt to quantify Pittsburgh smoke pollution over time using a variety of measures including coal consumption and weather bureau smoke observations. See also Gugliotta essay in this volume.

2. For early Pittsburgh smoke control efforts, see Robert Dale Grinder, "From Insurgency to Efficiency: The Smoke Abatement Campaign in Pittsburgh before World War I," *The Western Pennsylvania Historical Magazine* 61 (1978): 187–202; and David Stradling, *Smokestacks and Progressives: Environmentalists, Engineers, and Air Quality in America, 1881–1951* (Baltimore: Johns Hopkins University Press, 1999), 38–44, 76–77, 138–39.

3. Victor J. Azbe, "Rationalizing Smoke Abatement," in *Proceedings of the Third International Conference on Bituminous Coal*, 2 vols. (Pittsburgh: Carnegie Institute of Technology, 1931), 2:603.

4. Osborn Monnett, *Smoke Abatement, Technical Paper 273, Bureau of Mines* (Washington, D.C.: GPO, 1923); H. B. Meller, "Smoke Abatement, Its Effects and Its Limitations," *Mechanical Engineering* 48 (November 1926): 1275–83.

5. Interview with Abraham Wolk, April 26, 1973, in "An Oral History of the Pittsburgh Renaissance," Archives of Industrial Society, University of Pittsburgh, hereafter referred to as "Renaissance Oral History."

6. *Pittsburgh Press*, February 9, 1941, hereafter referred to as *Press;* Jennie Herron to Dr. Edward Weidlein, September 26, 1939, in Edward Weidlein Papers, Mellon Institute of Research, Pittsburgh.

7. David L. Lawrence, "Rebirth," in Stefan Lorant, *Pittsburgh: The Story of an American City*, 2d ed. (Lenox, Mass.: Authors Edition, 1975). Dr. Alexander's involvement, said one commentator, was important because "he was able to generate some real fear on the part of the people that maybe after all this was dangerous to health as well as being and an economic proposition" (interview with William Willis, April 16, 1973, "Renaissance Oral History"). See also Dr. I. Hope Alexander, "Smoke and Health," United Smoke Council of Pittsburgh, 1941, pamphlet. Alexander noted that "The medical profession is in accord with the statement that smoke is a health menace of major proportions. . . . For the

present, however, there are few scientific facts to definitely establish a case of cause and effect."

8. Joel A. Tarr and Carl Zimring, "The Struggle for Smoke Control in St. Louis: Achievement and Emulation," in *Common Fields: An Environmental History of St. Louis,* ed. Andrew Hurley (St. Louis: Missouri Historical Society, 1997), 199–220; "Cities Fight Smoke," *Business Week,* April 6, 1940, 33–34.

9. *Press,* February 3, 4, 12, 16, 19, 20, 21, 22, 1941; *Business Week,* February 22, 1941, 30; "Smoke Meeting," February 20, 1941, Civic Club Records, Archives of Industrial Society, University of Pittsburgh; and Tarr and Zimring, "The Struggle for Smoke Control in St. Louis," 216–18.

10. Interview with Gilbert Love, December 19, 1972, "Renaissance Oral History"; Annette Giovengo, "The Cartoonist as Policy Influential: Cyrus C. Hungerford in Pittsburgh, 1933–1961" (unpublished senior thesis, Carnegie Mellon University, 1985).

11. See, for instance, *Press,* February 3–5, 8, 9, 14, and March 1, 2, 13, 20, 21, 1941.

12. *Report of the Mayor's Commission for the Elimination of Smoke* (Pittsburgh, 1941), in Civic Club Records, hereafter referred to as *Report of the Smoke Commission; Press,* February 19, 1941.

13. *Press,* February 19, March 13, 1941.

14. See, for example, *Press,* March 13, April 30, June 24, 1941; M. Jay Ream to ————, April 3, 1941, Civic Club Records; "Notes Taken on Smoke at Annual Meeting," May 8, 1941, Civic Club Records.

15. The comment is that of John P. Robin, the mayor's executive secretary, in "Fourth Meeting of the Smoke Commission," March 12, 1941, 74, Pittsburgh City Council Archives.

16. The third meeting was arranged by the Civic Club Smoke Committee.

17. "Hearings before the Smoke Commission," April 15, 1941, 49, City Council Archives.

18. Ibid., 38–39.

19. "Proceedings of the Tenth Meeting of the Smoke Commission," April 24, 1941, 57, City Council Archives.

20. See, for instance, "Fifth Meeting of the Smoke Commission," March 31, 1941, 23, 69–78; "Proceedings of the Sixth Meeting," April 7, 1941, 38–39, for a discussion of the benefits of smoke control to the working class. For aid to the poor, see, for instance, "Proceedings of the Fifth Meeting of the Pittsburgh Smoke Commission," March 31, 1941, 69; "Hearings before the Pittsburgh Smoke Commission," April 15, 1941, 49–50; and "Proceedings of the Twelfth Meeting," May 14, 1941, 22–32.

21. "Proceedings of the Twelfth Meeting of the Smoke Commission," May 14, 1941, 13–32.

22. *Press,* May 15, 1941.

23. See "Hearings of the Western Pennsylvania Coal Operators Association before the Mayor's Commission for Elimination of Smoke," May 13, 1941, Pittsburgh City Council Archives; "The Western Pennsylvania Coal Operators Association Reports on a Plan to Reduce Air Pollution in Greater Pittsburgh," in Civic Club Records, Archives of Industrial Society.

24. *Report of the Mayor's Commission,* 18.

25. Ibid., 18–19.

26. The Ringelmann Chart was a method of estimating smoke density through a visual comparison of a column of smoke with a shaded chart representing various densities. See L. S. Marks, "Inadequacy of the Ringelmann Chart," *Mechanical Engineering* 59 (September 1937): 681–85. The fly ash provision was also included in the St. Louis ordinance and represented an advance in air pollution control as compared to earlier ordinances that had focused on dense smoke only.

27. Quotation from *Report of the Smoke Commission, 37*. The railroads wanted an alteration in the amount of time they were allowed to produce dense smoke. Jones & Laughlin Steel Corporation opposed the provisions in regard to fly ash and fumes on the grounds that it would be "a burden to the steel business." Their representative argued that fly ash and fumes involved "air pollution" and not smoke. See Committee on Hearings, Pittsburgh City Council Records, June 24–25, 1941; *Press*, July 7, 1941.

28. *Press*, October 25, 1942, and April 25, 1943; "Memo of the Meeting of the Associated Municipalities," November 19, 1942, Civic Club Records; *Press*, January 20 and March 11, 1942.

29. See, for instance, *Press*, Nov. 5, 7, 1945; in its 1944 *Report for Stationary Stack Conditions*, the Bureau of Smoke Prevention noted that 75 percent of the heating equipment of nondomestic structures was "more or less antiquated" (5).

30. See "The United Smoke Council of the Allegheny Conference," in United Smoke Council Records, and "Minutes," meeting of the United Smoke Council of Pittsburgh and Allegheny County, October 18, 1945, United Smoke Council Records.

31. Roy Lubove, *Twentieth-Century Pittsburgh* (New York: John Wiley, 1969), 106–21; M. Jay Ream to Richard King Mellon, June 9, 1943, and Mellon to Ream, n.d., in Allegheny Conference on Community Development files, John Heinz III History Center, Pittsburgh, hereafter referred to as ACCD papers. Mellon's father, Richard Beatty Mellon, had provided funding for the original Mellon Institute Smoke Investigation in 1914.

32. "Minutes, Meeting of the United Smoke Council of Pittsburgh and Allegheny County," November 3, 1945.

33. Lorant, *Pittsburgh,* 390.

34. See C. K. Harvey, "Report to the Technical Committee on Smoke Abatement," February 1946, ACCD, in Abraham Wolk Papers, Archives of Industrial Society; C. K. Harvey to M. Jay Ream, January 17, 1946, United Smoke Council files, ACCD papers.

35. Harvey, "Report to the Technical Committee on Smoke Abatement," 1–2, 15. Park Martin, director of the Allegheny Conference, supported the October 1, 1946, date with the comment that "there probably never will be a 'just right time.'" "Minutes," Special Meeting of the United Smoke Council of the Allegheny Conference, February 23, 1946, Civic Club Records.

36. Dr. Robert Doherty to Park Martin, March 29, 1946, copy in "Miscellaneous Correspondence" of Dr. Edward Weidlein, Mellon Institute.

37. The Western Pennsylvania Conference on Air Pollution, *The Role of Coal in Smoke Abatement* (April 9, 1946), copy in Wolk Papers; Mrs. Gregg to members of the Executive Committee, March 29, 1946, Weidlein Papers.

38. "Proposed Solution of Smoke Abatement Problem," April 2, 1946, draft in papers of Dr. Edward Weidlein, Mellon Institute. See also Executive Minutes of the ACCD, April 2, 1946.

39. *Press,* April 17–18, 1946. The various petitions are available in the City Council archives.

40. There are discussions of methods of enforcement by Dr. Sumner B. Ely in "Minutes," United Smoke Council, December 13, 1945, and in *Report of Stationary Stacks,* Bureau of Smoke Prevention, Department of Public Health, Pittsburgh, 1948, 9–10. See also interview with Albert Brandon, July 21, 1972, "Renaissance Oral History." Brandon was assistant city solicitor in charge of the enforcement of smoke control.

41. Interview with John P. Robin, September 20, 1972, "Renaissance Oral History"; *Press,* December 16, 1947, January 13, 1948. For comparative costs of competing fuels, see Peoples Natural Gas Company, *Operating and Financial Statistics Years 1943–1972* (Pittsburgh, 1973), 23a. This source shows that in 1948 bituminous coal was $10.70 a ton while "Disco," or treated coal, was $17.10.

42. As shown in a U.S. Department of Labor tabulation of data from forty-two cities in 1940, and noted in "The Western Pennsylvania Coal Operators Association Report on a Plan to Reduce Air Pollution in Greater Pittsburgh," 15, in Civic Club Archives.

43. For discussion of these issues, see A. P. L. Turner to David L. Lawrence, October 31, 1947; T. B. Lappen, spiritual director, Society of St. Vincent de Paul, to Junction Coal & Coke Company, April 17, 1946; and Howard D. Gibbs, executive secretary, Retail Coal Merchants Association, March 24, 1946, all in Wolk Papers. The negative position on smoke control of the Pittsburgh Italian-American community is reported in Stefano Luconi, "The Enforcement of the 1941 Smoke-Control Ordinance and Italian-Americans in Pittsburgh," in *Pennsylvania History* 66 (autumn 1999): 580–94. According to Luconi, Italian-Americans were concerned about the effect of smoke control on the cost of living and on employment possibilities.

44. Interview with Ralph German, February 27, 1979; statement of John J. Grove, public relations director, ACCD, in "Oral History"; and Bureau of Smoke Prevention, Department of Public Health, *Report on Stationary Stacks 1948* (Pittsburgh, 1948), 11.

45. *Press,* February 2, 1948; United Smoke Council, *That New Look in Pittsburgh* (n.p., n.d.). On hours of smoke, see City of Pittsburgh, Department of Public Health, Bureau of Smoke Prevention, *Report 1955* (Pittsburgh, 1955), 6.

46. *Report of the Mayor's Commission,* 10; Bureau of Smoke Prevention, Department of Public Health, *Report on Stationary Stacks 1951* (Pittsburgh, 1951), 13.

47. *Press,* June 22, 1947, and August 29, 1948. In 1947 the n=460; in 1948, no "n" was given. In the 1949 Democratic primary election, Edward J. Leonard, who had voted against the Smoke Control Ordinance in 1941 on the grounds that it would hurt the little man, ran against David Lawrence. Lawrence was renominated by a vote of approximately 77,000 to 50,000 in a hard campaign, with Leonard winning many of the labor wards. Smoke control, however, was not the only issue in the election.

48. Arno C. Fieldner, *Recent Developments in Fuel Supply and Demand,* U.S. Department of the Interior, Bureau of Mines (November 1943), 11. For discussions

of the high price and erratic supply conditions of natural gas in 1941, see transcripts of the Mayor's Commission for Smoke Elimination, March 12, 1941, 17–19, 60; for March 28, 1941, 7–8; and March 31, 1941, 74–76. On April 19, 1946, the *Press* cited higher prices for home heating by natural gas as compared to coal.

49. *Press,* April 7, 1946, February 15, 1947.

50. See "Jobs for Inches," *Business Week,* December 29, 1945, 19; "Natural Gas Is on the Up," ibid., March 13, 1948, 26; *Annual Reports of the Philadelphia Company [Equitable Gas Company], for 1946,* 15, for 1948, 16–17, and for 1949, 21–22; Christopher James Castaneda, *Regulated Enterprise: Natural Gas Pipelines and Northeastern Markets, 1938–1954* (Columbus: Ohio State University Press, 1993), 75–89, 118.

51. Data on household fuel use is available from the 1940 and 1950 Censuses of Housing. See U.S. Department of Commerce, Bureau of the Census, *Housing: Characteristics by Type of Structure, 16th Census of the U.S.* (Washington, D.C.: GPO, 1945) and *Census of Housing: 1950,* vol. 1, *General Characteristics 17th Census* (Washington, D.C.: GPO, 1953). The conversion to gas was also accelerated by several coal strikes from 1946 through 1949 which caused uncertainty in regard to bituminous supplies and price.

52. See *Press,* September 29, October 4, 1949, and March 8, 22, 1950.

53. Even in St. Louis the rate of change to natural gas and oil was slower, but here a "maze of contracts of affiliated utilities" caused problems on the supply side. See Tarr and Zimring, "The Struggle for Smoke Control in St. Louis," 218.

54. Representatives of the United Mine Workers charged in the postwar period that there was a conspiracy in Pittsburgh to drive out coal in favor of natural gas. See *Press,* December 21, 1945; March 8, 9; April 23; December 2, 5, 1947; and July 3, 1948. In its 1949 annual report, the Equitable Gas Company, Pittsburgh's largest gas utility, observed that smoke abatement legislation and the high cost of coal were increasing their domestic sales.

55. The ACCD and the USC favored rapid implementation of the city law in 1946, hoping that such action would create momentum in favor of countywide smoke regulation. See minutes of the Smoke Abatement Committee, ACCD, January 7, 1945, in "Smoke Control—Allegheny Conf. (USC)" file, ACCD Archives.

56. The 1947 Census of Manufactures recorded 1,083 manufacturing establishments in Pittsburgh and 1,581 in Allegheny County, giving the city a 68.5 percent share of the county total, but the city accounted for only 36.6 percent of county manufacturing employment. See Bureau of the Census, United States Department of Commerce, *Census of Manufactures: 1947,* vol. 3 (Washington, D.C.: GPO, 1950), table 2, 514, 516.

57. Joel A. Tarr and Kenneth E. Koons, "Railroad Smoke Control: The Regulation of a Mobile Pollution Source," in *Energy and Transport: Historical Perspectives on Policy Issues,* ed. George H. Daniels and Mark H. Rose (Beverly Hills, Calif.: Sage Publications, 1982), 75–78; David Stradling and Joel A. Tarr, "Environmental Activism, Locomotive Smoke, and the Corporate Response: The Case of the Pennsylvania Railroad and Chicago Smoke Control," *Business History Review* 73 (winter 1999): 677–704; *Press,* September 21, 1946; R. H. Flinn, letter to Sumner B. Ely, March 12, 1946, in "Smoke Control—Allegheny Conf. (United Smoke Council)" file, ACCD Archives; "Railroads Ask for Workable Smoke Law,"

Pennsylvania Railroad press release, March 22, 1947, in "Smoke Control—General" file, ACCD Archives.

58. "The Pennsy's Predicament," *Fortune* 37 (March 1948): 202–3; Tarr and Koons, "Railroad Smoke Control," 72–73. In 1946, as a result of skyrocketing costs for labor and materials, the Pennsylvania Railroad had run a deficit for the first time in its history. See J. M. Symes, "The Big Squeeze," *Greater Pittsburgh* (November 1947): 8–9.

59. Transcript, Smoke Abatement Law Hearing, 66; *Post-Gazette,* November 28, 1946.

60. Untitled listing of "Pittsburgh Package" bills, n.d., in "Miscellaneous" file, ACCD Archives; Park H. Martin, "Narrative of the Allegheny Conference on Community Development and the Pittsburgh Renaissance, 1943–1958" (Camp Hill, Pa: author's manuscript, March 1964), 24–26; M. Jay Ream, letter to Park H. Martin, January 30, 1947, in "Legislation—Pittsburgh Package" file, ACCD Archives; *Post-Gazette,* January 16, 1947; and *Press,* January 21, 1947.

61. Martin, "Narrative of the Allegheny Conference," 26–27; *Press,* March 19, 23, 1947; *Post-Gazette,* March 21, 1947.

62. M. Jay Ream, USC form letter, 20 March 1947, in "Smoke Control—General" file, ACCD Archives; *Post-Gazette,* March 22, 1947; Martin, "Narrative of the Allegheny Conference," 27; interview with John Walker, "Renaissance Oral History," 6:2142–43.

63. For testimony on the effects of this publicity upon the railroad executives, see William Block, transcript of interview by Cutler Andrews, April 24, 1971, in "Renaissance Oral History," vol. 1 (Pittsburgh: Graduate School of Public and International Affairs, University of Pittsburgh, 1973), 281–83; and Edward R. Weidlein, transcript of interview by Nancy Mason, September 14, 1972, in "Renaissance Oral History," 6:2173.

64. Chamber of Commerce of Pittsburgh, press release, March 24, 1947, in "Smoke Control—County of Allegheny" file, ACCD Archives; *Post-Gazette,* March 24, 1947; *Press,* March 25, April 16, and May 9, 1947; *Post-Gazette,* May 10, 1947.

65. Charles O. Jones, *Clean Air: The Policies and Politics of Pollution Control* (Pittsburgh: University of Pittsburgh Press, 1975), 46, 94–96.

66. The industrial and commercial members of the Advisory Committee were Charles T. Campbell of United Barge Line; Charles R. Cox of Carnegie-Illinois Steel; Howard D. Gibbs of the Retail Coal Merchants Association; George E. Kelly of W. Earl Bothwell, Inc.; George H. Love of Pittsburgh Consolidation Coal; Benjamin Moreell of Jones & Laughlin Steel; F. E. Schuchman of the Homestead Valve Company (also the chair of the United Smoke Council); and Curtis M. Yohe of the Pittsburgh & Lake Erie Railroad. The labor members were John P. Busarello of the United Mine Workers; Louis J. Gizzi of the Teamsters; and John J. Mullen of the United Steelworkers (also the mayor of the city of Clairton). Representing civic organizations were Mrs. Ira W. Marshall of the Congress of Women's Clubs; M. Jay Ream of the Chamber of Commerce and the United Smoke Council; Leslie J. Reese of the Pennsylvania Economy League; and Edward Weidlein of the ACCD. Mrs. Frank D'Ascenzo was a board member of the Gumbert School for Girls, and Mrs. Robert L. Vann was the president of the *Pittsburgh Courier.*

67. County of Allegheny, Bureau of Smoke Control, "A Review of Program," June 18, 1951, 2, in "Smoke Control—County of Allegheny" file, ACCD Archives; Thomas C. Wurts, "The Pittsburgh Plan and Its Implementation" (paper presented to Pittsburgh Section, American Society of Mechanical Engineers, April 20, 1959), 2–3, in "Smoke Control—General" file, ACCD Archives; Edward R. Weidlein, "Organizing for Effective Air Pollution Control," *Journal of the Franklin Institute* 263 (February 1957): 103.

68. County of Allegheny, "Smoke Control Ordinance of Allegheny County, Pennsylvania," May 1949, 6, copy in "Smoke Control—County of Allegheny" file, ACCD Archives. The following paragraphs are based upon this document.

69. "Smoke Control Ordinance," 9.

70. The ACCD Executive Committee strongly recommended this course of action after sponsoring a study that pointed to a potential shortage of clean-burning fuels and equipment. See Robert J. Thomas, "Domestic Requirements for Solid Fuel in Pittsburgh and Allegheny County as of January 1, 1948," February 26, 1948, in "Smoke Control—Allegheny Conference," in "United Smoke Council" file; Minutes, ACCD Executive Committee, August 9, 1948, 7–8, in "1947–49 Executive Committee Minute Book"; and "Subject: Resolution Passed by the Executive Committee of the Allegheny Conference at Its Meeting on August 9, 1948, with Instructions for the Executive Director to Transmit It to the Interested Parties," in "Smoke Control—County of Allegheny" file, ACCD Archives; and Weidlein, "Effective Air Pollution Control," 105.

71. Thomas C. Wurts, to W. G. Willis, December 7, 1950; County of Allegheny, "Review of Program," 3–5; Allegheny County Bureau of Smoke Control, *Ninth Annual Report of Activities,* 1958, 6; County of Allegheny, "Review of Program," 9; and *Press,* June 15, 1952.

72. County of Allegheny, "Review of Program," 4; F. E. Schuchman to William A. White, February 27, 1954, and F. E. Schuchman to Admiral Ben Moreell, August 20, 1953, both in "Smoke Control—Allegheny County" file, ACCD Archives; Jones, *Clean Air,* 93–94.

73. *Post-Gazette,* March 11, 1949; "The Pennsy's Predicament," 201; and "Railroad Motive Power Data—County of Allegheny," in "Air Pollution Control Progress," April 1953, copy in "Smoke Control—County of Allegheny" file, ACCD Archives.

74. *Press,* November 22, 1950; United States Steel, press release, April 23, 1952, in "Smoke Control—County of Allegheny" file, ACCD Archives; "Information on Pittsburgh's Smoke Control Program," n.d., in "Smoke Control—General" file, ACCD Archives; "Why You're Getting Gas This Winter," *Greater Pittsburgh* 37 (January 1955): 36–37, 105. Virtually every major iron and steel company operating in Allegheny County invested extensively in new or improved plants during the first decade and a half after World War II. See Benjamin R. Fairless, "The Steel Industry Marches On," *Greater Pittsburgh* 30 (January 1948): 32.

75. *Press,* May 19, 1953.

76. Wurts, "Pittsburgh Plan," 5–6.

77. C. A. Bishop and W. W. Campbell, "Pittsburgh Looks to the Future— Research Program" (paper presented to the Pittsburgh Section of the American Society of Mechanical Engineers, April 20–21, 1959), in "Smoke Control— General" file, ACCD Archives; Pittsburgh Bureau of Smoke Prevention, "Pitts-

burgh Open Hearth Dust Problem," November 1955, in ACCD Archives. After research indicated that electrostatic precipitators offered the most likely solution to open-hearth pollution, U.S. Steel and J & L Steel made commitments to install these devices in the late 1950s. See *Press*, June 5 and April 19, 1959. By mid-1959, however, only 13 of the 102 open-hearth furnaces operating in Allegheny County had any kind of pollution-control equipment (*Post-Gazette*, August 19, 1959).

78. *Press*, October 26, 1954.

79. T. C. Wurts to John J. Grove, September 22, 1952; Pressly H. McCance to Sumner B. Ely, July 16, 1953; and Ely to M. Jay Ream, March 3, 1954, in "Smoke Control—County of Allegheny" file, ACCD Archives; *Post-Gazette*, July 24, 1955; *Press*, May 26, 1958; *Sun-Telegraph*, June 17, 1959.

80. Minutes, ACCD Executive Committee, May 16, 1955, 6, in "1955 Executive Committee Minute Book," ACCD Archives.

81. *Post-Gazette*, April 10, 1957; *Sun-Telegraph*, April 10, 1957; and Bureau of Smoke Control, *Ninth Annual Report*, 6.

82. *Press*, February 17 and October 23, 1956; *Post-Gazette*, June 8 and October 24, 1956, November 19, 1957, February 6, 1959; Jones, *Clean Air*, 47; and *Press*, April 29, 1959. Of the thirteen members of the 1959 Citizens Advisory Committee, six were executives of industrial corporations and three came from academic circles. Joseph Yablonski of the United Mine Workers was the sole union representative. Three members represented the community at large.

83. In June 1959, the ACCAAP presented the County Commissioners with 747 letters of protest from residents in forty-seven different neighborhoods. See *Press*, May 21, April 25, and June 17, 1959; *Post-Gazette*, June 17, 1959.

Slag in the Park

1. The slag is made up of silica and alumina from the original ore. For every ton of iron produced, more than a half ton of blast furnace slag was produced. Steelmaking produced a quarter ton of slag for every ton of steel. Because of the volumes and the weight of the slag produced by Jones & Laughlin, disposal was a major concern. In recent years, slag material has been used as roadbed, fill, and for other uses. In the early twentieth century, however, such uses were seldom explored. Instead, the material was dumped in as inexpensive a fashion as possible. See G. W. Josephson, F. Sillers Jr., and D. G. Runner, *Iron Blast-Furnace Slag: Production, Processing, Properties and Uses* (Washington, D.C.: GPO, 1949).

2. Joel A. Tarr, "Infrastructure and City Building," in *City at the Point: Essays on the Social History of Pittsburgh*, ed. Samuel P. Hays (Pittsburgh: University of Pittsburgh Press, 1989), 213–61.

3. See Howard Stewart, comp., *Historical Data: Pittsburgh Public Parks* (Pittsburgh: Greater Pittsburgh Parks Association, 1943); Barbara Judd, "Edward M. Bigelow: Creator of Pittsburgh's Arcadian Parks," *Western Pennsylvania Historical Magazine* 58 (January 1975): 53–67; and Marianne Maxwell, "Pittsburgh's Frick Park: A Unique Addition to the City's Park System," *Western Pennsylvania Historical Magazine* 68 (July 1985): 243–64.

4. Roy Lubove, *Twentieth-Century Pittsburgh: Government, Business, and Environmental Change* (New York: John Wiley & Sons, 1969), 1–58; Joel A. Tarr, "The Pittsburgh Survey as an Environmental Statement," in *Pittsburgh Surveyed: Social*

Science and Social Reform in the Early Twentieth Century, ed. Maurine W. Greenwald and Margo Anderson (Pittsburgh: University of Pittsburgh Press, 1996), 181–83.

5. John Paul and Molly Davidson-Welling, "Brownfield Development Case Study: Nine Mile Run" (Pittsburgh: Carnegie Mellon University, 1996, photocopy). For pictures of the valley before slag dumping, see Citizens' Committee on City Plan, *Parks Report* (Pittsburgh: Citizens' Committee on City Plan, 1923), 65, 67.

6. Lubove, *Twentieth-Century Pittsburgh,* 34–35.

7. For discussions of the Survey, see ibid., 6–33, and Greenwald and Anderson, *Pittsburgh Surveyed.*

8. Frederick Law Olmsted Jr., *Main Thoroughfares and the Down Town District,* report no. 8 (Pittsburgh: Pittsburgh Civic Commission, 1911), 119–20; Bion J. Arnold, John R. Freeman, and Frederick Law Olmsted, *City Planning for Pittsburgh* (Pittsburgh: Pittsburgh Civic Commission, 1909), 5.

9. John F. Bauman and Margaret Spratt, "Civic Leaders and Environmental Reform," in Greenwald and Anderson, *Pittsburgh Surveyed,* 154.

10. Tarr, "The Pittsburgh Survey as an Environmental Statement," 177–78

11. Lubove, *Twentieth-Century Pittsburgh,* 54; Pittsburgh Department of City Planning, *Report of the Department of City Planning for the Year Ending January 31, 1913* (Pittsburgh, 1913), 13–18, 25.

12. Interview with Frank Kurtik, Heinz family historian, February 26, 1997, Heinz Family Office, Pittsburgh, Pa.

13. Pittsburgh Regional Planning Commission, *Prelude to the Future* (Pittsburgh: Pittsburgh Regional Planning Commission, 1968), 4–6; Lubove, *Twentieth-Century Pittsburgh,* 87.

14. Lubove, *Twentieth-Century Pittsburgh,* 87–91; John F. Bauman and Edward K. Muller, "The Planning Technician as Urban Visionary: Frederick Bigger and American Planning, 1913–1954," *Planning History Studies* 10, nos. 1–2 (1996): 21–39.

15. Citizens' Committee on City Plan, *Parks: A Part of the Pittsburgh Plan,* report no. 4 (Pittsburgh: Citizens' Committee on City Plan, September 1923), 11–15, 65.

16. Ibid., 15, 64–71.

17. Lubove, *Twentieth-Century Pittsburgh,* 94–95

18. Anne Lloyd, "Pittsburgh's 1923 Zoning Ordinance," *Western Pennsylvania Historical Magazine* 57 (July 1974): 289–306; Janet R. Daly, "Zoning: Its Historical Context and Importance in the Development of Pittsburgh, 1900–1923," *Western Pennsylvania Historical Magazine* 71 (April 1988): 99–126.

19. Pittsburgh Department of City Planning, *Arguments against the Proposed Zoning Ordinance* (Pittsburgh: Department of City Planning, 1923), 3–4, 20; "Zoning Bill to Govern Building Operations Here Sent to Council," *Pittsburgh Press,* January 22, 1923, 7.

20. Pittsburgh Regional Planning Association, *Prelude to the Future,* 246.

21. Lubove, *Twentieth-Century Pittsburgh,* 95.

22. Pittsburgh Department of City Planning, Map of Pittsburgh Zoning (Pittsburgh: Department of City Planning, 1923), n.p., interview with Howard Shubel, former Duquesne Slag Products Company employee, March 18, 1997, Pittsburgh, Pa.; Chester Environmental, Nine Mile Run Phase I Environmental Assessment Report (Pittsburgh: Chester Environmental, 1995), appendix B, 1–5;

and map of Nine Mile Run valley properties, from the collection of Mr. and Mrs. Thomas J. Horrocks, Pittsburgh, Pa., used by permission of Mr. Samuel Edelman.

23. CCCP, *Parks*, 71.

24. Map of Nine Mile Run Properties, from the collection of Mr. and Mrs. Thomas J. Horrocks, Pittsburgh, Pa.; used by permission of Mr. Samuel Edelman.

25. Testimony of Duquesne Slag Products Company before the City Council of Pittsburgh, April 5, 1953, in *Pittsburgh City Council Hearing Book, 1953* (Pittsburgh: Pittsburgh City Council, 1953), 291; testimony of William A. Robinson before the City Council of Pittsburgh, April 3, 1953, *Pittsburgh City Council Hearing Book, 1953,* 295–96.

26. Interview with Swisshelm Park resident Al Protheroe, April 24, 1997, Pittsburgh, Pa. Chester Environmental, Nine Mile Run Phase I Environmental Assessment Report, 5; see also appendix A, 8–9.

27. See the Articles of Incorporation, Swisshelm Park Civic Association, 1937, from the collection of Mr. and Mrs. Thomas Horrocks, correspondence of Richard H. Dick, Swisshelm Park Board of Trade, to C. L McKenzie, president, Duquesne Slag Products Company, November 7, 1939, Horrocks collection.

28. Decision of the Board of Zoning Adjustment, January 20, 1947, from the Horrocks collection; correspondence of Mrs. Thomas Horrocks to Charles F. Miller, Board of Zoning Adjustment, January 21, 1947, Horrocks collection; correspondence of W. B. Jones, president, Duquesne Slag Products Company to Swisshelm Park Civic Association, October 17, 1946, Horrocks collection.

29. Testimony of Duquesne Slag Products Company before the City Council of Pittsburgh, May 3, 1950, in *Pittsburgh City Council Hearing Book, 1950* (Pittsburgh: Pittsburgh City Council, 1950), 508–9; testimony of Paul Good before the City Council of Pittsburgh, May 3, 1950, *Pittsburgh City Council Hearing Book,* 1950, 510.

30. Minutes of the Emergency Meeting of the Swisshelm Park Civic Association, May 28, 1950, from the Horrocks collection.

31. Testimony of Duquesne Slag Products Company before the City Council of Pittsburgh, June 5, 1950, in *Pittsburgh City Council Hearing Book, 1950* (Pittsburgh: Pittsburgh City Council, 1950), 520–21; testimony of Thomas Horrocks et al. before the City Council of Pittsburgh, June 5, 1950, in *Pittsburgh City Council Hearing Book, 1950,* 522.

32. Correspondence of J. Frank McKenna, Pittsburgh solicitor, to City Council, February 14, 1955, from the Horrocks collection. Unpublished transcript of Pittsburgh City Council Hearings on Nine Mile Run, March 29, 1954, Horrocks collection.

33. Correspondence of Frank J. Gaffney, Esq., to the Swisshelm Park Civic Association, December 19, 1955, and March 23, 1956, Horrocks collection; and undated notes of Mrs. Thomas J. Horrocks, Horrocks collection.

34. Interview with Nancy Horrocks Thomas, former Swisshelm Park resident, April 17 and 22, 1997, Pittsburgh, Pa. See also Testimony of Duquesne Slag Products Company before the City Council of Pittsburgh, February 15, 1957, from the Horrocks collection. Construction debris from Interstate 376, the Parkway East, was also reported to have been dumped in Nine Mile Run.

35. Paul and Davidson-Welling, "Brownfield Development Case Study," 4–5; Tom Barnes, "City Buying Slag Pile," *Pittsburgh Post-Gazette,* October 13, 1995.

36. Cooper, Robertson & Partners, *Master Plan Report: Nine Mile Run, Pittsburgh, Pennsylvania,* prepared for City of Pittsburgh, Department of City Planning (Pittsburgh, 1996).

37. *Summerset at Frick Park: A New Traditional Neighborhood* (Summerset Land Development Associates, Pittsburgh, 2001).

Beyond Celebration

1. Relevant documents gathered during this lifetime of observation and writing about environmental affairs are now located in the Samuel P. and Barbara D. Hays Environmental Collection at the Archives of Industrial Society at the University of Pittsburgh (henceforth cited as Pitt Environmental Archives) and are fully available to the public. For a description of the archives, see Dominic LaCava and Ruth C. Carter, "Documenting Social Action: Environmental Archives at the University of Pittsburgh," in *Pennsylvania History* 66 (Autumn 1999): 595–600.

2. It seems quite obvious that many experiences of seemingly limited significance should be involved in developing conclusions about the environmental affairs of the city and the region. These are too numerous to mention, but one still remains rather prominent in my memory. During a talk at the 1980 Earth Day activities at the Carnegie, I mentioned that when my department was hiring in 1960, we worried that haze and limited visibility as seen from the department offices on the twenty-ninth floor of the Cathedral of Learning would drive candidates away. An official of the U.S. Steel Corporation was on the same panel and apparently he reported my comments to his CEO; the university chancellor later in casual conversation conveyed to me that the CEO had mentioned the incident to him with disapproval.

3. For the role of the Adirondacks in shaping the initial interest in Pennsylvania forest programs, see Lester A. DeCoster, *The Legacy of Penn's Woods: A History of the Pennsylvania Bureau of Forestry* (Harrisburg, Pa.: Pennsylvania Historical and Museum Commission and Pennsylvania Department of Conservation and Natural Resources, 1995).

4. The most extensive comparative analysis of city parks in the United States, including Pittsburgh, is Peter Harnik, *Inside City Parks* (Washington, D.C.: Urban Land Institute, 2000).

5. The best comparative state environmental data comes from the Institute of Southern Studies located in Durham, North Carolina. Its latest analysis is *Gold and Green 2000* (Durham: Institute for Southern Studies, 2001), and it indicates that since its analysis a decade previously, Pennsylvania's environmental rank among states has declined.

6. For a fuller elaboration of both the concept of environmental culture and the strategy of identifying the culture of a given region by widespread comparisons, see Samuel P. Hays, "Environmental Politics Culture and Environmental Political Development: An Analysis of Legislative Voting, 1971–1989," *Environmental History Review* 16 (summer 1992): 1–22.

7. Comparative state park data can be derived from the annual reports of the Association of State Park Directors.

8. See my paper on the potential management of the Presidential Oil Tract

(presented to the Western Pennsylvania Conservancy), located in the Pitt Environmental Archives.

9. The description of environmental affairs in Pennsylvania presented here is derived from the author's personal experience but is augmented by extensive interviews in 1980 with William Eichbaum, former head of enforcement for the Department of Environmental Resources.

10. The roles of Pennsylvania environmentalists in shaping the Surface Mining Act of 1977, including my own role in the proceedings leading up to the act, are reflected in dossiers in my environmental files in the Pitt Environmental Archives. See, especially, my paper, "The Federal Surface Mining Act: The Pennsylvania Input."

11. Paragraph based on observations at meetings on the Allegheny County air pollution control ordinance in the early 1970s and from interviews with the staff of Representative Joe Gaydos of the Monongahela Valley. See also the early issues of the GASP newsletter, Pitt Environmental Archives.

12. This issue can be followed in detail in the pages of the *Pittsburgh Post-Gazette* and the publications of the AAA of Western Pennsylvania, both of which can be found in the Pitt Environmental Archives.

13. While the administrative agencies in Pennsylvania continue to tout the Environmental Rights Amendment, they know full well that the courts have deprived it of its enforcement influence, especially compared with other states such as Washington.

14. The Natural History Surveys in Illinois and Ohio have played an important role in various nature-oriented programs in those states which are much more fully advanced than Pennsylvania. Especially noticeable is the distinction between the Illinois and Pennsylvania forest stewardship programs, the one in Illinois being strongly influenced by ecological scientists and association with the Illinois Arboretum, while the one in Pennsylvania is equally strongly influenced by the leaders of a complex of wood products organizations and institutions.

15. The mythology of smoke reduction in Pittsburgh has several quite separate questions, many of which are blurred together amid the continual reiteration of the myth. They are: (1) To what extent was smoke reduction an action distinctive to Pittsburgh or due more to trends in all the inland cities of the northeast? (2) To what extent was smoke reduction due to action by the Pittsburgh City Council and a few community leaders or to changes in the fuel market? (3) To what extent did the emphasis by the city's leadership on the importance of clearer air to the region's economic development represent a permanent rather than a temporary commitment to community environmental objectives?

16. Joel A. Tarr, *The Search for the Ultimate Sink: Urban Pollution in Historical Perspective* (Akron: University of Akron Press, 1996), 227–61, and Joel A. Tarr and Carl Zimring, "The Struggle for Smoke Control in St. Louis: Achievement and Emulation," in *Common Fields: An Environmental History of St. Louis*, ed. Andrew Hurley (St. Louis: Missouri Historical Society Press, 1997), 199–220.

17. The records of the Group against Smog and Pollution (GASP) are in the Pitt Environmental Archives; a dissertation dealing with the history of GASP and based on these records is now underway in the CMU Graduate History Program (James Longhurst, "I Belong Here!": Environmental Activism, Community Politics, and Air Pollution Control in Pittsburgh, 1965–1975").

18. A comprehensive account of pesticide issues is John Wargo, *Our Children's Toxic Legacy: How Science and Law Fail to Protect Us from Pesticides,* 2d ed. (New Haven, Conn.: Yale University Press, 1998); pesticide issues can be followed in two periodicals, *Journal of Pesticide Reform* (Eugene, Ore.: Northwest Coalition for Alternatives to Pesticides, 1980–), and *Pesticides and You* (Washington, D.C.: National Coalition against the Misuse of Pesticides, 1980–).

19. Issues involving implementation of the Food Safety Act of 1996 can be followed in *Risk Policy Report* (Washington, D.C.: Inside Washington Publishers, 1993–).

20. The Earth Day celebration at the Carnegie Museum of Natural History in 1980 was constrained by the insistence of one major source of funding that antienvironmental speakers appear on the program. I was a member of the advisory committee and assisted the director in tracking down the qualifications of speakers proposed by the funding agencies.

21. The Frick Environmental Center was destroyed by fire in summer 2002. Plans are being made to rebuild it.

22. See environmental items clipped from the Pittsburgh newspapers in the Pitt Environmental Archives.

23. Haurwitz has since commented to me that the climate for environmental reporting at his Austin, Texas, newspaper, in contrast with that at the *Pittsburgh Press,* was like the difference between "night and day."

24. Excellent environmental reporting on broad national issues was rare in the city's press.

25. Somewhat further away, but still within the region, was the McKeever Environmental Center, which played a more limited role in the city's environmental activities.

26. I reviewed this curriculum for the Pennsylvania chapter of the Sierra Club and outlined in detail the way in which it involved a strong bias toward commodity wood production and failed to include in a parallel way elements of ecological and environmental forestry. This review is in the Pitt Environmental Archives.

27. In recent years a more formally organized bachelor of arts in environmental studies was instituted at the University of Pittsburgh, housed in the Department of Geology and Planetary Science and based primarily on existing university courses. It involves a limited number of course offerings with environmental content, a voluntary internship and advising program and, because of the continuing lack of support from the administration, faces a future that is rather problematical. See the brochure, "Bachelor of Arts in Environmental Studies: A Liberal Arts Education with a Focus on Our Planet and Its Environment" (Department of Geology and Planetary Science, University of Pittsburgh).

28. During the 1970s and 1980s when the program was active, I was the main advisor to the "self-designed" environmental majors, and served as advisor to the student environmental group during its various incarnations over several years.

29. I was a member of the group that met to discuss these possibilities. An event that illustrates dramatically the indifference of the University of Pittsburgh to environmental education is the Talloires Declaration, produced by twenty leaders of universities throughout the world after a meeting in Talloires, France, in which they affirmed the necessity of comprehensive environmental curricula in every institution of higher education. Of the twenty leaders, one was

Wesley W. Posvar, chancellor of the University of Pittsburgh. I never heard this declaration or Chancellor Posvar's contribution to it mentioned on the Pitt campus.

30. This, for example, was the case with the limited environmental program at Duquesne University.

31. At the graduate level, the most conspicuous university program was in the School of Public Health. No city university had a broad-based liberal arts curriculum. At the University of Pittsburgh the major exception was the annual summer program sponsored by the Honors College which focused on Yellowstone National Park and its surrounding area. I served as a faculty member of the Yellowstone seminar in 1991, directing the public policy segment of the course, and was in close contact with the program throughout subsequent years.

32. Carnegie Mellon University has an undergraduate major in environmental policy and a minor in environmental studies. However, it only has a limited number of humanities and social science faculty dealing with environmental issues.

33. A major event in the life of the Rachel Carson Institute was a conference featuring prominent women in national environmental affairs. The institute, however, failed to maintain the momentum provided by the conference for a major direction toward enhancing the role of women in environmental affairs. One can place the performance of Chatham College as well as that of other colleges and universities in Pittsburgh in context through the excellent report by the National Wildlife Federation about the environmental performance of such institutions throughout the United States: See *State of the Campus Environment: A National Report Card on Environmental Performance and Sustainability in Higher Education* (Washington, D.C.: National Wildlife Federation, 2001).

34. The Rachel Carson Institute, under the direction of Ellen Dorsey, is presently attempting to focus new attention on issues relating to the use of toxic chemicals on campus. See Don Hopey, "Alma Mater Pays Heed to Rachel Carson's Warnings,' *Pittsburgh Post-Gazette,* September 27, 2002. In 2002, the college hired Michael Shriberg from the University of Michigan School of Natural Resources and Environment to be a member of the faculty and director of their Environmental Studies Program.

35. Environmental programs at a number of institutions in Pennsylvania stand in marked contrast to the absence of such programs at the city's colleges and universities. Among these were Allegheny College, Dickinson College, and Indiana University of Pennsylvania. A benchmark against which to measure university acceptance and performance about environmental education is in an excellent survey of the "state of environmental education affairs," Wynn Calder and Richard M. Clugston, "Higher Education," in *Stumbling toward Sustainability,* ed. John C. Dernbach (Washington, D.C.: Environmental Law Institute, 2002), chapter 27.

36. The Carnegie contributed in a larger way when it sponsored the city's 1980 Earth Day activities, but this momentary interest soon languished amid evidence of misgivings by the institution's major donors. The newly established Science Center provides the most significant opportunity to bring environmental science to the public, but its exhibits seemed to avoid opportunities to do so.

37. I attended the public meetings on the county's new air pollution ordinance and witnessed this opposition firsthand.

38. This conclusion comes both from the public relations campaigns of the AEI and conversations with an individual in the firm that organized those publicity campaigns.

39. Many records of the Pennsylvania Environmental Council have been deposited in the Pitt Environmental Archives.

40. In the early 1970s I explored the citizen's environmental organizations in Pennsylvania and discussed the mission of the projected Pennsylvania Environmental Council with its main promoter, Curt Winsor of Philadelphia. I found that the citizen-based form of organization was not to be followed in this new Pennsylvania venture but that the tripartitite form of organization, with directors chosen to represent business, industry, and environmental professionals, was to be the pattern.

41. Major disagreements developed between the PEC and citizen environmental groups over several pieces of legislation, such as the returnable container or "bottle" bill, which citizen groups promoted year after year in the Pennsylvania legislature.

42. West Virginia and its very active organization, the West Virginia Highlands Conservancy, was quite attractive to a number of Pittsburgh leaders in nature-oriented activities, such as backpacking, and who devoted considerable attention to wilderness proposals for the Monongahela National Forest. This focus of interest led them to be less interested in the more problematic environmental circumstances in the Pittsburgh area in favor of interest in the more promising West Virginia scene.

43. The Allegheny Trails Alliance has actively pushed trails construction in the Pittsburgh region.

44. I had been following the EPA-sponsored relative risk program throughout the country via its centers in Vermont and Colorado from which information about the various state and local relative risk projects was reported regularly. I attended all of the meetings about the Pittsburgh project and was struck by how limited the entire venture was. The budget of the Pittsburgh project doomed it to failure at the start, and the leaders seemed to be relatively uninterested in learning from the projects elsewhere to improve the Pittsburgh venture. In fact, they seemed not to know much at all about the broader EPA relative-risk program. On several occasions in these meetings I attempted to broaden the perspective of the program in the light of similar relative risk projects elsewhere, but obtained no positive response from the program's leaders. In order to understand the project in more detail I wrote the director of the Pittsburgh program, a faculty member at Carnegie Mellon, asking for a copy of the contract agreed on between the program and the EPA. One letter and two follow-up letters with the same request produced no reply. This secrecy only confirmed my assumption derived from the way the public meetings were held that the leaders were not interested in conducting an open, "transparent" process involving people outside its relatively close circle of program managers.

45. *Editor's Note:* In 1999, the nonprofit group Sustainable Pittsburgh evolved out of the High Technology Council's environmental program. The group

sponsors symposium and speakers on environmental issues related to the quality of life in the Pittsburgh region.

46. See, for instance, the *Pittsburgh Green Directory,* compiled by Environmental City Initiative, which omits citizens advocacy groups.

47. The current "Green Map" program for Pittsburgh as well as other cities is on the relevant website under the "Green Cities" title; it identifies a number of so-called "green sites" in the Pittsburgh region. Its earlier version, no longer on the Web, emphasized tourist destinations rather than environmental and ecological sites. Its September 2002 version included a wider range of items with little or no environmental content and exaggerated the number of sites. The list of environmental organizations is marked by an absence of citizen environmental groups such as Clean Water Action, the Sierra Club, GASP, and the Audubon Society. It appears that the Pittsburgh Green Map is an exercise in pretension rather than an example of reliable information.

48. Leaders of the Pittsburgh High Technology Council were continually advertising their activities as attempts to make Pittsburgh a "world environmental leader." This only confirmed the city's penchant to emphasize "celebration" via media images rather than environmental performance.

Afterword

1. For the contemporary problems with sewage pollution, see *Investing in Clean Water: A Report from the Southwestern Pennsylvania Water and Sewer Infrastructure Project Steering Committee* (Pittsburgh: Pennsylvania Economy League, 2002).

2. Possible topics for historical investigation include examination of the region's historical ecology and natural history, detailed study of the region's rivers, post–smoke control air pollution problems and policy, environmental justice issues, and matters relating to environment and health.

CONTRIBUTORS

Nicholas Casner received his Ph.D. from Carnegie Mellon University in 1994. He has published articles on environmental and public health issues. He is currently working as an independent historical consultant.

Angela Gugliotta received her Ph.D. at the University of Notre Dame in 2003. She currently is a lecturer in environmental studies in the Humanities Collegiate Division and a research associate in the humanities at the University of Chicago. She recently published "Class, Gender, and Coal Smoke: Gender Ideology and Environmental Injustice in Pittsburgh," *Environmental History* (April 2000).

Samuel P. Hays has written extensively in environmental politics; he lived in Pittsburgh between 1960 and 2000 where he was a close observer of and participant in environmental affairs in the city, the region, and the state. In 2000 he retired to Boulder, Colorado. Most recently he published *A History of Environmental Politics since 1945* (2000).

Andrew McElwaine is president of the Pennsylvania Environmental Council, a nonprofit environmental education and advocacy organization. He holds an M.S. in history and policy from Carnegie Mellon University and an M.A. in history from George Mason University.

Sherie R. Mershon received her Ph.D. in history and policy from Carnegie Mellon University, where she is presently a research fellow at the Center for History and Policy. She is co-author, with Steven Schlossman, of *Foxholes and Color Lines: Desegregating the U.S. Armed Forces* (1998).

Edward K. Muller is professor of history and director of the Urban Studies Program, University of Pittsburgh. He received his Ph.D. in geography at the University of Wisconsin, Madison. He was the co-editor of *The Atlas of Pennsylvania* and *North America: The Geography of a Changing Continent*.

Lynne Page Snyder works as a program officer in the Division of Health Care Services of the Institute of Medicine, National Academy of Sciences. She earned her doctorate in the history and sociology of science from the University of Pennsylvania and received her M.P.H. from the Johns Hopkins School of Hygiene and Public Health.

Joel A. Tarr is the Richard S. Caliguiri Professor of History and Policy at Carnegie Mellon University. He is the author of *The Search for the Ultimate Sink: Urban Pollution in Historical Perspective* (1996), and recently published "The Metabolism of the Industrial City: The Case of Pittsburgh," *Journal of Urban History* (July 2002).

Terry F. Yosie is currently a vice president of the American Chemistry Council responsible for environmental, health, safety, and security performance, and formerly served as a senior official at the U.S. Environmental Protection Agency. He received his doctorate from Carnegie Mellon University. He has written widely in the area of environmental policy.

INDEX

ACCAAP: *See* Allegheny County
    Citizens against Air Pollution
    (ACCAAP)
ACCD: *See* Allegheny Conference on
    Community Development (ACCD)
acid mine drainage: corrosive effects,
    94–96; drinking water quality, 94;
    economic costs, 79, 95–98; environ-
    mental impacts, 19, 55, 92–93, 198;
    formation, 89–91, 104; legal cases,
    98–102; mine sealing, 103–8;
    neutralization procedures, 91, 96–
    97, 104
AEI: *See* Americans for Energy
    Independence (AEI)
air pollution: air quality sampling, 131–
    32, 134–35, 138–43; coking process,
    21–22; Donora, Pennsylvania, 129–
    44; emissions reductions, 199, 211;
    environmental impacts, 26, 112–13,
    131; environmental reform efforts,
    198–99, 201; epidemiological
    approach, 138–39; federal interven-
    tion, 128–29, 137–39, 141–43;
    government legislation, 149, 198–
    200; government policies, 143–44,
    155–62, 166; industrial compliance,
    199; industrial pollution, 163, 166–67,
    170–71, 198; industrial self-gover-
    nance, 166–68, 171–73; ozone
    emissions, 199; public health issues,
    116, 118–21, 123, 126–44; smog, 126–
    44; soot fall, 118–21; St. Louis,
    Missouri, 148–49; test smog, 139–40,
    142; weather observations, 131–32,

135–36, 138–43; zinc smelter effluent,
    130–34, 139, 141–43. *See also* pollution;
    smoke; smoke control
ALCOSAN: *See* Allegheny County
    Sanitary Authority (ALCOSAN)
Alexander, I. Hope, 148–50, 252n7
Allegheny Bridge, 32
Allegheny City, 48
Allegheny Conference on Community
    Development (ACCD), 80, 156–59,
    163–66, 170–71, 185–86, 191
Allegheny County: air pollution, 141,
    148; beautification projects, 33–35;
    bridges, 33, 49–50; environmental
    improvements, 58, 211; smoke
    control efforts, 162–73
Allegheny County Citizens against Air
    Pollution (ACCAAP), 172
Allegheny County Health Department,
    171, 199, 214
Allegheny County Sanitary Authority
    (ALCOSAN), 35, 81–88, 237n66
Allegheny County Smoke Abatement
    Advisory Committee, 166–68,
    257n66
Allegheny Defense Project, 203
Allegheny Landing and Sculpture
    Garden, 36, 61
Allegheny Mountains, 45
Allegheny River: bridges, 49–50;
    flooding, 56; geological history, 13,
    43; historical background, 6, 45;
    locks and dams, 53; navigation
    issues, 47, 53; pollution, 49, 106;
    recreational activities, 50–51;

redevelopment efforts, 37, 59–62; sewage discharge, 25, 70–74; as trade route, 43–47, 52; urban-industrial development, 15, 48–49; waste disposal, 49, 52; as water supply, 49, 52, 65–66 See also rivers

Allegheny Valley Railroad, 18

American Lung Association, 203

Americans for Energy Independence (AEI), 212

American Steel & Wire Company, 131, 134, 136–37, 139–41, 143

Appalachian Mountains, 12–13, 15–16

Army Corps of Engineers: acid mine drainage, 93; bridges, 49–50; flood control dams, 35, 47, 52–53, 231n49; pollution survey, 95; wetland construction, 191

Armstrong, Charles, 181

Art Commission, 31, 35, 50

Baltimore & Ohio Railroad, 18, 97

Bardwell, R. C., 97

Beaver River, 43, 47

Becks Run, 25, 66

Beechwood Farms, 202, 204, 206

beehive coke ovens, 20–22, 225n33

Bell, Thomas, 132

Bendel, Joseph, 61

Bernard, John, 111

Bigelow Boulevard, 27, 34

Bigelow, Edward, 1, 2, 72, 176, 234n26

Bigger, Frederick, 181, 183–84

bituminous coal: acidic water formation, 90–91; air pollution, 111–14, 123, 147; coking process, 19–20; production rates, 92. See also smokeless fuel

Blough, Roger M., 133

Board of Health, 67, 69, 71, 132–34

Board of Zoning Adjustment, 184, 187–88, 192

Boulevard of the Allies, 27

Brackenridge, Hugh Henry, 111

Braley, S. A., 107

Breckenridge, Mrs. H. K., 150

bridges, 27, 30–33, 49–50

brownfields, 36–38, 60–62, 215, 217

Buncher, Jack, 188–89

Bureau of Engineering, 27, 69

Bureau of Forestry, 207

Bureau of Health, 68

Bureau of Recreation, 180

Bureau of Smoke Control, Allegheny County, 168, 171, 173

Bureau of Smoke Prevention, 155, 159–61

Bureau of Smoke Regulation, 121, 148

Bureau of Steps and Boardwalks, 29

Burns, Allen T., 32

Bussarello, John P., 154, 257n66

by-product coke ovens, 21–22

Campbell, John, 44

canals, 47–48, 53–54

carbon dioxide, 131

carbon monoxide, 131, 142

Carnegie, Andrew, 1, 30–31, 53

Carnegie Library, 210

Carnegie Mellon University, 37, 190–91, 208–9, 214

Carnegie Science Center, 210

Carson, Rachel, 202, 209

CCCP: See Citizens' Committee on City Plan (CCCP)

Celapino, Abe, 138–39

Chamber of Commerce, 33–34, 56, 71, 123–24, 148, 176, 199, 211

Chatham College, 208–9

Chestnut ridge, 13, 16

cholera, 67

Citizens Advisory Committee, 171–72, 259n82

Citizen's Coal Project, 203

Citizens' Committee on City Plan (CCCP), 181–85, 191

city beautification projects, 33–35

City Planning Commission, 35

city planning efforts, 33–34, 45, 176–83

City Water Commission, 67

Civic Club, 33–34, 148–51, 156, 176, 179–80

Civic Commission, 35, 177–80, 182–83, 191

Civilian Conservation Corps, 103

Civil Works Administration, 77, 106

opposition influence, 211–13; university professional community, 214

Hump: *See* Grant's Hill

Hungerford, Cy, 150

Hurley, Andrew, 5

hydrological patterns, 25

inclines, 29

Indian Creek watershed, 72, 100–102, 104

Industrial Hygiene Foundation, 135–136, 142

industrialization: environmental impacts, 19–23, 51–57, 63, 92–93, 130–32, 136–37; historical background, 15–18; public perception, 17–18; rivers, 51–54; suburbanization, 114–15; World War I, 121; World War II, 122

industrial pollution: acid mine drainage, 19, 55, 89–109; air quality, 163, 166–67, 170–71, 198; Donora, Pennsylvania, 129–44; government legislation, 91; policy development, 101–3, 108–9; public health issues, 93–96; smoke, 15, 198; toxic wastes, 38, 60; water supply, 94, 100–102

infectious diseases, 93–94, 116, 127–28

iron manufacturing, 16, 20, 51–52, 174, 184

Izaak Walton League, 102–3, 105–6, 108

Jones & Laughlin Steel (J&L): beehive coke ovens, 22, 225*n*33; industrial era, 51; redevelopment efforts, 37; slag wastes, 184, 189, 259*n*1; smoke control regulation, 155, 171

Jones, Benjamin F., 51

Kane, John J., 80, 163, 165

Kaufmann, Edgar J., 182

Kehoe, Robert, 136, 140, 143

Kellog, Paul U., 17–18

Kennywood Amusement Park, 182

Ketchum, George, 181

Kettering Laboratory of Applied Physiology, 136, 139–43

Kiskiminetas River, 43, 47, 106

Knowles, Morris, 72

Koruzo, John, 78–79

Krebs, Otto, 16

Kudlik, John, 46

Laboon, John P., 81–85

Ladies Health Protective Association (LHPA), 116

landscapes: artistic representations, 14–16; bridges, 30–33; city beautification projects, 33–35; coal industry, 19–22; construction activities, 24–30; environmental reform efforts, 39, 177–92; geological history, 12–13; human impact, 14; hydrological patterns, 25; mining, 19–20; Pittsburgh Renaissance, 35; railroads, 18–19; topography, 24–31; urban-industrial development, 12, 15–18, 53–54; urban renewal projects, 35–37, 176–77. *See also* hillsides; rivers

Laurel ridge, 13, 16

Lawrence, David L., 82–85, 157–58, 165, 200, 255*n*47

League of Women Voters, 151, 159

Leech, Edward T., 148–50

Leighton, Henry, 43

Leitch, R. D., 104–5

Leonard, Edward, 155, 255*n*47

LHPA: *See* Ladies Health Protective Association (LHPA)

Liberty Bridge, 27

Liberty Tunnel, 27

Lindenthal, Gustav, 32

locks and dams, 47, 53–54, 231*n*49

Love, George, 158, 257*n*66

Love, Gilbert, 150, 153

Lower Hill renewal project, 35–36

low-income residents: disease mortality rates, 70–73, 118–19; employment concerns, 148; environmental impacts, 218; environmental involvement, 39; fuel costs, 152, 154, 160, 172–73; housing, 20, 30. *See also* working class

Lubove, Roy, 182–83, 192

Magee, Christopher L., 178
Magee, William A., 31, 100, 178–81, 183
Martin, Park, 165, 170
May, Herbert, 182
McCabe, Louis, 138
McKeesport, Pennsylvania, 61, 94–95
Meller, Herbert, 121
Mellon, Andrew, 181
Mellon family, 118, 121–25
Mellon Institute for Industrial
    Research, 107
Mellon Institute Smoke Investigation
    (MISI), 118–22, 136, 148
Mellon, Ralph, 120
Mellon, Richard B., 181
Mellon, Richard King, 156, 165, 200–201
Mellon, Thomas, 181
Mencken, H. L., 29
Mesta Machine Corporation, 61
Miller, Char, 5
Mills, Clarence, 135, 139, 141–42
mining: acid mine drainage, 19, 55, 79,
    89–109; environmental impacts, 19–
    20, 92–93; historical background,
    91–92; mine sealing, 103–8; waste
    dumps, 19, 31. *See also* coal industry
MISI: *See* Mellon Institute Smoke
    Investigation (MISI)
Monongahela Bridge, 32
Monongahela Incline, 29
Monongahela River: acid mine
    drainage, 93, 106; bridges, 32, 49;
    environmental impacts, 59, 212; fish
    population, 93; flooding, 56;
    geological history, 13, 43; historical
    background, 6, 44–45; locks and
    dams, 47, 53; navigation issues, 47,
    53; recreational activities, 51;
    redevelopment efforts, 37; sewage
    discharge, 25, 70; slack water
    projects, 23; as trade routes, 43–47,
    52; urban-industrial development,
    48–49; waste disposal, 52; as water
    supply, 52, 66; wharf district, 15, 22–
    23, 45–46, 48, 51–52, 59. *See also* rivers
Moretti, Giuseppe, 2
Morrow, J. D., 158

mortality rates: diarrhea, 79; enteritis,
    79; infectious diseases, 127–28;
    typhoid fever, 70–71, 73, 79, 94–95;
    waterborne diseases, 93–95. *See also*
    germ theory
Mount Washington, 26, 29, 42
Murphy, Tom, 61
Murray, Phil, 135

National Audubon Society, 204
National Aviary, 210
National Industry Recovery Act
    (NIRA), 105
National Tube Company, 97
National Wildlife Federation, 204
Native American population: environ-
    mental impacts, 14; Pittsburgh
    region, 7; river usage, 43–44
natural environment: assets, 194–95;
    coal industry, 19–22; interactions
    with human-built environment, 4–
    5, 11–12. *See also* landscapes; rivers
natural gas, 114–16, 123, 146, 162, 170, 198
nature centers, 206
Neale, M. M., 132–33
Neville, Presley, 112
Nine Mile Run, 25, 174–75, 177–80, 182–
    92, 215
NIRA: *See* National Industry Recovery
    Act (NIRA)
nitrogen oxides, 130, 132, 142
North Shore Corridor, 62
nuclear industry, 207, 212

O'Connor, John, 120
Ogden, George W., 16
Ohio River: acid mine drainage, 93,
    106; geological history, 13; historical
    background, 6; importance, 41, 43–
    44; locks and dams, 53; navigation
    issues, 47, 53; sewage discharge, 25,
    70; as trade routes, 52; waste load,
    236*n*52. *See also* rivers
Ohio River Valley Water Sanitation
    Commission (ORSANCO), 85
Oliver, A. K., 150, 154
Oliver, Henry, 50, 56

population estimates, 6, 21, 53, 175–76
privy vaults, 49, 66–69
Progress, 181, 184
Project Z, 83
public health issues: air pollution, 116, 118–21, 123, 126–44; environmental reform efforts, 116–22; government policies, 128–29; health effects survey, 134–40; smoke, 149; water pollution, 55, 67–77, 79, 93–95, 100–102
public school curriculum, 206–7
pulmonary anthracosis, 119
Purity of Waters Act, 74, 98–99
Pyle, Ernie, 24

Rachel Carson Homestead, 202, 206
Rachel Carson Institute, 202, 209
railroads: bridges, 32; combustion technology, 169; cultural impacts, 51; environmental impacts, 18–19, 26; fuel changes, 169, 201; importance, 51–54; legal cases, 100–102; smoke control regulation, 163–67, 169; water treatment costs, 97–98
Ream, M. Jay, 156, 257n66
Reed, David, 183
Regional Industrial Development Corporation (RIDC), 37
Reid, Kenneth A., 78, 102–3, 106
Reiser, Catherine, 46
Renaissance II, 36
Research and Development Park, 37
retaining walls, 27, 28
Richardson, George, 32
Richardson, Henry Hobson, 27
RIDC: See Regional Industrial Development Corporation (RIDC)
Ridge, Mrs. W. C., 150
Riverlife Task Force, 37–38, 62
rivers: bacterial contamination, 55, 68, 70–75, 79, 86–87; environmental impacts, 22–23, 48–49, 54–57; fish population, 7, 50, 55, 92–93; fluvial processes, 54; geological history, 43; importance, 41–47, 51–53; industrial functions, 51–54, 59; locks and dams,

47, 53–54; navigation issues, 46–47, 53–54; public perception, 51, 57–61; recreational activities, 38, 50–51, 56–63; redevelopment efforts, 36–38, 58–63; riverbanks, 23, 48, 50, 53–63; sewage discharge, 65–80; shipyards, 48, 52; slack water projects, 23, 47; as trade routes, 43–47, 52–53; urban-industrial development, 22–23, 48–49; waste disposal, 52, 54–56; as water supply, 49, 52–55. *See also* acid mine drainage; mining
road construction, 26, 58–59
Roberto Clemente Park, 59
Roberts, Thomas P., 93
Robin, John P., 151, 153
Robinson, William H., 182
Roddy, Jim, 199
Roebling, John, 32, 49
Rongaus, William, 132–34
Roosevelt, Franklin D., 103
Russell Sage Foundation, 178
Sanderson case, 98–99
sand filtration system, 55–56, 71–74, 93–94
Sanitary Water Board, 77–81, 99–100, 101, 107
Saw Mill Run, 25
Schaeffer, Raymond, 197, 201
Schenley, Mary, 1, 176
Schenley Park, 1–3, 30–31, 34, 176
Schrenk, H. H., 142
Schuchman, William, 16
Schultz, Christian, 111
Scully, Cornelius, 78, 148–50, 152
Sedgwick, William T., 72
sewage: overflow points, 87, 217; public health issues, 67–74, 87; river pollution, 65–80, 87; treatment efforts, 74–86; water supply, 65–67
sewer systems: Allegheny County Sanitary Authority (ALCOSAN), 35; connected households, 236n44; construction activities, 25, 68–79, 81–83; financing issues, 69–70, 82–86, 233n18; government legislation, 74–75; legacy systems, 87; redevelop-

construction activities, 24–26; Pittsburgh region, 42–43; sewer systems, 81–82
toxic wastes, 38, 60
Trax, Edward, 95
tree planting projects, 33–34
tuberculosis, 119
Tucker, Raymond R., 149
tunnels, 26–27
typhoid fever, 55, 68, 70–75, 79, 94

United Mine Workers (UMW), 152
United Smoke Council (USC), 156–59, 163, 165–66
United States Bureau of Mines, 104–5, 108, 137–38, 162
United States Geological Survey, 93, 95, 103
United States Public Health Service, 93, 95, 128–30, 134–39, 141–43
United Steelworkers (USW), 134–35, 137, 199, 201
University of Pittsburgh, 37, 190, 208, 210, 214
urban-environmental history, 5
urban-industrial development: coal industry, 19–22; deindustrialization, 36, 57, 212; environmental impacts, 15–18, 25; floodplain, 23, 24, 28–30, 48–49, 53–54; housing, 20; natural resources, 15–16; topographical impact, 24–26; urban renewal projects, 35–37, 58–59, 79–80, 176. *See also* sewer systems
Urban Redevelopment Authority, 37, 61, 191
urban renewal projects, 35–37, 79–80
USC: *See* United Smoke Council (USC)
U.S. Steel: air pollution, 22, 131, 133, 141, 144; housing, 66; slag wastes, 184; smoke control regulation, 167, 170–71
USW: *See* United Steelworkers (USW)

Van Buskirk, Arthur B., 158
Vann, Mrs. Robert L., 257*n*66
Van Swearingen, John Q., 100

Vaux, Calvert, 1
vegetation: along riverbanks, 23, 60, 92; destruction, 26, 54–55; environmental impacts, 26; restoration projects, 198; tree planting projects, 33–34
Vikeroy, Thomas, 45

War Department, 50
War for Empire, 44
Waring, George E., Jr., 69
Washington, George, 6
Washington Post, 205
Washington's Landing, 37, 61, 215
waste dumps: Allegheny River, 49, 52; environmental impacts, 184–89; Nine Mile Run, 174–75, 184–91; ravines, 30–31; rivers, 52, 54–56; urban renewal projects, 38
wastewater disposal, 25, 49, 55–56, 67–69, 81–88
waterborne diseases, 69, 79, 93–94
water pollution: *See* acid mine drainage; industrial pollution; pollution control; rivers; water supply
Water Pollution Control Act, 103
water quality: environmental activism, 78, 102–3; environmental impacts, 55, 78–79, 198; environmental improvements, 59–61, 80; government legislation, 74–75, 77–78, 198; sewage pollution, 71–79, 234*n*26
water supply: bacterial contamination, 55, 68, 70–75, 79, 86–87, 93–95; industrial pollution, 94, 100–102; neighborhood access, 66–67; Pennsylvania Railroad, 100–102; potability, 94; rivers, 49, 52–55; sewage pollution, 71–79; sources, 65–66
water treatment: chlorination, 73, 79, 94–95; disease eradication efforts, 55–56, 93–94; environmental improvements, 59–61, 80; financing issues, 65–66, 72–74, 80–86; McKeesport, Pennsylvania, 94–95; political disputes, 72–74, 82–84, 86–87, 234*n*26;